SISTERS IN PEACE

THE WOMEN'S INTERNATIONAL LEAGUE FOR
PEACE AND FREEDOM IN AUSTRALIA, 1915–2015

SISTERS IN PEACE

THE WOMEN'S INTERNATIONAL LEAGUE FOR
PEACE AND FREEDOM IN AUSTRALIA, 1915–2015

KATE LAING

ANU PRESS

… At once a convention of all wives through Hellas here for a serious purpose was held,

To determine how husbands might yet back to wisdom despite their reluctance in time be compelled.

Why then delay any longer? It's settled. For the future you'll take up our old occupation.

Now in turn you're to hold tongue, as we did, and listen while we show the way to recover the nation.

Aristophanes, *Lysistrata*, 411 BCE,
Jack Lindsay translation 1925.

ANU PRESS

Published by ANU Press
The Australian National University
Canberra ACT 2600, Australia
Email: anupress@anu.edu.au

Available to download for free at press.anu.edu.au

ISBN (print): 9781760465995
ISBN (online): 9781760466008

WorldCat (print): 1395061309
WorldCat (online): 1395062214

DOI: 10.22459/SP.2023

This title is published under a Creative Commons Attribution-NonCommercial-NoDerivatives 4.0 International (CC BY-NC-ND 4.0) licence.

The full licence terms are available at creativecommons.org/licenses/by-nc-nd/4.0/legalcode

Cover design and layout by ANU Press. Cover photograph: 'Women's International League for Peace and Freedom', held in Photographs and slides relating to the peace movement in Australia, ca. 1930–1982, created by the Association for International Co-operation and Disarmament (N.S.W.) Mitchell Library, State Library of NSW, PXE 1463.

This book is published under the aegis of the Social Sciences editorial board of ANU Press.

This edition © 2023 ANU Press

Contents

Foreword	ix
Abbreviations	xi
Introduction	1
1. World War I and the founding of WILPF	27
2. The feminist side of the League of Nations	61
3. White Australia and regional relationships	83
4. 'Our struggle is not only one for peace but also for freedom'	115
5. The United Nations and Indigenous rights	155
6. The Cold War and nuclear disarmament	187
7. The anti-Vietnam War movement and women's liberation	227
8. Women, peace and security: The United Nations Women's conferences and Security Council Resolution 1325	261
Conclusion	299
Appendix: Biographies of WILPF leaders	309
Acknowledgements	319
Bibliography	321

Foreword

This is a very important book because it details the history of Australian women working for peace as members of the oldest international feminist organisation, 'Women's International League for Peace and Freedom' (WILPF), which grew out of women's opposition to World War I.

This global organisation has persisted *with its peace advocacy* against a background of war and conflict in political environments where the majority of decision-makers choose military might rather than rational dialogue to find solutions.

It is women who have created a strong backbone of resistance to government propaganda that tries to convince communities that a so-called just war will bring lasting peace. Yet after decades of modern warfare peace remains as elusive as ever and civilians, mainly women and children, have become disproportionate victims of war.

I was politicised by Australia's entry into the Vietnam War in 1965 when the Australian Government imposed conscription of 19-year-old men as soldiers for that war. I was a young mum with a baby son and could not imagine how I would feel if he were ever to be conscripted. I joined 'Save our Sons', a newly formed organisation established in Melbourne that aimed to overturn conscription policy and support conscientious objectors and others actively working against Australia's participation in the Vietnam War.

Years later, as an Australian Senator, I was able to participate in a range of foreign policy debates that focused on peacebuilding. During the years I was in government, the first Minister for Disarmament was appointed and played a major role negotiating for the development of an International Chemical Weapons Convention. I joined some of my colleagues in campaigning against Australia's involvement in the US MX Missile Defence Program, and Australia's promotion of a Nuclear Free Pacific.

In 1989, as Minister for the Status of Women, I welcomed 300 women from around the world to WILPF's International Congress in Sydney: Women: Building a Common and Secure Future.

This book is a major contribution to the historiography of the Australian peace movement so it should be read widely to influence debate about Australia's future role in international relations.

We can continue to view militarisation as our standard response, or we can become respected negotiators valued for our professionalism in conflict resolution and peacebuilding.

Margaret Reynolds
President of Woman's International League for Peace
and Freedom Australia.

Abbreviations

ABC	Australian Broadcasting Commission
ADB	Australian Dictionary of Biography
AICD	Association for International Cooperation and Disarmament
AIDEX	Australian International Defence Equipment Exhibition
AIF	Australian Imperial Force
AJDS	Australian Jewish Democratic Society
ALP	Australian Labor Party
APA	Australian Peace Alliance
APC	Australian Peace Council
ASIO	Australian Security Intelligence Organisation
AWNL	Australian Women's National League
CICD	Congress for International Cooperation and Disarmament
CPA	Communist Party of Australia
CPD	Commonwealth Parliamentary Debates
CSW	Commission on the Status of Women
ECOSOC	Economic and Social Council of the United Nations
GPS	global positioning system
IAW	International Alliance of Women
ICW	International Council of Women
ICWPP	International Committee of Women for Permanent Peace
ILO	International Labour Organization
IPC	International Peace Campaign
IWY	International Women's Year
MAW&F	Movement Against War and Fascism

NCW	National Council of Women
NGO	non-government organisation
NLA	National Library of Australia
NWAC	National Women's Advisory Council
Peace Army	Women's Peace Army
PLC	Presbyterian Ladies' College
PLO	Palestinian Liberation Organisation
PPWA	Pan-Pacific Women's Association
Sisterhood	Sisterhood of International Peace
SIP	Sisterhood of International Peace (in footnotes)
SLNSW	State Library of NSW
SLV	State Library of Victoria
SOS	Save Our Sons
THC	Trades Hall Council
UAW	Union of Australian Women
UN	United Nations
UNAA	United Nations Association of Australia
UNESCO	United Nations Educational, Scientific and Cultural Organisation
UNSCR	United Nations Security Council Resolution
WAP	White Australia Policy
WCTU	Woman's Christian Temperance Union
WFP	Women for Peace
WIDF	Women's International Democratic Federation
WIL	Women's International League
WILPF	Women's International League for Peace and Freedom
WLM	Women's Liberation Movement
WPA	Women's Political Association
WSG	Women's Service Guild
WSP	Women Strike for Peace
WWPP	World Women Parliamentarians for Peace
YWCA	Young Women's Christian Association

Introduction

'Is preparation for war the best means of preserving peace?'[1] This was the question posed to the Australian federal government in 1947 by Doris Blackburn, the second woman elected to the House of Representatives. It was a pertinent question. Australia had recently entered into an agreement with the British Government, the Long-Range Weapons Project, to begin testing rockets on Australian soil at Woomera in South Australia. Blackburn was worried over signs of postwar militarism. She was not alone in her concerns, but even so they were brushed aside as Cold War anxieties created bipartisan support for armaments. 'We appear to be dominated by the military machine—and that is a hideous admission to make after we have fought two great wars to end war', she lamented.[2]

Blackburn's lone protest was prescient in expressing the potential long-term dangers of the project. The agreement saw the eventual testing of rockets and atomic bombs in the Australian outback during the 1950s and 1960s. Remote areas in South Australia, including Maralinga, were offered up for this purpose. Nine atomic explosions took place, cratering and contaminating the land and displacing the Anangu traditional owners of the Maralinga Tjarutja lands.[3] In 2021 a group of scientists, led by Monash University researchers, published a study looking into the lasting effects on the environment of plutonium (Pu) and toxic uranium (U) fallout.[4] Their findings established that the particles 'are actually more complex and varied than previously thought' and, far from being stable and inert,

---

1   Doris Blackburn, *Commonwealth Parliamentary Debates (CPD)* vol. 190, 1 May 1947, 1826–45 in *Great Words: Speeches That Stirred Australia,* ed. Michael Cathcart and Kate Darian-Smith (Melbourne: Melbourne University Press, 1998), 218.
2   Blackburn in *Great Words*, 218.
3   See *Maralinga Tjarutja,* directed by Larissa Behrendt, ABC Blackfella Films, 2020.
4   Megan Cook et al., 'The Nature of Pu-Bearing Particles from the Maralinga Nuclear Testing Site, Australia', *Scientific Reports* 11, no. 1 (May 21, 2021): 10698, doi.org/10.1038/s41598-021-89757-5.

react to the harsh arid environment and continue to slowly release Pu into the environment. Despite the millions of dollars that have been spent over several decades to remediate radioactive fallout, lead researcher Megan Cook recently recognised that 'the resulting radioactive contamination and cover-up continues to haunt us'.[5]

With such deleterious effects on the landscape and environment persisting for almost 70 years after the event, many have wondered how approval for the testing could have been so freely given and why there was such a broad consensus for the project among the political establishment. When the proposal for the Woomera Prohibited Area, which included Maralinga, was debated in parliament in 1946, it was in an environment of secrecy and fear created by the continuing scars of World War II and the emerging realities of Cold War politics. Seeking self-reliance, the British Government invested in a weapons program that was not dependent on information from the US.[6] In Australia, the Chifley Labor Government, concerned with Pacific strategic planning and wanting to affirm the bonds of empire, 'did not quibble about money, materials and men' and gave every support to the joint military project.[7] Though there were grumblings and 'lukewarm dissent from Canberra's party politicians' on the issue, the party discipline characteristic of Australian politics, and the path dependence of decision-making once funding started to pour into the program combined to ensure that almost all parliamentarians supported the deal.[8] All except Doris Blackburn.

Elected in 1946 as an independent Labor candidate for the Melbourne seat of Bourke, formerly held by her late husband Maurice Blackburn, she stood apart. An independent unconstrained by party discipline, Blackburn possessed the opportunity and felt the concomitant responsibility to raise objections publicly to policy she disagreed with. Through her longstanding involvement with organisations in the women's peace movement she had acquired the language and critical perspective to evaluate and challenge prevailing orthodoxies around war and militarism. Her first contribution

---

5   Gillian Aeria and Evelyn Leckie, 'Fallout from Nuclear Tests at Maralinga Worse than Previously Thought', *ABC News*, 22 May 2021, accessed 11 April 2022, www.abc.net.au/news/2021-05-22/maralinga-nuclear-particles-more-reactive/100157478.
6   Margaret Gowing, *Reflections on Atomic Energy History*, The Rede Lecture (Cambridge: Cambridge University Press, 1978), 12.
7   LF Crisp, *Ben Chifley: A Biography* (London: Longmans, 1961), 282.
8   Deborah Wilson, 'Different White People: Communists, Unionists and Aboriginal Rights 1946–1972' (PhD thesis, University of Tasmania, 2013), 105.

to parliamentary debate was to question the rocket testing in Australia, articulating her concern that work had commenced without debate.⁹ She moved a motion in March 1947 and gave two passionate speeches to the parliament elucidating the impact the testing of rockets would have on Aboriginal communities and lamenting the secrecy and militarisation of society in a time of peace.¹⁰

The major parties circumscribed debate and her motion was defeated. Yet without Blackburn's intervention the use of Australian territory as a laboratory for the detonation and subsequent study of irradiating weapons of mass destruction would have gone without scrutiny. The Australian parliament does not constitutionally have a defined role in approving military decisions; they can be unilaterally announced by the prime minister. Her opposition, though lonely, was insistent. When near the end of her term in 1949 rumours surfaced that the atomic bomb might soon be tested in Australia, she forthrightly asked if this was true, reminding the government that the defence minister had said in 1946 'reports that huge areas in central Australia will be blasted by explosives are highly coloured figments of the imagination.'¹¹ But the imaginary soon became real as an election saw policy priorities change, and the limited restraint of the Chifley Labor Government gave way to the imperial enthusiasm of the Menzies Coalition Government. Meanwhile, Blackburn had lost her seat after an electoral redistribution.

Blackburn's stand reminds us of the nuance, sophistication and resolution of opposition to militarism and war in Australian history. Far from being marginal, as many have characterised opposition groups, Blackburn made her protest in the parliament. Politicians had no defence of ignorance. Blackburn's actions are of a piece with the cohort of Australian women who embraced an internationalist perspective that oriented their values and priorities towards humanitarianism. Blackburn continued her activism on the issue through the Women's International League for Peace and Freedom (WILPF), an organisation of which she had been president from 1928 to 1930, and which she again took leadership of during the 1950s.

---

9   Carolyn Rasmussen, *The Blackburns: Private Lives, Public Ambition* (South Carlton: Melbourne University Publishing, 2019), 278.
10 Doris Blackburn, *CPD*, vol. 190, 1 May 1947, 1826–45 in Cathcart and Darian-Smith, *Great Words*, 218.
11 Doris Blackburn, 'Question Atomic Energy Speech', *CPD*, House of Representatives, Thursday, 6 October 1949, 1048. See also: JL Symonds, *A History of British Atomic Tests in Australia* (Canberra: Australian Government Publishing Service, 1985), 62.

She continued to hold public meetings about atomic weapons and used WILPF as an organisation to persist with her political activism. This book is a detailed history of the Australian branch of the WILPF. First established during the Great War, campaigning against militarism and particularly the development of nuclear weapons has been part of WILPF's agenda for action that has engaged many women over more than a century.

Throughout the twentieth century, the women of WILPF have challenged politicians, and the public more broadly, to consider a different path on issues of arms production, violence and war. Understanding the history of WILPF's activism against nuclear weapons remains relevant today, as a new generation of activists continue the campaign. In 2007 the International Campaign to Abolish Nuclear Weapons (ICAN) was established in Melbourne, becoming a key international coalition of lobby groups including representatives from WILPF.[12] ICAN was awarded the Nobel Peace Prize in 2017 for its advocacy at the United Nations (UN). In October 2020 the aim of its campaign was realised when the Treaty on the Prohibition of Nuclear Weapons become international law, entering into force in January 2021.[13] It was the first legally binding agreement to prohibit nuclear weapons globally.

While WILPF's international advocacy remains relevant, the story of WILPF in Australia is as much about its impact on individual lives as its effect on international law. This is a history of women, like Blackburn, who committed to local and international peace activism over extended periods. They gave their energy to promoting WILPF's message in a variety of forums and in disparate contexts as Australia's national identity and military allegiances shifted over time. Providing a place and a reason to encourage women to become active and take political leadership roles is a defining part of WILPF's legacy. Knowing about the tactics and activities of WILPF extends our understanding of women's place in politics over the twentieth century.

War, and its all-encompassing impact on society, led many women to consider political involvement, even at times when there was significant discrimination around the world against women's involvement in policymaking. While WILPF has not realised its foundational goal to abolish war, the organisation's persistence in promoting its message in the

---

12 Ray Acheson, *Banning the Bomb, Smashing the Patriarchy* (Rowman & Littlefield, 2021), 57.
13 Acheson, *Banning the Bomb, Smashing the Patriarchy*, xxi.

face of many difficulties has been a defining aspect of its role and legacy. Since World War I it has provided something greater than an organisation for protesting the horrors of war: it became a network that encouraged women to consider their power in politics, at a time when they were often marginalised from the inner workings of power and policymaking. With a need to look once more at how to mediate conflicts across the world, understanding the history of WILPF may encourage us to ask what gender has to do with complex global problems and to revisit the solutions offered by women in the past.

***

In Melbourne, in 1915, a small group of women came together to express their opposition to their country's rush towards militarist nationalism and imperialism. They questioned the legitimacy of the Great War and, perhaps, all war. Brought together in the liberal Australian Church, they formed the Sisterhood of International Peace (the Sisterhood). A few weeks later, the Women's Political Association (WPA) created the Women's Peace Army (the Peace Army) to similarly register their dissatisfaction and find a political space to express anti-war dissent. The two groups both collaborated and disagreed; their differences anticipated divisions to come.

The Sisterhood focused on education to change public opinion through reasoned argument and the provision of information. In their monthly newsletter, *Peacewards*, the Sisterhood wrote of their intention to 'unite Australian women among themselves, and with women throughout the world, in throwing the weight of Woman's influence into the scale of international goodwill.'[14] This meant creating a 'new international ideal and spirit', which they felt women were uniquely positioned to advocate, 'in the family, in the social circle, in the school, in shops and factories, in churches, on the platform, and at the polling-booth'.[15] Many of these Australian women found a spirit of kinship and support among women overseas, who had similarly turned their minds to organising internationally against war.

---

14 'Annual Report of the Sisterhood of International Peace', *Peacewards*, published as a supplement to the Australian Church's *Commonweal*, 1 May 1916, State Library of Victoria (SLV), 13.
15 'Annual Report of the Sisterhood of International Peace', *Peacewards*, 1 May 1916, 13.

In the same year the Sisterhood and the Peace Army were established, a call went out to convene a Women's International Congress at The Hague, and over 1,200 women from neutral and belligerent nations made the difficult wartime journey to discuss ending the war. They formed the International Committee of Women for Permanent Peace (ICWPP) and opened an office in Amsterdam.[16] In 1919, after the war had ended, they convened another conference in Zurich, where the organisation formally became known as WILPF. Their aims were to 'support movements to further peace, internationalism and the freedom of women', and to organise protest 'against the madness and the horror of war'.[17] Their method was to focus on international lobbying for peace by encouraging the new League of Nations to settle disputes through arbitration, conciliation and universal disarmament. The international bureau, later affectionately named the Maison Internationale, was established in Geneva specifically to be close to the new League of Nations headquarters.[18] It became the base for operations as well as a hostel and meeting place for women visiting from all over the world. The national sections of WILPF gained their funding from membership fees, journal subscriptions and fundraising. Each section then paid a yearly affiliation fee of 50 Swiss francs that contributed to the financial support of WILPF's international office. During the 1919 conference, the two Australian groups, the Sisterhood and the Peace Army, became affiliated and formed a cohesive national section of WILPF.

The inaugural president of WILPF International was Jane Addams (1860–1935), an American based in Chicago with a long and illustrious record as a Progressive-era social reformer committed to the welfare of the poor, the sick, women and children. Her fellow countrywoman Emily Greene Balch was elected the secretary general, moving to Geneva to establish the office. Both subsequently won Nobel Peace Prizes for their international work.[19]

---

16   GC Bussey and Margaret Tims, *Pioneers for Peace: Women's International League for Peace and Freedom, 1915-1965*, 2nd ed. (London: Allen & Unwin, 1965). Information about the 1915 congress was published immediately after by Jane Addams, Emily G Balch and Alice Hamilton, *Women at The Hague: The International Congress of Women and Its Results* (Urbana, Ill.: University of Illinois Press, 1915).
17   WILPF, Geneva Switzerland, 'Report of the Second International Congress of Women', Zurich 1919, accessed through database edited by Kathryn Kish Sklar and Thomas Dublin, *Women and Social Movements, International—1840 to Present*, 280.
18   'Report of the Second International Congress of Women', Zurich 1919, 287.
19   Laura Beers, 'Advocating for a Feminist Internationalism Between the Wars', in *Women, Diplomacy and International Politics since 1500*, ed. Glenda Sluga and Carolyn James (New York: Routledge, 2015), 202.

Every nation was eligible to create a national section. Though it was born international, WILPF 'has never been a homogenous organisation, even within individual sections' and the development of sections across the world has been distinctive, making branch histories different across the world.[20] An executive committee was elected at the international congress that met once a year, appointing subcommittees when necessary. A consultative committee was also formed, which consisted of two people from each national section who attended the executive committee meetings to keep all groups informed of the organisation's progress.[21] The highest decision-making body was the international congress held every three years that elected the president and the executive committee. The first constitution gave each national section 20 delegates and 10 alternate delegates. In 1915, there were 13 national sections, increasing to 19 by 1919, when Australia became a national section.[22] In 2022 there were 52 national sections, the largest and most inclusive the organisation has been.[23] WILPF has held consultative status with the UN Economic and Social Council since 1948, as well as with other international bodies such as the International Labour Organization (ILO), and the UN Children's fund in New York.[24]

---

20 Rhona Ovedoff, WILPF profile in *Australian Feminism: A Companion*, ed. Barbara Caine (Melbourne: Oxford University Press, 1998), 522. Various national section histories have been completed on the US, Canada, UK and New Zealand such as: Harriet Hyman Alonso, *Peace as a Women's Issue: A History of the U.S. Movement for World Peace and Women's Rights* (Syracuse, NY: Syracuse University Press, 1993); Carrie A Foster, *The Women and the Warriors: The U.S. Section of the Women's International League for Peace and Freedom, 1915–1946* (Syracuse, NY: Syracuse University Press, 1995); Joyce Blackwell, *No Peace Without Freedom: Race and the Women's International League for Peace and Freedom, 1915–1975* (Carbondale, Ill.; London: Southern Illinois University Press, 2004); Melinda Plastas, *A Band of Noble Women: Racial Politics in the Women's Peace Movement* (Syracuse, NY: Syracuse University Press, 2011); Beverly Lynn Boutilier, 'Educating for Peace and Co-Operation: The Women's International League for Peace and Freedom in Canada, 1919–1929' (MA thesis, Carleton University (Canada), 1988); Megan Hutching, 'Turn Back this Tide of Barbarism: New Zealand Women who were Opposed to War, 1896–1919' (MA thesis, University of Auckland, 1990); Betty Holt, *Women for Peace and Freedom: A History of the Women's International League for Peace and Freedom in New Zealand* (Wellington: The League, 1985); Elise Locke, *Peace People: A History of Peace Activities in New Zealand* (Christchurch: Hazard Press, 1992).
21 Ovedoff in Caine, *Australian Feminism*, 522.
22 Leila J Rupp, *Worlds of Women: The Making of an International Women's Movement* (Princeton: Princeton University Press, 1997), 17, doi.org/10.1515/9780691221816.
23 'WILPF National Sections', accessed 5 October 2020, wilpf.org/wilpf/sections/.
24 Cynthia Cockburn, *From Where We Stand: War, Women's Activism and Feminist Analysis* (London: Zed Books, 2007), 136, doi.org/10.5040/9781350220287.

There has been a considerable amount of historical research into WILPF's international office and activities, particularly on the way in which the international sphere offered space, experience and networks of support for women's voices and activism.[25] There has been less work on the Australian section. Though formed in the same year as the 'birth' of the Anzac legend, the history of the WILPF has been overshadowed by the increasing glorification of the Anzacs over the twentieth century. Indeed, military history has often trumped the history of anti-war and peace movements. The most wholehearted supporters of Anzac condemn challenges to its importance or its centrality to understanding modern 'Australian values'. Buoyed by massive funding from government and the private sector, in the past 20 years Anzac commemoration has militarised Australia's popular history—encouraging school children and communities more generally to honour the landing at Gallipoli in 1915 as the birthplace of the nation.[26] More recently, the Liberal/National federal government committed to investing $500 million to expand the War Memorial in Canberra, turning the space into what some critics are calling a militarised 'Disneyland', where exhibits are sponsored by armaments manufacturers.[27]

Anzac Day parades and celebrations have historically struggled to incorporate uncomfortable truths about the realities of war. In the 1980s when women activists challenged commemorators to remember women

---

25   For example see: Rupp, *Worlds of Women*; Bussey and Tims, *Pioneers for Peace*; Catherine Foster, *Women For All Seasons: The Story of the Women's International League for Peace and Freedom* (Athens: University of Georgia Press, 1989); Linda K Schott, *Reconstructing Women's Thoughts: The Women's International League for Peace and Freedom before World War II* (Stanford, California: Stanford University Press, 1997), doi.org/10.1515/9781503623873; Catia Cecilia Confortini, *Intelligent Compassion: The Women's International League for Peace and Freedom and Feminist Peace* (Oxford: Oxford University Press, 2012), doi.org/10.1093/acprof:oso/9780199845231.001.0001; Carol Miller, '"Geneva – the Key to Equality": Inter-war Feminists and the League of Nations', *Women's History Review* 3, no. 2 (1994): 219–45, doi.org/10.1080/09612029400200051.
26   Marilyn Lake and Henry Reynolds, *What's Wrong With Anzac? The Militarisation of Australian History* (Sydney: UNSW Press, 2010).
27   Paul Daley, 'We Demean our History When We Turn the Australian War Memorial into Disneyland', *The Guardian*, 5 September 2019, www.theguardian.com/australia-news/postcolonial-blog/2019/sep/05/we-demean-our-history-when-we-turn-the-australian-war-memorial-into-disneyland, accessed 6 September 2019. See also Paul Daley, 'An Australian War Memorial Sponsored by Weapons Dealers is No Place for Quiet Reflection on Anzac Day', *The Guardian*, 25 April 2022, accessed 26 April 2022, www.theguardian.com/australia-news/postcolonial-blog/2022/apr/25/an-australian-war-memorial-sponsored-by-weapons-dealers-is-no-place-for-quiet-reflection-on-anzac-day.

raped in war they were threatened with sexual violence and arrested.[28] In Canberra in 1981 the 'threat' to Anzac Day from protests by women led the Minister for the Capital Territory, Michael Hodgman, to amend the local traffic ordinance so that anyone 'likely to give offense or cause insult' to the 'official' commemorators could be charged. This prompted a debate about who had the right to participate.[29] Labor senator for the Australian Capital Territory, Susan Ryan, decried the move to 'deny the rights of people to participate in the Anzac Day ceremony in the way they wished' as a misguided objective and called out the 'prejudice and viciousness' of Hodgman's 'attack on the women's movement—indeed on any women who do not happen to meet his peculiarly narrow and repressive view of what women ought to do.'[30] In such ways, Anzac Day was contested even while some sought to guard an authorised narrative through the exclusion of dissent.

In the immediate aftermath of World War I, Anzac Day was a more sombre and solemn occasion. The glorification of war was distasteful to many who were recovering from the trauma of wartime service and the loss of loved ones. It was also less common in 1919 to see Gallipoli as a defining moment in the making of the Australian nation.[31] Many wanted to recover and move on from the destruction of the war and Anzac Day was an occasion of mourning. WILPF women wrote of sending 'sympathies … to the many whose homes were on that day darkened, and whose hearts were torn', noting that the commemoration should 'impress on us more deeply the folly and crime of war, and stir us up to wage ceaseless war against it, as the enemy of mankind!'[32]

---

28 Meredith Burgmann, 'The Women Against Rape in War Collective's Protests against ANZAC Day in Sydney, 1983 and 1984', *Cosmopolitan Civil Societies Journal* 6, no. 3 (2014): 4222, doi.org/10.5130/ccs.v6i3.4222. See also Amy Way, 'Best We Forget: Excluding Women, Rape and Protest From the Anzac Myth and Memorial', *Making History at Macquarie,* 18 November 2013, makinghistoryatmacquarie.wordpress.com/2013/11/18/best-we-forget-excluding-women-rape-and-protest-from-the-anzac-myth-and-memorial/, accessed 20 October 2022. Adrian Howe, 'Anzac Mythology and the Feminist Challenge' in *Gender and War: Australians at War in the Twentieth Century*, ed. Joy Damousi and Marilyn Lake (New York, Melbourne: Cambridge University Press, 1995), 304. See also Sarah Dowse and Patricia Giles, 'Australia: Women in a Warrior Society', in *Sisterhood is Global: The International Women's Movement Anthology*, ed. Robin Morgan (Garden City, NY: Anchor Press/Doubleday, 1984).
29 Dowse and Giles, 'Australia: Women in a Warrior Society'; Morgan, *Sisterhood is Global,* 113.
30 Senator Ryan, *CPD*, 'Traffic (Amendment) Ordinance', Senate, 8 September 1981, 520.
31 Carolyn Holbrook, *Anzac: The Unauthorised Biography* (Sydney: NewSouth Publishing, 2014), 211. Lake and Reynolds, *What's Wrong With Anzac?,* 73.
32 'ANZAC DAY', *Peacewards,* 1 May, 1918, Box 1731/6 Papers, WILPF, MS 9377, SLV.

Women's march on Anzac Day in Canberra, Anzac Parade, 1981.
Source: Photo courtesy of Margaret Bearlin.

If there is not a nuanced engagement with the history and commemoration of war in Australia, including understanding opposition to it, there are real world consequences. Excessive cultural veneration of the military that imbues national forces with 'moral and military exceptionalism', has facilitated war crimes and shielded perpetrators from investigation.[33] A disproportionate focus on military engagements in Australian history obscures how women, and organisations like WILPF in the peace movement, have engaged with and helped change Australian democracy over time. The meaning of warfare has until recently been understood by narrowly defining the contributions of men and women in traditional gender roles, where the idealised masculine attributes of soldiers and combatant men were given primary importance.[34] WILPF women at times reinforced the dichotomies, portraying women as in need of male protection, yet they always tried to articulate the different experiences women had of war and to determine whether this stemmed from innate characteristics or socialisation. Their willingness to question the

---

33   Mia Martin Hobbs, 'Why Soldiers Commit War Crimes—and What We Can Do About It', in *Lessons from History*, ed. Carolyn Holbrook, Lyndon Megarrity and David Lowe (Sydney: NewSouth Publishing, 2022), 228, 236. Kevin Foster, 'The Diseased Orchard: Australia's Collective Moral Failures in Afghanistan', *Australian Book Review*, no. 446 (September 2022): 18.
34   Damousi and Lake, *Gender and War*, 3.

gendered experiences of war and recognise power imbalances between the sexes complicates our understanding of women in wartime in Australia and provides a counterpoint to the prevailing narrative of sacrifice and mateship.

WILPF was defined, in an Australian context, by both its longevity and its internationalism. It occupies a significant place in the history of the Australian peace movement, in part, because it has endured. Undertaking its activities in war as well as peace has distinguished WILPF from other peace organisations that rose and fell in rhythm with the crises that instigated their birth. WILPF Australia is also significant historically because its professed internationalism often, though not invariably, set it at odds with national priorities and interests. An internationalist orientation, as well as networks and connections with the League of Nations and the UN, meant that WILPF women usually adopted a distinctive perspective on local politics and international relations. Moreover, being a women-only organisation allowed many women to take on leadership roles within the wider peace movement, which was otherwise dominated by men's organisations such as the Australian Peace Alliance (APA) and trade unions.

WILPF also supported and encouraged women to take leadership in society more generally. Many prominent female politicians have been members or supporters of the organisation. Despite higher ideals of internationalism, they recognised the need to institute change through domestic political forums and pioneered ways of doing so. In 1962, Lynda Heaven was the first Labor woman elected to the Tasmanian House of Assembly. After her term in office, she found an outlet for her political energy by becoming Tasmanian WILPF president in 1966. Federally, Doris Blackburn was elected as an independent Labor Member of the House of Representatives in 1946 and was president of WILPF both before and after. Carolyn Jakobsen was elected in the House of Representatives for the seat of Cowan in Western Australia (WA) for the Australian Labor Party (ALP) in 1984 until 1993, and served as the chair of the Federal Parliamentary Labor Party while an active WILPF member.[35] Jakobsen, Elaine Darling and Margaret Reynolds refused to support military intervention in the Persian Gulf in 1991 leading to their censure by the ALP Caucus for dissenting against the government on the war. Margaret Reynolds was elected a senator for Queensland for the ALP in 1983, and she is currently (2023) serving as national president of the Australian WILPF section.

---

35 Marian Sawer, *A Woman's Place: Women and Politics in Australia,* 2nd ed. (Sydney: Allen & Unwin, 1993), 173.

With more women entering parliament around the world by the 1980s, an organisation called the World Women Parliamentarians for Peace (WWPP) was established in Stockholm in 1985 with 580 members from 63 countries.[36] Western Australian Senator Pat Giles, elected for the ALP in 1974, became the president of WWPP in 1988 and hosted the annual conference in Parliament House. Pacifist women were beginning to find electoral success in democratic institutions, insistent on having their voices heard in military decisions and creating global organisations to support feminist interventions in parliamentary debates. Yet despite hosting the event at Parliament House with elected representatives from around the world, their gathering was still considered 'unofficial'.[37] Giles was mentored by leading WILPF woman Irene Greenwood, and became a 'confirmed internationalist' when she attended the 1975 UN women's conference in Mexico City in Greenwood's place.[38] Other examples of female politicians being connected with WILPF include the senator for WA Jo Vallentine, elected in 1984 for the Nuclear Disarmament Party, and sitting from 1985 as an independent and later for the Greens WA; the senator for Queensland (QLD) Cheryl Kernot, first elected in 1990 for the Australian Democrats, later joining Labor; the senator for New South Wales (NSW) Irina Dunn, a Nuclear Disarmament Party candidate who would sit as an independent from 1988 until 1990 after filling a casual vacancy; and the senator for QLD Claire Moore, first elected 2001 for the ALP and retiring in 2019. The Labor senator for Tasmania (TAS), Lisa Singh, who was first elected in 2011, singled out WILPF out for the positivity many of their members brought into the cynical world of politics: 'despite all the atrocities going on in the world, they start their meetings by acknowledging all the good things, and the wins, however small, that have taken place in the name of peace'.[39]

---

36 Senator Patricia Giles, 'World Women Parliamentarians for Peace', press release, 7 September 1990, accessed 11 April 2022, parlinfo.aph.gov.au/parlInfo/download/media/pressrel/HNC062015050919/upload_binary/HNC062015050919.pdf;fileType=application%2Fpdf#search=%22world%20women%20parliamentarians%20for%20peace%22.
37 Department of the House of Representatives, *Annual Report 1988–89* (Canberra: Australian Government Publishing Service, 1989), 18.
38 Lekkie Hopkins and Lynn Roarty, *Among the Chosen: The Life Story of Pat Giles* (Fremantle: Fremantle Press, 2010), 42.
39 Senator Hon. Lisa Singh, 'Foreword', in *Prevailing for Peace: The History of the WILPF Tasmanian Branch 1920–2013*, ed. Linley Grant et al. (North Hobart: WILPF, 2015).

INTRODUCTION

Anti–Gulf War demonstration on lawns at Parliament House: Senator Jo Vallentine (Greens Party) talking to anti-war demonstrators, 31 January 1991.
Source: Image courtesy of the National Archives of Australia. NAA: A13966, 910006.

Despite acknowledged gender bias in the nomination for Australia Day honours, prominent members have received honours for their work associated with WILPF. They include women such as Edith Waterworth OBE (1935), Lynda Heaven MBE (1968), Joyce Clague MBE (1977), Margaret Forte OAM (1986), Stella Cornelius AO (1987), Evelyn Rothfield OAM (1988), Elizabeth Mattick OAM (1993) and Margaret Holmes AM (2001), just to name a few. It is an impressive list, even if it pales compared with the numbers receiving military honours. Margot Roe was entered on the Tasmanian Honour Roll of Women in 2005 to celebrate her commitment to human rights through WILPF activity.[40] Irene Greenwood AM (1975) even had a flagship of the WA state fleet named in her honour.[41]

The organisation provided a place for such women to have their words recorded and amplified when opportunities in public life were severely limited. It was therefore often a vehicle for political women to gain access to power and a platform to lobby throughout the twentieth century, whether they were committed life members, or transient activists utilising an organisation's reputation and strength. Exploring the extensive archives of WILPF illuminates both how Australian women engaged in international political action, and what the distinctive challenges of internationalism were throughout the century, as well as its promise and rewards. Engaging in international politics for most women was structurally different from official diplomatic forms of internationalism, usually dominated by men 'doing internationalism' as an extension of their official roles in national politics, requiring an immense personal commitment of funds and energy. Official internationalism was more exclusive, elite and well-funded by governments prioritising national interest in international arenas with carefully chosen delegates.[42] The lack of funding and insecurity of travel for non-state actors, particularly those representing women's organisations, meant their experiences were different, more self-conscious and potentially

---

40 Linley Grant, Kay Binet and Alison Alexander, 'Margot Roe: An Appreciation', *Tasmanian Historical Research Association Papers and Proceedings* 63, no. 2 (July 2016): 102.
41 Irene Greenwood, Australian Women's Register, accessed 16 May 2017, www.womenaustralia.info/biogs/AWE0805b.htm. See biography in Appendix.
42 Glenda Sluga has written extensively on internationalism as a political movement in Glenda Sluga, *Internationalism in the Age of Nationalism* (Philadelphia: University of Pennsylvania Press, 2013), doi.org/10.9783/9780812207781. Glenda Sluga, 'Add Women and Stir: Gender and the History of International Politics', *Humanities Australia*, no. 5 (2014): 65–72; Marilyn Lake, 'Women's International Leadership', in *Diversity in Leadership: Australian Women, Past and Present*, ed. Joy Damousi, Kim Rubenstein and Mary Tomsic (Canberra: ANU Press, 2014): 71–90, doi.org/10.22459/DL.11.2014.04.

more personally transformative. They did not primarily see internationalism in terms of globalisation or imperialism, which they felt compelled to 'fight against'.[43] Rather, their understanding of the political ideal was focused on worldwide humanitarianism and democracy and could encompass constructive national patriotism. Australian democracy has changed dramatically over the last century, most significantly in the way women have been able to engage in the political process. This study looks at the women active in WILPF to observe their role in this transformation, questioning the boundaries of inclusion and the purposes for which democracy should be harnessed.

WILPF's international structure was tailored towards encouraging women to put aside national loyalties and find common identity in their condition and values as women.[44] They wished to reform the League of Nations rather than model their operation on its more formal traditional diplomatic style. Yet just as official delegations had difficulty considering international policy without taking national interests into account, WILPF women also found that the world of nation-states and national interests compromised and at times clashed with their commitment to international idealism. At the same time the practical experience of international politics often shaped approaches to national politics and policy. This work does not shy away from mapping the tensions and contradictions between international visions and national commitments, asking how the women dealt with them to shape a coherent political message and how this message changed over time.

Women's groups have always balanced interest in internationalism with the reality that many political decisions were made, and political action taken, at the national level. However, at times, the international sphere operated as a distinct arena where women could gain more power to implement their political ideas nationally. As WILPF was primarily interested in foreign policy and founded at a time when dominions such as Australia still deferred many decisions about international relations to the imperial government, internationalism offered a pathway for pressuring the network

---

43   The *Woman Voter* would state in the header and footer of their paper that they were 'For Internationalism, Against Imperialism', 3 July 1919, 3.
44   For example, at international congresses, despite being elected by national sections, women were not 'expected to promote the interests of their own respective countries'. Jo Vellacott, 'A Place for Pacifism and Transnationalism in Feminist Theory: The Early Work of the Women's International League for Peace and Freedom', *Women's History Review* 2, no. 1 (March 1993): 33, doi.org/10.1080/09612029300200021.

of British nations and for amplifying their collective voice in the world. While members joined for different reasons, and many did aspire to a cosmopolitanism they felt Australia lacked, this organisation was not about leaving Australia in search of culture overseas. It was organised politically to achieve national peace when wars were an international affair. This book takes their organisation seriously as a legitimate place of political action and activity. While few members were able to hold positions of influence and political power because of the structural barriers placed on their sex, they nonetheless contributed time, energy and thought to problems that confronted humanity in the twentieth century.

There is a large range of archival sources about WILPF available in Melbourne, Sydney and Canberra as well as internationally. The central narrative of this work centres on activities in Melbourne and Sydney as women in these cities dominated most of the communication between the section branches and the international office. To balance the dominance of the eastern state members I have researched the activities and views of women from other states wherever possible. An investigation into the membership reveals how WILPF was influenced by dominant personalities who had the means to make a heavy commitment to its work. Researching WILPF across several decades shows the importance of family dynasties, with daughters, nieces, sisters-in-law all appearing in the archives, supporting an organisational structure almost matrilineal in nature. For instance the president of WILPF in the 1970s, Elspeth Christiansen, had aunts who were involved in the founding of the Sisterhood in 1915.[45] Margaret Holmes, Anna Vroland and Doris Blackburn all persuaded their family members to become office bearers. WILPF was an organisation fired by radical ambitions and attitudes, yet it drew on a profoundly domestic heritage.

---

45 Elspeth Christiansen, WILPF personality profile, *Peace and Freedom* 22, no. 4, December 1985, Box 5/35 Meredith Stokes papers, NLA.

INTRODUCTION

WILPF Poster: 'It will be a great day when our schools get all the money they need and the air force has to hold a cake stall to buy a bomber', undated, but likely authorised in the 1980s when Elizabeth Mattick was the branch president.
Source: WILPF, Australian Section, 1943-2014 [manuscript] Box 8 Folder 57 MS 7755 NLA.

When it came to politics WILPF followed a broad-church approach, always aiming to bring people of different political persuasions together in the struggle for peace. As an organisation it was never absolutely pacifist, though many of its members were. Nor was it explicitly feminist, organising as a women's-only group because it articulated how women experienced war differently. This illustrated the complexities over the decades of the twentieth century with categorising and labelling women's political activity. Many women were wealthy, but even if they had to work they nonetheless were usually well educated and had the confidence to build networks and speak out about their ideas. Irene Greenwood acknowledged the criticism of their class composition in 1975:

> I don't disguise the fact that they were middle class, nor apologise for it because they had the privilege to do these things. We were very effective in our time for this very reason. We served our purpose against our historical and class background at the time.[46]

Internationalism was an expensive exercise. While many self-funded trips overseas, their fundraising helped others to attend conferences. Each woman shared their experiences of her journey through lectures and speaking engagements, through which WILPF in its local incarnation helped to connect not just the travelling elite who could afford it, but the Australian-bound yet politically interested membership who were less mobile.

WILPF members were intensely productive, both nationally and internationally. They formulated positions on almost all conflicts in the world, with members writing papers, histories and letters, and delivering public talks on all sorts of topics. These archives reveal much about the issues that caught their imagination and the dynamics of the peace movement. The women who speak loudest through the records are those who wrote and signed letters. Undoubtedly, there were many more members who actively participated at several levels. Although WILPF remains an active political group today, I have not used oral histories as a main source for my study, deciding rather to research the texts that comprise the voluminous archives. The aim was primarily to write a political history rather than provide an exploration of contemporary memory. I have nevertheless been the beneficiary of much assistance from WILPF members who have facilitated my research efforts in unlikely places.

---

46   Irene Greenwood, 'A Lifetime of Political Activity', *Women and Politics Conference Volume 1* (Canberra: Australian Government Publishing Service, 1977), 60.

Activists meticulously documented their activities and archived their papers expecting, or hoping, that their work would one day be of interest. Eleanor Moore published a memoir of her experiences in the peace movement in 1948, utilising the vast archives of peace material she had amassed throughout her decades of involvement in the movement.[47] Moore's work was self-published, and is limited in many ways as a source—it did not have a wide release and arguably portrayed events as she hoped they had been, as she reflected on them years after. She had given the manuscript to fellow well-known pacifist Kenneth Rivett for comment but then proceeded to ignore all his recommended changes before publication.[48] Nonetheless, it remains a crucial source in understanding the history of WILPF, providing rare insight into Moore's thinking and, as she led the organisation for three decades, it lays out the progression of their activities throughout the early twentieth century.

In their lifelong commitments, which they considered 'as patriotic as [those] of the warriors on the battlefield', WILPF members believed they would receive appropriate historical recognition.[49] This book aims to offer such recognition and provide a critical assessment of the Australian section of WILPF's extensive commitment to anti-war activism. Existing studies of WILPF in Australia have been partial and missed the rich resources of its international archive.[50] There have been biographical studies of individual Australian members and WILPF has featured in various studies of the women's movement through its interaction with other organisations, but not as the focus of a separate study.[51]

---

47 Eleanor M Moore, *The Quest for Peace, As I Have Known It in Australia* (Melbourne, 1948).
48 Malcolm Saunders, *Quiet Dissenter: The Life and Thought of an Australian Pacifist: Eleanor May Moore 1875–1949* (Canberra: Peace Research Centre, Australian National University, 1993), 351.
49 'Annual Report of the Sisterhood of International Peace', *Peacewards*, 1 May 1916, accessed SLV, 13.
50 Saunders, *Quiet Dissenter*; Malcolm Saunders, 'Are Women More Peaceful than Men? The Experience of the Australian Section of the Women's International League for Peace and Freedom, 1915–39', *Interdisciplinary Peace Research* 3, no. 1 (1 May 1991): 45–61, doi.org/10.1080/14781159108412732; Malcolm Saunders, 'The Early Years of the Australian Section of the Women's International League for Peace and Freedom: 1915–49', *Journal of the Royal Australian Historical Society* 82, no. 2 (December 1996): 180–91; Malcolm Saunders and Ralph Summy, 'Odd Ones Out: The Australian Section of the Women's International League for Peace and Freedom: 1919–41', *Australian Journal of Politics & History* 40, no. 1 (7 April 2008): 83–97, doi.org/10.1111/j.1467-8497.1994.tb00093.x.
51 Such as: Janet Morice, *Six-Bob-a-Day Tourist* (Ringwood, Vic: Penguin Books, 1985); Kay Murray, *Voice for Peace: The Spirit of Social Activist Irene Greenwood 1898–1992* (Bayswater, WA: Kay Murray Productions, 2005); Hilary Summy, *Peace Angel of World War I: Dissent of Margaret Thorp* ([Brisbane]: Australian Centre for Peace and Conflict Studies, 2006); Michelle Cavanagh, *Margaret Holmes: The Life and Times of an Australian Peace Campaigner* (Sydney: New Holland, 2006). See also: Fiona Paisley, *Glamour in the Pacific: Cultural Internationalism and Race Politics in the Women's Pan-Pacific* (Honolulu: University of Hawai'i Press, 2009), doi.org/10.21313/hawaii/9780824833428.001.0001; Judith Smart and Marian Quartly, *Respectable Radicals: A History of the National Council of Women of Australia 1896–2006* (Melbourne: Monash University Publishing, 2015). Marilyn Lake, *Getting Equal: The History of Australian Feminism* (St Leonards, NSW: Allen & Unwin, 1999).

While WILPF women wanted their own activism known and understood, they also hoped for a more academic focus on peaceful strategies to resolve conflict. WILPF constantly advocated for peace research in universities, otherwise known as the study of irenology. In Australia the aptly named Irene Greenwood led a campaign to implement a Chair in Peace Studies at Murdoch University, for which she was awarded an honorary doctorate by the institution in 1981.[52] This political pressure around the world helped build the discipline of feminist international relations, pioneered by international scholars such as Ann Tickner and Cynthia Enloe who challenged international relations theorists to consider women, peace and security.[53] Tertiary institutions across the globe started to incorporate the women, peace and security agenda into departments and schools. WILPF established an academic network to encourage scholars working on gender and war to connect their research with interested activists and inform their campaigns.[54] Current members include Jacqui True, director of Monash University's Centre for Gender, Peace and Security and leading scholar of gender and international relations.

***

Each chapter of this book chronicles a particular phase of WILPF's organising in Australia. Chapter 1 examines how WILPF formed in Australia during World War I and analyses its internationalist ideology, shaped by maternalist thinking that stressed gendered difference. Two peace groups in Melbourne, the Sisterhood of International Peace (the Sisterhood) and the Women's Peace Army (Peace Army), affiliated separately with the international council. Both were keen to join a network of women who provided support and disseminated information across borders in time of war. The organisations often clashed over different ideas about tactics and tone. Yet both were moved to question imperial loyalty and Australia's involvement in the war because of their commitment to international cooperation and goodwill—a significant departure from the dominant pro-empire sentiment promoted during wartime.

---

52   Cora V Baldock, 'Irene Adelaide Greenwood 1992', *Australian Feminist Studies* 8, no. 17 (1 March 1993): 1–4, doi.org/10.1080/08164649.1993.9994672.
53   Cynthia Enloe, *Bananas, Beaches and Bases: Making Feminist Sense of International Politics* (London: Pandora, 1989); Ann Tickner, *Gender in International Relations: Feminist Perspectives on Achieving Global Security* (New York: Columbia University Press, 1992).
54   WILPF academic network accessed 26 September 2020, www.wilpf.org/members/; Jacqui True, *The Political Economy of Violence against Women* (Oxford, New York: Oxford University Press, 2012), doi.org/10.1093/acprof:oso/9780199755929.001.0001.

Chapter 2 charts the journey of founding WILPF women Eleanor Moore, Vida Goldstein and Cecilia John from Melbourne to the women's congress in Zurich in 1919. Their voyages illustrate many of the challenges of travel for unaccompanied political women in the early twentieth century, especially in a world recovering from total war. Looking at the practical impediments and enabling factors that surrounded their journeys, such as the funding provided by other women and their organisations, extends our understanding of the personal investments made by these women in internationalism. It was a community-funded commitment built on collective support, quite different from the official forms of government-supported internationalism that were overwhelmingly dominated by men. At the conference, the women negotiated the demands of an international organisation trying to facilitate the cooperation of participants from different nations, language groups and cultures. Each participant tended to speak from a national perspective and prioritise national interests, as did the Australians who sat together as a national section. Yet the international organisation departed from the methods of similar institutions by encouraging participation separate from national affiliation. Despite the tensions between the national and the international, the women strove to arrive at a position that allowed coexistence of different identities and interests.

Chapter 3 analyses how WILPF in Australia inspired shifts in racial thought among its members, as cosmopolitan and liberalising encounters challenged assumptions about the rationale of White Australia. The internationalism of WILPF made many of these women reconsider the White Australia project. Their personal experiences made them alert to overt racism which they found increasingly distasteful. Yet the entangled policies of labour protectionism and racial exclusion left them unable to denounce the White Australia Policy (WAP) entirely. This chapter examines the efforts of Australian members, generally on the left of the political spectrum, to navigate the tension between the labour progressivism they admired and the racism that was so intertwined with its advancement through the WAP.

Chapter 4 brings the tension between national interests and international commitments into closer focus during the 1930s, when WILPF women were confronted by the fascist threat. At first they were buoyed by mainstream support for pacifism. The Kellogg–Briand Pact outlawed war and the League of Nations convened a World Disarmament Conference in Geneva that gave hope to millions that war could be avoided in future. But during the lead-up to the outbreak of World War II, the WILPF in Australia came close to rupturing over incompatible ideas and strategies as the rise of fascism challenged many women's commitment to nonviolence. There were disagreements with the wider peace movement and, most damagingly, with the international head office. At this point the dominating personality of Eleanor Moore proved to be a real obstacle to recruitment. Membership dwindled and a core few prioritised absolute pacifism and purity over constructive engagement with anti-war campaigns that approved of violence. They persevered, leaving open a path for new members to tread after the war as they worked to reconstruct the national section.

For many women, internationalism as a political identity was attractive as they yearned for a more cosmopolitan and inclusive Australia and pursued experiences outside of the nation. Moore felt deeply Australia's 'insularity' when exposed to an international conference and its 'cosmopolitan atmosphere'.[55] Edith Abbott, when travelling in 1949, came to realise how 'isolated' Australia was and how important the 'few seeking souls' were who thought about world affairs.[56] Paradoxically, many members reasserted their Australian identity through their travels and were at pains to encourage a particularly Australian vision of international engagement. Moore also articulated how overseas travel heightened her love of country, and on returning from months abroad she noted how 'the burning blast of the north wind made the English people on board wonder what sort of an inferno they were coming to, but to me it was the breath of paradise regained.'[57] Greenwood similarly urged in 1975 that when histories of the women's movement were written, they should come:

> from the struggles of the early women in Australia, and not [be] a derivative of the work of the suffragettes in England, though it greatly influenced it, nor the American suffragette movement into which the young new liberationist women are digging for their background.[58]

The foundations for such a story were 'our diaries, our history, our literature about women'.[59] The significant involvement of WILPF in campaigns for Aboriginal rights in the mid-twentieth century are an example of a specific Australian agenda to which WILPF members applied their technique of the international campaign.

---

55 Moore, *Quest for Peace*, 97.
56 Edith M Abbott, report to the Australian Section of WILPF, 28 March 1950, Box 1728/3 Papers, WILPF, MS 9377, SLV.
57 Moore, *Quest for Peace*, 64.
58 Greenwood, 'A Lifetime of Political Activity', *Women and Politics Conference Volume 1*, 63.
59 Greenwood, 'A Lifetime of Political Activity', *Women and Politics Conference Volume 1*, 63.

Chapter 5 examines how WILPF adapted to changes in the discourse of internationalism with the creation of the United Nations (UN). New definitions of human rights allowed WILPF members to reconceptualise their ideas on peace and security. That also created a tension between recognising group rights and collective identity in a context where rights were increasingly seen as universal. WILPF wanted an end to race-based discrimination, while grappling with the complexities of cultural difference. Significantly, WILPF in Australia used new international structures, conventions and norms to call for greater international attention to Aboriginal rights in Australia, making local concerns international as they raised them in the meeting rooms of New York. Anna Vroland, a Victorian teacher and advocate of Aboriginal rights, led this shift in emphasis when she became leader of the Melbourne group.

The twentieth century has seen the rise and strengthening of national security institutions. In Australia, the forerunner to the Australian Security Intelligence Organisation (ASIO) was established during World War I, utilising the *War Precautions Act* of 1914 (Cth), while ASIO itself was founded in 1949. Passports and visas were introduced in a much more systematic way and border controls became more rigid. These governmental agencies, with increased funding and powers to conduct surveillance and record keeping of their citizens, increased the militarisation of civilian society, which allowed governments to justify prosecuting and spying on their national citizens. This new paradigm led to the criminalisation of activist activity, or at least the sense that participation in activism could be dangerous and lead to trouble with authorities. WILPF sought to resist these developments by working against this grain of the national security state.

Chapter 6 examines the new challenges posed by the Cold War and WILPF's negotiation of neutrality. New international women's groups, notably the Women's International Democratic Federation (WIDF) changed the dynamics of the international women's sphere. WILPF became anxious, guarding its heritage and position for fear of being subsumed into groups with alleged 'communist sympathies'. During the 1950s and 1960s WILPF in Australia focused on campaigns against nuclear testing and US military bases in Australia, and were more inclined to work within mainstream structures, especially under the leadership of Blackburn. In campaigning against militarism in the 'atomic age', campaigns again aimed to acknowledge women's power and position within the family as caregivers and protectors. This was in part due to the material conditions of women activists, many of whom were mothers concerned with their children's future. Some were only able to find the time to be politically active by bringing their children along to marches.

Chapter 7 charts the ways in which WILPF in Australia protested against the Vietnam War by using international connections that gave them detailed information ahead of national media. Organising during this time of renewed radicalism in Australian society forced WILPF to diversify in order to survive. The burgeoning women's liberation movement of the 1960s and 1970s caused a paradigm shift in theorising women's oppression. New feminists did not just ignore WILPF's activism of earlier decades, they called it out as anti-feminist. This was confronting, but after engagement in the UN Decade for Women, WILPF's ideology was modified through connections with the wider feminist movement, other non-government organisations (NGOs), international civil servants and national delegations. WILPF absorbed the new language of women's liberation. The concept of 'patriarchy', popularised by feminist scholars such as Kate Millett, helped them to adapt and renew their radical critique. Rather than claim that women were more peaceful or maternal than men, they described how the 'patriarchy' deformed both sexes, conditioning men and women into performing traditional gender roles that were conducive to violence and war.

After the fall of the Berlin Wall WILPF had to adapt its campaign focus. Chapter 8 continues the discussion of WILPF and the UN Decade for Women. Although the decade had 'peace' as one of its three themes, the UN conferences failed in WILPF's eyes to adequately address the issues of women and war. Peace, however, was discussed in relation to the Arab–Israeli conflict, something that WILPF members themselves had divided opinions on. WILPF internationally continued to focus energy and funds on their relationship with the UN. In the 2000s it was central to lobbying efforts for the UN Security Council Resolution (UNSCR) 1325 on Women, Peace and Security, which was the first resolution to focus on women and armed conflict, recognising gendered experiences of war and the need to have women contribute to the peacebuilding process.[60] National branches

---

60   Australian WILPF member Felicity Hill was director of the WILPF office in New York during the lobbying of this resolution, and has written about promoting UNSCR 1325 in her Masters thesis: Felicity Hill, 'How and When Has Security Council Resolution 1325 (2000) on Women, Peace and Security Impacted Negotiations Outside the Security Council?' (Masters thesis, Uppsala University Programme of International Studies, 2004).

took on the campaign to push governments to create National Action Plans for local implementation of 1325 goals, and continued to promote feminist foreign policy priorities.[61]

Trying to articulate the relationship between gender and peace was something WILPF constantly re-evaluated throughout its years of organising as a women-only group. War could have the effect of exacerbating the binary categories of gender roles, though modern campaigns for gender equality on the battlefield have complicated the strict gender roles of the combatant and those in need of protection.[62] By the 1970s WILPF desired to broaden its theoretical understanding of gender and peace, connecting issues of domestic violence and violence against women to the normalisation of militarism in society and broad acceptance of war. While women's liberation activists saw gender roles as something to be escaped from, WILPF connected its understanding of maternal citizenship to earlier ideas that saw care as the basis of a new social order. Australian member Stella Cornelius, who established a conflict resolution network, mused in 1975:

> We're concerned about peace, between person and person and peace between group and group and peace between nation and nation, [and] we often wonder if there is any difference between them.[63]

WILPF's message was, and continues to be, to encourage the creation of a culture of peace rather than simply an absence of war.

---

61 Confortini, *Intelligent Compassion*, 133.
62 Cynthia Enloe, *The Big Push: Exposing and Challenging the Persistence of Patriarchy* (Oxford: Myriad Editions, 2017), 81, doi.org/10.1525/9780520969193.
63 Stella Cornelius, 'Women Peace and Politics', *Women and Politics Conference Volume 1*, 66.

1
World War I and the founding of WILPF

On 28 April 1915 over one thousand women from warring and neutral nations came together at The Hague in the Netherlands for four days to discuss how to bring about peace.[1] Barred from commanding heights of power, these women nonetheless insisted on their capacity to deliberate on and seek to influence global events. Political women around the world looked on with interest. The very decision of these women to move across the borders of nations at war, was worthy of note. Some of the women's home nations prohibited them from travelling—the British Government refused permits to 180 women and the French government arrested women trying to attend.[2] Australian journalist and feminist Miles Franklin, at the time living in the United States, described the delegation of American women as the 'latest crusaders to formulate the idea of peace amid the fumes of war madness'.[3]

---

1   See Harriet Alonso, 'Introduction', in *Women at The Hague: The International Congress of Women and Its Results*, ed. Jane Addams, Emily G Balch and Alice Hamilton, 2003 ed. (Urbana, Ill.: University of Illinois Press, 1915), vii; and Kate Laing, 'World War and Worldly Women: The Great War and the Formation of the Women's International League for Peace and Freedom in Australia', *La Trobe Journal*, no. 96 (2015): 117–34, an article which informs this and the subsequent chapter.
2   J Ann Tickner and Jacqui True, 'A Century of International Relations Feminism: From World War I Women's Peace Pragmatism to the Women, Peace and Security Agenda', *International Studies Quarterly* 62, no. 2 (1 June 2018): 223, doi.org/10.1093/isq/sqx091.
3   Miles Franklin, 'Peace Ahoy! Crusaders of 1915', *Life and Labor* (April 1915): 66–67. Quoted in Jill Roe and Margaret Bettison, *A Gregarious Culture: Topical Writings of Miles Franklin* (St Lucia: University of Queensland Press, 2001), 55.

> There is something dramatic and inspiring in the S.S. Noordam slipping through the war-infested water lanes flying a little white flag bearing in blue letters the legend PEACE, when all the dominant flags on the seas today signify nothing better than hell let loose.[4]

Writing in the National Women's Trade Union League of America's journal, *Life and Labor*, Franklin did not want to 'worship them as heroes' noting they were 'a group of comfortable women, able to set sail on an adventurous and entertaining holiday, while lesser mortals are tied to the inconspicuous and monotonous grind which upholds the social fabric'.[5] Despite this, and pleased that a trade union representative was among them to put forward the plight of working woman at the conference, she encouraged readers to support the action for peace amid global turmoil. The motivation for the conference demonstrated how 'a shred of the developing sisterhood remained though brothers fought like fiends'. Franklin's hope was tinged with dismay that some in the British suffrage movement had chosen instead to support the nationalist war effort over the worldwide movement they had instigated before the war. She ended with a rallying call:

> Those contemptuous of the childish simplicity and apparent lack of practicality in asking for anything so violently repudiated as peace may be reminded that it was a bewildering intricacy of gymnastic reasoning on the premise that the only way to preserve peace is to prepare for war which is in part responsible for the present debacle … send forth our gallant band of crusaders with a blessing and a cheer.[6]

This first Hague Congress of Women has become emblematic of the internationalism the Women's International League for Peace and Freedom (WILPF) aspired to, both then and now. Women crossed borders, defied nationalistic chauvinism and greeted each other as sisters with common interests.[7] It is a story of pride in the WILPF. Yet, as significant as the conference was for the history of the WILPF, the women's peace movement in Australia was more homegrown, first developing independently and only later merging with the international assembly. No Australians were able to attend that conference in 1915 because of distance and geography, though many, including Franklin, watched closely. The organisations that formed

---

4   Franklin, 'Peace Ahoy! Crusaders of 1915', Roe and Bettison, *A Gregarious Culture*, 55.
5   Franklin, 'Peace Ahoy! Crusaders of 1915', Roe and Bettison, *A Gregarious Culture*, 55.
6   Franklin, 'Peace Ahoy! Crusaders of 1915', Roe and Bettison, *A Gregarious Culture*, 55.
7   GC Bussey and Margaret Tims, *Pioneers for Peace: Women's International League for Peace and Freedom, 1915-1965*, 2nd ed. (London: Allen & Unwin, 1965); Catherine Foster, *Women For All Seasons: The Story of the Women's International League for Peace and Freedom* (Athens: University of Georgia Press, 1989).

locally, the Sisterhood of International Peace and the Women's Peace Army, were influenced by the resolutions and ideas sent around the world after its conclusion and the optimism of that conference became foundation for local activity.

***

The formation of Australia's two major women's peace groups, the Sisterhood of International Peace and the Women's Peace Army, was initially spurred on by the Australian domestic political landscape. They subsequently widened their interest to international action and politics, drawing inspiration from the Hague Conference. Internationalism was a popular political movement at the turn of the century and the growing threat of war made it an attractive instrument for those trying to achieve permanent peace, especially for those activists and intellectuals who abhorred the atrocities they believed were committed in the name of nation and empire.[8]

Australian women had a markedly different experience of World War I from those in Europe and North America. Physical distance from the 'front line' shaped the opportunities available to women and shielded them from the full-scale transformative dislocation of total war mobilisation, as was experienced by civilians in Britain and Europe.[9] For the majority of women the strict gender division of labour was exacerbated and their contribution to the war effort defined by what was considered 'feminine', such as knitting for the troops overseas as part of the Australian Comforts Fund. Many women joined the Red Cross to feel useful in contributing to the war effort and, with children, were responsible for large-scale volunteer organising devoted to providing for the men at the front.[10] The sheer amount of volunteer work was unparalleled but because it was unpaid it has often been underrated, then and since.[11] There were few aspects of women's lives that were not affected by the war, and even social activities were curtailed due to the shame of associating with 'shirkers'. Some women felt it was their patriotic duty to encourage men to enlist.[12]

---

8 Glenda Sluga, *Internationalism in the Age of Nationalism* (Philadelphia: University of Pennsylvania Press, 2013), 2, doi.org/10.9783/9780812207781.
9 Michael McKernan, *The Australian People and the Great War* (Sydney; London: Collins, 1984), 65.
10 McKernan, *The Australian People and the Great War*, 75; Melanie Oppenheimer, *The Power of Humanity: 100 Years of Australian Red Cross 1914–2014* (Sydney: Harper Collins Australia, 2014), 27.
11 See discussion in Oppenheimer, *The Power of Humanity*, 27.
12 Carmel Shute, 'Heroines and Heroes: Sexual Mythology in Australia 1914–18', in *Gender and War: Australians at War in the Twentieth Century*, ed. Joy Damousi and Marilyn Lake (New York, Melbourne: Cambridge University Press, 1995), 27.

Many historians, including the official historian of the war, Ernest Scott, have focused on how the main motif of women's participation in the war was waiting.[13] Duty required many to 'wait and weep'—most having to deal with the loss of close friends, sons, brothers and husbands.[14] Even for those whose loved ones returned, the scars of war often ran deep.[15] In this environment, commitment to pacifism was a minority view. Mainstream opinion upheld loyalty to nation and empire, creating an inhospitable social and cultural environment for pacifism. It is partly for this reason that the establishment of anti-war groups is worthy of scholarly attention. World War I was the catalyst for the creation of women's peace groups in Australia. But their ability to connect so quickly with the international context was indebted to the strong networks that existed in the suffrage and women's rights movements that preceded the established peace movement.

Australian women and the tradition of internationalism

The domestic women's movement was familiar with international interactions and the exchange of ideas across borders. Formal organisations were set up for women to campaign internationally in the late nineteenth century, including the International Council of Women (ICW) formed in 1899, the International Alliance of Women (IAW) in 1904, and later the Woman Suffrage Union of the British Dominions in 1913.[16] Through domestic groups like the Woman's Christian Temperance Union (WCTU) and the National Councils of Women (NCW), which were in various ways affiliated to the ICW and the IAW, Australian women travelled and received international travellers to recruit, discuss and share ideas and experiences. They organised on political grounds, often focused on women's suffrage.

The ICW's primary goals were to facilitate communication between countries on the political position of women with a view to improvement and, as with the focus of other women's rights organisations of the time,

---

13 Shute, 'Heroines and Heroes', 31; Ernest Scott, *Australia During the War*, 1914–1918, volume 11 (Sydney: Angus & Robertson, 1936), 31.
14 McKernan, *The Australian People and the Great War*, 93.
15 Marina Larsson, *Shattered ANZACs: Living with the Scars of War* (Kensington: University of New South Wales Press, 2009).
16 Leila J Rupp, *Worlds of Women: The Making of an International Women's Movement* (Princeton: Princeton University Press, 1997), 16, doi.org/10.1515/9780691221816.

it promoted maternalism. The ICW's formation coincided with the development of the world peace movement, responding to concerns with new industrialised methods of warfare. Two mixed-gender peace conferences were held at The Hague in 1899 and 1907.[17] The ICW sent messages of support to The Hague in 1899 and recognised it as 'the first international women's association to identify itself with the Peace movement'.[18] However by World War I the NCWs in Australia that were affiliated with the ICW were unable to criticise the war effort and moved away from the peace movement. The NCW had separate council structures in each state, made up of local women's groups with different goals and political persuasions. With membership including the pro-empire Australian Women's National League (AWNL), the diversity of opinion on the council often inclined the leadership to avoid the discussion of peace activities during wartime.[19] As the war split feminists within the movement between those for and against the war, the need for a dedicated peace organisation became more pressing.

Understanding the tradition of women's internationalism indicates that the emergence of a peace-specific internationalism in 1915 was an extension of a pre-existing tradition. It drew on a history of Australian women proudly presenting to the world and using internationalism as a tactical political instrument for domestic gains. These representations were to become pivotal in connecting local peace groups with the International Committee of Women for Permanent Peace (ICWPP) after the women's congress at The Hague. One of their main organising methods was to send letters to every known and prominent internationalist they could reach to urge them to consider taking up the cause. Yet, when the ICWPP was created, later becoming WILPF, the impetus for internationalism had another layer. The focus was not simply on networking and sharing information on women's suffrage and maternal welfare, but rather it sought to encourage national governments to use arbitration instead of conflict to settle international disputes. It preceded a wider move to internationalism embodied in the creation of the League of Nations. The national sections of the international body ran in parallel with national governments, encouraging and lobbying them to embrace liberal internationalism as a new world order.

---

17   Sluga, *Internationalism in the Age of Nationalism*, 19.
18   Judith Smart and Marian Quartly, *Respectable Radicals: A History of the National Council of Women of Australia 1896–2006* (Melbourne: Monash University Publishing, 2015), 108.
19   Smart and Quartly, *Respectable Radicals*, 111.

The Federation of the Australian colonies in 1901 markedly changed women's engagement with the internationalism of the women's movement. Women who had previously situated themselves within the trans-Tasman world began to narrow their focus to the new nation-state.[20] Australian nationalism began to coalesce around the new federal parliament which legislated the White Australia Policy (WAP). A new national flag was also created and adopted. The new federal system was tightly bound to empire, preserving the right of appeal to the Privy Council in the United Kingdom. Women's activists were very interested in understanding the law, and the legal system of federation. Pacifists like Moore were aware that the constitution profoundly changed Australia's military system. It gave the Commonwealth power over 'the Naval and Military defence of the Commonwealth and of the several States, and the control of the forces to execute and maintain the laws of the Commonwealth.'[21] This provision was intended to 'remove from the States all means of making war upon one another', and Moore noted how after Federation all state-based military schemes ceased, including cadet training through schools. It was also important as it gave the legal power to the Commonwealth Government to defend Australia against attack, although the *Defence Act 1903* did not permit conscription for overseas service. But as the constitution reaffirmed the bonds of empire, Australians could be rallied to serve as volunteers if Great Britain was at war. That was precisely what happened in August 1914 with the formation and despatch of the Australian Imperial Force (AIF) as a volunteer army.

The women's movement's priorities post-Federation

Many of the organisations like the WCTU and the NCW that agitated for women's suffrage thought first and foremost about women's roles in the care of others, particularly children. They were maternalists who recognised the different life patterns of women and sought political acknowledgement of women's work.[22] It was a strategy characteristic of early Australian women's rights activists. Suffrage activists before Federation, such as the Womanhood Suffrage League (founded in 1891), with renowned members such as Rose Scott and Louisa Lawson, thought that the values of voting women would

---

20 James Keating, *Distant Sisters: Australasian Women and the International Struggle for the Vote, 1880–1914* (Manchester: Manchester University Press, 2020), 3, doi.org/10.7765/9781526140968.
21 Keating, *Distant Sisters*, 14.
22 Marilyn Lake, *Getting Equal: The History of Australian Feminism* (St Leonards, NSW: Allen & Unwin, 1999), 13.

bring a new experience and morality to public life. They believed that women lacked economic independence, not only by being denied access to fair working conditions and opportunities but also by the traditional division of labour within marriage.[23] Marriage for many activist women represented a degrading dependence on men. There were only narrow avenues of escape from abuses of husbands.

Women's rights campaigners agitated for the vote so that women would be able to have greater agency and bring into public life issues that were important to women and children but often unseen in politics because considered purely domestic or private. Especially once given the vote, beginning in South Australia in 1894, federally in 1902, and ending in Victoria in 1908, female reformers campaigned for welfare rights of women and children, to protect them from the abuses of men, and to help women better perform their nurturing roles.[24] Some believed that men's aggressive behaviour was exacerbated by alcoholism, tying women's rights movements with temperance as the WCTU did to encourage more harmonious family lives. When Vida Goldstein promoted the achievements of Australia abroad in 1902, her advocacy advanced the ideas of distinctive difference between men and women, noting that as mothers and wives women had different values and interests that should be prioritised and protected rather than to demand the same rights as men.[25] While maternalist feminism, and the way reformers encouraged women to use the vote, limited women's participation in the public sphere, it still had the potential to disrupt men's domination and posed a threat to male control over home life. Unsurprisingly, there was significant backlash among men against these calls for reform.

Maternalist campaigners did not necessarily link their nurturing agenda with peace, and the women's movement became divided over its involvement with the nascent peace movement. The war 'consolidated the idea of a sexually differentiated citizenship' and established the 'citizen solider' who was compensated for their sacrifice to the nation, an idea that women activists used to model the 'citizen mother' as a claim to greater state recognition and support.[26] Maternalist feminism, where the responsibility

---

23   Lake, *Getting Equal*, 3.
24   Marian Sawer, *A Woman's Place: Women and Politics in Australia*, 2nd ed. (Sydney: Allen & Unwin, 1993), 5.
25   Marilyn Lake, 'Women's International Leadership', in *Diversity in Leadership: Australian Women, Past and Present*, ed. Joy Damousi, Kim Rubenstein and Mary Tomsic (Canberra: ANU Press, 2014), 73, doi.org/10.22459/DL.11.2014.
26   Marilyn Lake, 'A Revolution in the Family', in *Mothers of a New World: Maternalist Politics and the Origins of Welfare States*, ed. Seth Koven and Sonya Michel (New York: Routledge, 1993), 382.

for caregiving was of primary importance, was repurposed for both the women's peace campaign and in support of the war. Supporters of the war believed it was a mother's duty to sacrifice sons in the interests of the nation, and some felt that their efforts should be compensated with state financial support. Women peace activists broadened the focus of the violence and control of men in the home to state violence and power of men in battle. At a time when society was sharply sexually segregated, the women's peace movement's appeal to women as mothers aimed to acknowledge the reality of women's work and daily lives while encouraging them to structurally consider where their power lay in the international economic system that caused and sustained wars.

Australian peace groups formed in World War I

In July 1914 tensions in Europe escalated and the military alliance system pulled the great European powers into war. When Britain declared war in August, it did so 'in the expectation that Australia and other Dominions would follow'.[27] The Australian Government, led by Prime Minister Joseph Cook, accepted the decision without question, reminding Australians that 'when the Empire is at war, so is Australia at war'.[28] Australia soon offered an initial expeditionary force of 20,000 men that increased to 33,000, all of whom had to be volunteers.[29] From a population of fewer than 5 million, this target was ambitious. The Australian Imperial Force (AIF) was created with bipartisan support from politicians. Australia's commitment to World War I, mainly uncontentious at first, would eventually ignite a nation-wide discussion about imperial loyalty. The issue of conscription in particular came to divide communities, and the imposition of wartime restrictions and general experiences of grief and loss caused an atmosphere of mistrust. The government, along with churches and other community groups, highlighted emotional and 'patriotic' identification with empire in recruitment campaigns. Men who chose not to enlist—nearly 70 per cent of eligible men between 18–60 years old—were labelled 'shirkers'.[30] It was

---

27 Joan Beaumont, *Broken Nation: Australians in the Great War* (Sydney: Allen & Unwin, 2013), 12.
28 Joseph Cook, Prime Minister, *The Argus*, 3 August 1914, 14.
29 Beaumont, *Broken Nation*, 16.
30 Beaumont, *Broken Nation*, xv.

in this political climate that the peace movement gained momentum, with some choosing to join peace societies to challenge unquestioning loyalty to empire and jingoistic patriotism.

In prewar Australia, peace activism had often taken root through the propagation of branches of groups that originated in England. The Society of Friends, whose religion was based on the Quaker Peace Testimony that refused militarism and violence, appeared in Australia from the 1880s, when individuals and families migrated from England.[31] For Quakers, pacifism was a way to 'reflect the spirit of Christ'.[32] The identity and following of the religion became stronger by the twentieth century and while the number of Quakers in Australia was never very large, they had an outsized presence in the peace movement.

One of the oldest peace groups in England was called the London Peace Society, formed by the Quakers in 1816.[33] Taking their lead from this, branches of the London Peace Society were established in Melbourne in 1905 and Sydney in 1907.[34] Other peace groups formed before the war included the Australian Freedom League, inaugurated in 1912 in Adelaide to oppose compulsory military training for young boys. There was also the Free Religious Fellowship, led by Reverend Frederick Sinclaire (who later became president of the Australian Peace Alliance), and the Peace, Humanity and Arbitration Society of Victoria, which was set up by Professor Lawrence Rentoul from Ormond College at Melbourne University to campaign specifically against the Boer War.[35] Many of these peace societies were connected with liberal religious organisations.

While peace groups became active in all Australian states during World War I, it was women's peace groups in Melbourne that were most energetic and outspoken. The establishment of the Australian Church, led by Rev. Dr Charles Strong, had exercised a great influence on social ideas in the city.[36] Having arrived from Scotland in 1875, Strong became a popular

---

31 Thomas D Hamm, 'Quaker Peace Testimony', in *The Oxford International Encyclopaedia of Peace*, ed. Nigel Young, online version (Oxford: Oxford University Press, 2010).
32 Hilary Summy, *Peace Angel of World War I: Dissent of Margaret Thorp* (Brisbane: Australian Centre for Peace and Conflict Studies, 2006), 12.
33 Patricia D'Itri, *Cross Currents in the International Women's Movement, 1848–1948* (Bowling Green, Ohio: Bowling Green State University Popular Press, 1999), 123.
34 Eleanor M Moore, *The Quest for Peace, As I Have Known It in Australia* (Melbourne, 1948), 22.
35 Mimi Colligan, 'Brothers and Sisters in Peace: The Peace Movement in Melbourne 1900–1918' (BA Honours thesis, Monash University, 1973), 6; Moore, *The Quest for Peace*, 18.
36 Malcolm Saunders, 'An Australian Pacifist: The Reverend Dr. Charles Strong, 1844–1942', *Biography* 18, no. 3 (1995): 242, doi.org/10.1353/bio.2010.0089.

and respected clergyman in the Victorian colony and the first president of the Peace Society.[37] His teachings were too liberal for the Presbyterian church and in 1885 he formed a new congregation he called the Australian Church, which was designed to engage 'in harmony with and expressive of, the free, democratic and progressive spirit of Australia'.[38] Standing on Flinders Street, Melbourne, the church and congregation grew to around 1,000, all comfortable, well-connected people from Melbourne's middle class, including the families of activists Eleanor Moore and Vida Goldstein.[39] Goldstein's father, Col. JRY Goldstein, was the church's first honorary secretary. By 1896 Alfred Deakin, a future Australian prime minister and close personal friend of Strong, had also joined.[40] Following in the tradition of theosophy, the Australian Church was suspicious of Christian orthodoxy and promoted liberalism and freedom of thought, and through Strong's personal conviction, anti-militarism.[41] It was a congregation of 'radicals and progressives, acutely aware of the social ills of their day, and determined to do something about them'.[42]

In January 1915 Strong gave an address to the church titled 'Women and War'.[43] He suggested that the:

> Women of Australia should form a League of Peace … think what a moral influence such a League would have … by exchange of literature, lectures, and conferences educating each other, and educating the young! … Woman helped to found Christianity. She was called now to aid in bringing the new patriotism, the new cosmopolitanism, with their new social conscience.[44]

---

37 Saunders, 'An Australian Pacifist', 241.
38 Dr Charles Strong, quoted in Saunders, 'An Australian Pacifist', 241.
39 Farley Kelly, 'Vida Goldstein: Political Woman', in *Doubletime: Women in Victoria, 150 Years*, ed. Marilyn Lake and Farley Kelly (Ringwood, Vic: Penguin, 1985), 170. See also: Janette M Bomford, *That Dangerous and Persuasive Woman: Vida Goldstein* (Carlton, Vic: Melbourne University Press, 1993); and Joy Damousi, 'An Absence of Anything Masculine: Vida Goldstein and Women's Public Speech', *Victorian Historical Journal* 79, no. 2 (November 2008): 251–64.
40 Colin Robert Badger, *The Reverend Charles Strong and the Australian Church*. (Melbourne: Abacada Press, 1971), 100.
41 Jill Roe, *Beyond Belief: Theosophy in Australia 1879–1939* (Kensington: New South Wales University Press, 1986), 33.
42 Marion Maddox, 'Charles Strong's Australian Church: A Network for Justice and Peace', in *Remembering Pioneer Australian Pacifist Charles Strong*, ed. Norman Habel (Melbourne: Morning Star Publishing, 2018), 74.
43 Dr Charles Strong, 'Pulpit and Platform', *Commonweal*, 1 February 1915, State Library of Victoria (SLV), 186.
44 Strong, 'Pulpit and Platform', 186.

Part of the attraction of the church to many members was the discussion of social theorists. Readings that greatly influenced the congregation included works by John Ruskin, Edward and John Caird, George D Herron, Thomas Carlyle and Alfred Russel Wallace.[45] Ruskin was particularly favoured. Indeed, Strong's lecture was inspired by Ruskin's words in *Sesame and Lilies* (1865):

> There is not a war in the world, no, nor an injustice, but you women are answerable for it; not in that you have provoked, but in that you have not hindered.

After the lecture the church publication *The Commonweal* published a 'suggested enrolment card' that promised to collect the names of interested readers.[46] On 25 March the first meeting of the Sisterhood was convened with 60 members under the motto 'Justice, Friendship, and Arbitration'.[47] Monthly meetings included guest lecturers which brought the women of the group into contact with many of the leading speakers on internationalism in Australia. Topics ranged from White Australia to peace, arbitration and conflicts around the world. The Sisterhood continued to grow and by 1918 members were designated as 'suburban secretaries' to encourage small reading groups around Melbourne, and sub-branches were formed in St Kilda and Footscray.[48]

Despite being barred from practising or studying law in some states, many political women were deeply interested in the law and the way the federal system shaped political involvement.[49] For women choosing to be active within the Australian Church and the Sisterhood, there was a desire to better understand how the federal system had led to Australia's involvement in the war. For some, the war illustrated how empire was fatal—their sons, brothers and husbands were killed in a far-off war front. The experience prompted a more critical stance toward imperialism. Their internationalism therefore arguably represented a shift away from empire and towards the global, as they sought to create a new system that would prevent war. In calling for justice and arbitration, the Sisterhood were focused on a practical legal solution to counteract the war system and called for an international court where national disputes would be settled.

---

45   MR Parnaby, 'The Socially Reforming Churchman: A Study of the Social Thought and Activity of Charles Strong in Melbourne 1890–1900' (BA Honours thesis, University of Melbourne, 1975), 13.
46   'Suggested Enrolment Card, the Sisterhood of Peace', *Commonweal*, 1 February 1915, 170.
47   Moore, *The Quest for Peace*, 27.
48   *Peacewards*, published as a supplement to the Australian Church's *Commonweal*, SLV, July 1918, 12. 'International Peace—Local Sisterhood Centre Formed', *Advertiser*, Footscray, 3 August 1918, 1.
49   Margaret Thornton, 'Women as Fringe Dwellers of the Jurisprudential Community' in *Sex, Power and Justice: Historical Perspectives of Law in Australia*, ed. Diane Kirkby (Melbourne: Oxford University Press, 1995), 189.

Committee of the Sisterhood of International Peace, 1919.

Back row from left to right: Mrs Slater, Miss Pierson, Mrs Jefferies, Mrs Levens, Miss Ferguson. Front row: Mrs Drummond, Miss Douglas, Mrs Warren Kerr, Mrs Paling, Miss H Milliard BA. (Eleanor Moore, abroad.) Mrs Janet Strong was also a founding member of the Sisterhood, but died in 1919 before this photo was taken.

Source: Records of the Women's International League for Peace and Freedom, MS 9377, State Library of Victoria.

When WILPF became more established internationally the official organisation was not connected to any religious order. However, as the connection to the Australian Church in Melbourne suggests, religious motivations played a large role in its establishment in Australia and overseas. Free-thinking nonconformist Christianity influenced both pacifism and women's activism in the early twentieth century and continued throughout with connections to the Society of Friends and individual Quakers. Spirituality contributed greatly to members' ideas about public and social theory, and their practical commitment to creating a better society. Eleanor Moore was closely aligned with the Australian Church. Educated at the Presbyterian Ladies College (PLC), the school for girls in East Melbourne, she followed other active political alumni including other women's peace activists such as Mabel Drummond, Vida Goldstein and Marion Phillips, who would be elected to the British parliament in 1929.[50] Moore's peace

---

50 For more information on PLC and the women educated there, see: Kathleen Fitzpatrick, *PLC Melbourne: The First Century, 1875–1975* (Burwood: Presbyterian Ladies' College, 1975), 113.

activism began in middle age. Her first engagement with peace campaigning was as a member of Strong's Peace Society, opposing the compulsory military training for cadets aged between 12 and 18 which had been introduced by the federal government in 1911.[51]

Moore's founding role in the Sisterhood was as corresponding secretary. Other prominent women involved included Mrs Lucy Paling as president, Mrs Janet Strong as general secretary, Mrs Mabel Drummond and Mrs Jane Kerr. The membership of the group grew to around 210.[52] They stayed in close contact with Dr Strong's Peace Society and the two organisations 'enjoyed a brother–sister relationship', jointly organising many activities and sharing responsibility for the monthly pacifist journal, *Peacewards*.[53] Joining the Sisterhood was a statement for many of the members. Jane Kerr was the wife of a prominent government adviser, Warren Kerr, who served as chairman of the Commonwealth War Savings Council and the Victorian War Savings Committee. Her outspoken commitment to the Sisterhood baffled some, not least the wartime censor who predictably dismissed women's anti-war activism and considered it 'somewhat remarkable that the husband of the President of the Women's Branch, W. Warren Kerr, takes a prominent part in patriotic movements here. Evidently a divided family.'[54] Mabel Drummond's activity was similarly disapproved of by her mother.[55] Both Drummond and Kerr had relatives in the war. Drummond's brother Thomas Gardner was her constant correspondent, and Kerr's son died at Gallipoli, inspiring her to continue organising against war. She 'scandalized some who talked of "avenging" their dead by declaring that she was at least thankful that her boy had died before he had had time to hurt anyone else.'[56] This statement was highly provocative even to those sympathetic to maternalist feminism.

---

51 LL Robson, *Australia and the Great War, 1914–1918: Narrative and Selection of Documents* (South Melbourne: Macmillan of Australia, 1969), 2.
52 Malcolm Saunders, 'Are Women More Peaceful than Men? The Experience of the Australian Section of the Women's International League for Peace and Freedom, 1915–39', *Interdisciplinary Peace Research* 3, no. 1 (1 May 1991): 47, doi.org/10.1080/14781159108412732.
53 Malcolm Saunders, 'The Early Years of the Australian Section of the Women's International League for Peace and Freedom', *Journal of the Royal Australian Historical Society* 82, no. 2 December 1996: 182.
54 T Miller to unknown, 1 July 1918, 're Sisterhood of International Peace (Melb)' Censor's notes, 169/26/34 MF1376 'Intelligence reports on enemy trading and other suspicious actions', MP95/1, National Archives of Australia (NAA).
55 Janet Morice, *Six-Bob-a-Day Tourist* (Ringwood, Vic: Penguin Books, 1985), 46.
56 Moore, *The Quest for Peace*, 40.

Eleanor M Moore, 1924.
Source: Eleanor M. Moore papers, 1887–1953, Mitchell Library, State Library of NSW PXE 1025. See Appendix for a short biography of Eleanor Moore.

The Sisterhood was proud of the status of Australian women as voters. Sisterhood followers also felt the weight of that responsibility and a corresponding need to have fully formed opinions and accurate information before making decisions:

> The situation of Australian women is peculiar. We are, as you know, fully enfranchised, therefore our actions have political significance, and since our country is one of the belligerents, it is by no means easy to know always what is the right and wise attitude for us to adopt.[57]

Overlooking the frontier wars as well as the war in South Africa (1899– 1902), members of the Sisterhood believed that, until the outbreak of World War I, Australia had always been at peace.[58] Their motivation to action was to counter the habit of 'always waiting for a lead from abroad' when discussing Australia's role in combat, which along with the focus on 'arbitration' showed their interest in foreign affairs policy.[59] Inspired by the Commonwealth Court of Conciliation and Arbitration that had been created in 1904, which set awards and settled political disputes between business and labour, Australian liberal pacifists believed that an international arbitration court would similarly be able to mediate differences between states without violence. Arbitration was a primary part of Australian progressivism that after Federation was promoted to the world alongside women's suffrage. Progressives concentrated on the domain of the international to understand the conflict and to insist that Australia should engage with diplomacy rather than blindly follow the empire. In a letter to American pacifist Jane Addams, Moore expressed how their group would be strengthened by joining the international community as women in general were 'torn by conflicting feelings'. As pacifist numbers were not great, they 'must be linked up in close bonds of sympathy and understanding with one another all over the world' if they were to have any influence.[60]

---

57   Moore to the ICWPP 1919 conference organising committee (undated), Papers, WILPF, 1723/1 MS 9377, SLV.
58   Moore, *The Quest for Peace*, 13.
59   Moore, *The Quest for Peace*, 14.
60   Moore to Jane Addams, Chicago, 5 May 1915, series III reel 54, WILPF International Papers 1915–1978, Sanford, NC: Microfilming Corp. of America, c 1983, accessed at the National Library of Australia (NLA). Hereafter referred to as WILPF Papers.

The Sisterhood were sceptical of any claim of women's innate peacefulness, acknowledging that there was no guarantee that women would automatically vote for peace.[61] However, in the wartime setting, the Sisterhood women were observant of the gendered division of labour that was exacerbated during the conflict, with eligible men being expected to fight while women were told to attend to the home and wait for the men to return. Echoing Ruskin's words, they realised that while women were not in the decision-making spaces directing men to war, they were still responsible for not 'hindering'. The Sisterhood wanted to use education to help women realise their power as a collective to stop war rather than accepting their subordinate status in voluntary organisations supporting the troops at the same time as nurturing the soldiers of the future in their homes. If adequately educated and informed, they would come to understand that a 'martial spirit was foreign to women's nature'.[62]

The Sisterhood was formed not just because of a belief that women might exercise a moderating influence on decisions about war. Its founders also believed that separate women's organisations allowed for greater autonomy and influence in the peace movement, as women in mixed organisations were rarely able to take on leading roles or feel as comfortable expressing their opinions. Moreover, they believed that women suffered more in war than men and had 'a special right to struggle for peace, but no special ability to achieve it'.[63]

The Sisterhood were not the only group to emerge in response to the horrors of World War I. Vida Goldstein and her Women's Political Association (WPA) turned their attention to peace in 1915. Goldstein's involvement in the Australian women's suffrage movement has been well documented.[64] In 1903, one year after Australian women were granted full political rights nationally, she formed the WPA and became its president. It was specifically a 'non-party' organisation which acted as a lobby group outside the major parties. The association supported Goldstein's several bids for parliament between 1903 and 1917. Yet, her electoral popularity declined with each election.[65] Moore noted that 'during the war, her outspoken

---

61 Saunders, 'Are Women More Peaceful than Men?', 55.
62 Moore to May Wright Sewall, 5 May 1915, Papers, WILPF, 1723/1 MS 9377, SLV.
63 Saunders, 'The Early Years of the Australian Section of the Women's International League for Peace and Freedom', 184.
64 Bomford, *That Dangerous and Persuasive Woman*; Kelly, 'Vida Goldstein: Political Woman', in Lake and Kelly, *Doubletime*, 170. See also Fitzpatrick, *PLC Melbourne*, 116.
65 Lake and Kelly, *Doubletime*, 176.

pacifist principles tended to lessen her popularity'.[66] In July 1915, the WPA formed a dedicated peace group, the Peace Army, to protest against the war and its impact on women.[67] Though a pacifist organisation that committed to 'fight for peace and internationalism', their decision to call themselves an 'army' was ironically anti-militarist. But they were influenced by socialist ideology and recognisably militant, modelling their activism on the British suffragettes. Their tactics were deliberately provocative.[68] The announcement of the group in the *Woman Voter* illustrated how the choice of name was embracing militaristic emotive rhetoric; 'the Peace Army would be a fighting body, and would fight for the destruction of militarism with the same spirit of self-sacrifice as soldiers showed on the battlefield'.[69] Members were called 'peace soldiers'. With Goldstein as the president, the Peace Army attracted other prominent women from the suffrage movement abroad. Adela Pankhurst, recently arrived from England with experience of suffragette militancy, became the secretary, and Cecilia John, an accomplished contralto singer, the treasurer.

The WPA argued that women's voting would change the nature of public life. Goldstein also hoped that women would vote for peace and, in the *Woman Voter*, she emphasised their responsibility to do so:

> The time has come for women to show that they, as givers of life, refuse to give their sons as material for slaughter, and that they recognise that human life must be the first consideration of nations … The enfranchised women of Australia are political units in the British Empire, and they ought to lead the world in sane methods of dealing with these conflicts.[70]

The political philosophy of the organisation focused on women's advancement and the leadership remained in women's hands, although the organisation allowed men to join as members.[71] In working for women's advancement, the WPA had previously promoted the benefits of women's internationalism. For example, the *Woman Voter* reprinted a 1913 article from *Jus Suffragii*, the journal of the International Woman Suffrage Alliance,

---

66 Moore, *The Quest for Peace*, 28.
67 For more on the Women's Peace Army, see Pat Gowland, 'The Women's Peace Army', in *Women, Class and History: Feminist Perspectives on Australia 1788–1978*, ed. Elizabeth Windschuttle (Melbourne: Fontana Books, 1980), 216.
68 Gowland, 'The Women's Peace Army', 217.
69 'Women's Peace Army', *Woman Voter*, 15 July 1915, 2.
70 Vida Goldstein, 'The War', *Woman Voter*, 11 August 1914, 2.
71 Vida Goldstein, 'Women's Peace Army', *Woman Voter*, 15 July 1915, 2.

declaring that: 'The curse of women has been her isolation … But at last the cry has sounded "Women of the world unite; you have nothing to lose but your chains".'[72] Following in this tradition, for the WPA, internationalism might thus provide a solution to the evils of imperialism, as well as to the general oppression of women.

Not all members of the WPA supported the new campaign for peace. In November 1914, three months after the outbreak of the war, two executive office bearers felt compelled to resign on the grounds 'they were out of sympathy with the anti-war campaign of the WPA', stating 'any opposition to compulsory military training and to militarism at this juncture might tend to weaken England's opportunities for obtaining volunteer military service in the present war'.[73] The WPA moved to establish the Peace Army as a separate organisation in part to accommodate internal differences. It meant that those 'who do not approve of our non-party political policy [could] unite with us in regards to peace'.[74] Labor Party women, proscribed from joining the WPA, could now join the Peace Army without risk of expulsion from the Political Labor Council of Victoria.

It was after the establishment of the Sisterhood and the Peace Army that news of the international women's congress in April 1915 reached Australian shores. This conference, initiated by Aletta Jacobs, a physician from the Netherlands, and led by Jane Addams and other US women from the Women's Peace Party, brought together 1,135 women from many different women's organisations with an interest in pacifism.[75] Australian women were not able to be present at this conference, though Australian-born Muriel Matters financially contributed and was listed in the report as representing the 'Union of Democratic Control, London Branch'.[76] She may very well have planned to attend but the majority of the British delegation was prevented from travelling by the British Government just days before they were due for departure.[77] The gathering had resolved to

---

72 Winifred Harper Cooley, 'Women and Internationalism', reprinted from *Jus Suffragii*, Official Journal of the International Woman Suffrage Alliance, *Woman Voter*, 16 September 1913, 3.
73 Hilda Moody and Doris Kerr, 'WPA Becomes Anti-militarist; Misses Moody and Kerr resign', *Woman Voter*, 10 November 1914, 1.
74 Goldstein to Ms Hobhouse, ICWPP secretary, Amsterdam, 3 November 1915, series III reel 54, WILPF Papers.
75 Carrie A Foster, *The Women and the Warriors: The U.S. Section of the Women's International League for Peace and Freedom, 1915–1946* (Syracuse, NY: Syracuse University Press, 1995), 11.
76 'International Congress of Women, 1915 Report', Amsterdam, database edited by Kathryn Kish Sklar and Thomas Dublin, *Women and Social Movements, International—1840 to Present*, 247.
77 'International Congress of Women, 1915 Report', 247.

convene another conference immediately after the war, and formed the committee called the International Committee of Women for Permanent Peace (ICWPP) to begin preparations.[78] They also delegated envoys to meet with national governments to 'urge the Governments of the world to put an end to this bloodshed and to establish a just and lasting peace'.[79]

The ICWPP began canvassing for support in each country by using the already established women's networks. They sent letters to all known women's rights campaigners to ask for sympathy with the peace cause, beginning the letter 'knowing that you are an active worker in the Women's movement we are sending you the enclosed papers in the hope that you will find yourself in sympathy with our work.'[80] The Sisterhood sent letters to Jane Addams before receiving the ICWPP circular, being able to contact her through Mrs Janet Strong's association with the NCW Victoria.[81] While it was through the NCW that the Sisterhood first reached out to international women, the NCW's balancing act of incorporating vastly different opinions made women of the Sisterhood feel they could no longer support the NCW. Strong and Moore both resigned from the council over their stance on peace. Strong had been the vice-president of the Victorian branch for 11 years, but took a stand, noting 'what is to be said of the officers of a National Council who return communications on Peace Work in America unread?'[82]

Many Australian women replied positively and the ICWPP began organising to put women in touch with one another. They circulated a memorandum that identified the leading women's rights campaigners they were corresponding with. There was a genuine effort to represent each state including Rose Scott from NSW and Edith Cowan from WA, though many of the women mentioned did not end up becoming extensively involved in the ICWPP or WILPF, as the Melbourne groups took on most of the responsibility for organising.[83] Rose Scott, however, was heavily involved in the peace movement as a foundation member of the NSW Peace

---

78   Addams, Balch and Hamilton, *Women at The Hague*, 77; Emily G Balch, *A Venture in Internationalism 1915–1938* (WILPF Switzerland, 1938); Sklar and Dublin, *Women and Social Movements*, 7.
79   Addams, Balch and Hamilton, *Women at The Hague*, 77.
80   IWCPP to M.A. Harwood, 8 January 1916, series III reel 54, WILPF Papers.
81   Moore, *The Quest for Peace*, 27.
82   *Peacewards*, 1 September 1915, 12.
83   Memorandum from the ICWPP, 8 January 1916, series III reel 54, WILPF Papers. For more information on Rose Scott see Judith Allen, *Rose Scott: Vision and Revision in Feminism* (Melbourne: Oxford University Press, 1994).

Society until her death in 1925.[84] The memorandum was intended to help organise a national structure to affiliate to the international committee, and to overcome communication difficulties. It demonstrated an alliance of practicality formed through established networks and is a reminder of the difficulties in communicating across such vast distances. Logistical rationality was required alongside affinity with the cause.[85]

Looking through the WILPF International archive, which has been divided into sections with each country's correspondence filed in order, Victoria's activities outstrip the action in other states.[86] After the initial contact with known campaigners sent by the ICWPP, most of the letters discuss the complexity of the engagement between the Sisterhood and the Peace Army and their efforts to find ways that both groups could affiliate separately.

They attempted an amalgamation but could not find common ground. Towards the end of 1915 the Peace Army suggested both groups use the title 'Victorian Branch of the ICWPP'. The Sisterhood agreed to form a provisional committee to discuss the proposal. The Peace Army sent Adela Pankhurst to Sydney and Brisbane to set up more branches, in the hope of forming a representative national committee that could affiliate to the international.[87] The ICWPP supported the move to set up a national structure and distributed a memorandum to help coordinate the interest in Australia.[88] Though the Peace Army saw the Sisterhood as a 'sort of Peace Kindergarten, as they themselves assert', they were happy to join together in order to smooth arrangements for international affiliation.[89] The Sisterhood, however, decided against amalgamation, fearing it would be subsumed into the Peace Army.

---

84 Malcolm Saunders, *Quiet Dissenter: The Life and Thought of an Australian Pacifist: Eleanor May Moore 1875–1949* (Canberra: Peace Research Centre, Australian National University, 1993), 6.
85 Memorandum from the ICWPP, 8 January 1916, series III reel 54, WILPF Papers.
86 Finding aid for this archive is: Mitchell Ducey, *The Women's International League for Peace and Freedom Papers, 1915–1978: A Guide to the Microfilm Edition* (Sanford, Microfilming Corp of America, 1983).
87 Goldstein to Hobhouse ICWPP Secretary, Amsterdam, 3 November 1915, series III reel 54, WILPF Papers.
88 'Memorandum on the progress of the organisation of an Australian National Committee to work in cooperation with the International Committee of Women for Permanent Peace', sent by the ICWPP to all Australian contacts, 8 January 1916, series III reel 54, WILPF Papers.
89 Goldstein to Hobhouse ICWPP Secretary, Amsterdam, 3 November 1915, series III reel 54, WILPF Papers.

The groups saw their purposes differently. The Sisterhood believed it would be most effective after the war had ended and was recruiting and engaging in the international struggle to put itself in a good position to educate once the war was over. Moore recognised the different attitudes of the groups, noting that the Sisterhood preferred persuasion through reason and education rather than provocation:

> When public opinion is inflamed, there are two ways of seeking to influence it. One is to be provocative, taking the risk of reprisals, in the hope of making converts on the recoil. The other is called educational.[90]

The women from the Sisterhood were also not as militant as the Peace Army in protesting the war. They saw their work as 'primarily educational' and advertised their 'non-sectarian and non-party' approach to spread knowledge of international affairs.[91] Care was taken to cultivate the image of respectability. They used discussion groups, reading material, letter writing and meetings in delegations with members of government to engage with the political debate. They only cautiously supported the 'no' campaigns during the conscription plebiscites because the engagements between pro- and anti-conscriptionists were characterised by hostility, aggression and disruption.[92] Monitoring school literature and encouraging internationalist reading for both adults and the young were the ways the Sisterhood chose to promote their anti-war philosophy.

Many of the women present at the founding of the Sisterhood had not been involved in political protest or activism. They did not wish to break the law or jeopardise their status within their communities. Their motivation to organise along gender lines was to give themselves a space for discussion they felt was not available to them through mixed-gender societies. They wanted to lead and control the direction of the group rather than being relegated to secretarial support work. Not all in the group were convinced that women were inherently peaceful. Nonetheless, especially in the education campaign targeting school children, their material adopted a maternalist rhetoric to

---

90   Moore, *The Quest for Peace*, 28.
91   'Sisterhood of International Peace', *The Age*, 21 December 1918, 15. See also Judith Smart, 'Women Waging War: The National Council of Women of Victoria 1914–1920', in *Victorian Historical Journal* 86, no. 1 (June 2015): 64.
92   Judith Smart, 'The Right to Speak and the Right to Be Heard: The Popular Disruption of Conscriptionist Meetings in Melbourne, 1916', *Australian Historical Studies* 23, no. 92 (1989): 203–19, doi.org/10.1080/10314618908595809.

claim authority in the debate.[93] As women were predominantly responsible for the welfare of children, their education and wellbeing, this area of reform was one in which the Sisterhood could claim a moral authority through their presentation of gender.

The Peace Army, on the other hand, wanted to protest the war as it was happening, preferring action and high-profile tactics. They believed that the 'timid' position of the Sisterhood meant they were left to do the real grunt work of opposing the war:

> The Sisterhood does not do any public propaganda in Victoria, let alone other states, and joint actions with them in Victoria can have little practical value. It is very nervous about being publicly criticised and ridiculed because of association with us, who are anathema to the militarists. Nevertheless it can do good educational work on ethical lines, in its quiet way, and we must carry on the political part of peace work, and continue our organising efforts in the other states.[94]

The Peace Army formed in direct response to a crisis and subsequently folded in 1919 with the conclusion of official hostilities, unable to sustain momentum when the immediacy of the situation had passed. This collapse contrasts with the Sisterhood, which continued its work after the war. While it might have been seen as more 'conservative' or 'cautious' in its approach and agenda, it was able to find a more enduring place in the peace movement with its more moderate views. Focusing on education and recruiting members that were more interested in the 'slow burn' of activism, they aimed to hold course in times of crisis and sustain interest when times were less fractious.

Both groups produced pamphlets and spoke at various public engagements. Moore and the other international secretary of the Sisterhood, Mabel Drummond, were regarded as good speakers and invited to address audiences along with the Peace Army, the Peace Society and the Australian Peace

---

93 In all pamphlets the SIP discussed bringing the 'humanising influence of women to bear on the bolition of war', Lucy Paling, 'SIP Call to Arms' pamphlet, May 1915, Box 30/4, WILPF, SCPC, University of Colorado at Boulder Archives (CU Archives). In a pamphlet Janie Kerr appealed to girls by expressing the grief and hopelessness women felt 'because of your very womanhood the maternal instinct made you cry aloud and ask yourselves was it hopeless to think of doing something to make impossible the horror and madness which had overtaken this world of yours', Janie Kerr, 'SIP Appeal to Girls', April 1916, Box 30/4, WILPF, SCPC, CU Archives.
94 Goldstein to the ICWPP, 27 April 1916, series III reel 54, WILPF Papers.

Alliance (APA).⁹⁵ Moore and the Sisterhood were more wary of disobeying the strict censorship laws imposed during the wartime than the Peace Army, releasing pamphlets that were only lightly censored due to a pragmatic choice of words. This contrasted with the WPA's publication *Woman Voter* which was heavily censored and even occasionally released with blank pages.⁹⁶ The Peace Army was more accustomed to public criticism. Their members had dealt with backlash from the public during the suffrage campaigns up to 1908 and in subsequent campaigns for public office. They were often criticised in the mainstream press, and by conservative groups organising recruitment efforts for the war. The conservative AWNL often spoke against them in their publication *The Woman*, with leader Eva Hughes chastising them for appearing unladylike:

> I have been to meetings for women only. What have I seen? A chance word, or a speaker, has transformed a quiet, nice looking face into that of a fury—womanhood, motherhood forgotten—clenched fists, stamping feet, curses on lips that should speak gently.⁹⁷

Both the Peace Army and the Sisterhood were prone to unfavourable press coverage during World War I. The *Argus* and the *Age* would both print reports of Peace Army and Sisterhood meetings in such a way that upset the women involved. Moore would always write correction letters, attempting to argue over the misrepresentations. For example, she wrote one to the *Argus* in 1916 requesting that they amend a report of a Sisterhood meeting where Moore felt they gave 'an impression' that the Sisterhood was encouraging men to request false medical certificates from doctors to avoid enlisting. She wrote:

> The only remark made in regard to certificates of medical unfitness was made by me, and I referred only to one medical man as having been asked to issue false certificates. I added that I was far from believing he or others would be guilty of doing such a thing, and that I had no sympathy whatever with men who sought to avoid military service in such a contemptible way.⁹⁸

---

95   Australian Peace Alliance Poster advertising a public meeting in Melbourne 18 March 1818 lists both Goldstein and Moore as prominent speakers on the topic 'Peace Terms—Australia's Part', Malcolm Saunders and Ralph Summy, *The Australian Peace Movement: A Short History* (Canberra: Peace Research Centre, Australian National University, 1986), 26.
96   Saunders, *Quiet Dissenter*, 90; Goldstein, 'The War', 2.
97   Eva Hughes, *The Woman*, 1 December 1916.
98   Eleanor Moore, 'A Correction—To the Editor of the Argus', *The Argus*, 5 May 1916.

Nonetheless, the *Argus*, known in Melbourne for its conservative coverage, frequently reported on the Sisterhood in unfavourable terms, despite their efforts to avoid controversy. Members of the Sisterhood and Peace Army were part of a deputation to the education minister in Victoria in 1917 requesting that *The School Paper* be less militaristic in tone. Responses concluded that 'these good ladies would find better use for their time knitting socks for the soldiers who will have to be heard later about the wisdom of shaking hands with our enemies'.[99] Their interest in the school syllabus was also a cause for concern for the censorship authorities. In 1918 a censor annotated a letter from Mabel Drummond on this subject: 'the pacifists are becoming more aggressive, and … intend to [sic] undermining the inculcation of healthy Patriotic ideals in State Schools … Is it not time that these dangerous Societies should be taught a lesson?'[100]

An *Argus* report in November 1915 noted that peace societies in Melbourne that discussed peace in the abstract were 'really railing at the British and Commonwealth Governments, and trying to discourage recruiting, and to bring about "peace at any price"'.[101] The article went on to describe the Sisterhood and the Peace Army, and printed quotes out of context written by the Sisterhood in *Peacewards*, and the Peace Army in *Woman Voter* to illustrate their unpatriotic beliefs. Similarly, letters to the editor offer insight into the perspective of some of the *Argus* readership. One reader signing off as 'Anti-Hypocrisy' wrote:

> A society calling itself the 'Sisterhood of International Peace' has passed a resolution of sympathy with the relatives of Nurse Cavell, who was executed by the Germans, the resolution goes on to say that the atrocity was the result of 'militarism and war'. Here you will notice this 'peace' society cunningly places the foul crime on militarism in general, and not 'German' militarism in particular. If I am not mistaken, this 'peace' society and the 'international socialists' society are identical, and their aims and sympathies are pro-German.[102]

---

99 'Peace! While There is No Peace', *Daily News*, Perth, 24 April 1917, 4.
100 Drummond, Hon. Sec. Sisterhood of International Peace, to T. Miller, Bentleigh, 'Coniston', 117 George Street, East Melbourne, undated, c. early July 1918, MP95/1, 169/17/25, MS1275, 'Intelligence reports on enemy trading and other suspicious actions', Censor notes, NAA.
101 'Peace Talk', *The Argus*, 27 November 1915.
102 'To the Editor of the Argus', *The Argus*, 9 November 1915.

The Peace Army not only had to deal with the press, but with scrutiny from the government which had increased powers to prosecute under the *War Precautions Act 1914*. This legislation, passed by the government of Prime Minister Andrew Fisher and subsequently extended in 1915 and 1916, gave the authorities wide-ranging powers to restrict civil liberties.[103] It allowed the censoring of media reports likely to cause disaffection or alarm and provided for the monitoring and prosecution of anyone deemed guilty of prejudicing recruiting.[104] The Act specified prohibited acts of protest, including tearing down recruiting posters and disturbing referendum meetings.[105] The Peace Army was prone to disagreements with the authorities over activities that allegedly contravened the Act. Cecilia John, Adela Pankhurst and Jennie Baines, all at times members of the Peace Army and the WPA, were summoned to court under this regulation for various peace-related activities.[106] The Peace Army held demonstrations against the unprecedented legislation. Pankhurst led a march on the Yarra Bank in Melbourne in January 1916 in defence of free speech, but the Sisterhood decided not to participate 'on the ground that the right of free speech on their part has not been assailed by the government'. Such a decision again reflected their desire to avoid being labelled as subversive.[107] At the end of the war, the Sisterhood joined delegations of peace activists who met the attorney-general with a petition to repeal the Act, showing their principled stance against it even if they were fearful of protest.[108]

While the Peace Army was accustomed to misrepresentation in the papers as well as prosecution from government and criticism from pro-war groups, they were not pleased to receive what they perceived as similar treatment

---

103 Diane Kirkby, 'When "Magna Carta Was Suspended": National Security and the Challenge to Freedom in Australia, 1914–1919', in *Challenges to Authority and the Recognition of Rights: From Magna Carta to Modernity*, ed. Catherine MacMillian and Charlotte Smith (Cambridge: Cambridge University Press, 2018), 322.
104 Kirkby, 'When "Magna Carta Was Suspended"', 322.
105 Scott, *Australia During the War*, 145.
106 Cecilia John was taken to court over printed material, see 'The Lasso Act Electors' Judgment Printer and Secretary—Another War Precautions Prosecution', *Daily Herald*, 5 December 1917. Baines and Pankhurst took their prosecutions to the high court, where they were charged with leading a protest to the steps of parliament. *Pankhurst v Porter* [1917] HCA 52 (2 October 1917); 'War Precautions Act Regulations Appeals Against Convictions Upheld by High Court', *The Ballarat Star*, 3 October 1917. For more information on the arrests, see: Judith Smart, 'Baines, Sarah Jane (1866–1951)', *Australian Dictionary of Biography* (ADB), National Centre of Biography, ANU, adb.anu.edu.au/biography/baines-sarah-jane-5100/text8519, published first in hardcopy 1979, accessed 14 January 2015.
107 Sisterhood Minutes of monthly committee meetings, discussing a demonstration at the Yarra Bank protesting the curtailing of free speech organised by Pankhurst in January 1916, quoted in Colligan, 'Brothers and Sisters in Peace', 50.
108 'Free Speech Repeal of Restrictions Urged by Deputation', *Daily News*, 20 October 1919, 6.

from the Sisterhood, who purported to share their goals. Moore had written a letter for inclusion in the circulated publication of the ICWPP called the *International*. It was designed to give an update on the state of affairs in Australia and explain the existence of two peace groups in Victoria, but unwittingly inflamed the animosity. She noted that two of the Peace Army meetings had 'ended in disorder' and that the group 'felt a duty to influence men not to enlist'.[109]

Moore apologised for the oversight and wrote again to the ICWPP to request they amend her paragraph.[110] Yet the incident again demonstrated how different the two groups were. The Sisterhood, not used to such a public performance, was inadvertently criticising the Peace Army in a similar way to the establishment, implying that they were unladylike and their methods disruptive. It revealed a deeper belief that women in the protest movement should be reserved. Considering the wide international circulation of the publication, some women who were members of both organisations saw it as an 'endeavour to aggrandise the Sisterhood at the expense of a sister society'.[111] Treasurer Cecilia John reacted with a sharp word written to the ICWPP:

> For your private information I may tell you that the Sisterhood of Peace is unknown even in our own city and has never held a public meeting. I could write at length about it but I do not desire to say more.[112]

While the Sisterhood used language that offended the Peace Army in describing its activities, Moore and the Sisterhood's membership saw themselves as justified in their fear of aggressive involvement by the intensity of the backlash. Many of the women who decided to become active in the Sisterhood were still reluctant to become publicly involved and the leadership felt that:

---

109 Cecilia John to the editor of the *International*, 14 June 1916, series III reel 54, WILPF Papers.
110 Moore to the secretary of the IWCPP, 19 September 1916, series III reel 54, WILPF Papers.
111 Clara Weekes, member of the Sisterhood and the Peace Army, letter to Mrs Strong secretary of the SIP copied in with the IWCPP, series III reel 54, WILPF Papers. See: Deborah Towns, '"Youth and Hope and Vigor in Her Heart": Clara Weekes, a "Born Teacher" and First-Wave Feminist', *Victorian Historical Journal* 79, no. 2 (November 2008): 277–95. Clara and her sister Edith were both Sisterhood treasurers in 1920, specifically concerning the publication *Peacewards*. Ina Higgins was another member of both societies, as the *Peacewards* treasurer of the SIP and member of the WPA. She was sister of Judge Henry B Higgins, see Deborah Jordan, '"Women's Time": Ina Higgins, Nettie Palmer and Aileen Palmer', *Victorian Historical Journal* 79, no. 2 (November 2008): 269–313.
112 John to Dr Aletta Jacobs, 14 June 1916, series III reel 54, WILPF Papers.

> There are many women who would sever their connection with the peace movement entirely if they thought it meant an open clash with their already harassed government. They nevertheless hold true peace ideals, their support is valuable, and the cause cannot afford to lose it.[113]

There was an increasing number of reports of violent behaviour on the part of returned soldiers who had become more threatening to women opposed to the war and conscription. One soldier reportedly interrupted a Peace Army demonstration and shouted: 'If the men here did as the Germans did to the Belgian women he would stand by and watch them with pleasure'.[114] The accusation is revealing of the ways in which those questioning militarised violence were often confronted by the 'violent defence of violence itself'.[115] Moore noted in her memoir the perceived need for a less threatening space for women to support their cause:

> There is a place for both, but they are better to work apart, especially at a time when a severe penalty may follow an unwise word. If one is to go to gaol for hindering recruiting (that was the sovereign offence in 1915), or to be ducked in the river by indignant men in uniform, it is something to know that the trouble springs from the assertion of one's own principle and not from the indiscretion of a colleague.[116]

The Sisterhood's insistence on differentiating itself from the Peace Army was entirely about approach, tone and tactics.

Conscription and the divided home front

The conscription campaigns exacerbated the tense public atmosphere. They also created new dangers for socialist women.[117] Women attempting to enter the male domain left themselves 'subject to sanctions ranging from ridicule to violence'.[118] Before the war outspoken political women such as Vida Goldstein and Rose Scott were often subject to ridicule, especially

---

113 Moore to *The International* March/April 1916, quoted in Saunders, *Quiet Dissenter*, 93.
114 Soldier addressing crowd after interrupting a meeting of WPA on Yarra bank, quoted in letter by FJ Riley to Hughes, 15 May 1916, quoted in Colligan, 'Brothers and Sisters in Peace', 41.
115 Colligan, 'Brothers and Sisters in Peace', 41. See also: Joy Damousi, 'Socialist Women and Gendered Space: The Anti-Conscription and Anti-War Campaigns of 1914–1918', *Labour History*, no. 60 (1 May 1991): 1–15.
116 Moore, *The Quest for Peace*, 29.
117 Damousi, 'Socialist Women and Gendered Space'.
118 Damousi, 'Socialist Women and Gendered Space'.

as their attempts at social reform clearly articulated criticism of traditional masculine values and behaviours. Even so, prior to the conscription campaigns of World War I, women had usually been able to engage in socialist movements without drawing actual physical violence. The conscription campaigns changed this situation, not least because women's support for the anti-conscription campaign directly 'challenged values associated with masculinity and manliness'.[119] The war, by its nature, reinforced conventional gender roles by defining who should fight the enemy and who should care for the home. Much government propaganda reinforced this division, playing on sentiments of masculinity to motivate men to enlist. Against this background, radical, anti-war and anti-conscriptionist political activity by women attracted male aggression. Soldiers would intimidate speaking women at rallies, tear down 'No' signs, and even resort to violence against the women as a way of reasserting their masculinity and enforcing their views.[120]

There were many tensions over masculinity in the gendered milieu of anxieties surrounding the conscription debates. Men dealing privately with the decision to enlist were faced with conflicting visions of ideal masculinities—negotiating their 'duty' to the nation with the more present and immediate 'duty' to the family as breadwinners and income earners.[121] But while the image of the ideal man, a physically strong and brave soldier, became increasingly obsolete and irrelevant when matched with artillery and machine guns, the conventional tropes and conventions of this ideal soldier remained central to patriotic propaganda.

Pro-conscription campaigners, returned soldiers and imperial patriots were also swept along with the aggressive sentiment against the women's campaigns in response to the unusual and threatening performance of femininity in the public sphere. Examples of such brazen expressions of femininity included an instance when young girls protesting against conscription 'tried to swing constables to dance with them' after a rowdy meeting was being shut down, as a nonviolent and good-natured way of undermining the social order and male authority.[122] At the same time the government campaigned for conscription in the same way they encouraged men to enlist—by playing into masculine stereotypes about duty and war. Pro-conscription rhetoric

---

119 Damousi, 'Socialist Women and Gendered Space', 8.
120 Damousi, 'Socialist Women and Gendered Space', 13.
121 Bart Ziino, 'Enlistment and Non-enlistment in Wartime Australia: Responses to the 1916 Call to Arms Appeal', *Australian Historical Studies* 41, no. 2 (2010): 217–32, doi.org/10.1080/10314611003713603.
122 Smart, 'The Right to Speak and the Right to Be Heard', 210.

and coercion to enlist became intertwined as labels such as 'shirkers' came to represent both people voting against the plebiscite and those refusing to enlist. Women of the AWNL saw the conscription votes as a way for women to publicly 'urge men to be strong in the courage of their fate', just as they had been encouraging women privately to do in persuading their men to volunteer.[123] Prime Minister Billy Hughes described the failed result of the plebiscite in 1916 as a 'triumph for the unworthy, the selfish and treacherous in our midst'.[124] But for the peace and anti-conscriptionist cause, it was a triumph for peace.

The violent behaviour of some soldiers who felt undermined by women's campaigns reinforced the gender divide. To women peace activists, their actions confirmed that women needed protection from the physical and sexual abuse of men, and that militarism and war cultivated these very behaviours. To the satisfaction of temperance-oriented women campaigners, all states imposed restrictions on hotel trading hours. Reports of brawls and looting by returned soldiers influenced these decisions, such as an incident early in the war where a soldier was shot dead in Sydney. The tragedy confirmed the 'horror the possible depredations of a drunken and licentious soldiery'.[125] Women active in the peace movement saw the negative impact of militaristic values on young men that encouraged their abuses of alcohol and made soldiers a force of social disorder. Each public riot and the abuse of dissenting women furthered their belief in the damaging social impact of war.

The question of conscription was put to a plebiscite by Prime Minister Hughes twice during the war, first on 28 October 1916 and later on 20 December 1917.[126] The year 1916 was therefore a very volatile one for public action, and once again highlighted a divide between the Sisterhood and the Peace Army in their responses. The Peace Army used the plebiscites as a core issue for action and held demonstrations on the Yarra Bank. One notable protest that Moore recounted was led by 'the striking figure of miss Cecilia John on horseback' with banners saying 'Gentle maiden, trust him not!' referring to Prime Minister Hughes' statement that married men or

---

123 Eva Hughes, 'AWNL Appeal to Women, Letter to the editor', *The Argus*, 24 October 1916.
124 William Hughes, quoted in Jeff Sparrow, *Radical Melbourne* (Carlton North, Vic: Vulgar Press, 2001), 216.
125 Robson, *Australia and the Great War, 1914–1918*, 12.
126 Saunders and Summy, *The Australian Peace Movement*, 20.

sole remaining sons would not be conscripted.[127] Cecilia John was renowned for singing 'I didn't raise my son to be a soldier/ I brought him up to be my pride and joy/ who dares to put a musket on his shoulder/ to kill some other mother's darling boy?'[128] The Sisterhood by contrast, hesitated. Moore wrote:

> Its members had been enrolled on the understanding that the society, as such, would not pronounce on questions directly connected with the waging of the war ... But, as controversy increased, everyone had to take one side or the other, and so it came about that all the most active members of the Sisterhood found themselves linked up with the anti-conscription movement.[129]

Fear of involvement and retribution from a tumultuous political environment was soon put to the side with the Sisterhood spurred on by public talks over the nature of war. Moore noted that the issue was so intensely debated that 'Yes' and 'No' buttons were almost universally worn, and 'wearers of the one eyed the others balefully in the street, silently thinking up epithets for use when conversation should so permit'.[130] Mabel Drummond wrote about the conscription meetings in her diary, giving some insight into the passion and controversy aroused by the political divisions. She noted in 1916 that, at one meeting, 'all rose to speak but they did not utter a word as the crowd howled them down, yelled and screamed TRAITOR and so on'. Furthermore, 'when some of us stood up against the motion of conscription, they howled around us like a pack of wolves'.[131] By the second vote in 1917, the Sisterhood and Moore had joined the Peace Army in stressing the gendered reasons to vote 'no', as seen in the piece she wrote for publication. 'I AM A WOMAN', wrote Moore,

> I can only be loyal in a woman's way. I cannot give to the State what is not mine. Giving away other people's money is not generosity; it is theft. Voting away other people's liberty is not patriotism; it is persecution. Forcing other people to risk their lives for me is not courage; it is cowardice.

---

127 Moore, *The Quest for Peace*, 36. See also Gavin Souter, *Lion and Kangaroo: The Initiation of Australia* (Melbourne: Text Publishing, 2001), 255.
128 Lyrics quoted in Shute, 'Heroines and Heroes', 29.
129 Moore, *The Quest for Peace*, 34.
130 Moore, *The Quest for Peace*, 36.
131 Drummond, 10 and 16 October 1916, quoted in Morice, *Six-Bob-a-Day Tourist*, 52.

> I AM A WOMAN. I was given a vote that I might impress my womanly feeling and point of view on public life. If I use that vote to strengthen men's faith in violence and revenge as against intelligence and moral force, my influence is worse than wasted …
>
> I AM A WOMAN. For the honour of womanhood, for the glory of Australia, and for the encouragement of men to be true to the highest in them, I mean to record a vote of WANT IN CONFIDENCE IN WAR, and VOTE NO!!![132]

In this excerpt Moore was debating the very foundations of the pro-conscription argument. Women in groups like the AWNL saw the responsibility of women to put their country above their family and sacrifice their sons and husbands for the war. Moore was also attempting to clarify the confused message that pro-conscriptionists peddled, by reiterating that voting away personal freedoms was wrong, and separate from the issue of encouraging enlistment. It also highlights her thorough commitment to personal liberty and individual freedoms. The establishment press appealed to women to do their duty by publishing opinions such as 'the mother who gives her son in war is noble, sublime … the noblest thing on earth today.'[133] Public sentiment began to acquire a coercive quality where women were told they should feel 'ashamed' of not having their men at the front. Another paper noted that 'any right-minded woman would rather be the mother or sister of a dead hero than a living shirker'.[134] This sentiment became so pervasive that activists called some childless women in the pro-conscription camp, who said they 'wished they had a dozen sons to send to the war', 'Vieilles Dames sans Merci' (old women without mercy).[135] Fairness and equity were in the minds of many women, who had already sacrificed and lost loved ones while watching bitterly as other men avoided a similar fate.[136]

---

132 Moore, 'Conscription and Woman's Loyalty', in *The McIvor Times and Rodney Advertiser*, 20 December 1917.
133 Excerpt from paper *National Leader*, June 1917, quoted in Shute, 'Heroines and Heroes', 29.
134 Excerpt from paper *Brisbane Courier*, 1916, quoted in Shute, 'Heroines and Heroes', 25. See also Patricia Grimshaw, Marilyn Lake, Marian Quartly, and Ann McGrath, *Creating a Nation* (Ringwood, Vic: McPhee Gribble, 1994), 212.
135 Moore, *The Quest for Peace*, 36.
136 For more on the discussion of loss and grief in World War I see: Joy Damousi, *The Labour of Loss: Mourning, Memory, and Wartime Bereavement in Australia* (Cambridge, UK; New York: Cambridge University Press, 1999), doi.org/10.1017/CBO9780511552335.

Both the pro- and anti-conscription campaigns attempted to appeal to maternal sentiments. The former portrayed ideal motherhood as a willingness to give up one's sons as a sacrifice to the war effort. The latter countered that the best kind of motherhood was to be found in a commitment to peace and the anti-conscription cause, based on the desire to protect young men from harm.[137] A contributing argument against conscription was that if men were forced to enlist, they would lose their jobs to women, as was occurring in Britain; something that concerned and shocked the AIF causing them to 'express the hope that Australia would never sink so low'.[138] The portrayal of women in these campaigns was often used as a tool for an anti-woman agenda. Prime Minister Hughes would speak at large patriotic women's meetings about the necessity of conscription, and women themselves promulgated the stereotyped duties of the patriotic woman.

The success of the anti-conscription campaigns was not entirely due to women's organising. Moore recognised that the influence of the women's campaign was limited. 'No one section', she explained, and 'certainly not the pacifists—could fairly claim to have exercised the dominating influence'.[139] A number of factors were important, including the commitment and backing from the labour movement and the collaboration of anti-war activists with moderate left-wing organisations that were at once anti-conscription and pro-war.[140] But the anti-conscription campaigns, and even the pro-conscription campaigns, provided a platform for women's groups to articulate what they saw as a connection between motherhood and a woman's responsibility with the vote. As women had only recently been enfranchised, and voting was not compulsory for the plebiscites, both sides were trying to mobilise women by appealing to their emotions and duties as mothers in a way that had not been seen previously. Not only were the people of Australia given a choice for conscription that no other participant country offered its citizens, the women of Australia were also a voice in whether their sons should be compelled to go to war.

**

---

137 Grimshaw et al., *Creating a Nation*, 214.
138 McKernan, *The Australian People and the Great War*, 89.
139 Moore, *The Quest for Peace*, 34.
140 Saunders and Summy, *The Australian Peace Movement*, 20.

The rift between the Sisterhood and the Peace Army was in many ways representative of the political culture at large in its response to World War I. The country was divided politically and socially, and not just because of conscription. The cost of living was increasing ahead of wages. Even so, strikers garnered bitter criticism from imperial patriots who despaired at their unwillingness to sacrifice mere material interests for the sake of King and country.[141] The anxiety around voluntary recruitment created a divide between men who enlisted and those who remained behind. The latter found themselves labelled 'shirkers', and 'slackers' for their lack of commitment to the war effort and they were harshly targeted by pro-war groups. At the same time, Australia's costly involvement in the war prompted questioning in some quarters about the pressing demands of empire and the nature of imperialism. While the initial commitment of the nation seemed to be 'almost unique in its touching simplicity', the naivety of 1914 had, by the war's end, given way to a more searching interrogation or to self-conscious reinforcement.[142]

While it seemed that women became more politically active during the conscription campaigns, not least because of their ability to vote, both the 'pro' and 'anti' positions reinforced the strongly defined sex roles that were upheld with Australian society. Active pacifist women were in the minority. In fact, holding such opinions was often seen as disloyal and unpatriotic, making the commitment of the groups that did speak out against the prevailing status quo all the more remarkable. They utilised women-specific internationalist traditions to gain political power in the domestic sphere, while also playing into the definitions of gender that were widely accepted. Both the Sisterhood and the Peace Army believed in the political philosophy of internationalism. They were affiliated with the ICWPP and committed to sending delegates to the international congress in 1919. As was the nature of an international network, women from other countries experienced the war very differently. The national political framework still dictated the experience of war for many of the women, and the need for local activism illuminated the tensions in campaigning nationally for an international ideal.

---

141 Robson, *Australia and the Great War, 1914–1918*, 13.
142 Governor-General Sir Ronald Munro-Ferguson, December 1915, quoted in Souter, *Lion and Kangaroo*, 245.

It was the Sisterhood that endured once the urgency of the war dissipated, and in 1919 it voted to change its name to the Australian section of WILPF. Yet both groups had played a pivotal role in the foundation of WILPF in Australia, as their collaboration and confrontation defined the Australian section during a globally tumultuous time. The establishment of WILPF in Australia was gradual, emerging out of transnational internationalist networks and building on maternal notions of women's rights and protections. It proceeded in various guises before settling on the WILPF. Those early incarnations laid the groundwork for gendered understandings of peace that prevailed during the turbulent war years, creating the pathways for women after the end of hostilities to travel and to experience international politics in the quest to implement their ideals.

2

The feminist side of the League of Nations

On 12 May 1919, Eleanor Moore arrived in Zurich after overcoming many hurdles in attempting to make the congress on time. She had sailed for 10 weeks on the *Themistocles* from Australia, and misplaced letters jeopardised her carefully planned accommodation bookings. When she arrived in Europe she discovered that the conference location had changed to an entirely different country, fortuitously finding the news in the London *Daily Express*.[1] Arriving finally in Switzerland she found no train to Zurich until the morning of the conference. It moved at a crawl because of postwar shortages.

By the afternoon she had entered the congress building. After months of planning and weeks of travelling, she had arrived on the afternoon of the first day of proceedings, ready to speak on behalf of pacifist women of Australia. She had with her a package with signatures of Australian subscribers to table with the secretariat, to show the genuine commitment of enfranchised Australian women to international peace and disarmament.[2] Moore was excited to meet the women of the organising committee, with whom she had corresponded for years but never seen.

---

1 Eleanor M Moore, *The Quest for Peace, As I Have Known It in Australia* (Melbourne, 1948), 48. Change of conference venue reported in 'The Need of the Moment', *Daily Express*, London, 30 April 1919.
2 Memorial from the Sisterhood, Melbourne Australia to the International Congress of Women, The Hague, May 1919, series III reel 54, WILPF International Papers 1915–1978, Sanford, NC: Microfilming Corp. of America, c 1983, accessed at the National Library of Australia (NLA). Hereafter referred to as WILPF Papers.

She slipped into the back of the gathering after giving her name and credentials, no doubt relieved she had only missed one morning and the trip generously funded by the women of the Sisterhood in Melbourne was not in vain. She watched in awe as the face she recognised from photos, Jane Addams, stood from her position as chairperson to interrupt the current speaker:

> I want to interrupt the business to make an announcement. A delegate from Australia has arrived after ten weeks of travel. Will Miss Moore come up on the platform and let us all look at her?[3]

'Such moments are unforgettable', she recalled.[4] Overcome with emotion she reflected: 'when I tried to respond to the words of greeting and the round of applause little would come but a whisper'.[5] Yet, this moment clarified in her mind the importance of her work. She had made it there 'and to the very day!' She was a 'crusader' for this new 'glowing religion' that would 'transform humanity'. Moore was now part of the group committed to rebuilding hope after such a devastating war. And she would commit all her effort to achieve this through internationalism, alongside the wonderful women of the world present at the 1919 conference in Zurich.

***

The fighting ended on 11 November 1918, which to Moore proved 'how completely the operation of war is within the control of its directors and how perfectly able men are to stop it whenever they will'.[6] After the Paris Peace Conference in 1919, internationalism was institutionalised with the creation of the League of Nations and the International Labour Organization (ILO), which were written into the Treaty of Versailles.[7] Involvement with internationalism was distinctly gendered. Government delegates, usually male, had their paths smoothed by institutional arrangements of state diplomacy. Independent women did not have this support. Many were required to self-fund their journeys, overcoming the hurdles of expense and distance with the force of their personal connection to expanding internationalism. They travelled 'to understand and change

---

3 Jane Addams at the International Women's Peace Congress, Zurich 1919, quoted in Moore, *The Quest for Peace*, 50.
4 Moore, *The Quest for Peace*, 50.
5 Moore, *The Quest for Peace*, 50.
6 Moore, *The Quest for Peace*, 45.
7 Glenda Sluga, *Internationalism in the Age of Nationalism* (Philadelphia: University of Pennsylvania Press, 2013), 50, doi.org/10.9783/9780812207781.

the world', refusing to be mere tourists with 'eyes fixed on monuments and ruins'.[8] Despite practical obstacles and their lack of official accreditation, many of which actually expanded their experiences and commitment to internationalism, their engagement with the League of Nations was much more fruitful than some have assumed. The League of Nations fostered a 'new paradigm of public diplomacy', that 'showcased the importance of informal connections and networks, of expertise and technical know-how'.[9] After the 1919 conference that formally established the Women's International League for Peace and Freedom (WILPF) structure, they were well placed to capitalise on this new paradigm. They clearly cultivated and utilised informal networks to influence the political agenda.

> An Australian delegate to a WILPF conference in 1926, Amelia Lambrick, saw WILPF as: really a feminist side of the League of Nations, and I try to imagine the secretary of the League of Nations attempting to carry on in anything like such circumstances as our secretaries have to accept and make best of.[10]

The international section enjoyed this characterisation, and agreed. '[T]his is a miniature League of Nations and therefore there is always the problem of how to make the different nationalities understand each other and come to an agreement'.[11] Their organisation ran in parallel, navigated similar organisational issues as the official League of Nations, and tried as best it could to have a presence on the main stage, despite knowledge that their dissent, and their contribution to the debate, may be ignored. It encouraged women to start questioning national interests to facilitate international agreement, something Australian WILPF women soon began to do.

This 'miniature League of Nations' preceded the official League of Nations by a full year, as the postwar meeting of the International Committee of Women for Permanent Peace (ICWPP), held in May 1919, was where the group was formally established. It was then that they took the new name Women's International League for Peace and Freedom, and voted on a new constitution. The significance of that postwar women's peace meeting, the first that Australian delegates were able to attend, calls for

---

8   Ros Pesman, *Duty Free: Australian Women Abroad* (Melbourne: Oxford University Press, 1996), 109.
9   Madeleine Herren, 'Gender and International Relations Through the Lens of the League of Nations (1919–1945)', in *Women, Diplomacy and International Politics since 1500*, ed. Carolyn James and Glenda Sluga (Abingdon, Oxon; New York: Routledge, 2016), 183, doi.org/10.4324/9781315713113-12.
10 Moore referring to Lambrick, letter to the Secretary of WILPF, 19 April 1927, series III reel 54, WILPF Papers.
11 International Secretary to Moore, 1 July 1927, series III reel 54, WILPF Papers.

closer attention. This chapter follows the journeys of three Australian delegates, Eleanor Moore, Vida Goldstein and Cecilia John, to understand how that formative conference solidified the legacy of WILPF organising in Australia. These women all navigated the practical pressures of being an internationalist after the war, from financial commitments and travel complications to issues of communication and cross-cultural relationships. Their experiences demonstrate that the journey was a very important aspect of their development as international citizens, as it presented the opportunity for an experiential engagement with political realities. What they saw and learned in their months of travel was as important as the experience of the three-day congress because it expanded and shaped their understanding of internationalism.

The ICWPP and the 1919 Congress

While the ICWPP organising committee gained purpose and strength during the war, setting out with determination to organise the Zurich congress, it was greatly constrained by the strict wartime controls and the limitations of global communication. The Sisterhood in Australia noted in its reports how the communication had become strained by conditions in Europe, with the international journal reduced in frequency by 'lack of funds' and 'difficulties of postal communication'.[12] Sea-lanes of communication were becoming precarious—in essence, nationalism was cutting the tendons and circulatory system of internationalism. This exacerbated the Australian section's sense of 'separateness' from the larger branches overseas.[13]

Women organising in other nations had been targeted for their pacifist activities during the war, which hampered recruitment. The Italian section fought against police action because of a petition they started, while German women returning from the 1915 congress were temporarily imprisoned.[14] Most sections experienced hostility for advocating peace and opposing the war effort. Yet despite the difficulty in organising during this time, many national sections managed to engage with the international committee

---

12   SIP Annual report 1917, 4 April 1917, WILPF papers Box 1730/9 MS 9377, State Library of Victoria (SLV).
13   Malcolm Saunders, 'Are Women More Peaceful than Men? The Experience of the Australian Section of the Women's International League for Peace and Freedom, 1915–39', *Interdisciplinary Peace Research* 3, no. 1 (1 May 1991): 58, doi.org/10.1080/14781159108412732.
14   GC Bussey, and Margaret Tims, *Pioneers for Peace: Women's International League for Peace and Freedom, 1915-1965*, 2nd ed. (London: Allen & Unwin, 1965), 28.

enough to encourage the organising of the 1919 congress, and to commit to sending delegates. The ICWPP even tried to reach out to other nations not represented, sending 'friendly correspondence with peace loving women of China and Japan' recognising their lack of racial diversity and the desire for an international organisation representative of all nations.[15] No Japanese women attended the Zurich conference, though Japan eventually joined WILPF as a national section in 1924.[16] The number of countries participating in the ICWPP had grown since 1915, with the largest delegations in 1919 coming from Germany, Britain and the USA.[17]

The huge workload of correspondence that the ICWPP sent and received to organise the conference shows how difficult the commitment to international organising was at this time. Distance exacerbated the logistical hurdles for the Australians, whose commitment to attend reveals the strength of their dedication to engage in the international arena. Sending and receiving mail could take months, while gaining access to telegrams and speedy communication were difficult due to their ad hoc office arrangements. There was no real office, just the homes of the most devoted, and subscribing to newsletters and funding work and travel was prohibitively expensive.[18] Yet none of this curbed the Sisterhood and the Peace Army's enthusiasm. The Sisterhood began preparations for the conference from the beginning of 1916, choosing and debating who should be the delegate.

Leading up to the announcement of the congress there was eager communication between Australia and the international committee. The ICWPP pursued collective decision-making by mailing ballots for voting for the chairman and vice-chairman, for increasing the Board of Officers, for electing delegates to that board, for decisions for the time of the meetings, and even for decisions on the country in which organising meetings should take place.[19] At this stage, the Sisterhood and the Peace Army were still communicating as separate organisations, and were not

---

15 SIP Annual report 1917, 4 April 1917, WILPF papers Box 1730/9 MS 9377, SLV.
16 Leila J Rupp, *Worlds of Women: The Making of an International Women's Movement* (Princeton: Princeton University Press, 1997), 18, doi.org/10.1515/9780691221816.
17 Bussey and Tims, *Pioneers for Peace*, 29.
18 Evidence in the WILPF international archive shows the 'Opened by the Censor' tags that were attached to all international mail that the SIP received, which would have prolonged the process of sending and receiving letters. Series III reel 54, WILPF Papers.
19 Ballot paper for the ICWPP, received by SIP, 7 March 1917, series III reel 54, WILPF Papers.

pooling resources to send the delegates. The Peace Army had begun a 'Peace Delegation Fund' in January 1919, identifying their delegates as Vida Goldstein and Cecilia John, who were elected in 1917.[20]

Australian women and their journeys

By January 1919, the ICWPP had sent cables notifying of the intention to call the conference, but without times, places or dates.[21] The Sisterhood and the Peace Army delegates braced themselves to receive notification at any time that would take them on their journeys. The Peace Army's funding plea for assistance appeared in the *Woman Voter* many times on the front page during 1919, as the urgency of finance became clear and they pressed the need to have Australia adequately represented by experienced women.[22]

These delegates were propelled on their trips by the collective mobilisation of small donations from committed individuals. This pattern of funding is revealing of the character of the organisation and its members. It also shows the major difference between official forms of international commitment, undertaken by men's and women's internationalism. These women's organisations worked outside of state sponsorship and had no access to official funding. They relied on membership fees and personal donations to operate their secretariats, organise their communication and fund their overseas representations. They all relied heavily on volunteer labour for the duties required to keep the organisations functioning. They had little access to office spaces and often the work (especially in the case of the Sisterhood) would be done in private residences, where all the material would also be stored, which fostered the dominance of a core group of the membership. Relying on private funding also had a gendered disadvantage, as most women involved were not independently wealthy and had limited access to paid work. The Sisterhood was in a similar situation to the Peace Army in needing to collect contributions, especially as Moore was not able to pay for the trip for herself. The Sisterhood similarly raised money from members.[23]

---

20   Vida Goldstein, 'Women's Peace Delegation to Europe', *Woman Voter*, 30 January 1919, 1.
21   Vida Goldstein, 'Women's Peace Congress, Australian Representation', *Woman Voter*, 16 January 1919, 1.
22   Goldstein, 'Women's Peace Delegation to Europe', 1.
23   £180 had been collected, plus private loans of £70 to be repaid. Moore, *The Quest for Peace*, 46.

The call came quickly for the delegates, and despite their anticipation, it still caught them off guard. Moore received the cablegram on 28 February 1919 to say that the congress would be on 19 May in Holland.[24] She frantically rushed to the shipping department and was able to gain passage to Europe on the *Themistocles*, which was scheduled to leave on 5 March, giving only five days for preparation, passport application and arrangements of appropriate funds. The Peace Army similarly scrambled to organise the timely passage of their delegates. They published in the *Woman Voter* how 'peace found us unready for the speedy sending of two delegates on the long and expensive journey necessary to land them at the European centre of deliberations'.[25] There seemed still to be confusion about the actual time and place of the congress, as the Peace Army believed the starting date to be 5 May, and thought the place was to be Berne, Switzerland.[26] Goldstein and John booked their passage on the *Orsova*, which left on 24 March.[27] Despite conflicting reports of the congress being in France, Holland or Switzerland, the three delegates sailed in the direction of Europe with the vague understanding of the congress opening around the beginning of May. Such haphazard communication and confirmation about details were clearly a major obstacle to their internationalism. Their travel itineraries were sorted on arrival and made more precarious considering their shoestring budgets.

Money remained a concern throughout the journey for all three Australians. The Peace Army continued to appeal for funds and donations after Goldstein and John had departed, noting 'the appeal … remains therefore, in view of the necessity for continued endeavour, and must remain until much more money than has yet been received is obtained'.[28] Both travelling parties recorded how on occasion, without the hospitality and generosity of others sympathetic of their cause, they would have found themselves without food or adequate accommodation.[29] Ros Pesman has noted how it 'has been customary to represent women's travel as transgression' despite women having always been on the move.[30] That many travelling WILPF women were older, confident and middle class made it easier for them to challenge the travelling woman taboo and assert their own agenda. But there were

---

24 Moore, *The Quest for Peace*, 46.
25 'Women's Peace Congress', *Woman Voter*, 27 March 1919, 1.
26 'Women's Peace Congress', *Woman Voter*, 27 March 1919, 1.
27 Moore, *The Quest for Peace*, 46.
28 Moore, *The Quest for Peace*, 48. 'Women's Peace Congress', *Woman Voter*, 27 March 1919, 1.
29 Goldstein, 'if it had not been for the kindness of a personal friend of mine, our predicament would have been trying', *Woman Voter*, 7 August 1919, 3.
30 Pesman, *Duty Free*, 6.

still limitations, as unaccompanied women travellers often had to balance societal concerns and anxieties about their welfare and protection. Goldstein and Moore made clear that, despite close calls and honest difficulties, their travels never compromised their respectability.

Travelling through Europe immediately after the war without official recognition and travel approval from the establishment was not easy. Moore described how 'days of great stress and anxiety followed, most of the time being fruitlessly spent in legations waiting for permits which did not come.'[31] Yet both parties were stoic about the obstacles that made their travels stressful and complicated. Goldstein recognised their privilege in spite of the hardship by stating 'it is a wonderful thing to go forth and see the world'.[32] She also wrote how unavoidable the inconveniences were, but not prohibitive to their goals, as internationalism was superior because it brought together the best from all parts of the world, and that was only possible with travel:

> to bring about the new thing requires the counsel of wise heads and of noble hearts. Such heads and hearts to come together in conclave require—shall we put it so?—the sinews of travel.[33]

Their commitment to internationalism was deepened by the incurred cost of physical hardship and sacrifice.

Moore's experiences in 1919 were in stark contrast to her previous travel from 1905. She had been to Europe with her sister and found that her identity as a white traveller allowed her to move from country to country without restriction: 'no official permission was needed for any movement anywhere. No passport was required, and from first to last not a single form had to be filled in.'[34] The situation had since changed. The experience of the war imposed visa restrictions, meaning paperwork, passport photos and having 'papers examined and fresh forms filled in' at every junction extended her journey, which was cause for significant worry.[35] It illustrated the hardship of self-sponsored internationalism, and the changed social conditions of Europe. World War I saw the strengthening of national borders

---

31 Moore, *The Quest for Peace*, 49.
32 Vida Goldstein, 'Letters from Miss Goldstein', *Woman Voter*, 3 July 1919, 2.
33 'Women's Peace Congress', *Woman Voter*, 27 March 1919, 1.
34 Moore, *The Quest for Peace*, 47.
35 Moore, *The Quest for Peace*, 49.

and tightened regulation of movement between countries. It also led to a sharp increase in the state's oversight of its citizens with the development of passports exemplifying this trend.[36]

After Moore had arrived in England, she was surprised to learn through reading a newspaper that the congress had been moved to Zurich. She quickly adjusted her plans so she would arrive in Geneva where she would be able to catch a train to Zurich and arrive at the conference on the afternoon that it opened.[37] Goldstein and John were not so lucky. There remains a detailed record of their journey, as Goldstein wrote many letters that were published in full in the *Woman Voter*, often given their own section titled 'Letters From Europe'.[38] Their ship had planned to arrive at Naples but was diverted, arriving instead in England, adding days to the journey. Their voyage was frequently held up at ports, because of new quarantine measures to stop the spread of influenza, which caused Goldstein to hold a 'grudge against the medical profession for the absurd laws it has laid down in its fear of influenza'.[39] Goldstein was annoyed at such an impediment to their journey. She was quite unused to such extreme measures to address medical issues, and as a Christian Scientist she disapproved of medical interventions on religious grounds, especially non-consensual and enforced examinations.[40]

The influenza pandemic of 1918–19, also known as the 'Spanish flu', was widespread and devastating, with some 40 to 50 million people dying of the infection in less than a year.[41] Australia introduced protective measures like the maritime quarantine that was effective in controlling the outbreak. The delay, exclusion and inspection of foreign ships limited the pandemic to less than 0.8 deaths per 1,000.[42] Again, like the experience Moore had with tighter controls on visas and movement across borders, rapid and radical changes to the way people moved around the world were being enforced as a result of the war. New Zealand was hit hard by the epidemic, and this gave Australia more resolve in instituting the tight restrictions: officials declared that 'there is no need for panic in Victoria, or in Australia generally, but

---

36 AJP Taylor, *English History, 1914–1945* (Oxford: Clarendon Press, 1966), 2.
37 Moore, *The Quest for Peace*, 49.
38 Vida Goldstein, 'Letters from Europe', *Woman Voter*, 7 August 1919, 3.
39 Vida Goldstein, 'Letter from Miss Goldstein', *Woman Voter*, 22 May 1919, 1.
40 Leslie Henderson, *The Goldstein Story* (North Melbourne: Stockland Press, 1973), 72.
41 Michael BA Oldstone, *Viruses, Plagues, and History: Past, Present, and Future* (Oxford; New York: Oxford University Press, 2010), 306.
42 Oldstone, *Viruses, Plagues, and History*, 308.

there is great need for preparedness.'[43] The restrictions affected not only the ability to travel, but the domestic political atmosphere by banning public gatherings, which interrupted the activities of the peace movement. The Sisterhood noted this in a letter to the international section: 'our work has been hampered by the influenza epidemic of 1919, during which all public meetings were forbidden.'[44]

Keeping in touch required careful monitoring of the timing of incoming and outgoing mail in each port. Goldstein constantly reported how difficult it was to receive messages and time the letters she was writing; 'if I am to catch tomorrow's mail, I must hurry on'.[45] On reaching London they were as surprised as Moore to find the place and city of the congress had changed, and the description of their efforts to make it to Zurich convey a similarly stressful experience of seeking permits and passages. With understanding officials, they were able to have their visas approved quickly, though again the process was trying: 'the passport business began downright in earnest. There we sat, row upon row, waiting our turn, first with one official, then with another, and with another, and with another, and so on, until one felt exactly like—well, I had better not say what, because my friends, the censors, might not allow it to pass!'[46] Through Paris, they arrived in Zurich by 15 May, four days after the opening. Goldstein acknowledged that Moore arrived before them, but perhaps in a moment of old rivalry was quick to point out that she left three weeks before them.[47]

The conference in Zurich

Benedict Anderson interpreted early twentieth-century internationalism as an expressive form of nationalism in his work *Imagined Communities*.[48] He saw the League of Nations as legitimising the nation-state as norm, a place where 'even the surviving imperial powers came dressed in national costume rather than imperial uniform.'[49] This perceived potential for exacerbating

---

43 'Spanish Influenza, Pneumonia Real Danger, Need for Precautions', *The Argus*, 23 November 1918, 21.
44 'WILPF Report, 1919–1921, Australian Section—branches Melbourne, Hobart, Rockhampton, Melbourne', 15 March 1931, WILPF papers Box 1730/9, MS 9377, SLV.
45 Goldstein, 'Letters from Europe', 3.
46 Goldstein, 'Letters from Europe', 3.
47 Goldstein, 'Letters from Europe', 3.
48 Benedict R O'G Anderson, *Imagined Communities: Reflections on the Origin and Spread of Nationalism* (London; New York: Verso, 1983), 113.
49 Anderson, *Imagined Communities*, 154.

national interests was one of the major concerns that WILPF had about the proposed League of Nations. It also represents one of the main anxieties that internationalists had about the theory of world government: that unless a genuine attempt at collaboration was enforced by the institution, it would never live up to that ideal. Therefore, in organising their own congress, WILPF was conscious of designing a space that represented more than the coming together of national sections. It specifically set up an international section as well as national sections to encourage a spirit of transnationalism.[50] Delegates and executive members, while elected by national sections, were not expected to promote their national interests, or speak as citizens of any country. Once the Zurich conference decided to take the name WILPF, the delegates determined that the international section would be set up in Geneva alongside the League of Nations headquarters, being 'from its foundation an international body and not simply a federation of national sections.'[51] As Eleanor Moore recalled, the atmosphere was one of cooperation, where there was 'a sense that something real has been achieved and that the occasion is epoch-making.'[52]

Every effort was made to overcome the impulse for nationalism in the international setting. Women from 'belligerent' countries were encouraged to be the ones to denounce the wrongs of their nations; 'it was the German women who denounced the invasion of Belgium, the deportations … it was the women from the Allied countries who denounced the blockade and the injustices of the Peace Treaty'.[53] This approach differed from the equivalent official conferences by actively encouraging the international perspective— incorporating views from neutral countries and countries on both sides of conflict. In contrast, the Paris Peace Conference ended with the 'Big Four'—the United States, France, the United Kingdom and Italy—making decisions, all nations from the Allied side. Some historians have even argued, echoing these women from the 1919 conference, that the groundwork for the Second World War was laid down at this stage by denying Germany a voice in negotiations, thereby disenfranchising them. WILPF prided itself on this exceptional origin and explicitly credited its success and cohesion

---

50   Jo Vellacott, 'A Place for Pacifism and Transnationalism in Feminist Theory: The Early Work of the Women's International League for Peace and Freedom', *Women's History Review* 2, no. 1 (March 1993): 33, doi.org/10.1080/09612029300200021.
51   Bussey and Tims, *Pioneers for Peace*, 32.
52   Moore, *The Quest for Peace*, 51.
53   Vellacott, 'A Place for Pacifism and Transnationalism in Feminist Theory', 33.

during the war to the fact that it was international first, and national only as a practicality. President Jane Addams explained this in a conference talk at Honolulu in 1928, which Moore recounted in a letter:

> Our League was different from other international societies, in that others usually were formed by a number of separate groups linking up to organise an international centre, but that ours began with an international centre or nucleus, and all the national groups have been formed from that. This peculiarity seems worth preserving, because it means that we are not a set of national bodies trying to be international if we can and liable to fly apart in times of special tensions (as so many so-called international societies did during the war), but we are international in our very nature and our only real reason for being 'national' at all is that we are trying to permeate the people we live amongst with the international spirit, and to get that spirit expressed in the enactments of the various governments.[54]

It was impossible to completely overcome nationalist tendencies. Moore noted how the congress overall was dominated by 'European-mindedness, or, to be exact, North-West-Central-European-mindedness'.[55] She saw this as understandable given the circumstances, but felt it necessary to draw attention to it when a resolution was accepted endorsing universal free trade without debate. Moore wrote a note after the congress that was published in the proceedings report outlining the detrimental effects this would have for Australia.[56] Her discussion of the idea of 'universal free trade', and the adherence to the issue of self-determination, shows how much her own national experience was present in her engagement with WILPF International. Despite their best intentions, in such a diverse group comprising so many different cultures, each delegate was shaped and influenced by their national experiences. Vestigial respect for national self-interest was difficult to dismiss.

The Zurich congress was an important gathering for the women's peace movement. But it also held wider significance as it was the first international gathering to consider the resolutions of the Paris Peace Conference and to provide comment on the Treaty of Versailles and the Covenant for the

---

54   Moore recounting a talk by Jane Addams, letter to WILPF secretary, 13 March 1929, series III reel 54, WILPF Papers.
55   Moore, *The Quest for Peace*, 53.
56   Eleanor Moore, 'A Note on Free Access to Raw Materials and Free Trade', in *The Women's International Congress, Zurich 12–17 May 1919: Towards Peace and Freedom*, WILPF Publication, accessed through database edited by Kathryn Kish Sklar and Thomas Dublin, *Women and Social Movements, International—1840 to Present*, 485.

League of Nations.[57] The women passed resolutions giving their thoughts on the treaty and covenant with recommendations for action to make them effective. Their unanimous verdict on the Peace Treaty was that it was harsh and detrimental, and that the discord it entrenched 'can only lead to future wars'.[58] There was more debate over the League of Nations Covenant, which proved to be the most contentious of all debates at Zurich. WILPF supported international government, thought to be one of the most effective ways to avert another war. It believed in the principles of a League of Nations as something that would exemplify their internationalism, creating a new stage for political development and a space that would command a higher loyalty than nationalism; 'not only of affection for the native land, but of loyalty to the Society of Nations'.[59]

However, what was proposed for the new League was a long way from what these women campaigned for. They felt it was far removed from the '14 points' proposed by US President Wilson, which they believed were greatly influenced by their resolutions from 1915.[60] The British delegation wrote their criticisms in the congress publication, which again showed how complex their engagement with these issues was—they understood the complexities of nationalism and internationalism working together, but saw a way for them to coexist, protecting each nation from the exploitation of another:

> We recognise first that the sentiment of nationality exists and manifests itself in many ways, political, linguistic, religious, racial, artistic; we take into account as actually existing this great factor in the motives of humanity, and many of us believe also that it greatly enriches thought and emotion, and do not wish to see it weakened ... We recognise in the second place, therefore, that international organisation of some kind is necessary in order to prevent the carious nationals from exploiting or oppressing each other.[61]

---

57 Bussey and Tims, *Pioneers for Peace*, 31.
58 Bussey and Tims, *Pioneers for Peace*, 31.
59 Vellacott, 'A Place for Pacifism and Transnationalism in Feminist Theory', 35.
60 Jane Addams quoted in *Woman Voter*, 1 September 1919, 1.
61 *The Women's International Congress, Zurich May 12–17 1919: Towards Peace and Freedom*, WILPF Publication, Sklar and Dublin, *Women and Social Movements*, 14. 'Democracy and the League of Nations' by HM Swanwick, MA, WILPF papers Box 1745, MS 9377, SLV.

Most at the congress were extremely disappointed with the proposed League of Nations. Some believed that in the form it was proposed, attached to the detrimental Peace Treaty, it would 'prove worse than useless as an international instrument' and should have been renounced by the congress.[62] Others were more optimistic, believing it was an imperfect step in the right direction and to be encouraged. After careful discussion the Zurich congress came to a resolution that proposed changes and recommendations to the covenant, which they intended to send to the official governments through elected envoys.

The Zurich conference also dealt with procedural matters, renaming the organisation, setting up the infrastructure for the newly named WILPF, electing office bearers Jane Addams (USA) as president, Helena Swanwick (UK) and Lida Gustava Heymann (Germany) as vice-presidents, and Emily Greene Balch (USA) as international secretary. Moore was very impressed with the women at the conference, even overwhelmed by the highly respected names of women leaders in their professional fields and made special note to say how much she admired them. Of note to her was Addams, who 'stands in [her] estimation as the greatest human being I have ever met', and others whom she had already corresponded with such as Jeannette Rankin from America, who was the first woman elected to the US Congress.[63]

The Sisterhood and Peace Army rivalry no longer seemed to be such a pertinent issue for the three Australian delegates. When they were at the Zurich congress together, they graciously shared notes to ensure the majority of people from Australia heard the news of the conference. As Moore had arrived earlier and was able to transcribe notes from the first few days, the *Woman Voter* acknowledged her for supplying them with articles, such as Addams' address that it printed in full.[64] Goldstein noted that they were encouraged and supported by each other, writing; 'It was good to see an Australian comrade in that great gathering. Seats were found for us with her, and we felt there was quite a home atmosphere around our table.'[65]

The Australians came prepared for the congress, putting together a memorial to be tabled that included reports from their meetings and petitions from Australian women in support of the conference

---

62 Vellacott, 'A Place for Pacifism and Transnationalism in Feminist Theory', 33.
63 Moore, *The Quest for Peace*, 50. Moore to Ms J Rankin, USA, 5 June 1917, WILPF papers Box 1723/3, MS 9377, SLV.
64 'Addams Address', *Woman Voter*, 1 September 1919, 1.
65 Vida Goldstein, 'Letters from Miss Goldstein', *Woman Voter*, 1 September 1919, 4.

2. THE FEMINIST SIDE OF THE LEAGUE OF NATIONS

deliberations.⁶⁶ As Australian women had the vote, their presence and expertise were seen as exotic and Moore was asked to give an evening speech on 13 May to a dinner about Australian Suffrage.⁶⁷ This speech was Moore's opportunity to convey her experience and doubts about the inherent peacefulness of women. Her talk began by noting how once women started to vote, none of the 'dreadful results predicted', that women would become unfeminine, or that it would destroy family life, came to pass. Nor would disaster ensure when all nations had given women the vote. But she then started on a more practical note arguing the suffrage did not fulfil all the prophecies women thought it would either:

> Woman suffrage having been once established among us, no one has ever raised an agitation to have it repealed. On the other hand, we cannot claim that the woman's vote has done all that some expected or hoped from it … A large section of the women had no confidence in their own judgement, and allowed the strength of their vote to be drawn wholly into the party politics of the day, in which any special value it might have had was lost.⁶⁸

Moore's solution was education. Her address concluded by stressing that women would only use the vote to their best ability when they had been educated on how to do so:

> To you younger women of Switzerland who eagerly look forward to voting, I would say, gain the right as soon as you can, use it, but do not overestimate its power. Think out now what your principles are to be on the great questions of the time, then remember that in giving you a vote, your country asks for *your* thought, not that of some relative, or orator, or newspaper. It has those already.⁶⁹

Despite these differences, the congress overall seemed to have deeply affected all the Australian delegates, shown in the way that they described the events to their constituents back home. They actively engaged in the deliberations and related their experiences. Overall they found the experience challenging and worthwhile, reaffirming their internationalism. Moore noted that the

---

66 Memorial from the Sisterhood, Melbourne Australia to the International Congress of Women, The Hague, May 1919, series III reel 54, WILPF Papers.
67 *The Women's International Congress, Zurich 12–17 May 1919: Towards Peace and Freedom*, WILPF Publication, Sklar and Dublin, *Women and Social Movements*, 199.
68 Eleanor Moore, 'Women Suffrage in Relation to Permanent Peace', speech given 13 May 1919, series III reel 54, WILPF Papers. Printed in *The Women's International Congress, Zurich 12–17 May 1919: Towards Peace and Freedom*, WILPF Publication, Sklar and Dublin, *Women and Social Movements*, 199.
69 Moore, 'Women Suffrage in Relation to Permanent Peace', speech given 13 May 1919, series III reel 54, WILPF Papers.

greatest thing to observe was that the debates and interactions between nationals were characterised by 'a persistent refusal to be dominated by inflamed race feeling', something that confirmed to her the potential for internationalism.[70]

Aside from the emotional significance of the congress, it was also productive in terms of output. Thirty-seven resolutions were passed, with twenty-two more proposals recommended for study that were unable to be voted on because of time constraints.[71] The resolutions were to be sent to the official governments as evidence of the work they had put in to create a lasting and constructive peace. However, like the output of the first conference in 1915, only US President Wilson acknowledged the resolutions.[72] While they were forwarded to all delegates and governments represented at Versailles, the silence made the women realise 'it is doubtful if it even raised a blush'.[73]

In addition to their rebuff from more official streams of international diplomacy, WILPF constantly struggled to make themselves heard as they were not part of official delegations. Organising exclusively along gender lines meant that they often had to battle the prejudiced view that women were inherently ill equipped to contribute to the complex world of international relations. Women involved in WILPF were aware of the pressure placed on them to prove their abilities to consider international relations and set about demonstrating them. According to Moore, the Sisterhood had taken the task very seriously since its inception:

> Urgent, indeed, was our need of all the knowledge we could gather, for at every utterance on this subject, whether in public or private, we were pelted with indignant objections and derisive questions. As a member once aptly remarked: 'pacifists are expected to be trained logicians, but anyone can be a militarist'.[74]

Regardless of their efforts, the establishment and even other women's groups did not usually see them in the light that they had hoped. They were constantly at risk of being sidelined into roles and issues that were seen as specific to women, matters that statesmen would expect to occupy their time. Once the Geneva office was set up it was constantly deluged by appeals

---

70   Malcolm Saunders, *Quiet Dissenter: The Life and Thought of an Australian Pacifist: Eleanor May Moore 1875–1949* (Canberra: Peace Research Centre, Australian National University, 1993), 124.
71   Moore, *The Quest for Peace*, 51.
72   Bussey and Tims, *Pioneers for Peace*, 33.
73   Bussey and Tims, *Pioneers for Peace*, 31.
74   Moore, *The Quest for Peace*, 41.

for humanitarian aid and for urgent reconstruction or postwar causes.[75] The international section of WILPF stressed that its role was political and not as an organisation for crisis relief. While they responded as best they could to these requests they only actively engaged where they could see an opportunity at a political level, as they knew their resources were better targeted at their core purpose rather than at direct services that would never be able to stretch to all that needed help. They also believed strongly that it would be better to 'tackle the causes of such tragedies, of which war was the greatest, rather than apply first aid after the event'.[76]

Travelling home

The 1919 congress was an important focal point for the women of WILPF as it brought them together to create the organisation that they would commit to advancing locally. Yet the organised proceedings were only scheduled for three days, and the pressures of time meant restrictions on debate and many motions were passed en bloc. As most delegates travelled for much longer than the allocated time they engaged, the personal connections and the travel proved to be just as revealing of their motivations, and the internationalising process, as the deliberations.

When the congress was over, getting home quickly was not guaranteed for the travelling Australians. Moore spent some time in Paris, after which she went back to London only to find that 'there was no hope of passage to Australia for months to come'.[77] Resigned to the fact that she would have to spend more time abroad waiting for news of a passage home, she undertook a Summer School at Cambridge, and another at Oxford. Spending time in different company, and again accepting the hospitality of acquaintances, she recalled many stories of people and fellow travellers that made her time memorable. Her insistence on recording the detail of people and places was to make the point that 'various nationalities and cultures can and do associate when they have opportunity to do so'.[78] She received an invitation from Emily Greene Balch, the new secretary of WILPF in Geneva, to volunteer at the international bureau, but once again had difficulty getting there. To Moore, the barrier of passports and borders was more than

---

75 Vellacott, 'A Place for Pacifism and Transnationalism in Feminist Theory', 41.
76 Vellacott, 'A Place for Pacifism and Transnationalism in Feminist Theory', 41.
77 Moore, *The Quest for Peace*, 57.
78 Moore, *The Quest for Peace*, 60.

just an inconvenience. It was 'obstruction-mongering' that intentionally thwarted the impulses found when people were able to 'move about freely, find affinities and form ties which are of lasting pleasure and benefit on both sides.'[79] This practical representation of nationalism demonstrated a 'hardening of the heart and a narrowing of the mind', causing her to muse 'we are meant to be servants one of another, not of abstract collectivities.'[80]

Moore made it once more to Switzerland, where she worked and lived with Balch for eight weeks. Together they readied material from the conference for publication. Her descriptions of this time show a sense of acceptance in the 'harmonious international circle' that she found around herself.[81] Her bond with Balch became a lasting friendship: she described their working styles as suiting each other 'excellently'. Moore began to have troubles with her health, and when she received notice that passage back to Australia was available she made the decision to return home. The time spent at the international headquarters elevated Moore's commitment to internationalism to new heights. The friendship she had with Balch became a motivation for activity. When they wrote to each other in their official capacities as secretaries of their respective sections, they discussed more than just business. They asked each other advice on decisions, gave lengthy descriptions of stories they thought would interest the other, and spoke with affection on receiving news of the other.[82] They did not meet again, but their friendship through correspondence remained strong and supportive.

It was to Balch that Moore mused about her disappointment at Australians not understanding their place in the world or realising the country's role in the wider international arena. Apathy towards international affairs by Australians was widely acknowledged.[83] Moore clearly saw how beneficial travelling was to her understanding of internationalism, and felt that the rest of Australia would benefit from the knowledge she gained.

> Coming back to this, and picking up again our old familiar newspapers, I feel at once our isolation and remoteness from the main currents of the world's affairs. Similar causes are producing similar effects, in a modified way, but there is very little sense of the vital importance to people abroad of what is done even in this

---

79   Moore, *The Quest for Peace*, 61.
80   Moore, *The Quest for Peace*, 62.
81   Moore, *The Quest for Peace*, 63.
82   Moore to Balch, 25 February 1920, series III reel 54, WILPF Papers.
83   Saunders, 'Are Women More Peaceful than Men?', 58.

'corner'. I am going to try and do what in me lies to stir not only the sense of world responsibility, but to open the eyes of Australians to their opportunities to give a lead, at least in some directions.[84]

Moore, Goldstein and John crossed paths again briefly in London after their harmonious interactions at the congress. Goldstein and John also found it difficult to return to Australia straight away due to shipping shortages. John had secured some of her travel funding from the People's Conservatorium of Melbourne, and so used her time to explore musical ideas in Paris, London and America.[85] She was the first of the three to return to Australia in October 1919, and once back she set her energies to using 'the common tongue of music [to] … bring together the common bond of peoples of the earth'.[86] She also became heavily involved in the Save the Children movement, inaugurating a local fund.[87]

Goldstein did not return to Australia for a long time. The Peace Delegation Fund of the Peace Army was unable to raise enough money for her return fare and she requested that no more money should be sent to her as she was severing her connection with the Women's Political Association (WPA).[88] Travelling around Europe after the conference allowed her to experience the impact of war on society, not just on women, but also the failure of governments to meet the needs of injured and returned soldiers in finding employment. She became profoundly disillusioned with the peace plans and the lack of influence the women's movement was able to have on them. Goldstein recalled that her decision to remain in England, rather than return to Australia, was partly because she felt she could 'no longer work in the political field because the people did not seem willing to tread this path'.[89] Goldstein had converted to Christian Science by the late 1890s, a religious movement that strongly disagreed with medical intervention and believed illness could be overcome with prayer.[90] At the Zurich congress Goldstein was a vocal opponent to a proposal that the congress support the creation of an International Health Bureau. She wrote:

---

84 Saunders, 'Are Women More Peaceful than Men?', 58.
85 'Miss John', *Woman Voter*, 6 November 1919, 3.
86 'Miss John', *Woman Voter*, 6 November 1919, 3.
87 Moore to Balch, 'My Dear Miss Balch', 25 February 1920, series III reel 54, WILPF Papers.
88 'International Women's Peace Congress', *Woman Voter*, 18 December 1919, 1.
89 Goldstein quoted in Janette M Bomford, *That Dangerous and Persuasive Woman: Vida Goldstein* (Carlton, Vic: Melbourne University Press, 1993), 199.
90 Goldstein along with her mother and sisters severed their religious connection with the Australian Church. Henderson, *The Goldstein Story*, 72.

> [S]ome people ... may think I am rather obsessed about this ... but to allow a medical bureaucracy to be established for the ostensible purpose of protecting the health of the people is to forge a weapon which will be used against the coming democracy in every country.[91]

The disillusionment she felt with the political process combined with the growing influence of her Christian Science beliefs led her to 'come to the conclusion that the world's ills could not be cured by political means, but only through religion'. She then became a Christian Science practitioner.[92]

Without Goldstein's oversight, and with public sentiment moving on from the crisis of the war, the Peace Army and the WPA decided to disband.[93] As the only woman-specific peace group left, the Sisterhood of International Peace became the natural inheritor of the WILPF functions and moved to adopt the title of 'Victorian Branch of the Australian Section of WILPF.'[94] It kept the Sisterhood motto as a subtitle and called itself the 'Victorian Branch', to encourage peace groups in other states to complete the Australian section. There ended the sometimes turbulent rivalry between the two colourful groups in the Australian peace movement. The new society that was officially part of the structure of the international organisation wasted no time in beginning its operations.[95]

***

The Zurich conference and the travels of the Australian women who participated represented a turning point for the women's peace organisation in Australia and reorganised the way Australian women participated in the international environment. Both the Sisterhood and the Peace Army waited until the end of the bitter, grinding and seemingly endless war to send their elected delegates to the conference, to help shape their contribution to world discussions for constructive peace. While only three women were able to attend, the experiences they reported back inspired and extended the understanding of internationalism as a political ideal for their followers and organisations. This congress also gave formal institutional support to the diverse groups in Australia.

---

91   Goldstein, quoted in *The Women's International Congress, Zurich 12–17 May 1919: Towards Peace and Freedom*, WILPF Publication, Sklar and Dublin, *Women and Social Movements*, 235.
92   Leslie M Henderson, 'Vida Goldstein 1869–1949 January 1966' [Manuscript], 1966, NLA.
93   'Miss Goldstein', *Woman Voter*, 18 December 1919, 4.
94   Sisterhood to Balch, 20 May 1920, series III reel 54, WILPF Papers.
95   WILPF Report, 1919–1921. Australian section—branches Melbourne, Hobart, Rockhampton. Melbourne, 15 March 1931, WILPF papers Box 1730/9, MS 9377, SLV.

Women peace activists understood that their conferences were 'unofficial'. Despite this, they organised them as best they could to approach the male-dominated arena with a 'strong and practical' platform to oppose national interests that did not prioritise peace.[96] They modelled their own 'unofficial' peace conference on the type of international institution they had hoped the League of Nations could be.

The travel experiences and hardships the women faced defined and challenged their political motivations. That they were unaccompanied women travelling with fluctuating itineraries highlighted their commitment, in a time when international travel was severely limited by the heightened sense of exclusionist nationalism in the aftermath of the conflict. The women's internationalism was deepened by their shared experiences and mutual collaborations in the flesh. The political ideal was always directed towards breaking down long-established views of war and militarism. The women developed lasting relationships that connected them across great divides, sharing personal stories and triumphs, providing mutual encouragement, and maintaining enthusiasm as 'kindred spirits'. They may not have had overwhelming support from the public at home, but they found solace in their shared beliefs across seas. This experience of internationalism motivated those individuals who were touched by it to commit even more of their time to the cause. Members often stayed involved in the organisation for significant lengths of their lives.

---

96 Sisterhood to WPP, ICWPP, 5 June 1918, WILPF papers Box 1723/3, MS 9377, SLV.

3

White Australia and regional relationships

During the war, Women's International League for Peace and Freedom (WILPF) members in Australia had joined international networks to promote world peace and arbitration. Not long afterwards they began to realise that an internationalist mindset demanded engagement with the politics of race. With this in mind, the women involved with WILPF held public meetings between the wars to discuss the White Australia Policy (WAP). 'Is our Internationalism only a word, or is it a fact?' challenged Mary Fullerton in 1919.[1]

These political women wished to ascertain if and how the economic policy of White Australia fostered militarism or otherwise represented an impediment to international understanding. They were willing to touch the 'thorny' issue of White Australia, normally seen as a 'nettle' that should be avoided.[2] Australian women in the peace movement drew attention to the hypocrisy of alliances with Asian and non-white countries during the war given the exclusionary policies of White Australia: 'if we make east and west one in time of war, we cannot make them two in time of peace'.[3] Similarly, some proclaimed how White Australia maintained a militarised

---

1 Mary Eliza Fullerton, 'White Australia Convention', *Woman Voter*, 3 July 1919, 3.
2 'Australasian Peace Conference, Interesting Melbourne Meeting, The White Australia Nettle', *Daily Standard*, 8 April 1921, 3.
3 'White Australia Policy Done For', *Woman Voter*, 27 October 1914, 2.

world. 'I am against the White Australia Policy,' explained Lucy Paling, 'because the arming of brothers against each other is the only way it can be preserved.'[4]

***

The women's groups confronted the inconsistencies in their own position regarding race and interrogated the implications of exclusionist policies of immigration. Their conclusions were complex, since the socially internalised assumptions that underpinned the WAP were hard to think beyond. Yet they asked a set of fundamental questions of the policy in a serious way that tested the tensions and contradictions of their own beliefs. Their deliberation was anxious, and their engagement with a policy supported across almost the entire political spectrum illustrated how discomforted they were by the realisation of its inconsistency with their aspirations for internationalism. Australian delegates at the League of Nations, meanwhile, argued vehemently in support of racial exclusion, placing supposed national interests above global cooperation and seeking to define an internationalism that could somehow encompass a racially exclusive immigration policy. They sought to harness the bureaucracy of international structures for the purposes of defending White Australia.

This chapter will focus on the way the women of WILPF confronted their understanding of racial politics between the wars. Many were motivated by a sense of unease at the way Australia was enacting national racial exclusivism and sought to engage practically with different countries whose people were excluded from Australia through the women's Pan-Pacific movement. It will focus on two meetings that occurred in Melbourne regarding the WAP: one in 1919 and the other in 1921. At these meetings there was an attempt to understand the complexity of the WAP and a push to dismantle it, a position that did not gain traction among politicians and the wider public until well into the middle of the twentieth century. Lastly, this chapter will explore how WILPF in Australia interacted with Pacific and Pacific Rim nations through the first Pan-Pacific Women's Conference in 1928. For this conference delegates travelled to Hawai'i and reported experiences that encouraged the section to prioritise regional engagement.

---

4   Lucy Paling, 'White Australia Convention', *Woman Voter*, 3 July 1919, 3. Mrs Lucy Paling was the founding president of the Sisterhood from 1915 to 1917.

WILPF considered racial politics through its interest in international relations. It was concerned more with cultural engagement with the outside world than with the treatment of Aboriginal Australians at this stage. In most of their discussion of White Australia, Indigenous issues were notably absent. This is not surprising, for the WAP was an immigration policy, not an approach to Aboriginal policy which, apart from in the Northern Territory, remained a state-based matter until 1967. As WILPF member Eleanor Moore noted later, 'by common consent, apparently, they were ignored as irrelevant'.[5]

The White Australia Policy

In 1901 the new federal parliament introduced the *Immigration Restriction Act* as the legislative expression of 'White Australia'.[6] Subsequent legislation and regulations complemented the initial Act and were aimed at restricting non-European immigration and promoting a racially white nation-state.[7] Many of the colonies had already implemented various forms of Asian immigration restriction and the WAP was a reinforcement of ideas and beliefs that were already widely held.[8] Within a global context, WAP proponents wanted to reinforce national unity through a mono-ethnic state in an attempt to avoid racial problems they perceived in other countries such as the United States of America. The labour movement, with its own industrial preoccupation with what they called 'cheap coloured labour', strongly endorsed this view. The implementation of 'White Australia' represented a foundational doctrine in international relations for Australia. It announced Australia's status as a self-governing dominion rather than a subservient colony.[9] Under the banner of White Australia, self-consciousness was cultivated within the community about who was considered white, and who was not. This manifested in concerns about interracial mixture, suspicion of cosmopolitanism and, in some sections of society, the adoption of an aggressive racially supremacist language.

---

5   Eleanor M Moore, *The Quest for Peace, As I Have Known It in Australia* (Melbourne, 1948), 70.
6   Marilyn Lake and Henry Reynolds, *Drawing the Global Colour Line: White Men's Countries and the Question of Racial Equality*, Australian ed. (Carlton, Vic: Melbourne University Press, 2008), 137.
7   Gwenda Tavan, *The Long, Slow Death of White Australia* (Carlton North, Vic: Scribe, 2005), 7.
8   Tavan, *The Long, Slow Death of White Australia*, 10.
9   Lake and Reynolds, *Drawing the Global Colour Line*, 144.

Not only was the policy supported by both major political parties, it was almost unanimously accepted by the public and by other institutions. The trade union movement supported exclusionary immigration to protect white workers from labour competition, while the press, employer groups, Returned Sailors' and Soldiers' Imperial League of Australia and church groups offered limited opposition.[10] Dissent was decidedly rare and cautious, though not absent. Petitions from the public were typically confined to individual cases of deportation, and rarely criticised the policy agenda as a whole. The WAP caused embarrassment to the British Government.[11] To ensure that there would be no interference from this direction, discretion was given to customs officials to keep 'undesirables' out by means of a literacy test in 'any European language'.[12] Designed so many would fail, this was an indirect form of racial exclusion. In effect, the WAP prevented Australia from engaging with the kind of international relations that utopian internationalism envisaged. It consciously looked to strengthen connections with other 'white men's countries'. The restriction of international conversations about interracial encounters to the sphere of 'white men's countries' only increased isolationism.[13]

Making connections during wartime, and the parliament for women debate White Australia

The Sisterhood of International Peace (the Sisterhood) took racial politics seriously throughout the war. In 1916 it published an article in its journal *Peacewards* which was clearly influenced by racial science and eugenics: 'we are opposed to the mixture of races at this state of human evolution'.[14] Even so the article went on to criticise a speech made by the prime minister which they felt was 'unwise, not to say unfeeling' in its discussion of 'coloured races'. '[C]ould anything be more likely to stir up racial feelings against Australia,

---

10 Tavan, *The Long, Slow Death of White Australia*, 14.
11 Lake and Reynolds, *Drawing the Global Colour Line*, 144.
12 Marilyn Lake, 'From Mississippi to Melbourne via Natal: The Invention of the Literacy Test as a Technology of Racial Exclusion', in *Connected Worlds: History in Transnational Perspective*, ed. Ann Curthoys and Marilyn Lake (Canberra: ANU Press, 2005), 222, doi.org/10.22459/CW.03.2006.
13 Lake and Reynolds, *Drawing the Global Colour Line*, 4.
14 'The Coloured Races' *Peacewards*, published as a supplement to the Australian Church's *Commonweal*, State Library of Victoria (SLV), 1 September 1916.

and to provoke future war, than to flaunt the flag of "White Australia"?'[15] The Sisterhood clearly made the connection between inflammatory uses of exclusion and overt discussions of race relations with the causes of international hatred and war. 'Thus wars are made, and if Australia is ever invaded those who thus stir up racial hatred will be responsible'. A Christian way of 'durable peace' was proposed as the way forward, and while separation was still preferred, it represented 'respect for fellow-men, whatever their colour, unselfish justice, and international, inter-racial goodwill'.[16]

Continuing on from the early considerations of race and war, the Peace Army held a public forum in June 1919 where it too put on record its concern with the WAP.[17] At this meeting women and men expressed concern about the policy that had until then provoked little opposition. *The Woman Voter* reported the meeting in full.[18] It was advertised as a 'Parliament for Women' convened specifically to discuss the WAP, which was an 'all important subject'.[19] Among the speakers were many prominent voices in the pacifist and progressive trade union movement. In the initial description, the editors recognised the significance of the question as a subject of continuing debate:

> The theme is a fruitful one; never more so than at the present time, when the world's politics have made it more alive than it has been in Australia at any time since the inauguration of the Commonwealth, with its restrictive legislation regarding the alien races. Everybody has ideas about a White Australia of some sort, and to that one must immediately add that few people who are not actually students of Internationalism, party politicians, or idealists, have any very absolute opinions upon this vital question.[20]

Recognising the complexity and sensitivity of emotions and opinions on the issue, they structured the meeting so that expressions of dissent and of approval of the WAP were equally acceptable. Opposition to the WAP was not presumed to be the orthodox position, or the one necessarily aligned with the Peace Army's ideology. The Sisterhood and the Peace Army had not yet merged, but they collaborated and both groups were participants. Both were ambivalent on the WAP. They were aware through

---

15 'The Coloured Races' *Peacewards*, 1 September 1916.
16 'The Coloured Races' *Peacewards*, 1 September 1916.
17 The Women's Peace Army 7 June 1919 meeting has been discussed in Marilyn Lake, *Getting Equal: The History of Australian Feminism* (St Leonards, NSW: Allen & Unwin, 1999), 162.
18 'White Australia Convention', *Woman Voter*, 3 July 1919, 3.
19 'White Australia Convention', *Woman Voter*, 3 July 1919, 3.
20 'White Australia Convention', *Woman Voter*, 3 July 1919, 3.

their internationalism that 'a change with us has taken place in the racial aspect of the question' and that Australia should be less opposed to 'the admission on a more generous basis than obtains of the coloured races'.[21]

Vida Goldstein, as the leader of the Peace Army, changed her views on the WAP over the period between 1911 and 1919. Goldstein's biographer, Janette Bomford, notes that Goldstein was 'in favour of White Australia'.[22] Early on, she supported many aspects of the WAP especially in relation to her political views on capitalism and labour rights. However, after observing race relations during the war and focusing more specifically on internationalism and anti-war activism, Goldstein began to change her views on the policy.

Goldstein and the members of the Peace Army always self-identified as non-party. This allowed the Peace Army to avoid any automatic adherence to a party position when reconsidering the benefits and limitations of immigration policy. After her travels in 1911 Goldstein keenly observed race relations and connected what she saw to her understanding of race in Australia. When in Colombo, Goldstein's experience reinforced in her mind that 'mixture' of races degraded them both and that Australia was not ready to deal with these complexities. She wrote:

> Every time I used a rickshaw I had a feeling of self-contempt. I could never get used to treating even the most degraded type of black man as an animal. I left Colombo believing more firmly than ever in the wisdom of a White Australia. At this stage of our civilisation the black and white cannot dwell together without both deteriorating—in spite of American experience. The coloured man takes all the vices of the white man, and the white man becomes dehumanised. He is so accustomed to being waited on hand and foot that he never does a thing for himself when he can get a coloured man to do it, and he is so full of contempt for the coloured man that he sees everything out of focus, and his tendency is to live only for himself and in himself.[23]

Goldstein, through such experiences, felt that in abandoning a White Australia, the nation would be creating a new underclass of exploited labour at the expense of the 'white man's' working conditions and that both whites and people of colour would be degraded in the process. This position

---

21 'White Australia Convention', *Woman Voter*, 3 July 1919, 3.
22 Janette M Bomford, *That Dangerous and Persuasive Woman: Vida Goldstein* (Carlton, Vic: Melbourne University Press, 1993), 60.
23 'Extracts From Miss Goldstein's Letter From Colombo', *Woman Voter*, 6 April 1911, 8.

revealed how Goldstein consciously enjoyed the privileges of whiteness, and as historian Angela Woollacott has observed, failed to see Australia as a 'racially structured society' like that of America despite the presence of Asians and Aboriginal peoples.[24] Her position was likely due to her own personal experience of urban Melbourne where she had 'probably never seen Aboriginal people working as employees or servants of white people as they did in pastoral areas'.[25] Urban progressives, many of whom grew up in middle-class families, often had a limited understanding of the issues of race in Australia. Travel encouraged Goldstein to consider the privilege of whiteness as part of the British Empire, which, despite her criticism of some aspects of colonialism, she sought to protect and uphold.

While Goldstein approved of the WAP and the culture of whiteness it enshrined, the Women's Political Association (WPA) did not support it unconditionally. When the Maternity Allowance Bill was passed in 1912 the WPA spoke out about the exclusion of the benefit to 'women who are Asiatics or aboriginal natives'.[26] Reasoning that the 'Asiatic' women in question gave birth to their children within the Commonwealth, and were therefore 'British subjects', they believed that this was 'the White Australia Policy run mad. Maternity is maternity, whatever the race.'[27] Evidently the WPA's position on White Australia was nuanced, and set between other pillars of its moral architecture, notably respect and recognition of motherhood. Their support for the policy focused upon immigration restriction, not discriminating against those already within the Commonwealth.

By 1914 Goldstein and the WPA identified another major inconsistency within the WAP caused by the war effort. They believed that once Japan became an ally of the Commonwealth, and 'coloured troops' were used in the armies, any arguments in favour of White Australia were voided. The *Woman Voter* carried the headline 'White Australia Policy Done For' in October 1914.[28] The article explained that the association supported White Australia on 'economic grounds without a thought of racial hatred', but felt that the economic argument no longer applied and 'self-respect will no

---

24 Angela Woollacott, *To Try Her Fortune in London: Australian Women, Colonialism, and Modernity* (Oxford: Oxford University Press, 2001), 44.
25 Woollacott, *To Try Her Fortune in London*, 45.
26 'Maternity Grant', *Woman Voter*, 9 October 1912, 1.
27 'Maternity Grant', *Woman Voter*, 9 October 1912, 1. See also Lake, *Getting Equal*, 75.
28 'White Australia Policy Done For', *Woman Voter*, 27 October 1914, 2.

longer allow [us] to uphold the principle' because of the way that 'coloured people' were being asked to fight alongside 'whites' as equals.[29] The article continued:

> If we consider coloured people good enough to use for the purpose of helping us to kill our enemies and expand our Empire, then we cannot refuse them the opportunity of using us for their purposes.[30]

Wartime and Commonwealth interaction with non-white Allied countries prompted these women to reconsider their ideas about the WAP. It revealed to them the 'racial hatred' behind the policy that they had defended on economic grounds until now. This racism made them uneasy and conflicted with their views on internationalism.

At the 1919 Parliament for Women meeting, these issues were re-examined. With such a strong representation of voices from the trade union movement, it was clear the biggest concern was the issue of the white working man's wage—perhaps the central pillar of the WAP's justification among the Australian progressive movement. It was assumed that any influx of migrants would have an undercutting effect as 'coloured labour' had the tendency to 'bring down the wage'.[31] Many examples of where this had occurred in other countries were cited, showing an international framing of the debate on both sides. In this matter the women of the Peace Army sided with the trade union movement, as those representatives, likewise avowed pacifists, identified themselves as the progressive side of politics. In an attempt to rationalise this stance in a non-racialised way, the Peace Army noted:

> It is not so much a war against colour as against Capital and its machinations, that holds our working class to the principles of our present legislation.[32]

This meeting was hosted and chaired by women but was open for men to join in the general debate. Many of the participants in the meeting were undecided about their position on the WAP, or how they should discuss it. Alfred Foster frankly stated 'I do not seek to justify the White Australia Policy, but I accept it'.[33] Some reiterated the concerns of the unions, as many of the women were involved in peace activism because of their

---

29 'White Australia Policy Done For', *Woman Voter*, 27 October 1914, 2.
30 'White Australia Policy Done For', *Woman Voter*, 17 November 1914, 2.
31 'White Australia Convention', *Woman Voter*, 3 July 1919, 3.
32 'White Australia Convention', *Woman Voter*, 3 July 1919, 3.
33 Alfred Foster quoted in 'White Australia Convention', *Woman Voter*, 3 July 1919, 3.

activities in women's rights movements interested in protecting the position of mothers and children, presumed beneficiaries of the WAP settlement. These maternalist feminists deferred to the masculinism of the trade union movement and those who reasserted rights for men to earn a family wage. Maternalist welfare feminists campaigned for state support for mothers, to enshrine the idea of domestic work as paid work and ensure that poor mothers would not be forced to undertake waged work and neglect their children.[34]

In the workplace women were limited to earning between 50 and 60 per cent of the male wage, so while campaigners argued for equal and fair wages, they too wanted women out of the workforce, which was in line with policies of male labour activists.[35] Labour women therefore strongly believed in both having state recognition for women's work and enshrining the bedrock of the 'civilized man's wage'. In practice, any support by the state such as the maternity allowance introduced in 1912 was exclusively intended for white mothers.[36] Australian women invoked motherhood when demanding more rights for women by demonstrating 'women's value to the nation … in the breeding of a stronger and sturdier race'.[37] Most interwar feminist activists were not as willing to question race-based immigration exclusion. Vida Goldstein and the WPA opposed the exclusions of the maternity allowance and called for non-white mothers to have access, but many other feminist activists in support of White Australia did not comment.[38]

The 'civilised man's wage' had only recently been sanctified by the Harvester judgement decided on by the Commonwealth Conciliation and Arbitration Court with Justice HB Higgins as president in 1907. This judgement set a minimum wage as a 'fair and reasonable' living wage that assumed men should support their families.[39] To threaten the breadwinning capabilities of husbands would destitute women and children and force them into the workplace. So many of the women's ideas of wage labour were tied,

---

34 Lake, *Getting Equal*, 72.
35 Shurlee Swain, Patricia Grimshaw and Ellen Warne, 'Whiteness, Maternal Feminism and the Working Mother 1900–1960', in *Creating White Australia*, ed. Jane Carey and Claire McLisky (Sydney: Sydney University Press, 2009): 214–29.
36 Lake, *Getting Equal*, 76.
37 Marilyn Lake, 'A Revolution in the Family' in *Mothers of a New World: Maternalist Politics and the Origins of Welfare States*, ed. Seth Koven and Sonya Michel (New York: Routledge, 1993), 379.
38 Lake, *Getting Equal*, 76.
39 John Rickard, 'Higgins, Henry Bournes (1851–1929)', *Australian Dictionary of Biography* (ADB), National Centre of Biography, ANU, adb.anu.edu.au/biography/higgins-henry-bournes-6662/text11483, accessed online 1 April 2014.

tangentially, to racism and class issues. Higgins was a pacifist supportive of international attempts at diplomacy and peace negotiation. While his judgement was not explicitly racial, but class-based, he still saw no tension between the WAP and wider pacifism.

Other women at the 1919 meeting were more radical and rejected the nexus between the claims of 'civilized labour', maternal and child welfare, and the WAP. One participant, Mrs Griffin, said 'imperialism is the menace, not the people', and 'our moral superiority is a joke'.[40] Another, Mabel Singleton, remarked that 'The Japanese do not seek to flood Australia, only to have our recognition of their "equality"'.[41] These women, along with Fullerton, Paling, and others who represented WILPF symbolised the element within the meeting that pushed for a rejection of the WAP. Their views were forcefully articulated. In the words of Paling from the Sisterhood: 'if we want to keep our nation on a high standard, we should banish the undesirable of our own race'.[42] One solution, suggested by Amelia Lambrick, was to 'let the coloured men bring their women, and there is no racial problem'.[43] Lambrick, who was active in the peace movement and a future president of WILPF, was vocal about the White Australia issue from as early as 1907. She wrote for the *Socialist* under the pseudonym 'Hypatia' and criticised the socialist movement for not understanding the meaning of 'brotherhood': 'we shout "brotherhood" in the major and "White Australia" in the minor and seem quite unconscious of the discord'.[44] However, her own position on racism still seemed equivocal and ill-defined. '[R]acial instincts', noted Lambrick, 'will prevent marriage save in the very lowest strata of society ... if we are superior beings we will not intermarry with an inferior race.'[45]

Given the range of contradictory positions among such a diverse group of delegates, the meeting concluded without a definitive pronouncement. The deep reservations that the participants of the meeting had with the idea of actually removing the WAP were apparent in the evasive words of the report:

---

40 Mrs Griffin, 'White Australia Convention', *Woman Voter*, 3 July 1919, 3.
41 Mabel Singleton, 'White Australia Convention', *Woman Voter*, 3 July 1919, 3.
42 Lucy Paling, 'White Australia Convention', *Woman Voter*, 3 July 1919, 3.
43 Amelia Lambrick, 'White Australia Convention', *Woman Voter*, 3 July 1919, 3. Lambrick was president of WILPF from 1932 to 1936 and attended the 1926 WILPF Congress held in Dublin.
44 Hypatia (Amelia Lambrick), 'The Cry for Freedom', *Socialist*, 9 March 1907, quoted in Graeme Osborne, 'A Socialist Dilemma', *Labour History*, no. 35 (1 January 1978): 114.
45 Osborne, 'A Socialist Dilemma', 114.

> The golden precipitate gathered from the convention is the growth of internationalism and of brotherhood that the tone of the proceedings marked. We are, despite economic fears and purity of blood considerations, learning that 'colour caste's a lie', and that 'a man's a man a' that.'[46]

This result was complicated. It recognised the force of the principle of racial equality but found no way to reconcile it with the WAP, and the suspicion that capitalism would exploit any change. Yet it was still pro-internationalist and assumed with time attitudes could change. What was made clear was how prominent figures in the peace and trade union movements believed the WAP to be necessary and not inconsistent with their call for peace. It was the specific international dimension of peace activism that prompted criticism of race-based exclusion among the women of the Sisterhood and the Peace Army.

White Australia and the world stage

Australia's postwar engagement with international governance was dominated by the strictures of White Australia and its preservation. The Peace Army folded in 1919 and the Sisterhood became the Australian section of WILPF, effectively allowing the two membership bases to merge and connect with the international section of WILPF. In November 1920, Australia sent Nationalist Party Senator Edward Millen as part of a national delegation to the first League of Nations Assembly. The newly reconstituted Australian section of WILPF sent a letter of introduction about Millen to their international comrades as a way of sharing information about how best to approach him. This initial letter encouraged WILPF International to spend time 'beguiling him into the international atmosphere' showing how it saw the diplomatic positions of each nation as a vital part of the international decision-making machine.[47] The women's groups invested time and energy in meeting and discussing issues with the chosen national representatives.

---

46 'White Australia Convention', *Woman Voter*, 3 July 1919, 3.
47 Moore as secretary of the APA to Balch, Geneva, 29 September 1920, series III reel 54, WILPF International Papers 1915–1978, Sanford, NC: Microfilming Corp. of America, c 1983, accessed at the National Library of Australia (NLA). Hereafter referred to as WILPF Papers.

However, there was a profound disconnect between how the women wished the delegates to approach their roles and how the delegates themselves planned on engaging with this first, very modest, gesture toward international government. Millen saw his job as defending Australian interests against any internationalism that would encroach on national policy. It has been well noted how Prime Minister Billy Hughes defended the WAP at the Paris Peace Conference, calling his successful attempt to prevent a racial equality clause being inserted in the League of Nations Covenant a victory despite aggravating diplomatic relations with Japan.[48] Millen was a close colleague of the prime minister and at the League of Nations he promoted the WAP as sacrosanct, just as Hughes desired.[49]

For the government of Australia, the idea of the League of Nations was threatening. Their involvement with the League was defined by an intention to monitor and curtail pressure to change White Australia. Hughes was quoted in the *Sydney Morning Herald*, describing how Australians should be suspicious about this type of internationalism:

> Australia was a signatory to the covenant of the League, and she had, perhaps, more than any other nation to lose by the League's decision, because many of the things for which her soldiers fought had not yet assumed as definite a shape as was desired ... Australia could not even listen, for instance, to anyone who suggested any encroachment on the policy of the White Australia.[50]

The international section of WILPF was not impressed with the Australian delegation at the first League of Nations meeting in 1920. The reports about Millen became something of an embarrassment to Australian WILPF women, and perhaps encouraged them to see the disadvantages in the WAP, especially when Australian representatives such as Millen used the policy as a way of disrupting and derailing progress at the conference. When the international section of WILPF approached the official Australian delegation as part of their commitment to lobbying all national sections for peace, the distrust Millen had for the goals of the League of Nations was apparent. As detailed in letters to the Australian section of WILPF, this attitude left them underwhelmed:

---

48   Lake and Reynolds, *Drawing the Global Colour Line*, 150.
49   Martha Rutledge, 'Millen, Edward Davis (1860–1923)', ADB, National Centre of Biography, ANU, adb.anu.edu.au/biography/millen-edward-davis-7577/text13227, accessed online 2 April 2014.
50   'League of Nations: Senator Millen a Delegate', *Sydney Morning Herald*, 18 September 1920, 13.

> Mr Millen kept us for two hours and was very urgent about seeing us again. He did most of the talking and the burden of it was 1) that he himself looked out for his own people first … and that 2) the delegates of the League of Nations were a contemptible crew who were not ready to sacrifice their particular national interests for the general welfare. There was not a glimmer of perception that there was an inconsistency in this. I regret to say he was the most ill considered and most disliked personality in the Assembly. [He had a] frank contempt for every race but his own. Is it not too bad that Australia to whom we all look with such high expectations should have to suffer being represented in such a fashion.[51]

Millen's crude style was provocative and highlighted to the Australian women the political vulgarity of the WAP. To the women of WILPF, the League of Nations was a crucial part of their internationalism and the promise for disarmament and peace. They realised the organisation would only succeed if all nations were able to engage by moderating national chauvinism. They criticised the drafting of the covenant for giving too much emphasis to national sections. To receive letters describing Australian delegates in the above terms would have prompted many in the internationalist movement to reconsider the way Australia was projecting itself to the world. Soon after hearing the critique, WILPF actively participated in the organising of an interstate Australian peace conference to be held in Melbourne that devoted the majority of its time to considering the WAP. Millen's appearance at the League of Nations suggests a tension between his representations of the national interest, and the priority of Australian WILPF who hoped to represent Australia's international goodwill.

The interstate peace conference, 1921

In 1921 the Australian Peace Alliance (APA) organised an interstate peace conference that brought together 38 peace societies from across Australia and New Zealand. Eleanor Moore, secretary of Melbourne WILPF, had taken up a part-time paid secretary position with the APA, and was centrally involved in the administration of the meeting. Held in Melbourne in March it met to discuss the 'new theme' of the WAP.[52] The timing of this conference was significant. It came directly after Australia's engagement with the first League

---

51 Balch to Moore, 11 January 1921, series III reel 54, WILPF Papers.
52 Moore, *The Quest for Peace*, 69.

of Nations meeting. The APA had held many public meetings in 1920 to discuss Australia's contribution to the international forum, which through the efforts of Senator Millen, had been a studied exercise in the obstruction of internationalists' goals.[53] The participants believed the issue was 'new' as it had 'been the accepted policy of all political parties for over 20 years' and the conference claimed that it was 'now, for the first time since Federation, made the subject open for public discussion'.[54] As historians David Walker and Agnieszka Sobocinska have pointed out, this idea of looking to Asia as being something 'new' for Australia has had a long history.[55] It was a tactic used to ignore difficult issues and convert 'those who are concerned with Australia's Asian future into visionaries, bravely going where none have gone before.'[56]

Disarmament Sunday, Yarra Park, Sunday 6 November 1921.
Source: Records of the Women's International League for Peace and Freedom, MS 9377 State Library of Victoria.

---

53 Moore, *The Quest for Peace*, 69.
54 Moore, *The Quest for Peace*, 69.
55 David Walker and Agnieszka Sobocinska, eds, *Australia's Asia: From Yellow Peril to Asian Century* (Crawley, Western Australia: UWA Publishing, 2012), 2.
56 Walker and Sobocinska, *Australia's Asia*, 2.

At this large Melbourne meeting, two speakers were there by special invitation, Dr W Lowe from Melbourne and Rev. Sydney Strong from the US. Two representatives of the trade union movement, RS Ross and Don Cameron, were vocal participants, and had been present at the earlier Peace Army meeting of 1919 where White Australia was questioned.[57] As representatives of the trade union movement, they felt it important to reinforce the need for the policy on the grounds of protecting white wage labour. At the 1921 meeting, only six women were present out of thirty-eight participants, and four officially represented WILPF's various branches.[58] Three were recorded as speaking, and those women were the only participants who pointed to the issue of racial exclusion as a potential cause of war. Isabel Swann, who was in Melbourne representing a small WILPF branch in Sydney, directly linked the rise of militarism in Australia with the narrow worldview promoted by the WAP:

> Why was the White Australia Policy ever introduced? We were not getting swamped with Asiatics. Behind it was the desire to create fear in the mind of the worker, so as to allow military power to be foisted on Australia.[59]

Swann's position showed how she believed the focus on White Australia encouraged people to prioritise defending it with violence and war. Eleanor Moore spoke out about the damage of nationalism and the fostering of war sentiment, but her position remained within the orthodox framework of language used to understand whiteness:

> The present policy makes for war. War will do nothing to settle this question, but will embitter it, and further weaken the white race. It should be made widely known that we are dissatisfied with the present position, and we are seeking a just solution.[60]

The 'present position' she referred to was the tension between the policy and the use of it by nationalists in the international setting. According to Moore's biographer, Malcolm Saunders, Moore was a faithful supporter of the WAP, and though her position softened after prolonged engagement with women

---

57 Report of the Fourth Interstate Peace Conference, held at the Friends' Meeting House, Melbourne, 25–28 March 1921, series III reel 54, WILPF Papers.
58 Report of the Fourth Interstate Peace Conference, held at the Friends' Meeting House, Melbourne, 25–28 March 1921, series III reel 54, WILPF Papers.
59 Isabel Swann, quoted in Report of the Fourth Interstate Peace Conference, held at the Friends' Meeting House, Melbourne, 25–28 March 1921, series III reel 54, WILPF Papers.
60 Moore, quoted in Report of the Fourth Interstate Peace Conference, held at the Friends' Meeting House, Melbourne, 25–28 March 1921, series III reel 54, WILPF Papers.

from across all regions of the world, she never fully renounced it.[61] Moore compared Australia with the US and its racial problems, and believed the mixture of races led to 'the blight of a fearful civil war', therefore signalling a belief that racial difference was prone to stir up violence.[62] This perspective was not unusual. Higgins, an important public figure even before his historic 'Harvester' judgement, considered himself a pacifist and had articulated similar sentiments when the WAP was introduced. Looking to the United States, he noted the country had experienced the 'greatest racial trouble ever known in the history of the world' and told the parliament that Australia should 'take warning and guard ourselves against similar complications'.[63]

Moore's argument represented a strong current of thought on nationalism and ethnicity in the early interwar period, even among the most liberal. Ethnically, religiously and linguistically homogeneous states were preferable to the social unrest caused by 'mixing' races and difference. The connection of ethnicity to nation was central to some perspectives of how to secure global peace. The rest of the participants debated issues of miscegenation and social mixture of races, Christian morality, industrial and capitalist threats to white wages and racial pseudoscience. Kathleen Hotson from Queensland representing the Children's Peace Army challenged the anxiety of trade unions by stating; 'Are we too weak and narrow to organise coloured workers if they come here? Why are they necessarily the asset of capitalism only?'[64]

Participants attempted to answer her statement, citing the illustrative example of 'Kanakas' in Queensland, or the different standards of living of other 'black or yellow peoples'. Ross explained that he felt the policy complemented rather than complicated his pacifism by categorising the WAP as a call for self-determination: 'Japan for the Japanese, Australia for the Australians'.[65] Ross put forward his own motion that urged conference delegates to recognise that under the capitalist system coloured immigration would 'produce enmity, unrest and war within'.[66] Fearful too that 'coloured races' would be used to break strikes, he acknowledged the racism of

---

61 Malcolm Saunders, *Quiet Dissenter: The Life and Thought of an Australian Pacifist: Eleanor May Moore 1875–1949* (Canberra: Peace Research Centre, Australian National University, 1993), 331.
62 Saunders, *Quiet Dissenter*, 332.
63 HB Higgins, *Commonwealth Parliamentary Debates (CPD)*, House of Representatives, 6 September 1901, quoted in Lake and Reynolds, *Drawing the Global Colour Line*, 143.
64 Kathleen Hotson, quoted in Report of the Fourth Interstate Peace Conference, 25–28 March 1921, series III reel 54, WILPF Papers.
65 Moore, *The Quest for Peace*, Appendix 9, 183.
66 Osborne, 'A Socialist Dilemma', 125.

his argument, especially when countering another speaker discussing miscegenation; 'keep your races pure'.[67] The historian Graeme Osborne has written about Ross's involvement in this meeting, recognising that as a leader of the socialist movement of the time his promotion of the WAP led to the collapse of any possibility for the Victorian Socialist Party to become genuinely international.[68] Ross's position was hardline and strident. By contrast, the WILPF women were too reserved to fully denounce it but refused to support it unequivocally. WILPF's nebulous and variegated approach afforded a way through by recognising the contradiction. They used personal internationalism as a way forward, making connections and visiting excluded countries as a way to move beyond a grand national political impasse.

Like the 1919 meeting, the interstate peace conference was inconclusive and did not commit to any clear position on the WAP. In their failure to produce a workable alternative, the peace movement joined most other political movements that discussed the WAP in being unable to 'suggest anything more than a nominal relaxation of the restrictions'.[69] The interstate peace conference ended with resolutions that encouraged closer cultural understanding but avoided any recommendation to abolish the exclusionist immigration policy.[70]

While neither explicitly disagreeing with nor wholeheartedly denouncing the foundations of the WAP, these recommendations were still radical at the time. They looked to address anxieties of labour activists by suggesting the unions should prioritise organising Asian workers and repudiated the idea of any 'intrinsic superiority' of the white race. They stated that cultural understanding and exchange needed to be pursued, recognising that the policy itself, regardless of the initial reasons for its implementation, had encouraged prejudice between 'people of the East and West'.[71] It was radical enough that media such as *The Australian Worker* reported simply that 'the Peace Conference which recently sat in Melbourne carried a resolution against the White Australia policy.' It elaborated: 'Unquestionably the

---

67   Osborne, 'A Socialist Dilemma', 125.
68   Osborne, 'A Socialist Dilemma', 128.
69   AC Palfreeman, *The Administration of the White Australia Policy* (Carlton: Melbourne University Press, 1967), 119.
70   Report of the Fourth Interstate Peace Conference, 25–28 March 1921, series III reel 54, WILPF Papers.
71   Report of the Fourth Interstate Peace Conference, 25–28 March 1921, series III reel 54, WILPF Papers.

delegates concerned are men actuated by high ideals, but sometimes high ideals cannot, or should not be given precedence of vital and irrefutable facts'.[72] Incorrectly assuming all delegates were male, the article reiterated the unionist position that capitalism would exploit the 'vast differences' between races. Eagle-eyed Moore picked up on the article and responded, asking for it to be modified. Her letter was printed in full in the next edition. She maintained that no resolution was 'against' the WAP and that the output of the conference was 'by no means unconditional'. Moreover, 'the question whether some measure of exclusion may not, in the best interest of both races, be desirable, on economic or other grounds, is left entirely open'.[73]

Without the crisis of war, interest in peace organising did not seem as critical to many and the APA stopped meeting in 1922, though it never officially disbanded.[74] Therefore, the proposed 'inter-racial congress' to discuss the WAP in more depth was never convened. Enthusiasm for such cross-cultural exchanges seem to have only been seriously pursued by the women in the peace movement, who then looked for ways to fulfil the recommendations independently. They found a new forum in the Pan-Pacific movement which enabled them to personally interact and challenge their own prejudices, however obliquely.

Division over the policy within the progressive internationalist movement shows how deeply naturalised the principles of White Australia were in the 1920s. It is also revealing of the many competing visions that existed within WILPF on what could reasonably be considered 'progressive'. In the Australian political sphere, 'progressive' movements were steeped in issues of concern to the working class and often preoccupied with protecting white wage labour. Support for the logic of the Harvester Judgement of 1907, and the principle of racial exclusion its racialised understanding of civilised life entailed, was an article of faith for most Australian progressive movements.[75] Internationalism represented a different form of progressive engagement. While peace was at its core, the new complexities about race that it raised meant a re-evaluation of how new internationalists should engage with the other active progressives. The women involved in WILPF sometimes experienced the WAP as insufficient and stifling, but they did not know how to oppose it or what to replace it with. Their action, overall,

---

72   'Mainly Political', *The Australian Worker*, 7 April 1921, 1.
73   Moore, 'White Australia', *The Australian Worker*, 21 April 1921, 2.
74   Moore, *The Quest for Peace*, 72.
75   Lake and Reynolds, *Drawing the Global Colour Line*, 157.

might not have been drastic, and tended more to unnerve rather than dissent, but having debate and discussion where opposition was raised and recorded remains significant as it shows that while support across Australia was dominant, it was not universal.

WILPF ventures out of White Australia: The Pan-Pacific movement

Despite their inconsistent position on the issue of White Australia, the Australian section of WILPF was eager to prove that their views had nothing to do with the respect they held for other countries. It became a priority to find ways to engage with neighbouring countries through WILPF, and reinforce that although immigration remained a fraught topic, a close international relationship was still desired. WILPF International proposed a fact-finding trip to China, and the Australian section repeatedly communicated their interest in the expedition. The delegates, Camile Drevet from France and Edith Pye from England, both travelled to China in October 1927.[76] The Australian section raised a generous contribution of £5 for their expenses, and forwarded a contact list of sympathetic individuals given to them by a fellow pacifist in China as a missionary from the Society of Friends.[77] They asked the delegates to 'assure the women of China' that Australian women 'desire to see most peaceful and cordial relations established'. They reiterated that the WAP was not meant to offend and that any interpretation of the policy being based on 'enmity' was 'largely imaginary'.[78] Moore wrote:

> I do not mean to imply that the exclusion law is a dead letter—that is far from being so—but it would be quite a mistake to conclude that it necessarily means either insult or contempt to another people. We of the [WILPF] in Australia join with our sisters in all other countries in hoping the visit of our delegates to China will be productive of great good in the way of improved understanding on all sides, and the making of many personal friendships.[79]

---

76   Camile Drevet and Edith Pye, *Report of the WILPF Delegation to China*, Geneva 1928, P 172.4 DRE NLA.
77   Moore to Sheepshanks, Secretary of WILPF Geneva, 21 November 1927, series III reel 54, WILPF Papers.
78   Moore to Sheepshanks, Secretary of WILPF Geneva, 21 November 1927, series III reel 54, WILPF Papers.
79   Moore to Sheepshanks, Secretary of WILPF Geneva, 21 November 1927, series III reel 54, WILPF Papers.

There was no mention in the official report of any discussion that the delegates had with Chinese women about White Australia, but there was recognition of 'their awakening sensitiveness to treatment as an inferior nation from unenlightened and unimaginative foreigners'.[80]

During the 1920s the peace movement began to look for ways to interact with countries of the South Pacific. There was a realisation that internationalists had mistakenly ignored Australia's near neighbours. Meetings were held to discuss how to encourage 'friendship' to foster a peaceful region, such as the 'Pan-Pacific Friendship meeting' held in the Town Hall in Sydney in 1923 which was hosted by the NSW Branch of the London Peace Society.[81] As more was known about the region from experts and commentators discussing the peculiar issues of the area, WILPF too looked for ways to become involved. When the potential for a Pan-Pacific Women's conference was circulated among women's networks, the Australian section of WILPF enthusiastically pursued this opportunity to interact with neighbouring countries in a constructive way. They wished to show a different interpretation of the WAP, one that diverged from the crude exclusivism espoused by Hughes and Millen, and which did not aim to offend or reject interaction with neighbouring nations.

The Pan-Pacific Women's Conference movement began organising in the 1920s and arranged its inaugural conference in 1928. It was set up out of the Pan-Pacific Union, which had headquarters in Honolulu, Hawai'i.[82] Looking at the series of eight Pan-Pacific conferences that took place between 1928 and 1958, historian Fiona Paisley has analysed how the women involved in the organising built upon 'ideals of cross-cultural exchange and interracial harmony' across a period when the world grappled with decolonisation, economic depression and world war.[83] The political motivation for these women's conferences was inherently internationalist and seemed out of step with the dominant Australian approach to regional engagement. Because of the debates over the WAP, many 'women who sought to learn more about Asian women's lives and to cooperate with them

---

80   Drevet and Pye, *Report of the WILPF Delegation to China*, 49.
81   'A Short Account of the Pan-Pacific Friendship Meeting', 3 September 1923, series III reel 54, WILPF Papers.
82   Moore, *The Quest for Peace*, 96.
83   Fiona Paisley, *Glamour in the Pacific: Cultural Internationalism and Race Politics in the Women's Pan-Pacific* (Honolulu: University of Hawai'i Press, 2009), 425, doi.org/10.21313/hawaii/9780824833428.001.0001.

on women's issues were consciously at odds with their cultural context.'[84] They revelled in the idea of the network representing 'East meeting West' and encouraged the attendance of non-Western nations. The promotion of cultural diversity complicated understandings of nationalism throughout the network. As some Western participants hoped that internationalism would promote a 'world identity', it became clear that for some non-Western countries nationalism represented an important anti-colonial struggle in which Western women were implicated.[85] Paisley notes that many non-Western women joined the network and participated in the conferences because nationalist anti-colonial governments were still not enfranchising women. They hoped to find a way to improve the situation for women in their countries and to criticise their own government's militarism.[86]

The very real divide between 'east and west' was clear in the Western modes of political dominance present in the structures of the conference. The proceedings were conducted in English and the choice of place, Hawai'i, was accessible to westerners because of its ties to the US.[87] In 1928 that connection was clear with the closing remarks from the chairman, WILPF International's Jane Addams, who stated that 'Honolulu is an outpost of America in the midst of the Pacific'.[88] At the first conference the site of Honolulu was very specifically chosen not simply because it was the home of the Pan-Pacific Union, but because it was 'at the ocean's crossroads' and was 'a laboratory of social and racial relationships'.[89] Hawai'i was colloquially considered the 'Geneva' of the Pacific.[90] It was around this time that it was proclaimed to be 'the most successfully racially mixed society in the world'. The Pan-Pacific Women's Association (PPWA) believed that 'the youngest and oldest civilisations' exist side by side because 'the people of the Pacific are without great traditional hatreds'.[91] This perspective obscured the colonial history of Hawai'i itself while also promoting a more thoughtful and moderate approach of the mixture of races, one that they thought should be studied and replicated in Europe and around the world.

---

84 Angela Woollacott, 'Inventing Commonwealth and Pan-Pacific Feminisms: Australian Women's Internationalist Activism in the 1920s–30s', *Gender & History* 10, no. 3 (November 1998): 435, doi.org/10.1111/1468-0424.00112.
85 Paisley, *Glamour in the Pacific*, 25.
86 Paisley, *Glamour in the Pacific*, 25.
87 Hawai'i became a state of America in 1950. Bessie Rischbieth, *March of Australian Women: A Record of Fifty Years Struggle for Equal Citizenship* (Perth: Paterson Brokensha, 1964), 123.
88 Paisley, *Glamour in the Pacific*, 69.
89 *Report of the Australian Delegation 1928*, The Pan-Pacific Women's Conference Honolulu, August 1928, accessed NLA, 3.
90 Paisley, *Glamour in the Pacific*, 16.
91 Paisley, *Glamour in the Pacific*, 41. *Report of the Australian Delegation 1928*, 3.

Pan-Pacific Women's Conference, Honolulu 1928. Round table, government section, chaired by Miss Kikue Ide (Japan). Eleanor M Moore standing at left.

Source: Various photographic views and portraits of Eleanor May Moore, alone and with various pacifist groups she belonged to, taken in Australia and overseas at conferences and demonstrations, ca. 1918–1945 Mitchell Library, State Library of NSW MLMSS 4170 PXE 1025.

The gatherings were organised to 'measure up the prevailing standards of life in those nations bordering on this great ocean'.[92] The emphasis on development and health, education, social science, and industry meant the participating countries ensured their delegations were experts in their chosen fields. Twelve nations participated including Australia, Canada, China, Java, Fiji, Hawai'i, Japan, New Zealand, Philippines, Samoa and the United States, with around 150 delegates in total. Australia sent 13 delegates and some associates from a number of different societies and organisations. Eleanor Moore was elected as the representative for Australian WILPF, and again they diligently raised the funds for her travel.[93] Her nominated area of interest was 'women in government' and she was allocated to engage in a round table discussion.[94] Two of her colleagues from WILPF Victoria joined her. The first was Mrs Bryning, whose speciality was listed as 'associated with child welfare activities'. The other was Mrs BM Fowler who was listed as an associate without voting rights.[95] The journey of the delegation took 16 days,

---

92 *Report of the Australian Delegation 1928*, 3.
93 Moore, *The Quest for Peace*, 97.
94 Moore, *The Quest for Peace*, 97.
95 *Report of the Australian Delegation 1928*, 6–7.

which while seeming long, was substantially shorter than the journeys that were required to reach any WILPF congresses in Europe.[96] The delegates all travelled together and recognised that this international conference was unique and even a 'new phase of international representation' because it brought together delegates from more than one nationally organised body, and represented different world movements.[97]

The leader of the Australian delegation was Bessie Rischbieth from Western Australia, an active internationalist who had co-founded the British Commonwealth League of Women and was a board member of the International Alliance of Women (IAW). In 1935 she would be awarded an OBE for her work advancing women's rights.[98] Rischbieth became a mentor for many Western Australian WILPF women and had lobbied in the 1920s for women to attend the League of Nations as Australian supplementary delegates. She was later a substitute delegate in 1935.[99] Women's groups were pleased that a substitute delegate to the League of Nations became standard practice and WILPF member Edith Waterworth took on the honour in 1936, though it was often felt that government appointments were not prioritised or appropriately funded: 'with only one exception the appointment has never gone to a woman unless she was already on the other side of the world.'[100] Eleanor Hinder was another of the internationalists pursuing practical work in China before the Pan-Pacific conference. She was an Australian involved in the International Labour Organization (ILO) and was living in Shanghai working for the Young Women's Christian Association (YWCA) with American Viola Smith, who was the US Assistant Trade Commissioner in China.[101] Hinder was already known to WILPF, and had even been promoted by them as a potential delegate to a committee of the League of Nations because of her known international work in China.[102] Similarly, Hinder was supportive of WILPF, having arranged accommodation and assisted with travel for the two WILPF delegates in

---

96 *Report of the Australian Delegation 1928*, 6–7.
97 *Report of the Australian Delegation 1928*, 30.
98 Lake, *Getting Equal*, 157. Nancy Lutton, 'Rischbieth, Bessie Mabel (1874–1967)', ADB, National Centre of Biography, ANU, adb.anu.edu.au/biography/rischbieth-bessie-mabel-8214/text14373, published in hardcopy 1988, accessed online 2 April 2014.
99 Paisley, *Glamour in the Pacific*, 35.
100 Julia Rapke, 'Edith Waterworth', Papers on various Australia Women, Manuscript. Exact dates unknown, though Waterworth essay written between 1940 and 1945, NLA.
101 Meredith Foley and Heather Radi, 'Hinder, Eleanor Mary (1893–1963)', ADB, National Centre of Biography, ANU, adb.anu.edu.au/biography/hinder-eleanor-mary-6678/text11515, published in hardcopy 1983, accessed online 2 April 2014.
102 Moore to Secretary, 31 August 1927, series III reel 54, WILPF Papers.

China.[103] Hinder was involved in the 1928 conference through the Chinese delegation and although not officially present as an Australian delegate, she was able to represent the wide network of Australian professionals working for women's rights abroad.

At the second conference in 1930 the PPWA was inaugurated to take on the responsibility of organising and promoting future conferences.[104] The first president was an Australian woman, Dr Georgina Sweet. Though not part of the first delegation, she became a very important figure in the organisation and promotion of the conferences in Australia. Sweet was an academic from Melbourne University specialising in zoology who was a founding member of the Women's Graduate Association and the international vice-president of the YWCA from 1934. She too was later awarded an OBE for her international work. Another participant, Dr Ethel Osborne, was an 'industrial hygienist' who was directly invited by the Pan-Pacific Union to chair the health section of the conference because of her achievement in that area. Her involvement attests to the ambition of the conference consisting of professionals and experts from the Pacific who would be able to influence the proceedings with their expertise. Osborne studied medicine at the University of Melbourne, specialising in obstetrics and gynaecology.[105] All of these women directed their training and skills towards international agendas. They focused on the challenges faced by 'less developed' nations and sought to improve women's health, hygiene and status domestically, hoping that their influence would foster a unity that would transcend nationalism and promote internationalism. The close contact of these women with the women of WILPF, facilitated by their engagement with the Pan-Pacific conference movement, illustrates how WILPF became interconnected in the wider women's network. Many formed close collaborative ties to other women who were working as internationalists or promoting internationalism in other fields.

From the outset, the women from Australia saw the promotion of Pacific cooperation as paradigm-shifting and talked at length about how the will for such a cross-cultural gathering was due to the area being the 'new World

---

103 Drevet and Pye, *Report of the WILPF Delegation to China*, 17.
104 Paisley, *Glamour in the Pacific*, 2.
105 Osborne was a substitute delegate with the official Australian delegation to the League of Nations in 1931. Diane Langmore, 'Osborne, Ethel Elizabeth (1882–1968)', ADB, National Centre of Biography, ANU, adb.anu.edu.au/biography/osborne-ethel-elizabeth-7925/text13791, published in hardcopy 1988, accessed online 2 April 2014.

Focus'.[106] They believed the meeting was 'pioneering', as rarely had so many 'races and creeds met' to 'learn and exchange'.[107] 'Australians', wrote Moore, 'were slowly beginning to realize that this Dominion is not an island just off the coast of Europe, but a continent in the Southern Pacific Hemisphere.'[108] Hinder, who published a piece on the first conference in *Pacific Affairs*, also noted how the focus of most international women's organisations was Europe, to the detriment of women of the Pacific.

> The headquarters of the main international groupings of women … are in Europe. Their international conferences have been in Europe. It follows from this that women of Australia, New Zealand, and China and Japan are able to be present in very small numbers.[109]

The conferences did not start out as explicitly pacifist gatherings but the involvement of women like Moore and Addams allowed the issue of peace to permeate throughout all the round table discussions. Moore wrote a report for the new international WILPF publication *Pax International* that began distribution in 1926, discussing how peace became central to all discussions:

> It was not a Peace Conference; that is to say, the subject of international peace had no place on the agenda, but it was implied throughout all discussions. More and more it was recognised as the days went on, that in our times the problems of one country are the problems of all; that every question proves under examination to be an international question; and that no satisfactory solutions are possible except on a basis of peace and cooperation.[110]

The Australian Government had a different understanding of their place in the global and geographical context. In contrast to the women seeking out intellectual and cultural exchange, the Australian Government treated the Pacific through a prism of defence, strategy and security. After the Paris Peace Conference, Australia was mandated control over New Guinea. Rather than any developmental goals, Millen unequivocally acknowledged

---

106 *Report of the Australian Delegation 1928*, 3.
107 *Report of the Australian Delegation 1928*, 3.
108 Moore, *The Quest for Peace*, 96.
109 Eleanor M Hinder, 'Pacific Women', *Pacific Affairs* 1, no. 3 (1 July 1928): 9–12, doi.org/10.2307/3035494.
110 Eleanor Moore, 'Neighbours in the Pacific', *Pax International* 4, no. 3 (January 1929).

that the benefit of controlling the territory was to create a buffer between Australia and other Pacific nations. According to Millen, '[i]f Australia has any policy in the Pacific it is a somewhat nebulous desire for safety'.[111]

All the women involved were interested in promoting cultural understanding between nations. Even so the topic of immigration was skilfully avoided. Moore recalled in her memoir that 'etiquette forbade' the discussion in any programmed way.[112] According to Paisley the first real discussion of the White Australia question at the PPWA was not until the 1937 conference. As official Australian WILPF delegates only attended the 1928 and 1930 conferences, WILPF did not explicitly engage with any critique of the Women's Political Association (WPA) through the PPWA.[113] Yet, in all Moore's writing about her time at the conference, there is a very strong sense that she wanted to experience a more cosmopolitan world.

In Moore's memoir, published towards the end of her life, she recognised how much this meeting changed her opinions on race. Moore noted that the atmosphere and the 'artistic, poetic and religious tradition' of the Pacific nations 'had its silent influence upon the preconceived ideas of the "whites"'.[114] In her reflection, she also noted how much the WAP and the insularity that it had created stunted the cosmopolitan growth of Australia:

> Australians could not but recognise that, whatever values the 'White Australia' policy had conserved, these were seriously offset by impoverishment in cultural and artistic graces. In that cosmopolitan atmosphere Australians felt their own insularity … while it had lain on our consciences that we might be doing others an injustice in excluding them, it had not occurred to us that we ourselves might thereby be losers too.[115]

She was quick to add a caveat that it was also the affinity within the gathering that facilitated her interactions with like-minded people, and that these relationships of 'finer character' would always be easier on an individual level than between nation-states.[116] Nonetheless she was moved by her

---

111 Senator Millen, quoted in WJ Hudson, *Australia and the League of Nations* (Sydney: Sydney University Press in association with the Australian Institute of International Affairs, 1980), 140.
112 Moore, *The Quest for Peace*, 97.
113 Paisley, *Glamour in the Pacific*, 151.
114 Moore, *The Quest for Peace*, 98.
115 Moore, *The Quest for Peace*, 97.
116 Moore, *The Quest for Peace*, 98.

engagements with the Japanese delegations, recounting their conversations and noting a story told to her by the Japanese of how grateful they were to Australia for sending aid after a natural disaster. Again, none of these experiences led her to unequivocally oppose the WAP but they did prompt her to re-evaluate the racialised principles that underpinned it.

The Australian women involved in the PPWA in 1937, when the White Australia discussion occurred, had a similarly difficult time reconciling the policy with the ideas of cultural internationalism that the Pan-Pacific conferences promoted. With anxieties about an overcrowded Europe as well as problems of food security and potential territorial expansion, population pressure was believed to be an aggravating factor that had the potential to cause conflict or war. By the 1937 conference the PPWA had embraced the idea of addressing peace as one of the most important issues facing the Pacific and its people. In the population pressures panel, immigration and 'even distributions' were considered as an outlet for the pressing issue as the 'etiquette' that forbade discussion at earlier conferences was put aside. As the delegates were asked to give presentations on population and immigration in their own countries, the Australian delegate Jean Daley, a Labor member and committed unionist, used a map as a prop.[117] She attempted to illustrate the nature of the 'open space' that was often cited as showing how Australia was capable of taking more of a population burden, and she characterised the continent as dry and lacking water, to indicate how much of the space was uninhabitable.[118] Paisley noted this as 'defensiveness' on the Australian delegation's behalf, as it tried to justify the safeguarding of Anglo-Saxon culture without resorting to any cultural arguments for restriction that could be seen as offensive. In a self-conscious way, these women internationalists exhibited their anxiety about the 'superiority complex of the white race'. Instead of embodying racist ideology, they wished to be seen as embracing and enjoying the pleasures of cosmopolitan society.[119]

There remained two different views about how peace and immigration interacted. One articulated in the Melbourne meetings about White Australia supported the policy because many believed that unregulated immigration would cause social unrest and violence. It would jeopardise

---

117 Judith Smart, 'Daley, Jane (Jean) (1881–1948)', ADB, National Centre of Biography, Australian National University, adb.anu.edu.au/biography/daley-jane-jean-5866/text9977, published first in hardcopy 1981, accessed online 11 January 2022.
118 Paisley, *Glamour in the Pacific*, 154.
119 Paisley, *Glamour in the Pacific*, 154.

the 'character of the people'.[120] The perspective prevalent at these Pacific gatherings, however, recognised that overpopulation would invariably lead to war and underpopulated areas like Australia should be open to accepting immigrants. Both opinions were considered and debated by internationalist women. But again the complexity and the lack of any ready solution to the reconciling of national exclusivism with cosmopolitanism meant that their discussions did not translate into a platform for action. As they were in no position to change the policy, there was no real need to produce a solution. The organisation of the PPWA was also constantly criticised for being 'anglocentric' and for not reflecting the diversity of its ambitions in its internal hierarchy.[121] In these shortcomings, the ideal of internationalism was revealed as in tension with the more complex and difficult issues of integration and immigration.

WILPF had a large presence at the first Pan-Pacific in 1928, mainly because its international president, Jane Addams, presided as the conference international chairman, since Hawai'i was in United States territory.[122] WILPF also had a meeting alongside the gathering to capitalise on the fact that so many members were gathering from distant places, where delegates could not usually travel to European conferences.[123] This not only served the purpose of having WILPF members report on sections but also allowed the promotion of WILPF to those interested who were not members. In her report, Moore noted that many women were initially sceptical of WILPF and of putting peace on the agenda. Addams, however, in opening the conference, was skilfully able to promote WILPF without 'uttering a word from the chair that could be so construed'.[124] The WILPF meeting that convened after, hosted by the Honolulu branch, was open for observers where according to Moore, Addams gave a talk 'with such wisdom and wit that not only were the objectors silenced, but the local branch of the League enrolled about a hundred new members within a few days.'[125] Australian WILPF members were proud to showcase their organisation to other internationalists.

---

120 Report of the Fourth Interstate Peace Conference, held at the Friends' Meeting House, Melbourne, 25–28 March 1921, series III reel 54, WILPF Papers.
121 Paisley, *Glamour in the Pacific*, 70.
122 *Report of the Australian Delegation 1928*, 1.
123 'The W.I.L. Conference at Honolulu', *Pax International* 3, no. 11 (October 1928).
124 Moore, *The Quest for Peace*, 97.
125 Moore, 'Neighbours in the Pacific', *Pax International* 4, no. 3 (January 1929).

3. WHITE AUSTRALIA AND REGIONAL RELATIONSHIPS

How the Pan-Pacific experience changed WILPF Australia

On return from the conference, Moore and other WILPF women lectured on their experiences at the Pan-Pacific conferences. In 1930 Moore journeyed to New Zealand on a lecture tour about the Pacific and spoke at various places in Victoria and New South Wales. Several years later, in 1936, she embarked on a lecture tour for the Country Women's Association. Moore was always surprised to find that in rural towns, 'Australian training in exclusiveness had not lessened their willingness to hear and believe the best that could be said of peoples outside their own borders.'[126] After the experience of 'oriental' culture and close contact with women of similar minds from 'eastern' countries, Moore's critique of the WAP changed from it being about embarrassment and excluding other countries, to the idea that Australia was missing opportunities to enrich its own culture. WILPF Australia began to reiterate the need for 'good feeling' between different nations as a way to overcome the idea that the WAP was causing racism and xenophobia. They specifically credited the PPWA as a factor in Australian society that promoted greater understanding of Asian neighbours, as noted in this letter sent to the international section of WILPF:

> On account of our 'White Australia' policy, which excludes most Asiatics as undesirable aliens, people here know very little about India, and have a general feeling that it is not their business. But within the last few years there have been a great extension of interest and sympathy towards the peoples of Asia. The series of Pan-Pacific Congresses held in Honolulu have done much to foster this spirit.[127]

The constant reference to the WAP as the cause of Australia's insularity further complicated the women's attitude towards exclusionary immigration policies and their own internationalism. The women of WILPF argued that the policy was not entirely racial. Over time, however, they had to concede that their world view and the perspective of the Australian people had been changed by it in a way that limited their understanding of other nations. The benefit of their engagement in the PPWA was not just in further illustrating to themselves the inconsistency in their country's racial immigration policy. It also reoriented their internationalism towards regional issues rather than

---

126 Moore, *The Quest for Peace*, 101.
127 Moore to Zueblin, WILPF Geneva, 1 July 1930, series III reel 54, WILPF Papers.

maintaining the focus on Europe.[128] More WILPF representatives could be sent because it was closer to home and cheaper, which would have increased the interest and excitement at local meetings. Once they had arrived, delegates felt more involved in the conference proceedings, and more fully present as participants rather than as token antipodean curiosities. Moore expressed a feeling of comfort in a letter to WILPF International where she wrote of how the Australians and 'Orientals' felt more 'at ease, and more ready to express themselves'. The atmosphere was less foreign and they were 'literally more at home', while the content discussed was more directly relevant.[129]

The feeling of achievement from their involvement was such that WILPF Australia began to question the zeal with which they should engage with the European-centric organisation. In the same letter to WILPF in Geneva, Moore noted how the Australian sections were beginning to discuss how their contribution to the world movement could be best facilitated. They believed that focusing on 'peaceful fellowship in the Pacific' was more important than making an effort to send delegates to conferences in Europe at great expense.[130] A sense of self-consciousness about the place of Australia in the world movement emerged from their deliberations. Weighing up the ties to the British Empire with the impact Australia could have locally, Moore felt that Australia's contributions to Europe were not worth as much had they had once been. Strengthening regional ties in defiance of 'sanctions from Westminster' would be the most effective way for Australia to contribute to keeping a check on British militarism. A shortage of funds and the practicalities of internationalism played a large influence in their debate. As Moore wrote, 'might we not really help the peace cause more in the long run by using the money, say, to go to Japan, or to India, or even to western America, and trying to cultivate and consolidate peaceful contacts there?'[131]

---

128 For an overview of the various regionally focused groups see; Marie Sandell, 'Regional versus International: Women's Activism and Organisational Spaces in the Inter-War Period', *The International History Review* 33, no. 4 (2011): 607–25, doi.org/10.1080/07075332.2011.620737.
129 Moore to Sheepshanks, Secretary WILPF Geneva, 21 November 1928, series III reel 54, WILPF Papers.
130 Moore to Sheepshanks, Secretary WILPF Geneva, 21 November 1928, series III reel 54, WILPF Papers.
131 Moore to Sheepshanks, Secretary WILPF Geneva, 21 November 1928, series III reel 54, WILPF Papers.

As well as reorientating their internationalism, Pan-Pacific engagement gained credit among members for increasing the understanding of WILPF as an organisation within Australia. Such regional activity facilitated the networking of women involved with other groups who were not 'definitely pacifist' but were 'internationally broad-minded'. Moore happily noted how 'co-operation with other societies is open to us now as it never has been before, and it will be interesting to see what good comes of it.'[132] Relationships formed here continued after the series of conferences and contributed to the longevity of WILPF by establishing it as a respected organisation with wide-reaching networks.

***

The Pan-Pacific conferences brought WILPF Australia into a new internationalist circle and encouraged women who were working as internationalists in Pacific countries to join the peace cause. It represented a complex engagement with cultural imperialism and whiteness, especially as many Pacific countries saw nationalism as an anti-imperial struggle. Given their own reluctance to confront the restrictive immigration laws of Australia, WILPF tried to engage with what it saw as 'oriental' cultures on an individual basis. Their experience of living in Australia with the WAP had created a perceived dearth of understanding of neighbouring countries, for they had been socialised to accept that there was a wide barrier between themselves and Asian others. For many, their interactions with foreign nationals often surprised them, not least by stirring up feelings of empathy and friendship. By the late 1930s Eleanor Moore's view on the WAP was considerably more relaxed if not entirely transformed. In a report of the section from 1939 Moore explained how:

> Internationalists are turning from the disappointment of Geneva to the hopes of the Pan-Pacific movement; open-minded Australians, enlightened by personal meeting with cultured Orientals, are realizing their previous mistake in assuming that all Asiatics were of the ignorant coolie class, and have begun to question whether the total exclusion policy, which they had accepted as an axiom of national life, is after all quite sound.[133]

---

132 Moore to Sheepshanks, Secretary WILPF Geneva, 21 November 1928, series III reel 54, WILPF Papers.
133 Moore to Baer, 'Some points of Australian Policy', 1 May 1939, series III reel 54, WILPF Papers.

Having the WAP in place meant that the Australian section of WILPF had to clarify and deal with the racialised constraints of the interplay between nationalism and internationalism. The questions and debates that it initiated forced them to engage with very complex ideas regarding peace and exclusion. The WAP exposed the paradoxical relationship of liberal internationalism, nationalism and peace, and as a political organisation in Australia they were not the only ones confronted by it. They were however among the few who vocalised the confused evolution of their position. WILPF found it difficult to produce a clear and coherent dissent from the WAP because there was not one available to them that would coalesce their internationalism with the precepts of Australian progressive thought. The engagement with the WAP exposed the limits of WILPF's internationalist imagination and restricted their ability to engage with the region as the equals of women elsewhere. They mapped out the contradictions, and the paradox, that recognised national exclusivism as distasteful and discordant but they retained the assumption that it was somehow indispensable. They had no serious reform proposition to offer other than a softening of the edges of the policy; it remained a difficult topic of discussion until after World War II, when the local and international context had changed sufficiently for WILPF and the progressive movement of Australia to begin opposing the policy outright.

4

'Our struggle is not only one for peace but also for freedom'

When the Women's International League for Peace and Freedom (WILPF) adopted its constitution at their international conference in Zurich in 1919, it also settled on a new name. In contrast with the existing placeholding name of 'International Congress of Women for Permanent Peace', many felt that the new name was 'more inclusive, and looking more toward the future than that first proposed'.[1] Some disagreed, saying that they wished to retain the old name because of its focus on 'permanent' peace. In this exchange, the importance of both elements of the name became clear, and was highlighted when a delegate argued that 'women cannot work for peace unless they are freed'.[2] The motion was put to a vote and WILPF was adopted, confirming that the organisation was bound to work for peace *and* freedom. At the time of the naming, peace and freedom seemed naturally aligned and complementary. By stating that women needed freedom to work for peace they were focusing not on national freedom, but on freedom from gendered oppression, which limited their capacity to act autonomously and participate as full global citizens. By World War II, however, the tension between peace and freedom took on a new meaning in the fight against fascist ideology and totalitarian oppression. Peace or freedom then became

---

1 'The Women's International Congress, Zurich 12–17 May 1919, Towards Peace and Freedom', WILPF Publication, accessed through database edited by Kathryn Kish Sklar and Thomas Dublin, *Women and Social Movements, International—1840 to Present*, 146.
2 'The Women's International Congress, Zurich 12–17 May 1919, Towards Peace and Freedom', WILPF Publication, 146.

a choice, and WILPF's name seemed oddly symbolic of the deep divide the peace movement would be forced to consider in the face of the aggressions of the dictators.

***

WILPF domestically and internationally saw the period after World War I, marked by widespread antiwar sentiment, as the best time to advance their cause. They utilised and encouraged the symbolism of antimilitarism within society, and were even prompted by national governments. There appeared to be a moment between the wars where the agenda of the women's peace movement and government policy coincided, culminating in the 1932 World Disarmament Conference organised by the League of Nations, to which most national governments sent delegations. Internationally, WILPF's president Jane Addams was recognised with a Nobel Peace Prize in 1931, and domestically the Scullin Labor Government embraced WILPF's ideas for disarmament.[3] WILPF put its efforts into encouraging public pressure and presented the disarmament conference with a record-breaking petition. The brief period when some of its major views about peace coincided with those of a significant body of mainstream public opinion allowed WILPF to connect with those large sections of the community horrified by the devastation of the recent war. The new League of Nations Union, which had formed around 1920 in various states and which many prominent politicians had joined, surged in membership. Their mission included promoting peace and the new international organisation.[4] This moment of recognition and relaxed tension, as energising as it was for peace activists, was short lived and hope soon gave way to disillusionment after Labor lost power and it became increasingly likely that another world war was imminent.

Global disarmament proved difficult to implement and interwar frictions impeded the success of any proposals. Once again, the world descended into conflict and war. The precipitous rate at which the pacifist concern dissipated was alarming and took WILPF by surprise. WILPF Australia was decidedly absolute in its pacifism and struggled to negotiate the sudden change in opinion among the public and some of their members who began

---

3   Eleanor M Moore, *The Quest for Peace, As I Have Known It in Australia* (Melbourne, 1948), 105. Jane Addams generously donated the prize money to WILPF International, to further support the organisation.
4   Hilary Summy, 'From Hope … to Hope: Story of the Australian League of Nations Union, Featuring the Victorian Branch, 1921–1945' (PhD thesis, University of Queensland, 2007), 48.

approving of military action against the rising threat of fascism. The response to World War II by WILPF was one that divided the organisation and pushed WILPF in Australia almost to breaking point. It was the closest the organisation came to collapse. The Australian section continued to support the principle of absolute pacifism while European countries under fascist rule were supportive of more forceful measures to secure, and increasingly to protect, a threatened freedom. World War II challenged its ideas about nonviolence and forced an interrogation of the meaning of its name: was peace or freedom more important, and was peace meaningful without freedom? Focusing on Australian WILPF's response to the international section on a decision to support a boycott of Japan, we can see not only the breakdown of international networks because of the war, but also a new self-conscious positioning of Australia as a regional leader. Emboldened by its recent engagement with the region through the Pan-Pacific conferences, WILPF Australia demanded acknowledgement from the international section of its right to decide on WILPF's policy in the Pacific.

The Kellogg–Briand Pact

Between the wars, the Australian Government's involvement in various League of Nations conferences represented the first time the nation engaged separately in international forums from the British Empire. In the words of one historian, 'Australia came of age in the League of Nations'.[5] The significance of the League of Nations for self-governing dominions and smaller nations was clear to all involved, including WILPF, who recognised that it gave Australia greater prominence and the 'status of an independent great power as no great international action can be taken without them'.[6] However, the two decades of Australia's involvement with the League of Nations was presided over by conservative governments. Labor only held office for a single term between 1929 and 1932 with James Scullin as prime minister. As a result, while the nation engaged on the world stage independently for the first time, Australian governments promoted

---

5   WJ Hudson, *Australia and the League of Nations* (Sydney: Sydney University Press in association with the Australian Institute of International Affairs, 1980), 3.
6   Sheepshanks to Septimus Harwood, Sydney, 2 July 1928, series III reel 54, WILPF International Papers 1915–1978, Sanford, NC: Microfilming Corp. of America, c 1983, accessed at the National Library of Australia (NLA). Hereafter referred to as WILPF Papers.

pragmatism over any other moral or ideological considerations and pursued national policy 'with whatever weapons came to hand and without much regard for theory, philosophy, morality or even consistency'.[7]

After the Paris Peace Conference, the world turned to contemplating the issue of disarmament with a series of conferences aimed at negotiating a solution to any future arms race. On 27 August 1928, the US Secretary of State Frank B Kellogg agreed to a pact recommended by the French Foreign Minister, Aristide Briand, which encouraged other countries to join in outlawing war. This was known as the Kellogg–Briand Pact, or the Pact of Paris, and Australia was one of the original signatories.[8] The US section of WILPF played a role in lobbying for the adoption of the pact, with Jane Addams herself heading a delegation of women that met with US President Calvin Coolidge in 1927. They presented him with a petition of 30,000 signatures which was also sent to Briand for consideration.[9] The pact asserted that warfare should be declared a violation of international law. The fact that so many countries signed the pact gave a real sense of hope to many that wanted to protect the world from future wars as devastating as World War I. Moore noted that 'the pacifist's dream seemed to be coming true'.[10] The Australian Government at the time, a Nationalist–Country Party coalition led by Prime Minister Stanley Bruce, paid tribute to the historical significance of the treaty.[11]

After 1919 it was widely accepted that a conflict on any similar scale should be avoided in the future. On this point, pacifists and conservatives agreed. For WILPF both domestically and internationally, the Kellogg–Briand Pact represented a starting point for their campaign against war and they hoped it would mark 'the beginning of a series of steps towards the substitution of law for war ... As military measures are no longer to be taken, disarmament must be begun at once and carried out thoroughly.'[12] While the message of the pact was one welcomed by the international community, its weakness lay in the impossibility of enforcement. Instead of outlawing war, it outlawed the declaration of war and had many ambiguous clauses that allowed for the

---

7   Hudson, *Australia and the League of Nations*, 4.
8   Nigel Young, 'Kellogg–Briand Pact', in *The Oxford International Encyclopaedia of Peace*, ed. Nigel Young, online version (Oxford: Oxford University Press, 2010).
9   Robert H Ferrell, *Peace in Their Time: The Origins of the Kellogg–Briand Pact* (Hamden, Conn: Archon Books, 1968), 119.
10 Moore, *The Quest for Peace*, 86.
11 Alexander McLachlan, 'Speech: Renunciation of War: Treaty', *Commonwealth Parliamentary Debates (CPD)*, Senate, 20 February 1929, 360.
12 Mary Sheepshanks, 'The Kellogg Peace Pact and After', *Pax International* 3, no. 9 (August 1928).

justification of defensive wars.¹³ For this reason the pact led the worldwide disarmament movement to call for further measures that would practically implement what had now been in principle agreed upon.

WILPF Australia's activities in the aftermath of war

WILPF was concerned with Australia's continuing postwar hostility towards Germany. It advocated tolerance and understanding to prevent another war and thought the Versailles treaty unfairly targeted the country. In 1920 the Australian Peace Alliance sent a letter to the government, which was forwarded on to WILPF International, outlining how Australia remained the only country that refused to trade with Germany, a position that seemed unjustifiable on both moral and economic grounds.¹⁴ This prompted the international section of WILPF, concerned that 'relics of war hysteria' were clouding judgement, to single out Australia as having a particular problem in forgiving Germany. WILPF International noted:

> We have heard that the majority of the Australian people still cherishes as great a hatred of the German people to-day as during the war. French, Belgian and German women find this hard to understand. We who, since 1919, have worked together as comrades to re-establish understanding between our nations, beg our Australian sisters from our hearts to try to create understanding in their country in place of hatred.¹⁵

Moore wrote to the editor of *The Sun*, a Sydney daily newspaper, requesting that they discontinue using the word 'Hun' to describe the German people.

> Ethnologically, the term is incorrect; sentimentally, it is out-of-date; and as a sneer at a defeated and suffering people, it does no honour to the pen or voice that uses it.¹⁶

---

13 Young, 'Kellogg–Briand Pact'.
14 'Trade With Germany' letter sent to Australian Members of Parliament on behalf of the APA, date not specified—c 1920, series III reel 54, WILPF Papers. See also Moore, 30 November 1920, series III reel 54, WILPF Papers.
15 'To the Women of Australia', letter sent from WILPF International the Australian Section, 1923, series III reel 54, WILPF Papers.
16 Letter from Eleanor Moore to *The Sun* editor, 28 September 1923, Box 1724/1, Papers, WILPF, MS 9377, State Library of Victoria (SLV).

Mrs WJ Drummond speaking, 'No More War' Demonstration, 1923.
Source: Eleanor M. Moore papers, 1887–1953, Mitchell Library, State Library of NSW PXE 1025. See Appendix for a short biography of Mabel Drummond.

The paper refused the request, replying that 'they are not suffering half as much as they deserve, or as I hope they will suffer in the future'.[17] The hostilities of the war did not evaporate with the declaration of peace.

Despite this, WILPF continued to campaign for peace, and found a more receptive audience elsewhere. It coordinated a Peace Library that operated out of rooms at 376 Flinders Street in Melbourne. They maintained a full and vibrant schedule of speaking commitments and actively participated in the annual 'No More War' demonstrations on Armistice Day, often having speakers talk to large crowds at the Yarra Bank about international issues. With the help of other peace organisations coordinating efforts for the 'No More War' campaign, its promotion was widespread. Advertisements were displayed in picture theatres in Melbourne with lines such as: 'A mighty crusade against the whole war system is imperative. If we do not end war, war

---

17 Montague Grover *The Sun* editor, to Moore, 1 October 1923, Box 1724/1, Papers, WILPF, MS 9377, SLV; Sally O'Neill, 'Grover, Montague MacGregor (Monty) (1870–1943)', *Australian Dictionary of Biography* (ADB), National Centre of Biography, Australian National University, adb.anu.edu.au/biography/grover-montague-macgregor-monty-6500/text11147, published first in hardcopy 1983, accessed online 30 March 2022.

will end us'.[18] Posters promoting peace were even placed in bus shelters with the costs donated by the Trades Hall Council (THC).[19] WILPF entered into a phase of intense activity, seeing the coming of peace as the proper time not only to educate and campaign against war but also warn against future wars. Such campaigns were more problematic during a crisis when national fervour was at its peak. They continued with their yearly fete, held at Janie Kerr's residence, which would often raise valuable contributions to their running costs and helped to support the journal *Peacewards*.[20]

The election of Labor governments after the war led to more serious engagement with the peace movement. In July 1924, turmoil in Victorian state politics, and a vote of no confidence in the Premier, brought Labor to power with Premier George Prendergast at the helm.[21] As his ascension to the leadership was unexpected and few anticipated this government to have long-term prospects, Prendergast used the opportunity to implement Labor policy with symbolic importance.[22] Conscription debates during the war had caused deep divisions within the Australian Labor Party (ALP), including in Victoria where the federal government was based. Prendergast had strongly opposed conscription during the war and had called for a negotiated peace settlement rather than following those determined on a 'punitive humiliation of Germany.'[23] When he became premier, the issue of postwar militarism was one that he felt very strongly about, though it also continued to divide the party and the community. Reversing the policy of previous governments, Prendergast refused to honour a £50,000 contribution to the building of a Shrine of Remembrance, declaring he would prefer to fund a 'lasting memorial' like a hospital that would 'continue to do good as long as there is need'.[24] His government also refused to gazette Anzac Day as a public holiday. He told a gathering at Trades Hall that duty to the Labor movement required being 'saturated with the ideals of peace'.[25]

---

18   Sentences shown as advertisements on films at picture theatres, No More War Week, 1923, Melbourne Australia, series III reel 54, WILPF Papers.
19   Moore to Acting Secretary of WILPF International, 7 January 1924, series III reel 54, WILPF Papers.
20   *Advocate*, Thursday 7 December 1922, 13.
21   Geoffrey Serle, 'Prendergast, George Michael (1854–1937)', ADB, National Centre of Biography, ANU, adb.anu.edu.au/biography/prendergast-george-michael-8103/text14145, published first in hardcopy 1988, accessed online 25 July 2016.
22   Paul Strangio and Brian J Costar, eds, *The Victorian Premiers 1856–2006* (Annandale: Federation Press, 2006), 178.
23   Strangio and Costar, *The Victorian Premiers*, 177.
24   Bruce Scates, *A Place to Remember: A History of the Shrine of Remembrance* (Port Melbourne, Vic: Cambridge University Press, 2009), 45.
25   Scates, *A Place to Remember*, 45.

WILPF fete at 'Trenant', home of Mrs Warren Kerr (President), Kew, December 1923.
Source: Eleanor M. Moore papers, 1887–1953, Mitchell Library, State Library of NSW PXE 1025.

Though its term in office was brief, Prendergast's government was emblematic of the extent to which support for peace activities was brought into the mainstream after the war. The war-weary public, dealing with personal trauma after the war, was more accepting of internationalist sentiments, especially after the creation of the League of Nations. The Victorian ALP adopted into its constitution at the 1919 annual conference 'that peace and internationalism be inculcated in the minds of all children attending State schools'.[26] Historian Bruce Scates has noted that there was a spirit of 'militant internationalism' in the postwar years which divided the society 'along much the same lines as the conscription referenda of 1916–17'.[27] Conservatives still deplored the goals of the 'anaemic pacifists', yet there was a higher tolerance for 'subversive' perspectives during peacetime. Without the pressure of wartime scrutiny, WILPF was emboldened to contribute more actively to the public discussion. Eleanor Moore expressed her support

---

26   Australian Labor Party Platform and Constitution, Labor Call Print, 1919, papers of R. S. Ross, MS 3222, Box 1 File 27, NLA.
27   Scates, *A Place to Remember*, 45.

for Prendergast's agenda when writing to the international office of WILPF, describing an event where she was given 'the honour' of sharing the stage with Prendergast to represent WILPF at a speech evening. The supportive atmosphere for her pacifist sentiment shone through when she wrote of how 'one of the members of the Federal Parliament who was present asked afterwards for a copy of what I had said, that he might quote it in the House of Representatives.'[28]

In this climate, WILPF considered the best course was to influence the rising generation through schools, eventually deciding to establish an International Peace Scholarship in Victorian state schools to encourage students to think about peace and internationalism.[29] Open to all children under 14, the scholarship was administered with the authorisation of the Victorian Department of Education and had the subeditor of *The School Paper*, Gilbert Wallace, providing advice on formalities.[30] Students were asked to submit essays on topics chosen by WILPF and the Director of Education awarded the scholarship with both parties sharing the costs of the scholarship. WILPF provided the prize winnings of £4 for school requisites while the minister granted free tuition for four years at a district high school, a school of domestic arts or a technical school.[31] This cost the organisation £16 per year, which was raised through contributions from members and by hosting sewing meetings to make items for their annual fete where they sold them for a small profit. The purpose of the scholarship was to be a 'practical attempt to draw the attention of Australia's future citizens' to questions about the abolition of war, arbitration, and the promotion of goodwill and friendship. Education was the primary means through which WILPF believed they could achieve this end.

---

28 Moore to Glucklich WILPF Secretary Geneva, 1 October 1924, series III reel 54, WILPF Papers.
29 'International Peace Scholarship', *Education Gazette and Teachers Aid*, 16 September 1924, accessed SLV, 284. See also 'International Peace Scholarship' poster September 1924, series III reel 54, WILPF Papers. 'Peace Scholarship', *The Argus*, 4 August 1925.
30 Moore, *The Quest for Peace*, 76; LJ Blake, *Vision and Realisation: A Centenary History of State Education in Victoria* (Melbourne: Education Dept of Victoria, 1973), 1057.
31 Moore, *The Quest for Peace*, 76. 'International Peace Scholarship', *Education Gazette and Teachers Aid*, 16 September 1924, 284.

July Demonstration in Hyde Park, 1922.
Source: Eleanor M. Moore papers, 1887–1953, Mitchell Library, State Library of NSW PXE 1025.

The International Peace Scholarship was created around the same time the Trades Hall Council decided to provide funds for prizes to the Education Department. The prizes, awarded on Armistice Day, were to be distributed to Victorian primary school students who wrote essays on international peace. Both WILPF and the THC wrote to the Minister for Public Instruction, John Lemmon, asking that the government accept the proposals and agree to their administration. Forwarding both requests with approval to the director of the department, Lemmon requested that the paper reflect more peace-focused material to support students in their essays:

> I desire that prior to the competition appropriate articles may be published in the School Paper. It is the desire that the children may have an opportunity of obtaining material from which they may select ideas and thoughts that may be incorporated in their essays. The articles should seek to lead the minds of the children from ideas which may foster the war spirit and glorification of battles of conquest. They should inculcate high ideals of international peace and good will, and the brotherhood of man.[32]

---

32   Mr Lemmon, Victoria, *Parliamentary Debates,* Legislative Assembly, 28 CA vol. 167 July–October 1924, 9 September 1924, 313.

4. 'OUR STRUGGLE IS NOT ONLY ONE FOR PEACE BUT ALSO FOR FREEDOM'

The directive drew the attention of the press and *The School Paper* was in the spotlight. The *Age* ran a story titled 'Labor and Peace, No War Teaching in Schools, Decision of Minister' which quoted a resolution from the Labor policy platform they assumed underpinned the directive of Lemmon to the department:

> That no articles regarding or extolling wars, battles or heroes of past wars be printed in the State school papers or books, and that peace and international brotherhood be inculcated in the minds of all children attending state schools.[33]

Letters to the editor flooded in to the daily press from concerned citizens worried that Lemmon was tampering with the school paper and trying to 'prevent the rising generation of Australians from learning of the glorious deeds and self-sacrifice of their fathers'.[34] The Returned Sailors' and Soldiers' Imperial League cried censorship and felt that 'the feelings of the members of the League [had] been severely tried by the statements of many Ministers'.[35] Attempts at clarification were reported as creating more confusion, with officers from the department telling the press: 'in the absence of a definite Ministerial ruling, they did not know how far-reaching Mr Lemmon's order was intended to be'.[36] Peace groups sent in letters of support for Lemmon's approach, while other members of the community attacked it. The Presbyterian church wrote that 'the proposal is absurd. The Christian Church does not desire to glorify war, but war is a fact that has left its mark upon history'.[37] Professor Ernest Scott, chair of history at Melbourne University, weighed in to the debate with a long article in the Melbourne *Herald*, which was republished in other states, arguing that 'to eliminate war as a factor in national development—and, indeed, as a very substantial factor in national progress—would be to falsify history deliberately'.[38]

Lemmon clarified his position to the parliament maintaining he was misrepresented in the furore. A letter from Mabel Drummond on behalf of WILPF was tabled alongside the THC proposal as evidence of why he

---

33 'Labor and Peace, No War Teaching in Schools, Decision of Minister', *The Age*, 23 August 1924, 15.
34 'Tampering with School Paper, to the Editor of the Argus', *The Argus*, 27 August 1924, 21.
35 'Soldiers and the Ministry', *Portland Guardian*, 4 September 1924, 2.
36 'School Books—Labor Bans Wars', *The Weekly Times*, 30 August 1924, 15.
37 'School Books—Labor Bans Wars', *The Weekly Times*, 30 August 1924, 15. 'Peace Alliance Pleased', *The Argus*, 3 September 1924, 18.
38 Professor Ernest Scott, 'Labour Ukases—History, Without War!—The Lemmon–Brennan Policy', *The Telegraph*, reprinted from the Melbourne *Herald*, 9 September 1924, 6.

gave the directive to *The School Paper*.³⁹ Heated debate ensued with Labor members being likened to 'cold-footer[s] who stayed home, sheltering behind a woman.'⁴⁰ The comment is a classic example of the disparaging way women were sometimes characterised when entering into political debate. Unwittingly, the initiatives by WILPF and the THC caused intense public debate over the teaching of history in public schools and the role it played in advancing different political agendas. Lemmon reassured the chamber that no material alterations were made to *The School Paper*, but that he would encourage the principles of peace wherever he could.⁴¹

The Prendergast Government soon lost the support of the precarious coalition that sustained them. By November 1924, after disagreement over a budget that conservatives called 'class warfare' for its proposed tax increases for the rich, another motion of no confidence was passed and Labor lost power.⁴² Their term was short but intense, reprising divisions over militarism that had continued to simmer in Australian society after World War I. WILPF's Peace Scholarship, created during this intensive period, benefited from the high-profile public debate. It continued for a decade with enough interest and entries to award the prize annually. It lapsed in 1934 when WILPF felt there were no longer enough teachers encouraging their students to compete and the number of entrants became too small.⁴³

The disarmament movement

During the 1920s, arising from the view that arms manufacture itself had been a significant driver of the recent war, WILPF was surveying the problem of international trade in armaments. A report released by the Swedish section in 1928 analysed the defence budgets, and import and export trends

---

39 Lemmon, quoting letters from Mabel Drummond, WILPF and EJ Holloway of the Trades Hall Council, Victoria, *Parliamentary Debates*, Legislative Assembly, 28 CA vol. 167 July–October 1924, 9 September 1924, 313.
40 Victoria, *Parliamentary Debates*, vol. 167 9 September 1924, 332, quoted in Phillip Deery and Frank Bongiorno, 'Labor, Loyalty and Peace: Two Anzac Controversies of the 1920s', in *Labour History*, no. 106, (May 2014): 216.
41 Lemmon, quoting letters from Mabel Drummond, WILPF and EJ Holloway of the Trades Hall Council, Victoria, *Parliamentary Debates*, Legislative Assembly, 28 CA vol. 167 July–October 1924, 9 September 1924, 313.
42 Strangio and Costar, *The Victorian Premiers*, 178.
43 Moore, *The Quest for Peace*, 76.

around the world.⁴⁴ The findings reinforced to WILPF that disarmament and economic issues were intertwined, and in promoting disarmament they would have to develop a coherent response to the economic consequences of their demands. They also realised that the main opposition to disarmament would be from people with 'vested economic interests'.⁴⁵ In their campaign policy platform they noted that national governments should 'exclude all persons having an interest in the maintenance of armaments' from any conference discussing the issue.⁴⁶

Every active interwar peace group included disarmament in its program. It 'became a definite political plan and as such it fired the imagination of the civilized world'.⁴⁷ Domestically, League of Nations Union began operation from 1920 with high-profile members, including public servants and politicians, which helped to promote the anti-war agenda as a mainstream issue.⁴⁸ Other women's organisations that had shied away from a definite stance during the war returned to support the League of Nations and discussions on disarmament.⁴⁹ As a campaign with clear objectives commanding wide support, it was fitted to a collaborative approach. Internationally WILPF became part of a Liaison Committee of International Women's Organisations to facilitate the joint campaign for disarmament, which brought together the International Alliance of Women (IAW), International Council of Women (ICW) and International Federation of University Women, among others.⁵⁰ This joint committee sent deputations to the Eleventh Assembly of the League of Nations. By January 1931 the League of Nations announced its intention to convene the World Disarmament Conference to be held in February 1932. With only a year to prepare, the women's movement began organising what would become the world's biggest petition to be presented to political leaders at the conference.

---

44   GC Bussey and Margaret Tims, *Pioneers for Peace: Women's International League for Peace and Freedom, 1915-1965*, 2nd ed. (London: Allen & Unwin, 1965), 93.
45   Bussey and Tims, *Pioneers for Peace*, 93.
46   Bussey and Tims, *Pioneers for Peace*, 97.
47   Moore, *The Quest for Peace*, 85.
48   Summy, 'From Hope … to Hope', 47.
49   For example, the NCW began to support peace work through the League of Nations, by allowing the League of Nations Union to join the council. Judith Smart and Marian Quartly, *Respectable Radicals: A History of the National Council of Women of Australia 1896–2006* (Melbourne: Monash University Publishing, 2015), 119.
50   Bussey and Tims, *Pioneers for Peace*, 95. See also Leila J Rupp, *Worlds of Women: The Making of an International Women's Movement* (Princeton: Princeton University Press, 1997), 41, doi.org/10.1515/ 9780691221816.

In Australia the peace movement also came together in solidarity over disarmament. The World Disarmament Movement formed in 1928 as an umbrella organising group for more than 88 groups ranging from peace societies to church and labour groups. The first president was Henry Bournes Higgins, the judge best known for delivering the Harvester decision in 1907 and bereft at losing his only son in the war, who presided until his death in 1929.[51] The growing movement recognised that simply campaigning for the Australian Government to disarm would have 'very little bearing on the general question of world peace'.[52] They wanted to find a way to bind larger nations to a popular sentiment. Increasingly familiar with the dismissive approach adopted by national governments, they wanted to override the priorities of the conservative political leaders.

The Australian section of WILPF began drafting a proposal that they believed would bypass governments' hostility towards genuine engagement in diplomatic conferences. Along with the Australian Peace Alliance (APA), WILPF prepared a recommendation for world 'simultaneous referenda'.[53] They sent the proposal to over one thousand organisations and national governments. The reply from the international headquarters of WILPF showed interest and asked for Australia's experience with the process to see what it would be like if other countries were to follow.[54] The proposal for an international referendum drew directly on Australia's recent experience with the 1916 and 1917 plebiscites on conscription as well as on the referendum provisions in the nation's constitution. In her letter in reply, Moore noted how the referendum allowed Australia to avoid being bound by British foreign policy, and how the creation of the League of Nations gave Australia its own voice in international affairs. Yet she also recognised the long path to independence that still lay ahead, noting how the 'sentimental bias' was very strong, leading the wider public to believe that 'the average Australian thinks of all foreign policy as a matter with which he has no concern— that is England's business'.[55] It was thought that all nations conducting simultaneous referenda would be a way for people's opinion to be heard beyond the complexity of geopolitical realities. In the end the prospect of organising for all nations to participate in an international referendum

---

51 Moore, *The Quest for Peace*, 87.
52 Moore to Glucklich, 5 January 1923, series III reel 54, WILPF Papers.
53 Moore on behalf of the APA to Balch WILPF International, 10 July 1922, series III reel 54, WILPF Papers.
54 Glucklich to Moore, 25 September 1922, series III reel 54, WILPF Papers.
55 Moore on behalf of the APA to Glucklich, WILPF Geneva, 5 January 1923, series III reel 54, WILPF Papers.

seemed unfeasible and the joint committee of women's organisations decided instead on a petition. Beginning in 1931, and organised out of the WILPF office in Geneva, the disarmament petition reached across the world.[56]

While the commitment to Britain and empire remained strong in the Australian community at this time, WILPF's view that Australia should have an independent foreign policy was quite distinctive. They believed that average Australians lacking interest and information about the state of world affairs and relying on England to make decisions was 'a state of affairs that must pass'.[57] It also consciously linked Australia's dependence on empire with war by calling conflicts that Australia could be drawn into 'British wars' and noting that 'it is the Great Powers that make war'.[58] In 1925 Moore went further to say that 'this country has never engaged in war as a result of its own policy, nor has it ever been attacked. But three times in little more than a century of national life we have been pulled into war by our position as a dependency of Great Britain, and of course that is our great danger again.'[59] For the peace movement, empire and imperialism demanded an unquestioning commitment to wars that were not their own and threatened the nation's ability to make sovereign decisions about its involvement in armed conflict.

This tension was self-consciously recognised by the Australian section, especially as many other sections and nations did not understand the complex status of Australia as both a nation and a dominion. On many occasions WILPF women had to write and explain Australia's national policy to their international colleagues and make clear when the country could act independently and when it could not. WILPF therefore took the activities of Australian delegates to the League of Nations very seriously, as they knew in that forum Australia could act independently, but when it came to discussing the lobbying of governments about resisting war they had to acknowledge the limitations of a country that lacked a foreign service. Moore felt it was 'not easy' to formulate a 'next step to peace' because the government action was 'determined by instructions from England which we have no means of influencing.'[60]

---

56   Bussey and Tims, *Pioneers for Peace*, 95.
57   Moore on behalf of the APA to Glucklich, WILPF Geneva, 5 January 1923, series III reel 54, WILPF Papers.
58   Moore on behalf of the APA to Glucklich, WILPF Geneva, 5 January 1923, series III reel 54, WILPF Papers.
59   Moore to Doty, 8 December 1925, series III reel 54, WILPF Papers.
60   Moore to Doty, 8 December 1925, series III reel 54, WILPF Papers.

The petition and official government support

Committee groups of WILPF with the disarmament petition, ready to go to Geneva, 1931.
Source: Herald Feature Service, photographer. Records of the Women's International League for Peace and Freedom, MS 9377 State Library of Victoria.

Australian women began preparations for the petition straight away, using a modified version of the British section's form to collect signatures. They not only utilised the networks of the peace movement but those of church groups, other women's societies, the Woman's Christian Temperance Union (WCTU), the Australian Natives' Association, the League of Nations Union and more.[61] WILPF did not have any travel funding for the canvassing of signatures and a request to the government for a railway pass was refused. But they had the devotion of individuals who disseminated the information and gathered support. Miss Kathleen Singleton was sent by the Melbourne Branch to Ballarat to doorknock for support and Amy Wilkins, the president of the small Newcastle branch, addressed meetings and canvassed regional areas, while Mrs Young visited Sydney to campaign along with Miss Ruth Swann. Two more sympathisers, Mrs Brice and Miss Casely, were responsible for the petition in Queensland. The League of Nations Union and the Women's Non-Party Association canvassed South Australia.

---

61   Moore, *The Quest for Peace*, 90.

Tasmania felt the impact of the local and active WILPF membership.[62] In Western Australia, collaboration with the Women's Service Guild (WSG) yielded a significant proportion of signatures, though there was disagreement about adequate recognition for the WSG by WILPF.[63] The area of Australia covered showed that while the membership and branch structure remained small, their canvassing and collaboration had a wide reach. The Melbourne group of WILPF acted as the distribution point for Australia. After months of 'door to door, shop to shop, explaining and arguing, writing to friends far and near' where representatives gathered signatures at public meetings, in street stands and at town fetes, the reward for their effort materialised in the final number.[64] Australia ended up with 117,740 signatures, all checked and certified then packaged up ready to be sent to WILPF in Geneva.[65] They joined the worldwide collection, built up by over 40 countries contributing over 8 million names.[66] The array of significant signatories to the Australian petition reveals how much the political sphere had changed over the short period from 1915 to 1931. Prime Minister James Scullin did more than just sign the pledge; he was present at the sending of the parcels and looked for ways to translate the ambition into national policy.

Labor had come to power late in 1929. They were led by Scullin and replaced a Nationalist–Country coalition government that had been led by Stanley Melbourne Bruce.[67] Very soon after Scullin's election the New York stock market crashed and the world was pulled into a severe economic depression that would later become known as the Great Depression. The new government was immediately faced with very serious economic problems. Scullin had won the election on industrial relations but found unemployment dangerously high. With a need to cut expenditure, he implemented deep cuts to defence spending.[68] These cuts were ideologically driven, as Scullin had been an avowed anti-militarist throughout his political career, opposing conscription, speaking out against the harsh treatment of Germany in the

---

62 Moore, *The Quest for Peace*, 89.
63 WSG Executive meeting in July 1932 quoted in Dianne Davidson, *Women on the Warpath: Feminists of the First Wave* (Nedlands, WA: University of Western Australia Press, 1997), 127.
64 Moore, *The Quest for Peace*, 90.
65 Moore to Secretary WILPF, 20 January 1932, series III reel 54, WILPF Papers.
66 Moore, *The Quest for Peace*, 89.
67 JR Robertson, 'Scullin, James Henry (1876–1953)', ADB, National Centre of Biography, ANU, adb.anu.edu.au/biography/scullin-james-henry-8375/text14699, published in hardcopy 1988, accessed online 13 June 2014.
68 John Robertson, *J.H. Scullin: A Political Biography* (Nedlands, WA: University of Western Australia Press, 1974), 215.

Peace Treaty and recognising the importance of internationalism.[69] This was a departure from the priorities of previous Australian governments, who treated the League of Nations with suspicion. Scullin had a more optimistic attitude, believing it could settle 'international disputes within the forum of the League of Nations instead of on the battlefield.'[70]

The rhetoric of war changed within Australia in the 1920s and 1930s. Official and government sources were no longer in tension with the pacifist movement, but rather in chorus. Even the postmaster general, the future Prime Minister Joseph Lyons, approved pacifist propaganda displaying the World Peace Pact to be hung in money order offices in 1930.[71] For Scullin, internationalism was central to his governing philosophy and the League of Nations was an important forum to attain disarmament and peace. He sent ministers to all international conferences. James Fenton, the Minister for Trade and Customs, attended the five powers naval conference in London, January 1930, where he received a delegation of the British Women's Peace Crusade that included WILPF women.[72] Scullin also travelled and represented Australia at the eleventh session of the League in 1930 while also attending the Imperial Conference in London. The decision unsettled his cabinet as many domestic issues needed attention and the parliament had to be recalled by Acting Prime Minister Fenton in Scullin's absence.[73] Australian WILPF women were proud of their peace-loving leaders, and expressed their approval in letters sent to introduce the international section of WILPF to the Australian League of Nations delegates. Moore's letter reveals how the Australian women could give a local perspective of the politicians:

> All three are peace people. Mr [Francis] Brennan [Attorney General, and leading Catholic ALP member] especially was a pacifist even during the war, and in those days, when the present political eminence was hardly thought of, we were together on many a platform pleading this unpopular cause. Mrs Scullin and Mrs Brennan are both going with their husbands, and we have written to them asking them if possible to visit the Maison Internationale.

---

69 Robertson, *J.H. Scullin*, 59.
70 James Scullin, *CPD*, House of Representatives, 20 March 1930, vol. 123, 325 quoted in Robertson, *J.H. Scullin*, 216.
71 Moore, *The Quest for Peace*, 88.
72 Bussey and Tims, *Pioneers for Peace*, 91. JR Robertson, 'Fenton, James Edward (1864–1950)', ADB, National Centre of Biography, ANU, adb.anu.edu.au/biography/fenton-james-edward-6155/text10571, published in hardcopy 1981, accessed online 11 June 2014.
73 Hudson, *Australia and the League of Nations*, 195.

> I know you always make a special point of approaching the League of Nations delegates, and with these particular ones we think it would be specially worth while.[74]

For the women of WILPF in Melbourne a moment of recognition for their work and an endorsement that reinforced the legitimacy of their cause was exemplified in a town hall meeting attended by notable political figures. It was convened by the League of Nations Union and the World Disarmament Movement and held in the Town Hall on 30 November 1931.[75] The Lord Mayor of Melbourne opened proceedings before a procession of WILPF women presented the petition to the prime minister. The petition was endorsed by Scullin and had many other notable signatories, including that of Sir John Monash, Commander of the Australian Corps on the Western Front in World War I. On the stage were a variety of public leaders including the federal Opposition Leader Joseph Lyons, Attorney-General Frank Brennan, and the Chancellor of the University of Melbourne John Macfarland. Together they represented the highest level of state and federal politics and public office and they all stood in support of disarmament.[76] It was a moment of reflection for Moore who went on to write about the event in many WILPF publications. She understood the significance of having such institutional support and that it might not be seen again: 'it was the greatest public gesture for peace and disarmament ever yet officially made in Australia.'[77]

This meeting was held very close to the federal election, which took place on 19 December 1931. Scullin thought 'it might seem strange to some that they were gathered together for a disarmament conference, or a peace demonstration on the eve of a general election', but he reiterated its importance to his policy platform. The need to promote ideas of peace and internationalism even close to an election 'showed that the question before them transcended all other interests.'[78]

---

74 Moore to Sheepshanks, Geneva WILPF, 12 July 1930, series III reel 54, WILPF Papers.
75 Moore, *The Quest for Peace*, 91.
76 'Disarmament Demonstration', *The Argus*, 24 November, 1931; 'Disarmament. A Melbourne Meeting. November 30', *Townsville Daily Bulletin*, 1 December 1931, 4. Summy, 'From Hope … to Hope', 96.
77 Moore, 'Early days of the WILPF' compiled by CMR Crosland, issued by the Perth branch of WILPF, 1943, Box 1732/4-6, Papers, WILPF, MS 9377, SLV.
78 'Disarmament Meeting in Melbourne', *The Mercury*, 1 December 1931, 8.

The World Disarmament Conference 1932

The Scullin Government was not a stable one and after many tumultuous events, including the resignation of two cabinet ministers Lyons and Fenton, it lost government at the December 1931 elections. This put the newly formed United Australia Party in government. It was led by Lyons who, while generally supportive of disarmament and peace, was not as ideologically driven by these demands as Scullin. It was the Lyons Government that was responsible for sending a delegate to the much-feted World Disarmament Conference in February 1932, and it chose John Latham, who had represented Australia at the League of Nations General Assembly in 1926.[79] After the defeat of the Scullin Labor Government, WILPF was beginning to sense the cooperation and support they enjoyed for a brief period was ending, though they knew of the new government's previous commitment to disarmament and intended to pressure it to stay the course. When writing to the international section, they were realistic about the prospect of Latham as a representative, calling him 'exceedingly cautious'.[80] They expressed disappointment that the government could not be persuaded to send a woman to the conference, the excuse being 'they say they cannot afford to do so'.[81] Women were routinely excluded from the white men's club of international affairs.

The Lyons Government had only gained power a few weeks before the opening of the conference and as a result the Australian delegation was relatively unprepared. They were often inclined to follow the direction of Britain rather than make an independent Australian stand. The WILPF women were correct in their hesitation about Latham, who did not show much interest in preparing for the conference. According to historian WJ Hudson, Latham was more interested in using the time abroad in London discussing rearmament than being in Geneva to discuss disarmament.[82] The conference opened on 2 February, but Latham did not arrive until 27 April, having spent time from 9 April in London. Even then he only spent one week at the conference, travelling back to London for another month and returning to Geneva for one more week in mid-June, bringing his time engaged with the proceedings at only two weeks out of a possible 23.[83]

---

79   Stuart Macintyre, 'Latham, Sir John Greig (1877–1964)', ADB, National Centre of Biography, ANU, adb.anu.edu.au/biography/latham-sir-john-greig-7104/text12251, published in hardcopy 1986, accessed online 17 June 2014.
80   Moore to Drevet, WILPF, 15 March 1932, series III reel 54, WILPF Papers.
81   Moore to Drevet, WILPF, 15 March 1932, series III reel 54, WILPF Papers.
82   Hudson, *Australia and the League of Nations*, 102.
83   Hudson, *Australia and the League of Nations*, 109.

Scullin, now in opposition, asked in question time about Latham travelling away from the conference despite work at the conference being incomplete. He pressed Lyons: 'will he attend the further sittings of the Disarmament Conference?' to which Lyons answered, 'I hope so'.[84]

Fifty-nine delegations were represented at the conference, including the USA, the Soviet Union, China and Japan.[85] This impressive gathering of nations gave the disarmament movement great hope that serious negotiation would take place to reduce or abolish armaments. On Saturday 6 February, in the opening week of the conference, the joint Women's Disarmament Committee presented the WILPF petition to a specially convened extraordinary plenary meeting where it was read out country by country to show how widespread the petition was.[86] Many regarded it as the 'biggest international petition there has ever been; nothing approaching it in scale was ever tried, before or since.'[87] The presentation of the petition, and the recognition by the delegates to the conference that it represented a worldwide campaign that had been in motion for years, gave legitimacy and urgency to the proceedings. WILPF noted how it affected the delegates, many using it as an example of how much the combined people of the world desired peace and security and how important their roles at the conference subsequently were:

> The presentation of the petitions seems to have really made an impression on public opinion and on the delegates. Many of the delegates in their subsequent speeches spoke of the petitions ... and the delegates seem to feel the necessity of emphasising that they speak in the name of the peoples.[88]

The conference chairperson, Arthur Henderson of the British Labour Party, referenced this sentiment in his opening address: 'the world wants disarmament ... The conference itself is unique. Assembled here are the spokesmen of seventeen hundred million people ... I refuse to contemplate even the possibility of failure'.[89] This atmosphere of hope characterised the

---

84 Scullin to Lyons, *CPD*, House of Representatives, 20 May 1932, 1123.
85 Hudson, *Australia and the League of Nations*, 107.
86 Moore, *The Quest for Peace*, 92. See also: Verbatim record of the extraordinary plenary meeting, Saturday 6 February 1932, 'Records of the Conference for the Reduction and Limitation of Armaments Series', United Nations Archives Geneva, 187.
87 Philip Noel-Baker, *The First World Disarmament Conference, 1932–1933 and Why It Failed* (Oxford; New York: Pergamon Press, 1979), 68.
88 Anne Zueblin, to Moore, 12 March, 1932, series III reel 54, WILPF Papers.
89 Arthur Henderson, 'First Plenary Meeting Text of the Debates', Tuesday 2 February 1932, 'Records of the Conference for the Reduction and Limitation of Armaments Series: A Verbatim Records of Plenary meetings Volume 1, 2 February to 23 July 1932', United Nations Archives Geneva, 40.

beginning of the conference, but as the months went by, it was clear that the conference was going to be a disappointment. By July 1932 Germany had withdrawn from the negotiations. There was also disagreement among governments about the desired outcomes of the conference, which extended over years, seeing many electoral changes in national delegations that led to inconsistencies. Many acknowledged that the conference was convened too late to make a difference as Japanese and Italian attacks and annexations had already occurred in Manchuria and Abyssinia.[90] The delegates at the conference also began to register their dissatisfaction at the involvement of 'vested interests' or 'hawks' who were more interested in secret diplomacy and armament profits than a serious engagement with world disarmament.[91] This all contributed to the petering out of proceedings, as the conference was never officially terminated. It continued into mid-1934, when the chair, Henderson, reserved the authority to reconvene, but his death in 1935 meant there was no further meeting.

Aftermath of the conference, the rise of 'collective security', and the IPC

The peace movement worldwide was devastated by the failure of the disarmament conference. Moore noted how 'public interest and hope ebbed together', showing that without the profile and promise of success, it became harder to push for a peaceful solutions to world problems.[92] The peace movement could not believe that public interest could be so great, yet come to nothing so quickly. Scullin expressed his disbelief in the House of Representatives saying how disappointing the disarmament conference was:

> I have been disappointed with the results of the Disarmament Conference which has been sitting for two and a half years. When I was Prime Minister, I stood on the public platform in the biggest halls in Australia, in company with representatives of the then Opposition, and voiced Australia's views on the subject of disarmament.[93]

---

90 Hudson, *Australia and the League of Nations*, 110.
91 Noel-Baker, *The First World Disarmament Conference*, 11.
92 Moore, *The Quest for Peace*, 95.
93 James Scullin, 'Speech; Armaments and Munitions Renunciation of War', *CPD*, House of Representatives, 5 December 1934, 799.

Despite the conference's failure, WILPF was determined to capitalise on the work members had put into the petition and the wider disarmament effort. They began a 'People's Mandate to Governments' campaign in 1935 which involved having organisations representative of the wider population sign a pledge in favour of disarmament, including 'labour bodies, women's organisations, peace and anti-war societies, educational organisations, political clubs, reform and religious movements, literary, professional and business associations, and youth associations'.[94] The wording of the pledge was urgent, noting: 'to meet the present threat of world chaos we, the undersigned, having faith in the power of human intelligence, demand that our Governments in common action fulfil their international pledges.'[95] In Australia 104 organisations signed the mandate, which WILPF estimated represented around 100,000 people. This was sent to the British section of WILPF, who presented it in a 'Golden Book' in a delegation to the president of the League of Nations Assembly in 1936. The Australian Amy Wilkins from the Newcastle branch of WILPF joined the ceremony.[96] Once again, however, WILPF had to recognise that its efforts were unavailing, with Moore reporting that the mandate had 'no traceable effect upon practical policy anywhere'.[97]

At this time another campaign was gaining momentum. The International Peace Campaign (IPC) aimed to restore authority in the League of Nations. Led by Lord Robert Cecil, it galvanised support around the desire to prevent another war, and it signified a subtle but important shift in the demands of the peace movement.[98] The shift challenged WILPF to define its stance on absolute pacifism.[99] This became clear when the IPC released its 'four points', one of which centred on the new theory of 'collective security'. According to Moore, 'collective security' became fashionable after the dream of complete disarmament failed. She wrote:

---

94 'People's Mandate to Governments', Box 1727/2, Papers, WILPF, MS 9377, SLV. 'Peoples' Mandate to Governments', *Pax International* 10, no. 5 (July 1935).
95 'Peoples' Mandate to Governments', *Pax International* 10, no. 5 (July 1935).
96 Moore, *The Quest for Peace*, 111.
97 Moore, *The Quest for Peace*, 111.
98 Bussey and Tims, *Pioneers for Peace*, 148. See also RJ Overy, *The Morbid Age: Britain Between the Wars* (London: Allen Lane, 2009).
99 Malcolm Saunders and Ralph Summy, 'Odd Ones Out: The Australian Section of the Women's International League for Peace and Freedom: 1919–41', *Australian Journal of Politics & History* 40, no. 1 7 April 2008: 83, doi.org/10.1111/j.1467-8497.1994.tb00093.x.

many people found relief in this new discovery that, after all, another and an easier and shorter way to peace was open. Armaments, it seemed, need not be abolished; they could be pooled, and thus the world would be made safe from aggression.[100]

The idea that peace could be enforced with the threat of violence was the antithesis of Moore's beliefs. Others also recognised this change of emphasis and its implications. The League of Nations Union from which the IPC grew, attracted unsympathetic epithets such as its members being called 'bloodthirsty pacifists'.[101]

The IPC began in 1936, as an Anglo-French group initially called the 'Rassemblement Universel pour la Paix'.[102] It arranged an international congress called the World Peace Congress, held in Brussels in September 1936, to which an Australian delegation of nine was sent, including Rev. H Palmer Phillips and WILPF member Amy Wilkins.[103] Five thousand delegates attended the conference, and Lord Cecil had the delicate task of bringing together the disparate and contradictory elements within the peace movement. Lord Cecil, the son of Lord Salisbury, with family connections and public notoriety, was a capable public figure, becoming leader of the pro-League forces in Great Britain.[104] While he desired world peace, he felt that disarmament was not an end in itself, and that pacifists who believed so failed to understand the complexity of international politics.[105] Therefore when drafting the 'four points' for the IPC, the most controversial was number three: 'Strengthening the League of Nations for the prevention and stopping of war by the more effective organization of collective security and mutual assistance.'[106] WILPF internationally expressed reservations about this point when deciding to support the IPC, but still endorsed the campaign in 1936.[107]

WILPF in Australia were part of the small group of absolute pacifists who were unable to produce positive policy as they struggled to find a position against both war and fascism.[108] Australia and the US were the only two

---

100 Moore, *The Quest for Peace*, 106.
101 JA Thompson, 'Lord Cecil and the Pacifists in the League of Nations Union', *The Historical Journal* 20, no. 4 (1 December 1977): 949, doi.org/10.1017/S0018246X00011481.
102 Thompson, 'Lord Cecil and the Pacifists in the League of Nations Union', 949.
103 Moore, *The Quest for Peace*, 116. Summy, 'From Hope ... to Hope', 165.
104 Thompson, 'Lord Cecil and the Pacifists in the League of Nations Union', 950.
105 Thompson, 'Lord Cecil and the Pacifists in the League of Nations Union', 957.
106 Moore, *The Quest for Peace*, 116.
107 Bussey and Tims, *Pioneers for Peace*, 149.
108 Carolyn Rasmussen, *The Lesser Evil? Opposition to War and Fascism in Australia, 1920–1941*, Melbourne University history monographs (Melbourne: History Department, University of Melbourne, 1992), 105.

WILPF sections to publicly defy WILPF's international endorsement of the IPC, both then seemingly distant from direct threat of fascist aggression compared with Britain and Europe. They came out against the IPC, becoming part of the 'pure pacifist' wing of the movement that wanted to articulate their different approach to peace that did not include any acceptance of violence. Moore felt very strongly about making their position on the issue of collective security official and was not content simply to withdraw support. She wrote to the Victorian branch of the IPC to state officially WILPF Australia's reasons for refusing support:

> after full discussion, the committee recommends that no action be taken in the matter of affiliation with the I.P.C ... If you believe in the total abolition of all armaments, you cannot also believe in the retention of them for joint use as an overwhelming threat.[109]

This position set WILPF apart from other women active in the peace movement. For example, Bessie Rischbieth, who Moore knew from the Pan-Pacific conferences, was a supporter of the IPC in Australia and also became a supporter of the Movement Against War and Fascism (MAW&F), another group that WILPF differentiated themselves from.[110] Other prominent women such as Ruby Rich, Constance Duncan, Nettie Palmer and Adela Pankhurst Walsh were involved with the IPC, which had a women's commission and hosted conferences and discussions.[111] Doris Blackburn, previously a president of WILPF Australia in 1928–1930, distanced herself from WILPF to become a leader of the IPC.[112] Alice Syme, president of WILPF Australia, argued within executive meetings about the decision, and openly clashed with Moore in correspondence and meeting minutes. Syme disagreed with Moore over the defiance of Geneva and accused her of manipulating discussion on these issues. She felt their group was too reticent in cooperating with other peace organisations and wrote to Geneva accordingly, calling Moore's leadership 'undemocratic'.[113] Moore responded sharply:

---

109 Moore to Constance Duncan, Melbourne, 3 April 1937, series III reel 54, WILPF Papers.
110 Malcolm Saunders, *Quiet Dissenter: The Life and Thought of an Australian Pacifist: Eleanor May Moore 1875–1949* (Canberra: Peace Research Centre, Australian National University, 1993), 203.
111 Rasmussen, *The Lesser Evil?*, 102.
112 Carolyn Rasmussen, 'Blackburn, Doris Amelia (1889–1970)', ADB, National Centre of Biography, ANU, adb.anu.edu.au/biography/blackburn-doris-amelia-9517/text16755, published first in hardcopy 1993, accessed online 2 December 2014.
113 Saunders, *Quiet Dissenter*, 211.

> A graver charge against a secretary could scarcely be made. You are a rash woman to put such a thing in writing and sign it ... perhaps you scarcely realise the full import of your own words, but, as other members of the committee agree, you have impugned my integrity in a way that cannot be passed over.[114]

Despite the unpopularity of Moore's espousal of separation from the wider peace movement, WILPF Australia went with her, and refused to collaborate with IPC campaigns, along with other groups like MAW&F, the Victorian Council against War and Fascism and the United Peace Council during World War II. WILPF felt the other groups were not true peace workers, but communists who 'love not peace the less, but Russia the more'.[115] After such disagreements, Syme remained a member of WILPF, but became more involved with the international, rather than the Australian section. She wrote to Geneva again in 1941, suggesting that Australia had too much centralised control:

> Meetings last year were few ... The main reason for few meetings is due to the fact that Miss Moore controls everything, in fact, is the Melbourne Section. Some years ago I urged that provision should be made for eventualities—'if anything should happen to Miss Moore', I asked 'What is to become of WILPF in Melbourne' ... The President is always nothing more or less than a peg to hang the Secretary on, she is the Secretary's shadow and dare not disagree with the Secretary.[116]

Moore set out in a letter to WILPF International similar reasons for publicly refusing to join with the IPC, which she felt compelled to do as it was contradicting the official position of WILPF. She reiterated her opposition to the principle of collective security, noting that some WILPF members in Australia did not wish to jeopardise their reputation by joining with 'compromised' organisations, and even quoted to the Geneva section decisions made at the 1919 Zurich conference to illustrate how they had strayed from the core beliefs of WILPF: 'the decisions of the assembly should under no circumstances be enforced by military action or by cutting off a population from the necessities of life', a reference to the use of sanctions.[117] The response from WILPF International illustrated the effects of turmoil in Europe on pacifist sentiments. While all the points raised by Moore

---

114 Moore to Alice Syme, 17 April 1937, Box 1722/1 Papers, WILPF, MS 9377, SLV.
115 Moore, *The Quest for Peace*, 214.
116 Syme to Baer, 19 March 1941, series III reel 54, WILPF Papers.
117 Moore to Baer, 3 April 1937, series III reel 54, WILPF Papers.

4. 'OUR STRUGGLE IS NOT ONLY ONE FOR PEACE BUT ALSO FOR FREEDOM'

gained consideration and sympathy, the increasing threat to freedom caused many to revaluate 'absolute' pacifist principles for more practical outcomes. Clara Ragaz, acting as secretary in Geneva, responded, noting that WILPF had raised reservations about point three. However, the WILPF executive believed that there were many benefits to being involved with the campaign that outweighed the differences, such as allowing the IPC to unite many organisations in a large federation to have a louder voice for peace, which gave WILPF the ability to work with the IPC on issues they did agree on. WILPF also saw that the IPC meant in 'no way to propagate anything like a military spirit'.[118] Finally Ragaz included a personal note that highlights the internal struggle about weighing peace against freedom many European pacifists experienced in the late 1930s. She wrote:

> But to boast on the one side of the strength of one's armed forces and of the protection they mean to one's own land and to one's own people and to stand with folded arms and declare one's self unable to prevent wrongs done to others and to punish the breaking of solemnly given promises that is a contradiction which I find difficult to bear, and which I am sure will find its heavy punishment one day. Only that here like in so many other cases the peoples will have to bear the heaviest part of all.[119]

The decision to publicly disagree with the international section of the organisation was not a unanimous one, and within the active group in Melbourne, many spoke out against the uncompromising position. Moore acknowledged this to the headquarters, describing how 'for the first time there is ill will between us', and admitting that some members had charged her 'with disloyalty'.[120]

With division within the movement at all levels, this 'ill will' signified the beginning of a turbulent time for WILPF. Disagreement over the IPC was just one of the issues that brought the Australian section into conflict with the international section. It signified dissent and disunity within the organisation on what were considered foundational issues, their identity as an absolute pacifist group and the tension between what was at the heart of the struggle: peace or freedom.

---

118 Clara Ragaz to Moore, 12 May 1937, series III reel 54, WILPF Papers.
119 Clara Ragaz to Moore, 12 May 1937, series III reel 54, WILPF Papers.
120 Moore to the Chairmen, WILPF, 28 June 1937, series III reel 54, WILPF Papers.

Breakdown of international networks

WILPF was the most radical of the three major international women's organisations and was much more likely to be sceptical of the League of Nations than the others.[121] This was shown in debates in 1919 when factions within WILPF argued over whether the league should be cautiously supported or unequivocally denounced. The response to the failed disarmament conference and the recognition of impending war stirred up tensions within the organisation, which led to discussions of a restructuring. The origins of the Australian section, brought together through liberal Christian pacifism and the Australian Church rather than the suffrage movement, meant that while internationally WILPF was the most radical organisation of the women's movement, domestically the story was far more complicated.[122] During the war, WILPF Australia had declined to engage in provocative activism and refused to defy the censors. During peacetime, their organisation was a flurry of activity. However, with war once more consuming the world, the conservatism of their methods brought them into conflict, not just with domestic women's peace groups, but with their own international section.

In the late 1920s, there was discussion of a change to the constitution of WILPF, which triggered copious debate among the European sections. The Australian section, being so far away from the cause of the tension, was not entirely aware of the practical issues prompting discussion about the changes and gave input in a self-acknowledged theoretical way. The call for consultation on the issue of constitutional reform gave Moore an opportunity to discuss and reinforce opinions about how the international organisation should operate, and in particular that it should not privilege national sections over international cohesion. The reply frankly stated that the need for reform had more to do with fracturing politics, with the 'more radical, that is to say, communist' national sections in France and Germany.[123] The organisation was finding difficulty balancing these sections with the more conservative sections who were often 'shocked and upset' by the radical influences in the executive.

---

121 Rupp, *Worlds of Women*, 30.
122 Saunders and Summy, 'Odd Ones Out', 85.
123 Mary Sheepshanks to Moore, 16 July 1929, series III reel 54, WILPF Papers.

4. 'OUR STRUGGLE IS NOT ONLY ONE FOR PEACE BUT ALSO FOR FREEDOM'

The changing political atmosphere in Europe started to have a real effect on the cohesion of international societies. By 1933 the international section came under more strain when the secretary Camille Drevet from France was threatened with expulsion from Switzerland because of allegations that she was a 'communist propagandist', having visited Russia in her organising duties with WILPF.[124] The Australian section wrote a letter of support for Drevet, believing her actions to be 'in full harmony with the spirit and principles of our League'.[125]

For the Australian section, being labelled 'communist' was an insult. They identified as anti-communist, not only because they disagreed with any movement that condoned the use of violence to meet political ends, but because they were openly annoyed by what they perceived as the communist movement manipulating the peace movement through organisations such as the MAW&F. Moore wrote many times that they disassociated themselves from communist groups, and reiterated WILPF in Australia's moderate status within domestic politics by giving support to the government when they agreed with any policies. She noted:

> It does not follow that because we as an organisation are against the military policies fostered more or less by all our governments, we are necessarily against our governments in other respects.[126]

That the communist issue was beginning to affect the working conditions of the international organisation was of great concern to Australia. They recommended to the Geneva section that if Switzerland was no longer a free and suitable place to organise, the international headquarters should be moved elsewhere. This suggestion was put at various times during the 1930s, though not always well received. The US section offered to host the international office, but each time the European sections felt it would be 'deserting Europe'. Other sections felt the euro-centeredness of the decision, Dorothy Detzer from the US noting: 'It is curious when one lives in Europe how one gets a European "mentality".'[127]

Suspicion and difficulties with communication began to strain the cohesion of WILPF during the 1930s. The Great Depression had affected countries to different degrees, which at times undermined the capacity of national

---

124 Bussey and Tims, *Pioneers for Peace*, 119.
125 Moore to Secretary, WILPF Geneva, 23 August 1933, series III reel 54, WILPF Papers.
126 Moore to Balch, 24 July 1934, series III reel 54, WILPF Papers.
127 Dorothy Detzer to Moore, 15 April 1940, Box 1724/1 Papers, WILPF, MS 9377, SLV.

sections to send delegates to conferences. Gertrud Baer from Germany, secretary of WILPF during the late 1930s, sent a circular letter to remote sections that acknowledged how WILPF was 'afraid that our Congresses become more and more a European/United States affair'.[128] Similarly, the rising tensions in Europe made peace work in certain countries extremely dangerous. WILPF women were imprisoned or targeted for raids, especially in Germany with the rise of Nazism.[129] Letters between the sections began to illustrate the fear around peace organising: 'our friends who are still in Germany must be in a very precarious position.'[130]

Letters were sent from all sections to the German Government before much was known about the agenda of the Nazi regime. Unsurprisingly, their letters went unanswered; 'I hope that your telegram to Chancellor Hitler was noticed by him. We wrote to him last year but never had any reply.'[131] The tension, violence and difficulty with communication all contributed to an atmosphere of heightened emotions. While many national sections sincerely attempted to continue with peace work, there was a widening gulf between sections that still enjoyed democracy and freedom and those whose freedoms were being curtailed.

Boycotting Japan

The issue that caused the biggest rift between the international section and the Australian national section was a policy to accept a boycott of Japan. At the executive meeting in 1937 held in Basel, Switzerland, WILPF passed a resolution relating to the 'refusal to buy Japanese goods' because of the Japanese invasion of Manchuria, as advocated by the IPC.[132] They sent out an international press release about WILPF's position, which was referred to by a major Melbourne daily newspaper. With this publicity, the Australian section, disagreeing with the international position, felt compelled to set the record straight and Moore wrote to the *Argus* detailing that 'the Australian section of the League has not adopted this suggestion.'[133] She noted that they 'took no part in recommending it to others', and how:

---

128 Baer, circular letter sent to Sections: Australia, New Zealand, Japan, Canada, and Mexico, 20 February 1937, series III reel 54, WILPF Papers.
129 Zueblin to Murdock, Tasmania, 14 June 1933, series III reel 54, WILPF Papers.
130 Zueblin to Moore, 13 March 1933, series III reel 54, WILPF Papers.
131 Moore to Balch, 16 January 1935, series III reel 54, WILPF Papers.
132 Moore to Baer, 23 February 1938, series III reel 54, WILPF Papers.
133 Moore, 'Women and Boycott', *The Argus*, 17 January 1938, 10.

> The various branches of the organisation throughout the commonwealth gravely doubt whether such a policy would tend at all to promote peace and harmony between the Chinese and Japanese, or would help to remedy any of the evils of the present situation.[134]

As with the previous disagreement with the international section about the IPC, they wrote lengthy explanations for their bold decision in defying the example of the executive. However, this dispute was much more public, spilling over into the press, causing a series of angry letters to be sent back and forth that expressed frustration and dismay.

The Australian section had previously not caused a fuss over the issue of boycotts, and it supported the League of Nations' sanctions against Italy after its invasion of Abyssinia.[135] Moore noted the inconsistency of their position in her memoir, where she explained how boycotting Italy failed to show the effectiveness of sanctions and demonstrated how fundamentally flawed they were as a device for effecting peace, as they failed when not all countries upheld the restrictions.[136] Therefore, in 1938, when the Australian section of WILPF felt the acceptance of a boycott of the Japanese was being forced on them, their position against the use of sanctions and boycotts had solidified. Before the publication of WILPF International's position on the boycott, the Australian section had made their sentiments known. They echoed the words of Prime Minister Lyons who had issued an appeal to the public not to commit to the boycott or 'pre-judge' Japan's actions, which were under review by the League of Nations. Lyons felt it would not be in Australia's economic interests and could easily draw the country into a war for which it was unprepared.[137] Moore defended Lyons' position, noting: 'He is a man of decided peace sympathies, with no fascist tendency whatever. His appeal made a strong impression'.[138] Thus when the international press release reached Melbourne, Australian WILPF members were annoyed their objections were not noted.

The first attempt to explain their decision focused on the right of the section to develop autonomous policy, especially when it concerned issues closer to their region and further away from Europe. Moore explicitly noted:

---

134 Moore, 'Women and Boycott', 10.
135 Moore to Balch, 23 October 1935, series III reel 54, WILPF Papers.
136 Moore, *The Quest for Peace*, 112.
137 'Threat of Boycott, Appeal by Mr Lyons', *The Argus*, 4 October 1937, 1.
138 Moore to WILPF Chairmen, 30 November 1937, series III reel 54, WILPF Papers.

'in dealing with European affairs, the Australian section has always been willing to remain in the background ... But in the Pacific crisis, exactly the reverse is true.'[139] She pressed the point that Australia had more legitimacy in deciding policy for the region, because they had a deeper understanding of the economic situation and the possible military repercussions of these decisions. Central to their unease was the idea that a boycott of Japan might aggravate the country to further action, which would be a primary concern for Australia. 'It is we, and not Europe, who would have to bear the brunt of the trouble.'[140] She continued to explain that the section did not feel that the boycott would work, and that Australian trade would suffer for no material or peaceful gain. Having been involved for many years in the Pan-Pacific women's movement, Australian WILPF genuinely believed that they should have been seriously consulted as leaders in the Pacific before the international section committed to such a stance. Moore wrote that the actions of the international section may provoke aggression, noting that 'we do not intend to provoke it, and we object to others provoking it for us'.[141]

The response from the executive was to characterise Moore's points as 'purely practical national character' arguments and expressed regret that Australia felt the need to disagree publicly.[142] They felt it important to reiterate how each country should be prepared to bear economic losses in the short term to save other losses that would result from war, and that the solidarity of the peoples and 'not of the Government or of Industry' was a founding principle of WILPF to be upheld by all national sections. The Australian section made sure that their position would be seen as that of the national organisation and wrote in the 1938 annual report how other branches—Melbourne, Newcastle and Perth—had endorsed the sentiment published in Moore's letter to the *Argus*, reflecting the rising fear in Australia of a rapidly militarising Japan.[143] Australian WILPF wrote again to reiterate that their objection was not merely economic. They believed that sanctions and boycotts were tools of aggression and war, and in some ways were worse than outright military conflict because of the lasting effects they could have on generations of innocent women and children.[144]

---

139 Moore to Baer, Geneva WILPF, 23 February 1938, series III reel 54, WILPF Papers.
140 Moore to Baer, Geneva WILPF, 23 February 1938, series III reel 54, WILPF Papers.
141 Moore to Baer, Geneva WILPF, 23 February 1938, series III reel 54, WILPF Papers.
142 Baer to Moore, 31 March 1938, series III reel 54, WILPF Papers.
143 Annual report of the Australian Section, WILPF, March 1937 to April 1938, sent to Geneva 4 April 1938, series III reel 54, WILPF Papers.
144 Moore to Baer, 12 July 1938, series III reel 54, WILPF Papers.

The issue may have ended there, with an implicit agreement to disagree. However, it was again inflamed when the Geneva section sent a simple request for the Australian section to sign up more international members, so they would contribute more moral and monetary support while 'Europe is on the verge of collapse.'[145] Believing this to be an attempt to decentralise the authority of the Australian section, Moore replied by noting that they felt they could not ask people for money to support the boycott. This made the dispute not just moral, but financial. The Australian section openly disagreed with the position of WILPF International and discouraged an active recruitment campaign while the international section was discordant with the national.[146] In her letter, Moore specifically referred to the Australian section's identity as 'absolute pacifists' and claimed that any new members, and even existing members, would be bewildered to hear of the 'spirit of coercion' from Geneva.[147] The Australian section also believed that a degree of racism underpinned the economic boycotts against Japan. Moore wrote of how groups in Australia that supported the sanctions did so to inflame racial hatred, which was contrary to WILPF Australia's position on engagement and friendship with Pacific nations:

> Certain groups, however, have favoured the boycott, some from purely disinterested motives, some from race-hatred and political animosity. Pacifists like the WILPF found it impossible to align themselves with the movement, feeling that it contradicted the more liberal attitude which they had for years been striving for.[148]

In July 1937, the Pan-Pacific Women's Conference reconvened in Vancouver with delegates from both China and Japan present.[149] WILPF could not send a delegate, but received the report, as Moore was the treasurer of the Australian Pan-Pacific Women's Association.[150] Poring over the detail, Moore read about how the delegates' kindness towards one another, and the 'higher patriotism than mere devotion to one's country' they demonstrated

---

145 Baer to Moore, 21 January 1939, series III reel 54, WILPF Papers.
146 Tensions with headquarters also discussed in Paul Wilson, 'A Question of Conscience: Pacifism in Victoria 1938–1945' (Thesis, La Trobe University, 1984), 60; Summy, 'From Hope … to Hope', 186; Rasmussen, *The Lesser Evil?*
147 Moore to Baer, 16 May 1939, series III reel 54, WILPF Papers.
148 'Some points of Australian Policy', written by Moore, sent to WILPF Geneva, 1 May 1939, series III reel 54, WILPF Papers.
149 Fiona Paisley, *Glamour in the Pacific: Cultural Internationalism and Race Politics in the Women's Pan-Pacific* (Honolulu: University of Hawai'i Press, 2009), 137.
150 Pan-Pacific Women Conference (PPWC) 1937 report edited by Julia Rapke, series III reel 54, WILPF Papers. Report of PPWC, showing Moore as Treasurer in *Peacewards,* published as a supplement to the Australian Church's *Commonweal,* 2 May 1938, accessed SLV, 8.

by discussing their countries' conflicts, represented a purer way to engage.[151] In a letter later that year to the WILPF in Geneva, she wrote of how following their diplomatic peaceful example was preferable to 'men's crude, fierce notions of coercion and boycott.'[152]

This willingness to support rather than condemn Japan caused Moore's international colleagues to question her understanding of the severity of fascism. Clearly unimpressed with the continuing argument and the accusations that they were not honouring the principles of the league, the Joint Chairwomen of WILPF crafted a reply after formally debating the issues the previous letters had raised. The tone was brusque, illustrating how frustrated they had become. They questioned the membership of Australian WILPF: 'we have heard at several times that there were only a few hundred members over the whole country' and that many members may express themselves differently if they 'did not feel bound by group discipline'.[153]

Their annoyance at the Australian section not having understanding or empathy for the real hardship facing Europe and placing their pure pacifist ideology above the freedom of others was clear. Gertrud Baer, the corresponding secretary at Geneva, wrote

> our struggle is not only one for Peace but also for freedom. This concern is our fundamental concern in this moment where hundreds of our formerly most active members are under coercion and completely bereft of their freedom.[154]

To Moore's suggestion that more should be done to spread knowledge of 'what is beautiful and admirable in all peoples', Baer replied:

> Do we understand that this phrase of yours means that you think there are good aspects in the Fascist and National-Socialist regimes' administrations also? ... An administration based on the use of most cruel violence ... can never have anything good, however seducing it may look to people in far-away parts of the world.[155]

Moore's rhetoric continued using idealistic internationalist language, though for the international WILPF headquarters the time for this particular idealism had passed.

---

151 Pan-Pacific Women Conference 1937 report edited by Julia Rapke, series III reel 54, WILPF Papers.
152 Moore to WILPF Chairmen, 30 November 1937, series III reel 54, WILPF Papers.
153 Baer to Moore, 4 July 1939, series III reel 54, WILPF Papers.
154 Baer to Moore, 4 July 1939, series III reel 54, WILPF Papers.
155 Baer to Moore, 4 July 1939, series III reel 54, WILPF Papers.

The Australians were hurt by Baer's letter and told Geneva of their distress. They felt that 'in the task of achieving world peace and disarmament, we have all failed', giving no section the right to criticise another no matter the size of the membership.[156] Both the international and the national sections then apologised for any perceived slights and agreed to 'let old controversies lapse' so they could continue working for the same goals. While the organisation was able to settle the tension and continue without any resignations of membership, the dispute did represent a fundamental philosophical divide within the pacifist movement. Historians of the Australian peace movement, Malcolm Saunders and Ralph Summy, have documented the episode of dissent, writing about why the Australian section had such an absolute and unpopular position.[157] They recognised how the debate over boycotts highlighted a fundamental schism between those who 'tacitly and most reluctantly accepted the proposition that war was less of an evil than fascism', and those who 'unwaveringly adhered to the notion that nothing was or could be worse than war.'[158] The women in Europe, hearing stories of violence and experiencing fascism themselves, did not have the luxury to maintain uncompromising views.

The Australian section on the other hand was far removed from the brutality in Europe. Letters and packages took weeks to arrive, making correspondence slow and interrupted. Information sent by cable gave headline news but further detail took time to arrive. This isolation contributed to the Australian section's different response to the worsening war conditions. Other factors, however, were also at play. The physical distance from Europe alienated many WILPF members in Australia from the wider peace movement as well as from their own organisation. The Australian section was small and very coordinated, and the influence of Moore was obvious.[159] As the international corresponding secretary she was entirely responsible for the communication and all letters were received and written by her. Her own priorities were at times depicted as those of the organisation. Moore so tightly controlled the flow of information that when the section began to have disagreements over policy, she maintained her influence over the passage of correspondence, and chastised members for circumventing it.[160]

---

156 Moore to the Joint Chairmen of WILPF, 21 August 1939, series III reel 54, WILPF Papers.
157 Saunders and Summy, 'Odd Ones Out', 93.
158 Saunders and Summy, 'Odd Ones Out', 93.
159 Saunders and Summy, 'Odd Ones Out', 94.
160 Moore to Syme, 17 April 1937, Box 1722/1 Papers, WILPF, MS 9377, SLV.

Activities during World War II

By 1938 the government's increasing expenditure on armaments had provoked a WILPF letter campaign.[161] The outbreak of war in September 1939 shocked and disappointed the Australian section of WILPF, who sincerely believed that Europe would not 'again plunge civilized nations into the agony they had struggled out of twenty years before'. They were 'met with a sensation of being stunned', a reflection of how little they understood of the situation in Europe.[162] In 1941, when Australia also found itself at war with Japan, fears of conflict close to home were realised. Around this time, the Pan-Pacific Women's Association had to cancel their 1940 conference in New Zealand because of increasing conflict within the region. After the disagreements of the 1930s were smoothed over, WILPF Australia continued to try to cooperate with the international section. However, wartime conditions hampered their efforts to connect with the international, and their activities were restricted to local action and answering personal requests on behalf of members wanting to find support for refugees. WILPF members also began protesting against local expressions of fascism. Fleur Finnie recalled standing with placards outside the Town Hall to protest a Nazi speaking where 'supporters of fascism tried to grab our placards while others opposing fascism tried to protect us. A vivid memory is of standing between two young men fighting above my head.'[163] WILPF joined with church organisations to lobby on behalf of refugees and made a special effort to fundraise for relief purposes with the Society of Friends.[164] WILPF did not usually engage in relief fundraising, but with limited scope for other advocacy activities, they found it to be one of the only actions available.

Communication slowed between the international and the national during the 1940s, not least because of wartime delays with mail delivery. Even so, in November 1940, Gertrud Baer appealed to the Australian section to pay more in affiliation to help make up for 'the places of those who must necessarily now fall out as financial contributors to our cause'.[165] Detailing the hardships many WILPF members in Europe were in, Baer reiterated how 'they are clinging to the international not so much for material help but for moral support'. For Baer it was essential WILPF continue and

---

161 Moore, *The Quest for Peace*, 127.
162 'Annual report, WILPF Australia section, 1939–1940', series III reel 54, WILPF Papers.
163 Fleur Finnie, *Peace and Freedom* (1985), 9, Meredith Stokes papers Box 5/35, NLA.
164 Moore to Lotti Birch, WILPF Geneva, 11 October 1940, series III reel 54, WILPF Papers.
165 Baer (from NYC, US) to Moore, 19 November 1940, Box 1723/5 Papers, WILPF, MS 9377, SLV.

4. 'OUR STRUGGLE IS NOT ONLY ONE FOR PEACE BUT ALSO FOR FREEDOM'

she felt Australians could contribute since the 'physical' war had 'not yet touched those on the other sides of the oceans'.[166] But it was a request that the Australian section could not meet. The Australian Government had tightened capital controls as part of war mobilisation, and the affiliation fees of the section were 'disallowed, as it contravene[ed] the National Security Monetary Control Regulations'.[167] They were effectively cut off from the headquarters and unable to contribute financially to WILPF, which was in desperate need of funds for their operating costs. The WILPF sections began to hope that the Maison Internationale was a 'sleeping beauty' that would hopefully awake to a 'happy ever after'.[168] When war was declared with Japan, Australian WILPF's international activities slowed even further as they focused relief efforts closer to home. Many letters with requests for help and details of the suffering in the world were sent, but the section was less able to act on them.

Domestically, WILPF women still participated in town hall meetings with other peace groups, debating and discussing the problems of the war and the nature of fascism. In 1944, after one conference, Moore felt compelled to publish a pamphlet called *What Shall We Do with the Japanese?* that detailed the need to foster understanding and goodwill with the Japanese despite the conflict.[169] Pacifists and internationalists who had engaged with and travelled to Japan were shocked by the 'hate campaign' propaganda that was prevalent on radio and in the press. One notable sign said: 'We've always despised them—now we must smash them'. To many pacifist internationalists, such claims were blatantly untrue and deeply offensive.[170] Moore's pamphlet pleaded that Australians 'think independently, and act with moral courage'.[171]

On top of these hardships, the aging membership threatened WILPF's future. Moore herself was dealing with personal grief after her mother and sister died in 1941 as well as having health problems of her own. By this time, the branch in Newcastle had folded when Amy Wilkins, an active member in that city, could no longer give energy to the cause. The Tasmanian branch ended their activity in 1942 after leading member Lesley Murdoch resigned,

---

166 Baer (from NYC, US) to Moore, 19 November 1940, Box 1723/5 Papers, WILPF, MS 9377, SLV.
167 Moore to Birch, 19 October 1940, series III reel 54, WILPF Papers.
168 Moore to WILPF Geneva, 23 May 1941, series III reel 54, WILPF Papers.
169 Eleanor Moore, *What Shall We Do with the Japanese?* (North Fitzroy, Vic: Publications Dept., Federal Pacifist Council of Australia, 1944), NLA.
170 Moore, *The Quest for Peace*, 135.
171 Moore, *What Shall We Do with the Japanese?*

concerned about rising communist influence in the peace movement.[172] The Perth branch continued until 1948 when the main organiser, Mrs Creeth, was unable to continue the work because of old age. They regretted the need to dissolve the branch but noted that 'there were no young people offering to carry on the work'.[173] This left only the Melbourne section with the smallest membership in its history of operation. In 1949 there were only 50 members, and the branch acknowledged 'this is the lowest it has ever been.'[174] With Moore's death in 1949 at age 72, the section had to reorganise and recruit new members to reanimate the section.

***

The 1930s was a time of great hope, which, in a few short years, turned to extreme disappointment. The war represented an end to an operating style that WILPF had utilised since 1915. The pressures of fascism pushed to breaking point the ideological boundaries that drew so many different women together over that time. In their desperation to maintain consistent nonviolent views, the Australian section of WILPF was at loggerheads with the wider peace movement and their own headquarters. When some of their positions were embraced by mainstream society, shown in the widespread support for the disarmament petition, WILPF Australia were willing to cooperate with sections of the community they knew had contradicting beliefs about absolute pacifism. Those contradictions could be papered over when mainstream opinions aligned, but became a major cause for concern when tensions were heightened and military conflict in the Pacific region eventually materialised. So grave was the ideological rift that it led the organisation to question its very purpose.

World War II was a hard test for the peace movement which was forced to confront the epochal clash between freedom and peace. Most chose freedom, except the few in the Melbourne WILPF branch who preferred ideological purity in resisting violence as a means to preserve the peace and freedom that dictators were taking from many in distant lands. Their

---

172 Lorene Furmage, 'Making it to the Platform: The Involvement of Women in the Peace Movement in Tasmania From the Crimean War to the End of the Vietnam War' (Masters thesis, University of Tasmania, 1993), 70, eprints.utas.edu.au/19514/. For more on Murdoch, see Elizabeth B Jones, 'Murdoch, Lesley Elizabeth (1881–1961)', ADB, National Centre of Biography, ANU, adb.anu.edu.au/biography/murdoch-lesley-elizabeth-7811/text13473, published first in hardcopy 1986, accessed online 25 August 2015.
173 Moore to Louisa Jaques, Geneva WILPF, 11 February 1948, series III reel 54, WILPF Papers.
174 Moore to Bloch, 12 May 1949, series III reel 54, WILPF Papers.

recruitment stagnated and they haemorrhaged membership because of static views and principles that were seemingly impervious to a reality others were experiencing. This era of their organising shows how ardently they valued and upheld the belief in nonviolence. It also demonstrates how dramatic the turn from peace to war was, and how strongly people believed that another devastating war like the last could be avoided. The dominance of national politics, and the insistence of Japan and Germany in pursuing national priorities rather than international cooperation, successfully undermined international movements. WILPF in Australia, despite coming close to ideological rupture, nonetheless persevered and left the path for reform open for members after the war.

5

The United Nations and Indigenous rights

With the creation of the United Nations Organization at the San Francisco Conference in 1945, and the adoption of the Universal Declaration of Human Rights in 1948, the language of human rights began to permeate the peace movement and define the way Women's International League for Peace and Freedom (WILPF) activists engaged in the postwar world. The declaration became an 'instrument, as well as the most prominent symbol, of changes that would amplify the voices of the weak in the corridors of power'.[1] At a meeting to discuss 'Justice for Aborigines', supported by WILPF and held at the Australian Church in Melbourne, the Western Australian feminist Ada Bromham explained that this language set a 'new world standard':

> We feel heartened by the fact that the UNO in their Universal Declaration of Human Rights sets out this principle: 'All human beings are born equal'. These words include the conclusions of those people who have set a charter for the world. This new world standard should be something that we should be very thankful about. We should use this world standard to influence our own government because after all the Australian Government is one of the members of the United Nations.[2]

---

1 Mary Ann Glendon, *A World Made New: Eleanor Roosevelt and the Universal Declaration of Human Rights*, (New York: Random House, 2001), xvi.
2 Ada Bromham, 'Justice for Aborigines', 21 February 1951, Papers of A. Vroland Box 4/28, National Library of Australia (NLA).

Following WILPF's engagement with the White Australia Policy (WAP) during the interwar years, members continued to explore racial discrimination as a root cause of conflict. In the 1950s WILPF prioritised understanding Aboriginal policy, encouraged Indigenous women's involvement, and tried to connect local community issues with international politics.

From Federation onwards, in an era of self-conscious nation building, the history of Indigenous Australia was usually written out of the national story. In the words of the historian Ernest Scott in 1916: Australia 'begins with a blank space of the map, and ends with the record of a new name on the map, that of Anzac'.[3] Throughout the twentieth century, many Australians continued to overlook and even deny the violence wrought by colonisation, preferring the 'heroic' military story of the Anzacs as a foundational national myth. So widespread was the blindness to the country's darker colonial past that in 1968, in his watershed Boyer lectures, the historian WEH Stanner described a national 'cult of forgetfulness' and 'great Australian silence'.[4] WILPF's serious engagement with Aboriginal rights in the 1950s, well before Stanner's lectures, illustrates their commitment to an issue not popular in the mainstream.[5] Their engagement was shaped by their experiences as white middle-class women, and their rhetoric at times reflected an older paternalistic humanitarianism. Nevertheless, their commitment was uncommon. The WILPF were 'one of the most cogent non-communist critics of the colonial system'.[6] They insisted on seeking information about Aboriginal disadvantage and countering discrimination, even when the exclusion of Aboriginal history from mainstream teaching was structural and deliberate.

At the same time, changes in technology revolutionised the practicality of international travel. In the interwar years WILPF in Australia was typically on the fringe of the wider progressive movement. They were resistant to change and remained 'absolute' in their pacifism. The revival of the section in

---

3   Ernest Scott, *A Short History of Australia* (London: Oxford University Press, 1916), quoted in Anna Clark, 'Friday Essay: The "Great Australian Silence" 50 Years On', *The Conversation*, published and accessed 3 August 2018, theconversation.com/friday-essay-the-great-australian-silence-50-years-on-100737.
4   WEH Stanner, 'The Great Australian Silence', in *After the Dreaming: The 1968 Boyer Lectures* (Sydney: Australian Broadcasting Commission, 1969), 18–29.
5   Alison Holland, *Breaking the Silence: Aboriginal Defenders and the Settler State 1905–1939* (Carlton: Melbourne University Press, 2019). She illustrated how there 'may not have been an official history that supported the defenders' claims at the time but there was a vociferous politics, undergirded by memory, which included a critique of the conspiracy of silence on the matter', 7.
6   Laura Beers, 'Advocating for a Feminist Internationalism Between the Wars', in *Women, Diplomacy and International Politics Since 1500*, ed. Carolyn James and Glenda Sluga (New York: Routledge, 2015), 202, doi.org/10.4324/9781315713113-13.

the 1950s, however, saw dramatic changes instituted relatively quickly. One reason the organisation was able to survive such difficult times was because its established international networks remained desirable to new members and it was malleable when driven by new and different personalities in the wake of Moore's death at the end of the previous decade.

***

Several scholars have considered the interests and activities of feminists advocating for the rights of Aboriginal and Torres Strait Islander communities in the early twentieth century.[7] Often invoking the language of sisterhood over racial difference, feminists' activism remained largely assimilationist.[8] Nonetheless, the women's movement, strongly influenced by maternal ideas of care and welfare, was a prominent voice in advocating for Indigenous peoples after World War II. Indeed, activists from the women's movement helped found political organisations that worked for Aboriginal rights. Jessie Street co-founded the Federal Council for Aboriginal Advancement, which later became the Federal Council for the Advancement of Aborigines and Torres Strait Islanders, while Shirley Andrews helped form the Council for Aboriginal Rights in Victoria.[9] Women's leadership on this issue culminated in the 1967 referendum for Aboriginal rights. Jessie Street had in fact proposed the referendum to Faith Bandler a decade earlier, reflecting the women's movement's interest in constitutional law reform.[10] Street, Bandler, Bromham and Joyce Clague were all members of WILPF branches and used the organisation in their activism. Yagel woman Joyce Clague (née Mercy) was even supported by WILPF to attend conference in New Delhi in 1966, making her the first Indigenous Australian woman to attend an international UN-sponsored event.[11]

---

7   For example see: Fiona Paisley, *Loving Protection? Australian Feminism and Aboriginal Women's Rights 1919–1939* (Carlton South, Vic: Melbourne University Press, 2000); Alison Holland, 'Wives and Mothers Like Ourselves? Exploring White Women's Intervention in the Politics of Race, 1920s–1940s', *Australian Historical Studies* 32, no. 117 (1 October 2001): 292–310, doi.org/10.1080/10314610108596166.
8   Marilyn Lake, 'Between Old World "Barbarism" and Stone Age "Primitivism": The Double Difference of the White Australian Feminist', in *Australian Women: Contemporary Feminist Thought*, ed. Norma Grieve and Ailsa Burns (Melbourne: Oxford University Press, 1994), 90.
9   Sue Taffe, 'The Council for Aboriginal Rights (Victoria)', *Australian Dictionary of Biography* (ADB), National Centre of Biography, Australian National University, adb.anu.edu.au/essay/8/text29426, originally published 11 April 2014, accessed 10 February 2022.
10   Kate Laing and Lucy Davies, 'The Leadership of Women in the 1967 Referendum', *Agora* 56, no. 1 (March 2021).
11   For more on Joyce Clague and her activism with WILPF and the World Council of Churches see Kate Laing and Lucy Davies, 'Intersecting Paths of the Local and the International: Joyce Clague's Activist Journeys', *Women's History Review* (11 June 2020): 1–20.

While WILPF women collaborated with others who worked for Aboriginal and Torres Strait Islander rights between the 1920s and 1950s—women such as Bessie Rischbieth and Ada Bromham—they did not make Indigenous rights activism part of their core campaign platform until the 1950s. It was only after Anna Vroland combined WILPF's agenda with Aboriginal rights campaigns upon taking over as the secretary that WILPF made a real attempt to interact with women from Aboriginal and Torres Strait Islander communities. WILPF women connected the campaign with their internationalism, basing their theories of achieving racial equality on demanding the proper application of universal human rights. They saw the treatment of Aboriginal and Torres Strait Islander Australia as a prerequisite for peace and promoted the campaign internationally. With the Universal Declaration of Human Rights, the UN allowed a new discourse that solved some of WILPF's philosophical ambiguities. The language of human rights associated with the UN system focused on individual rights rather than nation-states and allowed WILPF a new framework.

WILPF reformed

During the late 1940s, WILPF in Australia was limited in its activities because of a small and aging membership. A core group remained interested in world affairs but were unable to recruit younger or more active members. Annual reports show that their activities mainly consisted of meetings or conferences with other organisations, such as collaborations with the Australian Peace Campaign, and the Federal Pacifist Council of Australia.[12] Internationally, after World War II, WILPF mourned the loss of many members including some who had died in exile or concentration camps.[13] The executive of the organisation was unable to meet throughout the war and was only able to reconvene in September 1945.[14] At the 1946 conference in Luxembourg, though no Australian delegate was able to attend, WILPF seriously questioned whether it should continue or dissolve.

---

12 'WILPF Australian Section annual report', 7 February 1949, series III reel 54, WILPF International Papers 1915–1978, Sanford, NC: Microfilming Corp. of America, c 1983, accessed NLA. Hereafter referred to as WILPF Papers.
13 Rosa Manus of Holland died in a German concentration camp, Anita Augspurg and Lida Gustava Heymann both from Germany died in exile in Switzerland. More WILPF wartime losses were outlined in GC Bussey, and Margaret Tims, *Pioneers for Peace: Women's International League for Peace and Freedom, 1915–1965*, 2nd ed. (London: Allen & Unwin, 1965), 180.
14 Bussey and Tims, *Pioneers for Peace*, 187.

Dutch member J Repelaer van Driel spoke to the dissolution of WILPF, questioning the gender essentialism of the organisation. Her experience of war showed that women were just as likely to be complicit in violence and oppression. She did not want WILPF to dissolve, but she felt a serious reappraisal of their aims should be undertaken. Continuing as a women's organisation after women had attained the right to vote in most countries showed 'women who separate themselves into groups for the advancement of universal goals, demonstrate clearly their own inferiority complex.'[15] In response to van Driel, US member Mildred Scott Olmsted spoke about women's peaceful nature. This exchange is revealing of the internal contradictions of WILPF's gendered organising, which were constantly negotiated and questioned. As Catia Confortini has observed, it was also at this conference that 'they recognised the tension between their prewar liberal ideals and those ideals' inability to prevent the Holocaust'.[16] Confortini argues that after this discussion WILPF refrained from interrogating the relationship between women and peace in the 1940s and 1950s beyond their activism on women's equal representation at the UN. In many ways it reflected the absence of 'an organised feminist movement that publicly resurfaced only later.'[17]

Despite the exhaustion and disillusionment of many after the war, the conference voted overwhelmingly for WILPF to continue. A new secretary general was appointed, Mrs Anne Bloch from the US, who actively tried to re-engage national sections of WILPF. She sent the Australian section letters urging that they focus on recruiting younger members: 'please try to give us a sign of life as often as you can'.[18] WILPF International needed local involvement to bolster their legitimacy.

In 1949 the WILPF triennial congress was held in Copenhagen, and Victorian member Mrs Edith Abbott acted as the Australian delegate. Abbott was an early member of WILPF who fell out of communication with the group when she moved to the country and joined the Country Women's Association

---

15   Bussey and Tims, *Pioneers for Peace*, 188. See also '10th International Congress of the WILPF', Congress report at Luxembourg, 4–9 August 1946, database edited by Kathryn Kish Sklar and Thomas Dublin, *Women and Social Movements, International—1840 to Present*, 182. Translated from French to English by Julie Johnson 2015.
16   Catia Cecilia Confortini, *Intelligent Compassion: The Women's International League for Peace and Freedom and Feminist Peace* (Oxford: Oxford University Press, 2012), 4, doi.org/10.1093/acprof:oso/ 9780199845231.001.0001.
17   Confortini, *Intelligent Compassion*, 43.
18   Bloch to Moore, 10 February 1949, series III reel 54, WILPF Papers.

(affiliated to the Associated Countrywomen of the World).[19] She agreed to be the Australian representative as she was preparing for a trip to England. The prospect of having Australia represented at WILPF conferences once again gave momentum to the small and disconnected section, who sensed their activities had been hampered by a feeling of isolation. As Moore noted in a letter to Bloch in 1948: 'the threads of communication broken by the war have never been quite picked up.'[20] The recent introduction of airmail relieved some anxieties, but international travel was still difficult with 'little money and no official priority'.[21] Air travel was prohibitively expensive. While Abbott's journey by ship was long and interrupted, she still made the August conference.

For Abbott, the experience of the conference was emotional and transformative. She wrote in a report to the Australian section how she felt attending the conference as a delegate was a 'privilege' that she deeply appreciated, believing 'there is no experience in life like that of attending an international conference.'[22] It allowed her to realise how 'isolated' Australia was and how important the 'few seeking souls' were who thought on world affairs.[23] While Abbott was abroad, Moore passed away and the future of the Australian section was uncertain. Abbott returned and pleaded with the remaining members to make 'every effort to carry on'.[24] At this time WILPF Australia received a generous bequest of £100 from the deceased estate of Mrs Lucy Creeth, who had been a devoted member of the Western Australian branch.[25] The injection of funds, the excitement of reconnecting with the rejuvenated international section, and the addition of new members allowed WILPF Australia not just to reform, but to refocus. The most important new additions to the membership were Anna Vroland who joined and became the honorary secretary, and Doris Blackburn who became the president, having rejoined after a lapse in engagement.

---

19   Moore to Bloch, 29 March 1949, series III reel 54, WILPF Papers.
20   Moore to Bloch, 11 December 1948, series III reel 54, WILPF Papers.
21   Moore to Bloch, 12 May 1949, series III reel 54, WILPF Papers.
22   Edith M Abbott, report to the Australian Section of WILPF, 28 March 1950, Box 1728/3 Papers, WILPF, MS 9377, State Library of Victoria (SLV).
23   Edith M Abbott, report to the Australian Section of WILPF, 28 March 1950, Box 1728/3 Papers, WILPF, MS 9377, SLV.
24   Australian section report, '12th International Congress of WILPF report', 4–8 August 1953, Paris, in Sklar and Dublin, eds, *Women and Social Movements,* 143.
25   Australian section report, '12th International Congress of WILPF report', 4–8 August 1953, Paris, 143. See also letter from the deceased estate of Lucy Creeth, 25 August 1950 in Box 1724/2 Papers, WILPF, MS 9377, SLV.

5. THE UNITED NATIONS AND INDIGENOUS RIGHTS

'(194-?) Portrait of Mrs. Doris Blackburn, M.H.R.'
Source: This photograph was taken by Jack Gallagher, who was a government photographer working for the Australia Department of Information. National Library of Australia. See Appendix for a short biography of Doris Blackburn.

The two world wars had radically changed Australian politics. The federal government was located in Melbourne until 1927, when it moved to Canberra and the city rapidly grew to accommodate the new administration. Women still faced many barriers to full political participation, most notably shown by the ban on married women in the public service which was not abolished until 1966.[26] World War II also had a profound effect on women's employment opportunities and changed ideas about femininity and sexuality. Women gained 'independence, self-reliance and autonomy', which came with taking on male jobs with higher wages.[27] The government established the Women's Employment Board to regulate the wages and conditions of women doing men's work, and to allay fears of employers and trade unions about women taking men's jobs.[28] The reality of women

---

26 Marian Sawer, *Removal of the Commonwealth Marriage Bar: A Documentary History* (Canberra: University of Canberra, Centre for Research in Public Sector Management, 1997).
27 Marilyn Lake, 'Female Desires: The Meaning of World War II', *Australian Historical Studies* 24, no. 95 (1 October 1990): 269, doi.org/10.1080/10314619008595846.
28 Lake, 'Female Desires', 269.

taking on roles traditionally considered masculine challenged traditional gender norms and provoked 'strenuous reaffirmations of sexual difference'.[29] As historian Jill Matthews has noted, the construction of femininity changed over the first half of the twentieth century and by the 1950s conceptions of women in society shifted from ideas about sacrifice and a role as 'mother of the race' to a culture of 'permissive consumerism'.[30] Women were increasingly 'purchasing managers' for the household rather than servants of private spaces.[31] Femininity and sexuality were defined by youthfulness and consumerism, as evident in the traditional gender roles advertisers increasingly directed towards women.[32]

The fear of Cold War politics after World War II and a backlash against new images of femininity 'fostered a deep suspicion of social change, sexual deviance and female autonomy'.[33] The image of the 'nuclear family' and the idealised housewife therefore took on a new significance, while families also became increasingly dependent on women's waged work to 'maintain a desired lifestyle based on the purchase of services and commodities.'[34] Coupled with this shift was the increasing importance placed on women's right to work by the women's movement. From the 1930s onwards the feminist agenda also shifted away from promoting sexual difference towards encouraging women to participate on equal terms in public life.[35] Maternalist feminism, popular when WILPF was first constituted, was beginning to be seen as 'anachronistic, prudish and divisive'.[36] By the late 1940s, WILPF had lost touch with these new expressions of feminism and understandings of sexuality. Maternal activists for women's rights had demonstrated little capacity in later years to adjust their position to take on this difference within the organisation. Many feminists of the interwar era were opposed to the new representations of femininity.[37]

---

29   Lake, 'Female Desires', 269.
30   Jill Julius Matthews, *Good and Mad Women: The Historical Construction of Femininity in Twentieth Century Australia* (Sydney: Allen & Unwin, 1984), 90.
31   Matthews, *Good and Mad Women*, 90.
32   Matthews, *Good and Mad Women*, 90; Lake, 'Female Desires', 272.
33   Gail Reekie, 'Market Research and the Post-War Housewife', *Australian Feminist Studies* 6, no. 14 (1 December 1991): 15, doi.org/10.1080/08164649.1991.9994625.
34   Reekie, 'Market Research and the Post-War Housewife', 15.
35   Marilyn Lake, *Getting Equal: The History of Australian Feminism* (St Leonards, NSW: Allen & Unwin, 1999), 174.
36   Lake, 'Female Desires', 284.
37   Matthews, *Good and Mad Women*, 90.

5. THE UNITED NATIONS AND INDIGENOUS RIGHTS

The revival of WILPF internationally after the war and the vacuum left following Moore's death in Australia brought forth a new wave of women willing to engage with some of these complexities. WILPF was able to bring together a variety of points of view with different party allegiances because the women were 'united by the belief that warfare should be eliminated and that economic and social justice was part and parcel of a system of peace'.[38] WILPF adapted because of its basis in the tradition of liberal internationalism, and because (despite what Moore believed and hoped) the organisation had itself never identified with absolute pacifism or feminism, though many members individually did.[39] When asked to make definitive statements on complex issues, WILPF leaders often opted instead to refer people to the 'WILPF principles showing that women of different political viewpoints are welcomed.'[40] The new president of the Australian section, Blackburn, reasserted this position when the section reformed and delineated their new philosophical and theoretical understanding of the Australian section of WILPF. One member from Western Australia wrote referring to the new direction: 'I agree with Mrs Blackburn that the WILPF is not a Pacifist Organisation. Quite a number of our members may be, certainly not everyone.'[41]

In Australia white women had had the right to vote federally since 1902. The right to stand for election, however, was not granted to every woman in every state until 1923 when Victorian women were finally awarded the right to stand for state parliament.[42] WILPF women were proud of Australia's international reputation as a pioneer in women's political rights. However, despite the right to stand for federal parliament being won so early, it took 41 years before women were elected to federal parliament.[43] The first, in 1943, were Dame Enid Lyons, widow of the former prime minister, elected for the United Australia Party to the House of Representatives, along with Dorothy Tangney, who would represent the Labor Party in the Senate.[44] Three years later, Doris Blackburn was elected to the House of Representatives in the seat of Bourke as independent Labor, meaning she

---

38   Confortini, *Intelligent Compassion*, 4.
39   Confortini, *Intelligent Compassion*, 12.
40   WILPF Executive record of discussion, 9 August 1952, series III reel 54, WILPF Papers.
41   Nancy Wilkinson, WILPF member from the WA branch, to Anna Vroland, 10 November 1953, Box 1722, Papers, WILPF, MS 9377, SLV.
42   Marian Sawer, *A Woman's Place: Women and Politics in Australia*, 2nd ed. (Sydney: Allen & Unwin, 1993), 5.
43   Sawer, *A Woman's Place*, 1.
44   Sawer, *A Woman's Place*, 197.

was elected on Labor principles but not bound by the Australian Labor Party (ALP) Caucus. As a leader in WILPF before and after World War II, Blackburn's election to parliament represented a moment of mainstreaming for WILPF's agenda.

Blackburn had been an early member of WILPF, joining the Sisterhood of International Peace in 1915.[45] She was also a member of the Women's Political Association (WPA), where she met her husband Maurice Blackburn, a lawyer and member of the Victorian and later the federal parliament. Doris had been a campaign manager for Vida Goldstein's senate election bid in 1913.[46] She was president of WILPF from 1928 to 1930, though her involvement during this time was limited by her caring responsibilities for young children.[47] In 1937 Blackburn threw her energies into the International Peace Campaign (IPC), for which she was suspended from the Labor Party. She had a very pragmatic political style and was not interested in putting her energies into organisations that she felt were too insular and not advancing the cause for peace. She rejected absolute pacifism in the face of fascism and was thus aligned with the WILPF headquarters rather than the Australian section during the disagreements at the beginning of the war. She distanced herself from the Melbourne WILPF group because they publicly denounced the IPC.[48] After electoral defeat in 1949, when the seat of Bourke was redistributed into the seat of Wills, Blackburn returned to WILPF and once more became president in 1950. WILPF, in need of new leadership after Moore's death, provided a platform for her activism after her brief time in parliament ended. She was particularly interested in re-engaging with the international network and wanted to align the policies of the national section once more with the headquarters in Geneva.

---

45   Carolyn Rasmussen, 'Falling In and Out of Love: Doris Hordern, Maurice Blackburn and the Women's Political Association 1911–1915', in *Fighting Against War: Peace Activism in the Twentieth Century*, ed. Phillip Deery and Julie Kimber (Albert Park, Vic: Leftbank Press, 2015), 47.
46   Carolyn Rasmussen, 'Blackburn, Doris Amelia (1889–1970)', ADB, National Centre of Biography, ANU, adb.anu.edu.au/biography/blackburn-doris-amelia-9517/text16755, published first in hardcopy 1993, accessed online 2 December 2014.
47   Rasmussen, 'Blackburn, Doris Amelia (1889–1970)', ADB.
48   Rasmussen, 'Falling In and Out of Love', 50.

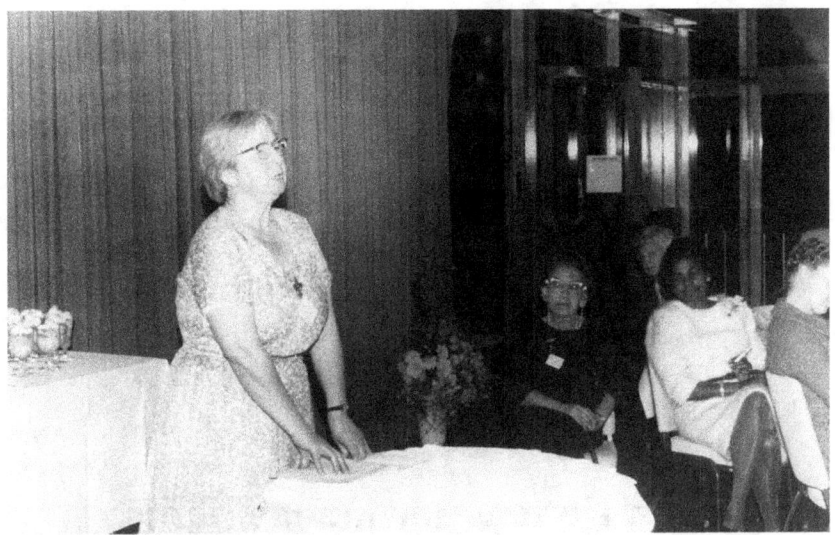

Anna Vroland speaking at the 50th Celebration of WILPF, Faith Bandler sitting in background. Celebration of 50th anniversary of Women's International League for Peace and Freedom, 28 April 1965.
Source: Compiled by Margaret Holmes, Mitchell Library, State Library of New South Wales and the Womens International League for Peace and Freedom (NSW Branch) [PXB 726]. See Appendix for a short biography of Anna Vroland.

Anna Vroland was, like Blackburn, involved in progressive causes in Melbourne, being an executive member of the Victorian Council Against War during the 1930s.[49] Vroland and her husband Anton, who married in 1947, were members of Charles Strong's Australian Church that founded the Sisterhood in 1915. Although no longer in its heyday, it still carried on in Melbourne organising and attracting nonconformist liberal intellectuals to progressive causes. Anton was secretary of the church from 1936 to 1955.[50] Well educated, Vroland was a teacher by profession, as was her husband. She had a great interest in internationalism and international relations and in 1938 acted as a commentator on international affairs for the radio station 3MA in Mildura. Her 12 broadcast talks were printed in a booklet called *Who Goes Where?*[51] Active alongside WILPF in World War II, she did not join as she 'had little tolerance for people whose ideas differed from

---

49 Sitarani Kerin, *'An Attitude of Respect': Anna Vroland and Aboriginal Rights, 1947–1957* (Clayton, Vic: Monash University, 1999).
50 Sitarani Kerin and Andrew Spaull, 'Vroland, Anna Fellowes (1902–1978)', ADB, National Centre of Biography, ANU, adb.anu.edu.au/biography/vroland-anna-fellowes-12108/text21371, published first in hardcopy 2002, accessed online 12 March 2015.
51 Anna White, *Who Goes Where?* (Mildura, Vic: Sunraysia Daily Print, 1938).

her own, and frequently worked alone', disagreeing with the anomalous position of WILPF during the war.[52] When she decided to join WILPF as it entered a new phase, she prioritised policy on Aboriginal affairs. She wrote in a letter to the headquarters of WILPF enclosing her policies about Aboriginal affairs that:

> for years, some of us have been presenting it to various organisations, hoping to interest some of them. It is because the WILPF women here took it seriously that I joined the organisation.[53]

WILPF had ratified her policy platform, but before Vroland's involvement with WILPF, their engagement with Aboriginal issues was limited to collaboration with sympathetic organisations.[54]

The United Nations and human rights

The League of Nations broke down during the 1930s and 1940s as nations withdrew and the organisation struggled to deal with state aggression.[55] Nonetheless, after World War II there was an increased investment in international solutions to world affairs which led to the creation of the United Nations.[56] Based in New York after 1945, the UN distinguished itself from the failed League of Nations experiment, but the League's organisational legacy was absorbed into the new institution and lessons of its shortcomings were taken on board. While the General Assembly represented internationally recognised states, and the Security Council gave veto rights to the US, China, the UK, France and the Soviet Union, which enshrined national sovereignty, its charter focused on 'fundamental freedoms without distinction as to race, sex, language or religion.'[57] This provided a way for marginalised groups to agitate to have their voices heard and introduced a 'human rights orientation to the concept of social

---

52 Kerin and Spaull, 'Vroland, Anna Fellowes (1902–1978)', ADB.
53 Vroland to Baer, 16 November 1953, series III reel 54, WILPF Papers. For example, the National Council of Women Australia did not have much interest in pursuing Aboriginal issues, 'there was not significant further discussion' until the 1960s. Judith Smart and Marian Quartly, *Respectable Radicals: A History of the National Council of Women of Australia 1896–2006* (Melbourne: Monash University Publishing, 2015), 319.
54 Eleanor M Moore, *The Quest for Peace, As I Have Known It in Australia* (Melbourne, 1948), 142.
55 Glenda Sluga, *Internationalism in the Age of Nationalism* (Philadelphia: University of Pennsylvania Press, 2013), 78, doi.org/10.9783/9780812207781.
56 Sluga, *Internationalism in the Age of Nationalism*, 78.
57 Sluga, *Internationalism in the Age of Nationalism*, 94.

justice'.[58] Internationally, WILPF fully supported the creation of the UN, despite its compromises and imperfections, as they believed that one of the root causes of war was 'the lack of legal instruments to resolve disputes peacefully. International law would be the antidote to the use of violence in international disputes'.[59] WILPF women also believed that any revision of the charter might lead to the dissolution of the organisation, so were reserved in their criticism.[60]

Historian Glenda Sluga defines this period as the 'apogee of internationalism' which, at the new UN, saw the creation of affiliated bodies such as the Commission on the Status of Women (CSW), formed in 1946, and the Human Rights Commission, which held its opening session in 1947.[61] After the horrors of two world wars, which increased sensitivity to race-based discrimination, the rights of the individual were put forward as a central issue. This shaped the new era's focus on human rights, reinforced in 1948 when the General Assembly adopted the Universal Declaration of Human Rights. The concept of human rights was not familiar in the mid-twentieth century, but after its incorporation into the central platforms of the UN it infused the language used to discuss world issues. The commission was flooded by demands for international attention and intervention on issues now characterised as violations of human rights.[62] Roland Burke has also shown how the human rights agenda helped the process of decolonisation as 'third world' delegates used the new discourse to push for the declaration to be truly universal.[63] This new international language gave WILPF in Australia a way to understand national and domestic issues in an international framework.

Australia was a conspicuous presence at the 1945 San Francisco Conference as Labor's Herbert Vere Evatt steered a delegation that included Jessie Street. Street was a well-travelled Australian woman with respected political skills and influence. Prominent in many progressive causes, she was part of a politically connected family as the 'daughter-in-law, wife, and mother of three Supreme Court Justices'.[64] Years earlier she had advocated for women's

---

58 Sluga, *Internationalism in the Age of Nationalism*, 94.
59 Confortini, *Intelligent Compassion*, 34.
60 Confortini, *Intelligent Compassion*, 36.
61 Sluga, *Internationalism in the Age of Nationalism*, 78.
62 Sluga, *Internationalism in the Age of Nationalism*, 100.
63 Roland Burke, *Decolonization and the Evolution of International Human Rights* (Philadelphia: University of Pennsylvania Press, 2010), doi.org/10.9783/9780812205329.
64 Jessie MG Street and Lenore Coltheart, *Jessie Street: A Revised Autobiography* (Annandale, NSW: Federation Press, 2004), vii.

rights as an alternate delegate for Australia at the League of Nations. She was then chosen as the only Australian female delegate at the San Francisco Conference and became a key player in the establishment of the CSW, before being elected as its vice-chairman in 1947.[65]

Street's appointment was not without criticism from other feminists. When she was appointed to the UN delegation by Evatt, Bessie Rischbieth and other activists protested to the prime minister, John Curtin, noting that there needed to be more transparency in the selection process.[66] In 1945, Street and Rischbieth, a prominent feminist from Western Australia, attended the founding conference in Paris of the Women's International Democratic Federation (WIDF), an organisation that became defined by its support for the Soviet Union. While there, Rischbieth became decidedly anti-communist. Later in a speech in Australia she defended democracy against 'the methods of the Soviet order (suppression of free speech, the imposition of uniformity and domination from the top).'[67] Street, however, showed sympathy towards the policies and practices of the Soviet Union. She wrote after her visit to the Soviet Russia in 1938 that she was 'very interested to find women had complete equality', and later became president of the Australian Soviet Friendship Society.[68] Rischbieth's and Street's philosophies on how to lead the women's movement in Australia became divided along Cold War lines.

When WILPF in Australia heard of Street's appointment to the UN meeting in 1945, they were pleased to have been part of the successful lobbying effort to have a female representative. Moore wrote to the international headquarters what she knew of Street, noting 'she was active in the IPC during its period of popularity and is to that extent peace-minded'.[69] Initially Australian WILPF had limited engagement with Street. Moore and her team were focused on Melbourne, and as Street was a well-known activist from Sydney she had not involved herself in the everyday working of the organisation. Yet, while the small Melbourne branch did not personally know Street in the 1940s, the headquarters in Geneva knew her well. In 1938 Street visited Geneva to attend the League of Nations and to work with women's organisations as president of the United Associations

---

65   Lake, *Getting Equal*, 204.
66   Lake, *Getting Equal*, 203.
67   Lake, *Getting Equal*, 203.
68   Street, 'Statement', New Delhi, 22 November 1954, Box 13/8, Jessie Street Papers, NLA.
69   Moore to Baer, 16 March 1945, series III reel 54, WILPF Papers.

5. THE UNITED NATIONS AND INDIGENOUS RIGHTS

of Women, which was affiliated to the International Alliance of Women (IAW). While there she attended WILPF International meetings to 'ensure the fullest understanding of women's issues around the world'.[70]

Street wrote in her autobiography how some delegates to the League of Nations were very patronising to women activists lobbying in the international sphere, noting:

> With few exceptions the male delegates were very backward in their attitude to women and in understanding the political, social and economic problems arising from sex discrimination. They listened to us with condescension and rather amused tolerance.[71]

Street was a member of WILPF internationally as well as many other international women's organisations, including the WIDF. In 1954 she addressed a WILPF forum to discuss the history of the disarmament campaign, drawing on her personal involvement with the international movement.[72] Her engagement with WILPF however was not through any Australian branches, but from abroad, communicating directly with European branches. From 1950 to 1956 she was effectively exiled from Australia when the Menzies Government withdrew her passport. This was because of her sympathy for the Soviet Union and the allegations of her communist associations, freezing her out of Australian politics at the height of the Cold War.[73]

Street maintained that she 'never was a communist' despite showing interest in the Soviet Union and its policies and attending Stalin's funeral as a guest in 1953.[74] She was very aware of the negative connotations evoked by any support for Soviet Russia and used her membership of various women's organisations strategically to counteract this. When necessary she promoted and organised within WIDF, helping to build the organisation into one of the largest international women's groups after World War II. Street had an interest in organising behind the 'Iron Curtain'. Yet, when she wanted to soften her image and distance herself from allegations of 'communist front'

---

70 Street and Coltheart, *Jessie Street*, 125.
71 Street and Coltheart, *Jessie Street*, 125.
72 Street, 'Disarmament?' Paper presented to WILPF, 1954, Jessie Street Papers, Box 13/2, NLA.
73 Street and Coltheart, *Jessie Street*, vii.
74 Nina Lowe to Vroland, 25 July 1956, reporting back from the Birmingham conference, Box 1722/25, Papers, WILPF, MS 9377, SLV; Ros Pesman, *Duty Free: Australian Women Abroad* (Melbourne: Oxford University Press, 1996), 138.

activities, she emphasised her membership to WILPF and downplayed her affiliation with WIDF by using the umbrella statement 'member of organisations working for equal rights for women'.[75]

In 1956 Street tried to convince the international leadership of WILPF to host a World Disarmament Conference with other peace organisations, noting 'I believe that the WILPF has a special spur to do this'.[76] She later clarified that the 'special spur' was that 'if you go to a peace congress now, you are called a communist and are cut off from your organisations. But if you have a conference organised by a body which is not suspect you may get somewhere.'[77] WILPF membership was therefore a tactical advantage in trying to give her message legitimacy. She utilised the jealously guarded and vigorously defended 'non-communist' image of WILPF while also freely associating with WIDF's subversiveness. Tensions caused by Cold War politics divided the women's movement and exacerbated personality clashes, to which women's organisations were vulnerable because of their non-hierarchical and unofficial structures.

Street was also present at the 1956 WILPF triennial congress in Birmingham. However, by then the Melbourne branch of WILPF, led by Vroland, were not appreciative of Street claiming membership of the section without involvement in the local network. Doris Blackburn, too, was often frustrated by Street's disorganised working style.[78] The section made a special effort to have their own delegate present who could provide a different perspective of the branch and report back to them. Nina Lowe was the chosen delegate who was able to be in England at the time, though she felt unqualified, writing to Vroland: 'I too wish you were here instead of an old noodle like me.'[79] Nonetheless, the Melbourne branch encouraged her to participate and to send information so they could get a better picture of Australia's standing within WILPF. The tension between Street and the Melbourne branch was clear when Lowe was unsure if the Australian section report had been received. Asking the secretariat who she should contact, they assumed Street was the official Australian delegate. Lowe wrote to

---

75 Street, 'Statement', New Delhi, 22 November 1954, Box 13/8, Jessie Street Papers, NLA.
76 Street, 'Minutes of Meeting with Peace Organisations', 29 July 1956, Birmingham, series I folder 13, reel 23, WILPF Papers.
77 Street, 'Minutes of Meeting with Peace Organisations', 29 July 1956, Birmingham, series I folder 13, reel 23, WILPF Papers.
78 Carolyn Rassmussen, *The Blackburns: Private Lives, Public Ambition* (Melbourne: Melbourne University Press, 2019), 296.
79 Lowe to Vroland, 22 July 1956, Box 1722/25, Papers, WILPF, MS 9377, SLV.

Vroland: 'I did not feel she was the one or that you would approve.'[80] The misunderstanding was rectified when Vroland's report was found, yet this incident highlighted another rivalry within the women's movement. There was a difference between the way members of the section felt about WILPF and how Street utilised it; they personally identified with the organisation while Street tactically engaged. Lowe described Street's contribution to the conference as 'provocative', recalling one discussion group where a prominent member from the UK section Kathleen Lonsdale 'almost lost her temper' with Street.[81] Nonetheless, WILPF International respected Street and her contribution to internationalism while the women's networks were in the process of re-engaging after the breakdown in communications during the war.

WILPF International connected with the UN and lobbied the national delegations just as they had done with the League of Nations. In 1948 they were eventually given consultative status B as a non-government organisation (NGO) to the Economic and Social Council (ECOSOC).[82] This was after much lobbying and a few rejected efforts on the grounds that the Liaison Committee of Women's International Organisations could represent them.[83] In 1949 they were also admitted to consultative status with the United Nations Educational, Scientific and Cultural Organisation (UNESCO). Both statuses remain with the organisation today. Gertrud Baer was appointed to be the consultant to the UN on behalf of WILPF.

It was towards Baer that Vroland directed her energy, encouraging her to use WILPF's newfound status with the UN to place Aboriginal rights on the international agenda, just as Street and Mary Bennett had tried to do earlier at the UN.[84] WILPF in Australia felt the need to approach international policymakers outside of the Australian delegation since Evatt and the Department of External Affairs did not take comments by WILPF into account. The government had a 'tendency to simply file comments from NGOs without subjecting them to detailed consideration.'[85] But with a new human rights language to discuss oppression and disadvantage, the

---

80 Lowe to Vroland, 22 July 1956, Box 1722/25, Papers, WILPF, MS 9377, SLV.
81 Lowe to Vroland, 25 July 1956, Box 1722/25, Papers, WILPF, MS 9377, SLV.
82 'NGO Branch ECOSOC, UN Website, WILPF Profile Special Consultative status since 1948', accessed 28 March 2015, esango.un.org/civilsociety/showProfileDetail.do?method=showProfileDetails&tab=1&profileCode=500.
83 Bussey and Tims, *Pioneers for Peace*, 197.
84 Marilyn Lake, *Faith: Faith Bandler, Gentle Activist* (NSW: Allen & Unwin, 2002), 66.
85 Annemarie Devereux, *Australia and the Birth of the International Bill of Human Rights, 1946–1966* (Annandale: Federation Press, 2005), 138.

Australian section of WILPF took a new direction, notably in making the injustice experienced by Aboriginal Australians an issue of international consequence.

Aboriginal rights

In the late nineteenth and early twentieth century, Social Darwinism heavily influenced policymakers who adopted a racialised vision of the world. Social Darwinists borrowed from Charles Darwin's theories on evolution in plants and animals and 'applied them, inappropriately, to change in human societies'.[86] The Australian Government or protection boards developed social policies that were motivated by the belief that Indigenous people were 'inferior races' who were 'doomed' to 'fade away'.[87] It eventually became clear, however, that Aboriginal people were not 'disappearing'. In fact, contrary to a belief that 'mixed race' people would become white and no longer identify with the Aboriginal community, many were instead 'identifying as Aboriginal, living with their Aboriginal relatives, and being identified by whites as Aboriginal.'[88] This led the protection boards in different states to develop new ways to categorise Indigenous people, which often had a significant impact on the way they were treated by state authorities as well as the status of their citizenship and the level of support they were entitled to. By 1900, 55 per cent of the Aboriginal population were of 'mixed' Aboriginal and European descent and were labelled as 'half-castes, quadroons, and octoroons'.[89] It was the anxiety about assimilating different 'categories' into the dominant 'white' culture that led to the removal of 'mixed' race children from families with the intention of separating them from their Aboriginal identity. These removals were, as is now widely recognised, a form of cultural genocide.

In a turn away from a paternalistic vision towards a more humanitarian approach, Vroland's focus was to understand Indigenous peoples' point of view rather than relying solely on 'expert' anthropologists who claimed to know what was in their interests. Historian Sitarani Kerin, in her work

---

[86] Heather Goodall, *Invasion to Embassy: Land in Aboriginal Politics in New South Wales, 1770–1972* (Sydney: Sydney University Press, 2008), 104.
[87] Goodall, *Invasion to Embassy*, 104.
[88] Goodall, *Invasion to Embassy*, 118.
[89] Goodall, *Invasion to Embassy*, 118.

on Vroland, argues that this approach set her activism apart from others.[90] Vroland's thinking on Aboriginal affairs influenced WILPF, while the organisation's focus on internationalism in turn led her to seek solutions within the UN. Vroland read widely about 'traditional' Aboriginal culture from anthropologists such as Professor AP Elkin. An Anglican clergyman and anthropologist, Elkin claimed that experts like himself were better able to interpret and administer Indigenous communities than they were themselves.[91] His work focused on the concept of how the traditional culture had 'shattered' under the impact of colonisation. Elkin believed that all that remained of the traditional culture were 'full-blooded Aborigines' and he therefore created an 'artificial division of Aboriginal society', delegitimising mixed-race and urban Indigenous communities.[92] When Vroland wrote to him in 1948 to request information about Victorian Aboriginal people from Lake Tyers and how to best encourage their adjustment to white society, his response was to say such people 'should be classed as members of the general community'.[93]

Vroland agreed with the consensus that Aboriginal peoples living in urban areas had 'lost' their culture. That said, she also recognised the inconsistency of treating them as part of the white community when they identified themselves as Aboriginal and were racially discriminated against by the rest of society. In a paper titled 'Towards Human Rights for Aborigines', Vroland noted that although these 'mixed descent' Aboriginal people were removed from their 'age old ancestors' they still 'speak of themselves as Aborigines though they are almost completely absorbed into the general community.'[94] She felt that much of the anthropological literature conflicted with the views of those Aboriginal and Torres Strait Islander peoples whom she had met and corresponded with. Her interaction with Victorian activists such as Margaret Tucker helped her to critique the dominant school of thought.[95] She wrote about the need to bring Aboriginal voices into the conversation about improving the lives of the urban Aboriginal communities in a way that acknowledged the common history of white oppression:

---

90 Kerin, 'An Attitude of Respect', xi. A description of Vroland's distinctive views is also discussed in Bain Attwood, *Rights for Aborigines* (Crows Nest, NSW: Allen & Unwin, 2003), 146.
91 Goodall, *Invasion to Embassy*, 235.
92 Kerin, 'An Attitude of Respect', 3.
93 Kerin, 'An Attitude of Respect', 5.
94 Kerin, 'An Attitude of Respect', 5.
95 John Farquharson, 'Tucker, Margaret Elizabeth (Auntie Marge) (1904–1996)', Obituaries Australia, National Centre of Biography, ANU, ia.anu.edu.au/biography/tucker-margaret-elizabeth-auntie-marge-1556/text1618, accessed 30 March 2015.

> Some time ago I met a very old man who had lived in Doncaster all his life. He remembered when red-coated soldiers used to ride out from Melbourne to shoot down aborigines, sometimes they took home a piccaninny for a pet. Such stories persist. And they are known abroad. Today, the public conscience is guilty about past treatment of aborigines ... Let us begin, as last, to try to understand these people. Let us hear what they have to say. Otherwise, what hypocrisy to talk about the rights of small nations![96]

Vroland sought to persuade Australians to take domestic action to improve the lives of Aboriginal people by exposing the country's poor national track record internationally, as well as by teaching white people about their thought, culture and hardships. To advance the latter cause, in 1951 she published a book called *Their Music Has Roots*, her own anthropological study of music and Victorian Indigenous communities.[97] It was an attempt to 'interpret to white people something of the thinking of dark Australians'. But Vroland believed that change would occur only when 'Aboriginal people were able to speak and struggle for themselves' and when white people were prepared to listen.[98] She sent her work around as an example of her advocacy and received many letters of recognition, including from Jessie Street who replied: 'I think it is a beautiful presentation of the aborigine outlook. Reading it has given me a clearer insight into their way of thinking'.[99]

Their Music Has Roots showcased the relationship Vroland had with the Aboriginal community. It focused on the lyrics of 10 songs and told the story of how Vroland herself first heard the music and what it meant to the person who sang it to her. This also gave her a platform to discuss other social and political problems faced by Aboriginal and Torres Strait Islander people. Margaret Tucker sang the first song, 'The Rough Road', and Vroland began the chapter with a simple instruction: 'Listen to Lulardia (Mrs Margaret Tucker)'. She then went on to explain her story: 'One of the first things I can remember is the singing of my dear old uncle. He used to sing me to sleep with songs in the old language.'[100] Tucker (Lulardia) was an Aboriginal activist born at Mooncullah in NSW before she was 'taken away

---

96 Vroland, 'The Aboriginal Questions—Aborigines I have Known', Undated, Vroland Papers MS 10301 Box 4336/4, SLV.
97 Anna F Vroland, *Their Music Has Roots* (Box Hill, Vic: Anna F. Vroland, 1951).
98 Kerin, '*An Attitude of Respect*', 7.
99 Street to Vroland, 30 July 1957, Papers of A. Vroland Box 3/20 NLA.
100 Margaret Tucker quoted in Vroland, *Their Music Has Roots*, 2.

by the police' to be 'educated'.[101] Hearing this personal history helped shape Vroland's understanding of Aboriginality as Tucker identified as Aboriginal despite being 'detribalised' or removed from the 'old' culture. Through her friendship with Tucker, Vroland recognised that Aboriginal women had an important role as spokespeople for their communities. She communicated by letter to many Aboriginal women and brought them into contact with the activities of WILPF.

In 1963 the anthropologist Diane Barwick submitted her doctoral thesis on the Victorian Aboriginal community, noting that many showed 'antipathy towards well-intentioned whites'.[102] Indigenous Australians interviewed by Barwick described three types of white 'do-gooders': 'the social worker type, the church people, and the type of women who had no children of their own and were in search of a good cause to fill the emptiness in their lives'.[103] Vroland could have been described as all three, but she was unusual in first earning the trust of Aboriginal women by helping only where needed and only when requested. She avoided speaking on anyone's behalf without their consent or collaboration. She also combined her charitable efforts with a 'critique of the system which perpetuated their impoverishment'.[104] In *Their Music Has Roots*, and in the Anton Vroland papers at the National Library of Australia, stories of how Vroland helped Aboriginal peoples are abundant. For example, she advocated on behalf of Edna Harrison who needed help getting the maternity allowance as she had been 'rejected on the grounds that [she was] an Aboriginal Native residing on an Aboriginal reserve [at Lake Tyers].'[105] She also sent a recommendation letter on behalf of Emma Bryant who, as a young Indigenous woman from East Gippsland, wanted special consideration to gain access to education to become a teacher.[106] In *Their Music Has Roots* Vroland explained how she had provided accommodation in her home to a woman named Mary Pepper, who was released from hospital in Melbourne but was gravely ill. She later died and Vroland helped her sister, Nellie Darby, by paying her fines and bail.[107]

---

101 For more information on Margaret Tucker, see documentary directed by Alec Morgan and Gerry Bostock, *Lousy Little Sixpence* (Ronin Films, 1982).
102 Diane Barwick, 'A Little More than Kin: Regional Affiliation and Group Identity Among Aboriginal Migrants in Melbourne' (PhD thesis, ANU, 1963), quoted in Kerin, '*An Attitude of Respect*', 30.
103 Kerin, '*An Attitude of Respect*', 30.
104 Kerin, '*An Attitude of Respect*', 33.
105 Director of Social Services to Edna Harrison, 'Maternity Allowance', 18 October 1950, Papers of A. Vroland, Box 3/20 NLA.
106 Vroland, to Mr Pederick on behalf of Emma Bryant, 19 September 1955, Papers of A. Vroland Box 3/20 NLA.
107 Vroland, *Their Music Has Roots,* 20.

According to Kerin, Vroland's ideas about the identity of 'part-Aboriginal' people were confused and complicated. She 'believed that Aboriginal culture no longer existed in Victoria' and yet her book was 'essentially an account of Aboriginal culture, a culture which, according to her own anthropologically-inspired understanding, did not exist.'[108] Similar to WILPF's early discussions on the WAP, Vroland had not quite arrived at a full paradigm shift, though she was aware of the flaws in the prevailing approach. This recognition, Kerin notes, predated the significant work by Barwick, who was the first scholar to recognise the so-called part-Aboriginal 'subculture'.[109] Vroland's divergence from official definitions of Aboriginality based on blood helped lay the groundwork for Barwick, as 'there needs to be a body of people thinking similar things before a new political discourse can truly emerge.'[110]

When Vroland became focused on WILPF, she encouraged the Australian section to accept a policy platform regarding Indigenous Australians that was based on the work of Donald Thomson from the University of Melbourne whom she greatly admired.[111] This set out a comprehensive 10-point agenda. It focused on seeking 'a recognition of the human rights of Aborigines, including land ownership and economic rights'. It also asked for a review into all Australian Native Policy, an anthropological and medical survey, and a royal commission to consider the facts revealed in the survey.[112] The agenda clearly identified the need to educate white Australians to increase 'awareness of their responsibility towards aborigines and descendants of aborigines [sic]', and a 'further fostering of essential elements of aboriginal culture', as well as the 'extension of full franchise but without compulsion'.[113] By ratifying the policy, WILPF also condemned the removal of Aboriginal children. As the Australian section explained in their policy statement: 'we oppose and seek a reversal of the policy of breaking up social and family life wherever this is customary' and they insisted that support should be given to mother and child rather than forced

---

108 Kerin, 'An Attitude of Respect', 12.
109 Kerin, 'An Attitude of Respect', 12.
110 Kerin, 'An Attitude of Respect', 14.
111 Howard Morphy, 'Thomson, Donald Finlay Fergusson (1901–1970)', ADB, National Centre of Biography, ANU, adb.anu.edu.au/biography/thomson-donald-finlay-fergusson-11851/text21213, published first in hardcopy 2002, accessed online 1 September 2016.
112 'Policy recommended by the Australian Section with regard to Australian Aborigines', sent to Baer, 16 November 1953, series III reel 54, WILPF Papers.
113 'Policy recommended by the Australian Section with regard to Australian Aborigines', sent to Baer, 16 November 1953, series III reel 54, WILPF Papers.

separation.¹¹⁴ WILPF held that 'people of mixed blood and those of full blood who are detribalised' needed special consideration and support to help them adapt to the general community. The policy document showed how WILPF believed there were two distinct groups of Indigenous people with different needs, the 'tribalised' communities in rural Australia who remained outside the white community, and the 'detribalised mixed-blood' communities who were having difficulty 'integrating' into white society.

WILPF Australia sent their policy statement to the headquarters in Geneva, suggesting to Baer that UNESCO or the Human Rights Commission might be interested in carrying out the proposal for the anthropological survey. She also sent it on behalf of WILPF to Paul Hasluck, Minister for Territories in Australia and a key architect of assimilation policy, with a memo stating her reasoning for approaching international organisations with issues concerning Aboriginal Australia: 'it is my failure to evoke any response within Australia that has made me think it necessary to raise the matter overseas.'¹¹⁵ From 1950 the Australian section began encouraging Baer to present their concerns about Australian Aboriginal human rights to the UN, mentioning the issue in most letters and all annual reports.¹¹⁶

Vroland kept Baer informed of the Indigenous women's responses to WILPF and noted their interest and cooperation with the organisation, describing how practical engagement in WILPF work was occurring:

> You may like to know that a half caste girl from an aboriginal reserve in Victoria helped me with the duplicating of your report, and that her dark aunt expressed great interest in a WILPF meeting they attended.¹¹⁷

Vroland's language remained within the lexicon that prevailed at the time, and was not in line with more modern terms coming into use in the international sphere. Indeed, Baer reacted strongly to the racial language that Vroland used to describe the different 'castes' of Aboriginal people. Internationally, the progressive movement came to believe that emphasis on racial difference was discriminatory, especially after the race-based horrors

---

114 'Policy recommended by the Australian Section with regard to Australian Aborigines', sent to Baer, 16 November 1953, series III reel 54, WILPF Papers.
115 Vroland, 'Memo to Minister for Territories', 21 November 1953, Anna F. Vroland (Mrs) re Welfare of Natives Northern Territory 1948–1954, National Archives of Australia (NAA): A431, 1950/730.
116 Vroland to Baer, 6 December 1950, series III reel 54, WILPF Papers.
117 Vroland to Baer, 6 December 1950, series III reel 54, WILPF Papers.

of the Holocaust, preferring the promotion of universalism over difference. This paralleled the change in the women's movement, where equality became more important than emphasising maternal difference.

Baer was a German of Jewish descent but was deprived of her German citizenship in 1933. She then became a permanent resident of Geneva, and later a US citizen, residing in New York.[118] Her thoughts on racial problems were influenced by a desire to move away from any idea of segregating minorities. Baer had seen the disastrous consequences of discrimination and more recently as an American she had been inculcated with new ideas about 'colour-blind' approaches to racial equality. She wrote:

> I never think of a person as being white or black of half-caste or pure race. There is no such thing as pure race any more. We have all mixed blood and for me there is only one thing which counts: integrity of character, warmth of heart and efficiency in work … I am quite convinced that every little bit we do to forget about all these differences helps to make them disappear. The most recent research of UNESCO resulted, as you know, in the definite findings that there is no such thing as a difference of race. No superiority and no inferiority. There are biological differences, but even those are disappearing more and more with civilisation expanding as it does. I wish you would have the UNESCO papers come in great numbers to hand them around to friends yet unconverted.[119]

Vroland, on the other hand, considered that ignoring race was not the way to improve the living standards of Indigenous people as a group. It was not that she believed white society was superior but that the 'Aboriginal way of life [was] *different but not inferior*' and she emphasised the need for special rights on account of that difference.[120]

This disagreement between Baer and Vroland highlighted a deeper philosophical tension in Australian society when discussing Aboriginality. Paul Hasluck, as Minister for the Territories, 'welcomed the United Nations' repudiation of racial distinctions' upon which he based his

---

118 Karl Holl, 'German Pacifist Women in Exile, 1933–1945', *Peace & Change* 20, no. 4 (1995): 491–500, doi.org/10.1111/j.1468-0130.1995.tb00248.x.

119 Baer to Vroland, 8 January 1951, series III reel 54, WILPF Papers. See also: Jean Hiernaux and Michael Banton, *Four Statements on the Race Question*, published by UNESCO, Paris, 1969. This text reproduced the four UN statements on the race question from 1950, 1951, 1964 and 1967. The 1950 and 1951 statements show the new research that Baer was referring to in her letter, accessed 16 April 2017, unesdoc.unesco.org/images/0012/001229/122962eo.pdf.

120 Vroland to Trades Hall Council, 18 February 1950, quoted in Kerin, '*An Attitude of Respect*', 22.

policy of assimilation.[121] He, too, saw 'race consciousness' as undermining national cohesion and hoped that 'there would soon be no distinction' as a result of assimilation policy, using the rhetoric of universal human rights that other progressives and feminists also adopted.[122] But Hasluck's focus on assimilation was based on the idea that Indigenous communities were 'crumbling' and 'fading'. His promotion of the new international discussion of human rights through 'non-discrimination' raised ambiguities that some women activists, such as Vroland, Street, Bennett and Bromham, resisted.[123]

Despite WILPF Australia's language and choice of terminology regarding 'castes', they too believed that it was 'incorrect biologically to speak of "Aboriginal blood"' and thought that there should be no distinction between those of 'full and mixed' descent.[124] They implored the Victorian Government to 'bring their ideas in line with the latest science and knowledge on the subject'.[125] The insistence that assimilation was a denial of difference led to terminology in the debate changing from 'race' to 'culture' which should be valued and protected, allowing 'Aboriginal peoples' the right to retain their identity.[126]

Despite their ambivalence towards the language of international human rights, which was so integral to their emancipatory cause, both emboldening women's international organising but disavowing sexual and cultural difference, the value of the international connection for the Australian activists in this debate was clear. Before joining WILPF, Vroland promoted her views in letters and communications with the government and other organisations with little response or acknowledgement. After demonstrating to the government that the policy ratified by WILPF had been sent to the Geneva headquarters, the potential international scrutiny pressured the government to respond seriously to their demands.

The Department of External Affairs in Canberra drafted a response to each of the 10 points raised in the WILPF paper for the minister. They noted the reason for the response was because the recommendations had been 'sent to the League's Headquarters at Geneva' and as there was 'a possibility that

---

121 Marilyn Lake, 'Paul Hasluck's Horror of the Two-Headed Calf', in *Contesting Assimilation*, ed. Tim Rowse and Richard Nile (Perth, WA: API Network, 2005), 253.
122 Lake, 'Paul Hasluck's Horror of the Two-Headed Calf', 253.
123 Lake, 'Paul Hasluck's Horror of the Two-Headed Calf', 265.
124 Vroland, 25 April 1957, quoted in Kerin, *'An Attitude of Respect'*, 25.
125 Kerin, *'An Attitude of Respect'*, 25.
126 Lake, 'Paul Hasluck's Horror of the Two-Headed Calf', 266.

these recommendations might be taken up with UNESCO the following departmental comments are made, if necessary, for your guidance.'[127] WILPF used the power of potential embarrassment. This was one of their greatest strategic tools, as they publicly forced officials to rebut their statements or persevere in the face of public criticism. They could also demonstrate that their activism had a wide reach. A WILPF member in Italy acknowledged 'various letters and the material on Aborigines have found their way to Rome and I have forwarded all reports to the Human Rights Commission this week.'[128]

The department's response included detailed reasons for the difficulties in dealing with this issue, including that the state governments bore responsibility for most of the problems. They cited a failed referendum in 1944 to give power to the Commonwealth parliament to legislate on behalf of Aboriginal Australians as being to blame for this and noted that Commonwealth–state conferences were not legally binding on the states thereby making cohesive national policy elusive. The government also rejected the recommendation of a royal commission, stating that there were 'inadequate reasons to support the appointment' and that setting aside land would mean 'either reverting to the old policy of protection or else it would mean segregation'.[129] Once again reiterating the policy of assimilation the government pursued the idea that Indigenous people should receive no special treatment or discrimination and wherever possible should be set up in 'economic undertakings with equal opportunities to Europeans'.[130] External Affairs argued that one point in the WILPF paper was 'misleading, as the welfare system does not involve a present practice of forcibly separating mother and child'. Separation, they claimed, was only used where the child was 'deemed to live under neglected conditions' and in need of care 'whether European or native'.[131] Concluding the report, the department claimed that WILPF's recommendations were theoretically inconsistent:

---

127 C.R. Lambert, Secretary of Department of External Affairs, to Minister, 15 January 1954, 'Anna F. Vroland (Mrs) re Welfare of Natives Northern Territory 1948–1954' NAA: A431, 1950/730.
128 Cedelardi Baker to Vroland, c/o US Embassy, Rome, Italy, 26 April 1963, Box 1723/16, Papers, WILPF, MS 9377, SLV.
129 C.R. Lambert, Secretary of Department of External Affairs, to Minister, 15 January 1954, 'Anna F. Vroland (Mrs) re Welfare of Natives Northern Territory 1948–1954' NAA: A431, 1950/730.
130 C.R. Lambert, Secretary of Department of External Affairs, to Minister, 15 January 1954, 'Anna F. Vroland (Mrs) re Welfare of Natives Northern Territory 1948–1954' NAA: A431, 1950/730.
131 C.R. Lambert, Secretary of Department of External Affairs, to Minister, 15 January 1954, 'Anna F. Vroland (Mrs) re Welfare of Natives Northern Territory 1948–1954' NAA: A431, 1950/730.

> Taking the recommendations as a whole they represent conflicting views, with no clear objective in mind. The League urges full social and economic recognition for aborigines, and on the other hand attempts to restrict advancement by preserving aboriginal life based on its ancient culture which has in fact largely disappeared from the Northern Territory. There exists an urgent need to fit these people into a new way of life through a constructive and vigorous policy which, however, the League has not presented.[132]

Despite the defensive response by the government, WILPF continued to promote their policy. Their agitation on the issue and the official responses show that they, along with other activist groups, were successful in keeping the discussion on the political agenda. This in turn forced officials to defend government positions.

Apart from encouraging the UN and international bodies to take up the fight for equality for Indigenous Australians, WILPF Australia committed locally to intervene and help where they could. In 1951 the section reported on how they contributed to a vigorous letter writing campaign to the Victorian Government about the Framlingham Aboriginal Reserve, where families were being threatened with eviction. Two WILPF members visited the reserve, including the treasurer Helen Strong, and cooperated with journalists and the Reserve Welfare Committee to have the evictions stopped.[133] Mrs Mary Clarke, a 'part-Aboriginal' woman from the Framlingham community, requested WILPF hold a meeting about what could be done about the issue and she spoke to the public about the conditions at the reserve. The meeting was chaired by Ada Bromham.[134] Among the speeches of note was the address by Shadrach James, a member of the Aborigines Protection Board and secretary of the Mooroopna Aborigines' Progress Association.[135] James' father, who was of Indian descent, was a dedicated advocate for Indigenous rights and a teacher at the Cummeragunja reserve, educating William Cooper, Margaret Tucker and Douglas Nicholls who all

---

132 C.R. Lambert, Secretary of Department of External Affairs, to Minister, 15 January 1954, 'Anna F. Vroland (Mrs) re Welfare of Natives Northern Territory 1948–1954' NAA: A431, 1950/730.
133 Anna Vroland, 'Australian Section Annual Report', 7 April 1951, series III reel 54, WILPF Papers.
134 For more information about Ada Bromham, internationalist and Aboriginal advocate see: Lake, *Getting Equal*, 53. Wendy Birman, 'Bromham, Ada (1880–1965)', ADB, National Centre of Biography, ANU, adb.anu.edu.au/biography/bromham-ada-5368/text9081, published first in hardcopy 1979, accessed online 9 April 2015.
135 'Justice for Aborigines', Minutes of meeting held in Australian Church, Russell Street Melbourne, 21 February 1951, Papers of A. Vroland Box 4/28 NLA.

went on to become leaders in the movement.[136] James' mother was Yorta Yorta woman Ada Cooper, sister of William. James assured the gathering that 'the Board have adopted a new attitude towards the people there' and confirmed that no more houses would be sold. The commitment conveyed a tension between not wanting to betray the confidence of the board while also reassuring the room of his activism.[137] James went on to passionately describe disadvantages communities faced: 'the aborigines [sic] are asked to pay taxes—well let them have the same privileges.'[138]

WILPF women kept close watch on any publicised instances of unjust imprisonment. On one occasion they attempted to correspond on behalf of a young girl from WA whose arrest was, they believed, 'due to the caprice of officials'.[139] Recognising that their interventions were showing no results, they decided to 'make a study of the legal position of aborigines' by collecting and surveying the various Acts relating to Aboriginal and Torres Strait Islanders in all parts of the Commonwealth.[140]

WILPF-sponsored survey of East Gippsland

WILPF realised that without proper information about the situation of the Indigenous communities, not much could be done in way of campaigning strategically. Therefore, following the example of WILPF's international fact-finding trips such as the delegation sent to China in 1927, the section decided to send three WILPF members to East Gippsland in 1951 to make a report of the conditions of Aboriginal communities. This included Dr Hilda Heffernan (née Greenshields), a retired doctor, Sister L Miller, a former matron of an industrial school, and Miss Cora Gilsenan, a social worker and Aboriginal rights advocate. The three women planned to write the report so that WILPF could use the information to 'publicise with

---

136 George E. Nelson, 'James, Thomas Shadrach (1859–1946)', ADB, National Centre of Biography, Australian National University, adb.anu.edu.au/biography/james-thomas-shadrach-10610/text18855, published first in hardcopy 1996, accessed online 12 April 2022.
137 'Justice for Aborigines', Minutes of meeting held in Australian Church, Russell Street Melbourne, 21 February 1951, Papers of A. Vroland Box 4/28 NLA.
138 'Justice for Aborigines', Minutes of meeting held in Australian Church, Russell Street Melbourne, 21 February 1951, Papers of A. Vroland Box 4/28 NLA. See also: 'Aborigines Give Black Views on White Australia', *The Age,* 22 February 1951, 4.
139 'Justice for Aborigines', Minutes of meeting held in Australian Church, Russell Street Melbourne, 21 February 1951, Papers of A. Vroland Box 4/28 NLA.
140 'Justice for Aborigines', Minutes of meeting held in Australian Church, Russell Street Melbourne, 21 February 1951, Papers of A. Vroland Box 4/28 NLA.

5. THE UNITED NATIONS AND INDIGENOUS RIGHTS

a view to having improvements made'.[141] Gilsenan acted as a guide, as she lived in East Gippsland in a town called Metung that was close to the Lake Tyers Aboriginal community.[142]

The three women stayed in East Gippsland for one weekend, acknowledging themselves that this was not enough time to complete an exhaustive study.[143] However, they observed 'the way people were living, and it was a shock, even to one, accustomed, as I have been to know about bad living conditions'.[144] Visiting six places where Aboriginal people were living, each woman wrote a small description of her experience. Child mortality, hygiene and maternal healthcare were a great concern for each of them. But they primarily discussed inadequate shelter and housing, noting that 'mothers are most prolific' and 'improved accommodation alone would save many children's lives.'[145]

Despite the alarming descriptions, all three reiterated how much effort was made by the communities to overcome such hardships. Gilsenan focused on stories of men trying hard to support families but being unable to find suitable employment, and recounted how a family spent all their money on an ambulance for their child with meningitis causing them to lose nearly all their possessions.[146] There was a shift in the 'discursive terrain' in the 1950s campaigns by white activists on Aboriginal issues with 'the reconceptualising of Aborigines as workers rather than as feminine victims' enabling 'labour men to identify more easily with the struggle for Aboriginal rights.'[147] The focus in the report on maternal welfare, arguing for state care for mothers and leftist assimilationism, as well as the recasting of Aboriginal men as workers desperately seeking employment, shows WILPF's attempts

---

141 Vroland to Baer, 19 April 1951, series III reel 54, WILPF Papers. Vroland to Prime Minister J.B Chifley, 14 February 1948, 'Anna F. Vroland (Mrs) re Welfare of Natives Northern Territory 1948–1954', NAA: A431, 1950/730.
142 Richard Broome, 'Tracing the Humanitarian Strain in Black-White Encounters', *Latrobe Journal* 43 (1989): 38.
143 'Conditions of Dark Children in East Gippsland', June 1951, WILPF Australian section, Box 4336/4, Vroland Papers, MS10301, SLV.
144 'Conditions of Dark Children in East Gippsland', June 1951, WILPF Australian section, Box 4336/4, Vroland Papers, MS10301, SLV.
145 'Conditions of Dark Children in East Gippsland', June 1951, WILPF Australian section, Box 4336/4, Vroland Papers, MS10301, SLV.
146 'Conditions of Dark Children in East Gippsland', June 1951, WILPF Australian section, Box 4336/4, Vroland Papers, MS10301, SLV.
147 Marilyn Lake, 'Feminism and the Gendered Politics of Antiracism, Australia 1927–1957: From Maternal Protectionism to Leftist Assimilationism', *Australian Historical Studies* 29, no. 110 (1 April 1998): 106, doi.org/10.1080/10314619808596062.

to broaden the appeal of the report for the widest support. These stories reinforced the idea that this was a failure of the state rather than of the individuals. As Sister Miller explained:

> The parents have belonged to a community that has lost the old aboriginal knowledge concerning care of children, and their way of living is completely different from the old way. They have been thrust into an alien culture without being provided with the sort of training that would enable them to adapt themselves successfully to the difficult position in which they find themselves. Surely they are not to be blamed overmuch for their shortcomings. Love of offspring and kin is theirs to a marked degree. Only the means and the knowledge of what to do for them is lacking. The community should be responsible for supplying those needs.[148]

Just as Vroland's politics were informed by the idea of 'mixed-race' living with no culture, so too were the politics of the women writing the report. The focus on how the children could be 'absorbed' into the community if given the 'proper environment' drew heavily on the language and policy of assimilation.[149] Still, WILPF also recognised that those 'mixed-race' were denied the opportunity to assimilate because of discriminatory community attitudes. WILPF gained publicity for this expedition and the public meeting they held after it. Their report was published in the *Argus*, where the paper focused on the issue of child mortality raised by the findings: 'children are dying of starvation and exposure in camps and shacks'.[150] Their discussion revealed an uneasiness with the policy of assimilation, and reaffirmed their belief that Aboriginal rights were a racial issue for UNESCO and for the world, not something to be hidden away or kept exclusively for the domestic agenda.

Various elements of the findings of this report influenced WILPF activities during the 1950s. The section continued to press for wider-ranging 'rights to petition' the UN, so that not only signatory states could approach the Human Rights Commission, but also 'minorities whose needs are the greatest'.[151] Despite their efforts, they would have to wait until the late 1960s before any significant breakthrough was made.

---

148 'Conditions of Dark Children in East Gipplsand', June 1951, WILPF Australian section, Box 4336/4, Vroland Papers, MS10301, SLV.
149 'Conditions of Dark Children in East Gipplsand', June 1951, WILPF Australian section, Box 4336/4, Vroland Papers, MS10301, SLV.
150 'What Goes On? A Melbourne News Diary', *The Argus*, 4 September 1951.
151 Vroland to Hon P.C. Spender, Minister to External Affairs, 14 February 1951, series III reel 54, WILPF Papers.

Doris Blackburn travelled to Europe in 1952 to engage with the international WILPF network. There was supposed to be a triennial congress in August that year, but it had to be moved to 1953.[152] Nonetheless, as her plans were in place, Blackburn travelled in August 1952 and attended the International Executive Committee in Geneva. It discussed various issues and adopted several resolutions presented by national sections for the policy platform. Blackburn and the Australian section proposed that WILPF 'requests the United Nations General Assembly to include among the functions of the UN and its Specialized Agencies and organs HOUSING as one of the most crying needs of the peoples of the world.'[153] This resolution, named the 'right to shelter', showed Australians engaging with the discussion about economic, social and cultural rights put forward in the Universal Declaration. It was a direct result of the Australian section's desire to place the issues of Aboriginal Australia in a global context, reflecting the main issue of inadequate housing for the disadvantaged brought up in the East Gippsland report. Blackburn continued as an advocate for the rights of Indigenous people, and in 1957 co-founded the Victorian Aborigines Advancement League to further this activism.[154]

***

The decade of the 1950s was one in which decolonisation, racial equality and Indigenous peoples' rights were given increased international attention. WILPF was inspired by other progressive activists working on Indigenous issues and quickly became committed to promoting the human rights of Indigenous communities in the international sphere. They worked alongside a community of activists that all utilised the new human rights framework to have the issue advanced in the Australian political sphere, eventually leading to the 1967 referendum on Aboriginal rights. Within the movement there was still a theoretical inconsistency as some argued for radical universalism (leading to approval of assimilation policies) while others wanted recognition of group rights and collective identity. WILPF Australia's argument in favour of presenting Aboriginal rights to international organisations was illustrated

---

152 Baer to Vroland, 14 February 1952, series III reel 54, WILPF Papers.
153 Resolutions adopted at the meeting of the International Executive Committee of WILPF in Geneva 6–11 August 1952, series I reel 12, WILPF Papers.
154 Richard Broome, *Fighting Hard: The Victorian Aborigines Advancement League* (Canberra: Aboriginal Studies Press, 2015).

in the International Labour Organization's 'Indigenous Tribal Populations Convention 107', drafted in 1957, which advocated 'integration' rather than assimilation of Indigenous peoples.

WILPF members in Australia were willing to collaborate with mainstream political parties at this time. Blackburn had been a member of federal parliament, and the public profile she brought to WILPF, as well as her political experience, were invaluable to their activities. Nancy Wilkinson from Western Australia ran for parliament for the Australian Labor Party, and other prominent women including Vroland and Mary Broun were ALP members, willing to criticise from within. Political involvement in the domestic sphere began to bring the message of WILPF to a wider audience and the politically involved women focused energy on domestic electoral politics as well as international networking. The use of the international arena continued to legitimise their work and provided a space for them to present their concerns if they could not find a response in the domestic sphere. It was also a means of applying pressure locally as Australia's policies and behaviour received wider scrutiny.

For the WILPF women, peace was not merely the absence of war. It included a detailed social and political agenda that was aimed at achieving gender and racial equality in an effort to extend to all individuals appropriate human rights and standards of living. Dealing with these issues shows how they connected the idea of 'peace' to a wider platform of social justice. They argued that by improving understanding of oppression and inequality they could create a more just and peaceful world.

After the breakdown of networks following the war, WILPF in Australia redefined and rebuilt its membership. That said, their membership was never large, and activities were often limited to holding public meetings, publishing pamphlets and petitions, and organising conferences. Nonetheless, this activity strengthened their purpose and cemented their presence in the Australian peace movement. By the 1960s the movement had an established platform to begin engaging the wider public when the Vietnam War brought issues of peace once more to mainstream attention.

6
The Cold War and nuclear disarmament

In 1952 the Women's International League for Peace and Freedom (WILPF) hosted a meeting to protest nuclear tests. 'If atom bombs make a country secure Americans should be serene and confident', opined Lillian Miller, president of the Victorian WILPF branch. 'But they have the jitters so badly that it is being seriously suggested that they should live and work underground'.[1] Miller believed Australians did not want the bomb. And yet the government was proposing collaboration with the British Government to test nuclear weapons in Australia. Pacifists had to be ever vigilant. As one war ended, new conflicts and more terrifying weapons continued to dominate world politics.

***

By the 1960s a new trend in WILPF's operating style was emerging. WILPF's international headquarters acknowledged that 'technical and political developments' were taking place at an 'unprecedented speed' which made the 'mass protests, manifestoes and petitions of the 1930s … no longer adequate'.[2] The headquarters in Geneva placed greater importance on the executive committee giving continuous attention to policy, and their UN consultants' 'constant attendance at history-making commissions

---

1   Mrs. L Miller, 'Report of the Public Meeting of Protest Against Atom Bomb Test', 18 March 1952, series III reel 54, WILPF International Papers 1915–1978, Sanford, NC: Microfilming Corp. of America, c 1983, accessed at the National Library of Australia (NLA). Hereafter referred to as WILPF Papers.
2   GC Bussey and Margaret Tims, *Pioneers for Peace: Women's International League for Peace and Freedom, 1915–1965*, 2nd ed. (London: Allen & Unwin, 1965), 203.

and assemblies'.[3] It saw the role of national sections in this new program as being 'never-sleeping watchdogs of governmental policies which might make or break the world'.[4] This emphasis, with the Geneva office focusing on lobbying the UN while the national sections acted as local governmental pressure groups, represented a subtle but significant shift in the identity of WILPF. A movement born out of and responding to crisis was transforming into a professional modern non-government organisation (NGO). It was a shift prompted by the Cold War tensions of global politics.

WILPF had to adapt to the Cold War era of the 1960s and early 1970s to focus their energy on nuclear disarmament through the channels that they felt they were most effective. The direction of campaigns became more about understanding and targeting militarism and its socialisation and exposure to children, shown with the 'no war toys' for children slogan, as well as wider campaigns against French nuclear testing in the Pacific. The Cold War and the constant nuclear threat provided the world with an incentive for institutionalised militarisation, and WILPF had to try to mobilise people against militarism, without the specific catalyst of combat or global warfare. This proved a much more complex environment within which to recruit and grow as an organisation. While it was a more complicated mobilisation, stalwarts in WILPF felt their work was now more urgent than ever, with the nuclear bomb and the apocalyptic threat presented by its future use reinforcing how necessary it was to intervene before a crisis. They wished not to 'protest when an international crime had been committed', but to 'anticipate the crisis and offer an alternative, practicable policy.'[5] Human survival seemed to depend on it in a nuclear age.

Working within the new Cold War environment, the Australian section during the 1960s also adapted and modified its organising style. After attending the 1959 Stockholm WILPF Congress, new member Margaret Holmes founded the Sydney branch of WILPF, which soon assumed responsibility for the organisational duties of the national section as the leaders of the aging Melbourne branch were unable to continue with their volunteer workload. Strengthening sections in South Australia, Tasmania, Queensland and Western Australia were able to connect with the New South Wales and Victorian branches to establish the first interstate network, adding another to the organising structure.

---

3   Bussey and Tims, *Pioneers for Peace*, 203.
4   Bussey and Tims, *Pioneers for Peace*, 203.
5   Bussey and Tims, *Pioneers for Peace*, 203.

While self-proclaimed progressive groups focused their energy on campaigning against the bomb, they also had to negotiate the divisive and often cynical politics of conservative politicians and commentators who claimed any campaign against the US was 'communist'. The peace cause became synonymous with communism, a problem exacerbated by the active campaigns of Cominform, and Comintern before it, to coopt the terminology of peace.[6] WILPF had a complex relationship with communism and a rhetorical challenge to maintain their image of neutrality. Other women's groups, such as the Women's International Democratic Federation (WIDF), were founded and further changed the dynamics of the women's international sphere. WILPF had to find a way to interact and cooperate despite a fundamental difference on 'communist sympathies'. Despite this, they still became part of the political targeting of communists in the Australian context. They were tracked by the Australian Security Intelligence Organisation (ASIO), questioned by politicians and harangued by anti-communists. This inevitably interfered with their organising, especially after the referendum to ban the Communist Party by the Menzies Government in 1951.

The atomic age: Nuclear testing in Australia

The world entered the atomic age after World War II, and the peace movement was dismayed by the 'shame and horror of the atomic bomb' after its use at Hiroshima and Nagasaki in August 1945.[7] In 1946 WILPF in Melbourne participated in a combined protest against the manufacture of atomic bombs, and demanded that:

> scientific research should be free from military and political control and that scientists should not be hindered from making known to one another and to the public the results of their investigations.[8]

---

6 Peace was a highly politicised term during the Cold War, and scholars such as Petra Goedde have noted how it was 'a controversial concept infused with multiple meanings in different geographical and political spheres'. Peace discourse both divided and united various parts of the international community, and the rhetoric of peace was 'used, altered and fought over', allowing some to assert the Soviets appropriated the idea, while Western leaders equated peace advocacy with communism. Unaligned peace groups struggled to uncouple these tensions in opposing militarism in the Cold War. Petra Goedde, *The Politics of Peace: A Global Cold War History,* (Oxford: Oxford University Press, 2019), 2, doi.org/10.1093/oso/9780195370836.001.0001.
7 Eleanor M Moore, *The Quest for Peace, As I Have Known It in Australia* (Melbourne, 1948), 150.
8 Moore, *The Quest for Peace*, 151.

However, the beginning of the Cold War and the sprint for many nations to become nuclear powers meant that scientific information was often classified. A number of countries all began nuclear weapons testing programs to develop and improve their capabilities. Britain was determined to become a nuclear power, believing that a strategy of deterrence would be economical and effective.[9] Excluded from sharing US nuclear secrets from 1946, the United Kingdom began its own nuclear program and enlisted Australia to provide land that could be used for bomb testing. This brought together the two issues that WILPF prioritised: protesting any increase in militarism and the manufacture of weapons intended for mass destruction, and the welfare of Indigenous communities, since the testing sites in Central Australia were inhabited by Aboriginal people.

The federal government's decision to allow British testing to occur on Australian soil was influenced by imperial identity and fears for Australia's own national security during the Cold War. The Australian government's 'extraordinary generosity' meant Britain performed 12 atmospheric atomic explosions between 1952 and 1957.[10] The aid was so 'freely given' by Australia because in the 1940s and 1950s, despite Australia's disappointment about the fall of Singapore in 1942 and Curtin's appeal to America, many Australians and their politicians still felt a strong sense of belonging to the British Empire. In 1946 Prime Minister Ben Chifley established, at Britain's request, the experimental Woomera Rocket Range. At 1,250 miles in length, it was the largest testing range in the Western world, covering areas in South Australia and Western Australia.[11] Chifley's statement to a 1946 London Conference concerning Pacific strategic planning reinforced the bonds of empire:

> the amount required has been provided and the plan is being carried out … we have great respect for our American friends, but we simply say: 'We are part of the British Empire and we are prepared to help the United Kingdom'.[12]

---

9   Lorna Arnold and Mark Smith, *Britain, Australia and the Bomb: The Nuclear Tests and Their Aftermath*, 2nd ed. (New York: Palgrave Macmillan, 2006), 5.
10 Arnold and Smith, *Britain, Australia and the Bomb*, xi.
11 Peter Dennis et al., 'Long Range Weapons Establishment, Woomera—Oxford Reference', *The Oxford Companion to Australian Military History*, online version (Oxford: Oxford University Press, 2008), doi.org/10.1093/acref/9780195517842.001.0001. For more information on this see: Peter Morton, *Fire Across the Desert: Woomera and the Anglo-Australian Joint Project 1946–1980* (Canberra: AGPS Press, 1989).
12 LF Crisp, *Ben Chifley: A Biography* (London: Longmans, 1961), 282.

This rocket range was named after an Aboriginal weapon, the woomera, which is used to launch spears. It encompassed areas known as Emu Field and Maralinga and was established only after Indigenous communities at nearby locations such as Ooldea, where a mission was in operation, were relocated.[13] This enclosed area was known to be Yankunytjatjara land, which concerned pacifists and Aboriginal rights activists.

At this time Doris Blackburn was a member of the House of Representatives, succeeding her late husband as a Labor independent. In 1947 she proposed a motion to parliament condemning the proposed Woomera Rocket Range and weapons testing.[14] Her criticism of the project was twofold: first, she was against the testing because of her firm belief in disarmament, and second, she was concerned about the impact it would have on Indigenous people and their land. The discussion around the impact on the Aboriginal community was focused on the 'tribalised' lifestyle of the population in the area, and much of the anxiety centred on their 'nomadic traditions', which would be curtailed by military personnel.[15] It was not just 'projectiles' falling over the area 'but the real danger to the natives' would be 'their probable contamination by the white people who will go into that area.'[16] With limited collegial support in the parliament particularly on this issue, and as an independent without a party, Blackburn turned to her connections and networks with women's organisations for support. As a member of parliament she frequently corresponded with Anna Vroland and WILPF to discuss the campaign against the rocket range. Blackburn encouraged WILPF to ramp up protests so public opinion could influence proceedings, though she lamented that 'it seems the matter is cut and dried with the government already' and complained of a gag being applied to her motion, 'effectively stopping everything. There had been other speakers waiting from both sides of the house', wrote Blackburn in a letter to Vroland. 'Since then I have been told that the prime minister said "we might perhaps have let her finish, but I could not allow other speakers on the subject"'.[17]

---

13 Heather Goodall, 'Colonialism and Catastrophe: Contested Memories of Nuclear Testing and Measles Epidemics at Ernabella' in *Memory and History in Twentieth-Century Australia*, ed. Kate Darian-Smith and Paula Hamilton (Melbourne: Oxford University Press, 1994), 71.
14 Richard Broome, *Fighting Hard: The Victorian Aborigines Advancement League* (Canberra: Aboriginal Studies Press, 2015), 40. See also discussion in Deborah Wilson, *Different White People: Radical Activism for Aboriginal Rights 1946–1972*, (Crawley: UWA Publishing, 2015), 95.
15 Wilson, *Different White People*, 95.
16 Doris Blackburn, 'Question, Guided Weapons, Speech', *Commonwealth Parliamentary Debates (CPD)*, House of Representatives, 1 May 1947, 1844.
17 Doris Blackburn to Mrs Vroland, 22 November 1946, 7 March, 1947, 14 May 1947, 4 March 1948, Box 1726, Papers, WILPF, MS 9377, SLV.

Prominent experts supported Blackburn in her opposition to the rocket range, including the Presbyterian doctor Charles Duguid and anthropologist Donald Thomson, who both travelled to the affected communities and published widely on their observations.[18] WILPF, through the efforts of Vroland, maintained consistent communication with Thomson and Duguid so that their information could directly inform WILPF's activism.[19] Duguid was responsible for establishing the Ernabella Aboriginal reserve in 1937 which was considered 'one of the most culturally sensitive ever established'.[20] Ernabella was directly affected by the creation of the rocket range. Collaborating with groups such as the WILPF against the testing, Thomson and Duguid convened a public forum in 1947. Thomson, as historian Bain Attwood has noted, intended to use his high standing and reputation in international circles as an anthropologist to give 'considered opinion' to the campaign.[21] The information Thomson and Duguid provided formed the basis of WILPF's opposition and was used by Blackburn in arguing against the range. Yet, as they operated within the Cold War discourse, their concern for the health of Aboriginal Australians was often discredited as being 'communist'.[22]

The government commissioned a report to outline the potential impact on the Aboriginal population, prepared by a panel which included Professor Elkin, an anthropologist from the University of Sydney. He accepted the assurances of the government that it would protect the Indigenous communities, and defended the project from all critics.[23] Thomson and Duguid, who both opposed the testing site, presented their arguments to the panel, but the report, in the words of Robert Menzies as leader of the opposition, 'entirely disposed of the criticisms made and of the alternatives

---

18   Donald Thomson, 'Aborigines and the Rocket Range' May 1947; and Thomson, 'The Black and White of the Rocket Range', produced by WILPF, the Peace Pledge Union, and the Christian Pacifist Movement, Papers of A. Vroland Box 6/44 NLA. See also Charles Duguid, 'The Rocket Range, Aborigines and War', transcript of address delivered at Melbourne Town Hall, 31 March 1947, series III reel 55, WILPF Papers.
19   Charles Duguid to Miss White (later Vroland), 21 December 1946, and Donald Thomson to Mrs Vroland, 6 March 1948, Box 1726, Papers, WILPF, MS 9377, SLV.
20   Rani Kerin, *Doctor Do-Good: Charles Duguid and Aboriginal Advancement, 1930s–1970s* (North Melbourne, Vic: Australian Scholarly Publishing, 2011), 16.
21   Bain Attwood, *Rights for Aborigines* (Crows Nest, NSW: Allen & Unwin, 2003), 121.
22   Goodall, 'Colonialism and Catastrophe' in Darian-Smith and Hamilton, *Memory and History in Twentieth-Century Australia*, 59.
23   Attwood, *Rights for Aborigines*, 122.

suggested.'[24] Blackburn had her dissent heard in parliament, reiterating her opposition to both the intrusion on Aboriginal land and the development of guided weapons. She stated:

> I maintain that we have committed, or propose to commit, an offence on a weaker people who cannot speak for themselves, and I maintain that in the spending of millions of pounds for war in time of peace we are doing a great disservice to the Australian people.[25]

Blackburn was one of the only Australian parliamentarians to object publicly.[26] At this stage, the parliament was assured that no atomic warheads would be used at the rocket range. WILPF released a flyer called 'The Black and White of the Rocket Range' noting 'it is incompatible with the spirit of the United Nations Charter'.[27] Their joint protest, supported by anthropologists and other protest groups, succeeded in so far as having the patrol officer Walter MacDougall appointed at Woomera to oversee the treatment of Aboriginal communities.[28]

The Menzies Government won power in 1949 and sought to strengthen its ties to the British Government. Australia became involved in Cold War conflicts in Korea in 1950, which had a multinational character under the auspices of the UN, and the government believed that a partnership with Britain to help produce a nuclear deterrent would be in Australia's best interest.[29] In February 1952 the British and Australian governments announced their intention to test atomic weapons in Australia. The first of these trials, codenamed *Hurricane*, took place in the Monte Bello Islands off the coast of Western Australia. The second series of tests, called *Totem*, took place in 1953 on mainland Australia at a place called Emu Field, within the Woomera Rocket Range.[30]

---

24 Robert Menzies, 'Question, Guided Weapons, Speech', *CPD*, House of Representatives, 1 May 1947, 1834. See also Wilson, *Different White People*, 105.
25 Blackburn, 'Question, Guided Weapons, Speech', *CPD*, House of Representatives, 1 May 1947, 1845.
26 Wilson, *Different White People*, 104.
27 Thomson, 'The Black and White of the Rocket Range', Papers of A. Vroland Box 6/44 NLA.
28 WH Edwards, 'Duguid, Charles (1884–1986)', *Australian Dictionary of Biography* (ADB), National Centre of Biography, ANU, adb.anu.edu.au/biography/duguid-charles-12440/text22369, published first in hardcopy 2007, accessed online 8 April 2015.
29 Arnold and Smith, *Britain, Australia and the Bomb*, 21.
30 Arnold and Smith, *Britain, Australia and the Bomb*, 50.

Protest against atomic bomb testing in Australia.

It is likely that the images are of the 1952 demonstration for disarmament, and protest against the testing of atomic bombs in Australia, organised by the Women's International League for Peace and Freedom. The protest meeting was held in the Assembly Hall, 156 Collins Street, Melbourne, 18 March 1952, and the demonstration appears to be near the Shrine of Remembrance, Melbourne.

Source: Records of the Women's International League for Peace and Freedom, MS 9377 State Library of Victoria.

Upgrading the site from conventional weapons testing to nuclear testing horrified but did not surprise the women of WILPF, who had never believed the assurances that no nuclear testing would take place at the site. The Aboriginal communities in the affected area had already been traumatised by an outbreak of measles in Ernabella in 1948, the first time that disease had struck Central Australia. It killed between one-quarter and one-third of the Anangu population who had no immunity.[31] WILPF organised a public meeting on 18 March 1952 to express their outrage, with flyers stating 'Atom Bomb Test—How do YOU view this threat to Australia … Help us to make a protest to be remembered—Tomorrow will be too late'.[32] The meeting, chaired by Blackburn and held at the Assembly Hall on Collins St, began with messages of support from many prominent

---

31 Goodall, 'Colonialism and Catastrophe' in Darian-Smith and Hamilton, *Memory and History in Twentieth-Century Australia*, 62.
32 WILPF Atom Bomb Test meeting flyer, 18 March 1952, series III reel 54, WILPF Papers.

people including Duguid.[33] His statement focused on the impossibility of the government guarantee that the affected areas would be cleared, noting 'no body of men however large, will be able to clear it of men, women and children, not to speak of animals'.[34] Blackburn addressed the crowd and raised her previous objections expressed in parliament:

> Some of you will remember that in 1946 I took up in Federal Parliament the matter of the range for testing guided missiles. We were told there were to be no war-heads. All the time I believed this step would follow.[35]

There were many speakers, including university lecturers, church leaders and pacifists, but the talk that was most widely reported in the *Argus* after the event was by Indigenous woman Margaret Tucker.[36] Her intimate connection with the problems of interventionist government policy resonated with the crowd:

> My people will be the last to have faith in the Government's promises not to hurt any living thing. We have been promised so much … When I was a child my sister and I were taken from our mother. No-one will ever be able to convince my mother, or my sister or me that that terrible separation helped anyone. I know people say that our aboriginal people did not develop Australia. According to other peoples' way of thinking I suppose this is true, but I don't think aborigines ever did so much harm to the country as atomic warfare of civilised nations will do.[37]

A representative from the Woman's Christian Temperance Union (WCTU) proposed a recommendation, unanimously accepted by the audience, expressing 'disapproval of the use of the atom bomb anywhere'.[38] The meeting believed it to be:

---

33 Edwards, 'Duguid, Charles (1884–1986)', ADB.
34 'Report Public Meeting of Protest Against Atom Bomb Test', 18 March 1952, series III reel 54, WILPF Papers.
35 'Report Public Meeting of Protest Against Atom Bomb Test', 18 March 1952, series III reel 54, WILPF Papers.
36 '"Lilardia" is Angered by Bomb Plans', *The Argus*, 19 March 1952.
37 '"Lilardia" is Angered by Bomb Plans', *The Argus*, 19 March 1952.
38 'Report Public Meeting of Protest Against Atom Bomb Test', 18 March 1952, series III reel 54, WILPF Papers.

> against the best interests of the whole of the people of the Commonwealth, and one more betrayal of our responsibilities to guard human rights, especially the rights of aborigines [sic] who have no voice in the ordering of their own lives and who cannot defend themselves.[39]

The meeting also recognised the international implications of Australia renewing its dependence on the empire in the age of rising decolonisation. Amelia Lambrick, who in the 1920s was a fierce opponent of the White Australia Policy (WAP), once more called for an end to the discriminatory policy and Rev. James Stuckey characterised the issue as a 'major insult' to our 'Asiatic neighbours': 'Do we imagine that these threats and insults will go unnoticed and un-remembered? Asia watches Australia'.[40]

WILPF continued their advocacy on this issue throughout the 1950s. They sent a petition to be tabled in parliament in 1955 and maintained an extensive letter writing campaign to all members of parliament, asking them to consider the safety of the world.[41] In 1956 they extended their campaign by writing to the British Prime Minister, Anthony Eden, requesting that he cancel the planned tests in Australia and the hydrogen bomb tests in the Pacific. WILPF noted that they should approach the Australian Government first, but stated: 'we address ourselves to you directly, because … we believe the initiative came from your Government, to which the Australian Government is so closely linked in matters of defence and foreign policy'.[42] WILPF only received a reply from the Office of the High Commissioner directed from Eden confirming that the UK was committed to the testing of nuclear weapons because they were 'the most powerful deterrent to war that exists in the world at the present time'. The letter included a statement from Eden, noting:

---

39 'Report Public Meeting of Protest Against Atom Bomb Test', 18 March 1952, series III reel 54, WILPF Papers.
40 Rev JM Stuckey, 'Report Public Meeting of Protest Against Atom Bomb Test', 18 March 1952, series III reel 54, WILPF Papers.
41 Mr Pollard, 'Atomic Weapons, Petition, Procedural Text', *CPD*, House of Representatives, 19 October 1955, 1659. See also WILPF Australia to all Members of Parliament, 'Those who use the sword—or the atom bomb—may well perish by the sword—or the atom bomb', 8 March 1952, series III reel 54, WILPF Papers.
42 WILPF Australia to UK PM Anthony Eden, 12 July 1956, series III reel 55, WILPF Papers.

the conviction that the radiation dose to human beings arising from the testing of megaton weapons at the present rate was insignificant compared with the radiation dose received from natural causes.[43]

WILPF International did not accept these types of arguments. In 1954 Japanese fishermen on *Daigo Fukuryū Maru (Lucky Dragon 5)* were contaminated by fallout from US nuclear testing at Bikini Atoll in the Marshall Islands, and one of the crew died of radiation poisoning that September. Immediately after this incident the Japanese section of WILPF helped with a mass petition drive, the 'Sugunami Appeal' led by 'housewives' calling for a 'ban on the A-bomb and H-bomb.'[44] The 'Lucky Dragon' incident was widely reported on in Australia and strengthened the case for caution.[45] In 1955 the WILPF International executive called on national sections to continue to prioritise mobilising public opinion against nuclear weapons, and at the 1956 congress it was the major topic of conversation.[46] The Australian section printed a pamphlet, originally written by the Swiss section, called *The Hydrogen Bomb: The World In Danger*, which used the example of the 'Lucky Dragon' incident to show the dangers of testing.[47] It described the health of the men 'whose state bears resemblance to those affected by the Hiroshima bombs, half of whom died', and detailed the fears WILPF had of food contamination, especially in the fishing industry.

Despite the protest, the Australian Government approved the Maralinga range as a permanent testing site in 1955. By 1957, however, Gallup polls showed public opinion was turning against the government's decision, with the majority against the testing in Australia.[48] In 1967 the agreement between Britain and Australia ended, and Australia was left to deal with radioactive contamination and fallout at the test sites. WILPF may not have successfully halted the testing at the time, but their sustained protests

---

43 WI McIndoe, Office of the High Commissioner for the UK in Canberra, to WILPF Au, 1 August 1956, series III reel 55, WILPF Papers.
44 Lawrence S Wittner, *The Struggle Against the Bomb* (Stanford, California: Stanford University Press, 1993), 8. See also Vera Mackie, 'Radical Objects: Origami and the Anti-Nuclear Movement', *History Workshop Online*, 3 August 2015, accessed 29 November 2022.
45 For example see: 'Luckless Crew of Lucky Dragon Saw "Something Larger than the Sun"', *The Argus*, 7 August 1954.
46 Wittner, *The Struggle Against the Bomb*, 4. See also '13th International Congress of WILPF', 1956 Birmingham England, accessed through database edited by Kathryn Kish Sklar and Thomas Dublin, *Women and Social Movements, International—1840 to Present*, 81.
47 *The Hydrogen Bomb: The World in Danger*, WILPF Australia section, 1955, accessed NLA.
48 In 1952, Gallup Poll showed 58 per cent in favour with 29 per cent opposed, by 1957 only 37 per cent were in favour, and 49 per cent opposed the testing. Arnold and Smith, *Britain, Australia and the Bomb*, 236.

kept the issue in the public arena and made the government constantly justify decisions that they would have preferred, and tried very hard, to keep quiet. In 1985 the government appointed the royal commission into British Nuclear Testing in Australia.[49] It found that the first atomic test on mainland soil in 1953 was ordered against meteorological advice that the plume of radioactive smoke would not disperse because of the strength of the wind, allowing the cloud to pass directly over known Indigenous communities of Mintabie, Wallatina and Welbourne Hill.[50] Eventually the Australian Government agreed to pay $13.5 million in compensation.[51]

WILPF and communism

Cold War tensions not only played out in the testing of weapons and in the willingness to cooperate with Britain. Throughout the 1950s, the contentious issue of communism dominated the political landscape, and protest groups had to determine how to engage with this political struggle. The persecution and suspicion around alleged communist activities set limits on the activities of progressive and pacifist movements. WILPF had been concerned by the potential for communist infiltration of their organisation internationally for some time and had restructured their constitution in the interwar period to allow national sections with different sympathies to continue working together.[52]

The 'not infrequent accusation that it was a "communist" organisation' was a problem for WILPF, having to deny allegations that it was linked with Comintern.[53] WILPF strongly rejected any link, and clarified that their only connection with Russia was through lobbying letters sent to delegations in Geneva, which were ignored.[54] This strenuous denial set the tone for

---

49 For discussion of the royal commission and impacts of the testing on Indigenous communities, see Wilson, *Different White People*, 180.
50 Goodall, 'Colonialism and Catastrophe' in Darian-Smith and Hamilton, *Memory and History in Twentieth-Century Australia*, 55.
51 Jan Palmowski, 'Woomera Rocket Range—Oxford Reference', *A Dictionary of Contemporary World History*, 3rd ed., online version (Oxford: Oxford University Press, 2008).
52 Sheepshanks to Moore, 16 July 1929, series III reel 54, WILPF Papers.
53 Bussey and Tims, *Pioneers for Peace*, 79.
54 Bussey and Tims, *Pioneers for Peace*, 79. In 1962 the US WILPF section hosted Soviet women at an informal conference to 'discuss methods of alleviating the acute tensions between our two countries'. However, despite feeling the meeting was able to 'differ without hostility', the press and establishment ignored the conference and the joint statement produced, and the meeting contributed to the assumption that WILPF was connected to communist activities. Agnes Meyer, 'Soviet and American Women Meet', *The Peacemaker* (reprinted from *Four Lights*) 24, no. 3 (March 1962): 1.

future responses to allegations of communist sympathies as WILPF wanted to maintain its non-party political 'neutral' stance. They were motivated in this course of action by their desire to keep together fracturing sections. In Germany in the early 1950s the WILPF branch split into two opposing segments, each claiming to be the official representative of WILPF in Germany.[55] These responses led WILPF to stop focusing on economic arguments in debates on disarmament, and they shied away from using and critiquing terms such as 'capitalism'.[56]

When Eleanor Moore led the Australian section, she shared the desire to distance the section from communist influences because she felt its promoters wanted to 'capture' pacifist groups for their own ends.[57] However in 1951, after Moore's death, the Australian section had to declare a public position on the Communist Party Dissolution Act and referendum which Prime Minister Robert Menzies made a significant political issue. This meant that while WILPF still asserted they were not affiliated with communism, they were obliged to campaign in favour of the Communist Party of Australia (CPA) when civil liberties and the concept of freedom of association were under attack. To Menzies and his supporters, communism was a dire threat to Australian democracy as CPA members were disloyal to the nation and aligning themselves instead with Moscow. He attempted to capitalise on the fear, prevalent in the community, to push for the party's suppression.[58] The Dissolution Act which passed parliament in 1950 declared the Communist Party to be illegal and had provisions that allowed the government to target 'bodies that supported or advocated communism, were affiliated with the Party, or whose policies were substantially shaped by members of the Party'.[59] These wide-ranging provisions were a threat to civil liberties, which is why the leader of the opposition, HV Evatt, argued against them despite being an avowed anti-communist.[60]

---

55 Catia Cecilia Confortini, *Intelligent Compassion: The Women's International League for Peace and Freedom and Feminist Peace* (Oxford: Oxford University Press, 2012), 38, doi.org/10.1093/acprof:oso/9780199845231.001.0001.
56 Confortini, *Intelligent Compassion*, 38.
57 Moore, *The Quest for Peace*, 118.
58 George Williams, 'Communist Party Case 1951', in *The Oxford Companion to the High Court of Australia*, ed. Michael Coper, Tony Blackshield and George Williams, 1st ed. (Oxford: Oxford University Press, 2001), 122.
59 Williams, 'Communist Party Case 1951', 122.
60 Williams, 'Communist Party Case 1951', 122.

WILPF also saw the legislation and the referendum as an attack on their freedom and joined the 'no' vote campaign in the referendum. They saw how its passing could affect their ability to organise, stating: '"Peace" work in Australia is very difficult and, I fear, will be more so, if the proposals in the forthcoming Referendum are carried.'[61] They acknowledged that the principle was too important to ignore and campaigned against the referendum despite the potential for being labelled as communist. In a pamphlet produced in September 1951, WILPF urged the public to 'MAINTAIN FREEDOM! Vote NO!'.[62] Clearly distancing themselves from being a 'communist front', they focused on how the referendum was 'complicated and confusing' and gave the government powers to 'label as "communist" any person or group who opposes the present drive to war'.[63] They campaigned on the idea that 'we are aware of the need to "cleanse and strengthen our political life" but this can be achieved only by free and intelligent citizens, not by police state methods.'[64] WILPF members were relieved when the referendum failed.

As most of the peace organisations in Australia were portrayed as 'communist front' organisations, many people were reluctant to associate with them, which only helped to keep the membership of WILPF and other organisations small during the Cold War years.[65] Histories of the 1950s peace movement often focus on the distraction caused by communist fears but WILPF women were nevertheless also working on serious campaign issues. WILPF decided to focus its activism on issues of disarmament, anti-conscription and Aboriginal rights, rather than heavily participating in the Australian Peace Council (APC), which prioritised the 'Stockholm Appeal' made at the World Peace Council meeting in March 1950.[66] Jessie Street and Faith Bandler were members of the APC, which they knew was seen as a 'dangerous Red organisation' by the Menzies Government.[67] WILPF

---

61 Helen Strong to Robinson WILPF Geneva, 12 September 1951, series III reel 54, WILPF Papers.
62 'Maintain Freedom! Vote No', WILPF Flyer, September 1951, Papers of Vivienne Abraham Box 64/8/2, NLA.
63 'Maintain Freedom! Vote No', WILPF Flyer, September 1951, Papers of Vivienne Abraham Box 64/8/2, NLA.
64 'Maintain Freedom! Vote No', WILPF Flyer, September 1951, Papers of Vivienne Abraham Box 64/8/2, NLA.
65 Barbara Carter, 'The Peace Movement in the 1950s', in *Better Dead Than Red: Australia's First Cold War, 1945–1953 Volume 2*, ed. Ann Curthoys and John Merritt (Sydney: George Allen & Unwin, 1984), 60.
66 The Stockholm Appeal made by the World Peace Council called for an absolute ban on all nuclear weapons, and societies affiliated to the WPC used it to campaign and collected signatures. Curthoys and Merritt, *Better Dead Than Red*, 61.
67 Marilyn Lake, *Faith: Faith Bandler, Gentle Activist* (NSW: Allen & Unwin, 2002), 33.

6. THE COLD WAR AND NUCLEAR DISARMAMENT

internationally did not support the Stockholm Appeal because of its communist influences and the difficulty it gave to their own legitimacy as a peace organisation.[68] However, WILPF members in Australia participated in the 1959 Melbourne Peace Congress organised by the APC, bringing the organisation to the attention of ASIO.

ASIO was established in 1949 in response to a US ban on passing intelligence to Australia on the grounds of lax security. It sought to improve the government's capacity to gather information about Soviet intelligence officers conducting espionage in Australia.[69] But it quickly extended its activities. Using covert surveillance and methods of infiltration, ASIO created comprehensive files on individual members of the CPA or those connected to 'communist front' organisations. A file on Vroland in the National Archives shows the level of scrutiny she was under. A 1959 report showed that WILPF was under surveillance, but was seen as a 'legitimate international pacifist organisation for women' that came 'into contact with communist "front" organisations'.[70] The report noted that 'there is nothing to suggest that the WLPF in Australia is under Communist control'. Nevertheless, they were still watched because 'some of its members are known to be Communist Party of Australia members or sympathisers'.[71] Vroland came to ASIO's notice specifically because of her association with WILPF. It was presumably the international nature of the organisation that kept WILPF under suspicion as well as an awareness of communist efforts to use the peace movement to advance its goals. ASIO kept notes on all their international travel, writing lists of each country the women visited.[72] It was noted that Vroland was 'interested in the Communist Party in the 1930s', but had 'never been chosen as a delegate to anything.'[73] By 1961,

---

68 Bussey and Tims, *Pioneers for Peace*, 196.
69 David Horner, *The Spy Catchers, Volume I: The Official History of ASIO, 1949–1963* (Crows Nest, NSW: Allen & Unwin, 2014), 1.
70 ASIO letter 13 January 1959, 'VROLAND Anna 1939-1970', National Archives of Australia (NAA): A6119, 2419.
71 ASIO letter 13 January 1959, 'VROLAND Anna 1939-1970', NAA: A6119, 2419.
72 Vroland file 21 March 1963, – 'Anna Vroland is now back in Australia after attending the WILPF conference in San Francisco USA. She then toured Canada, Europe and Asia.' ASIO file VROLAND Anna 1939-1970, NAA. In the US, WILPF similarly was not cited as a 'communist front' organisation, yet they were continually harassed by agencies such as the FBI because of their anti-war activities. See Helen Laville, *Cold War Women: The International Activities of American Women's Organisations* (Manchester, New York: Manchester University Press, Distributed in the USA by Palgrave, 2002), 131.
73 Report no. 1226 'Anna Fellows Vroland', 16 June 1959, ASIO file VROLAND Anna 1939-1970, NAA: A6119, 2419.

however, suspicions of communist sympathies related to her work with WILPF caused a scandal for her teaching career and she was dismissed from her employment.[74]

While WILPF remained vigilant about presenting a 'neutral' position and distancing themselves from communist activity, many members of the organisation felt that it needed to produce a definitive statement of their position. At 88 years old, Amelia Lambrick was a veteran WILPF member. In a letter to the Geneva headquarters she asked: 'what is to be our attitude towards communism?'[75] She was concerned that in an effort to remain neutral amidst the controversy, WILPF was failing to engage with an important debate about US world dominance. Lambrick wanted a statement on something 'deeper and wider than these [the CPA or Cominform] restricted groups'; she wanted the 'official attitude of the WILPF towards the spiritual concept of communism'.[76] Lambrick believed that if the US expanded its military presence in Asia from Korea to China, 'the whole of Asia will be behind China' and Australia would be forced to consider how to engage. This raised questions of racial inequality. Lambrick insisted that what was needed was to understand each other better, not to make restrictive decisions on the grounds of race, noting: 'We have insisted on our superiority in such a way that we have made ourselves ridiculous'.[77] She believed that blindly following the US on the grounds of race would be detrimental to Australia, as Australia did not realise 'how much the USA is hated in Asia.' Dismayed that the US blocked the People's Republic of China's entry to the Security Council of the UN, she saw the rise of communism in Asia as an extreme response to injustice and the unequal distribution of wealth. In proposing WILPF participate in this debate, Lambrick was insisting WILPF consider why communism was gaining such traction across the world and why capitalist nations so feared it.

---

74 Sitarani Kerin and Andrew Spaull, 'Vroland, Anna Fellowes (1902–1978)', ADB, National Centre of Biography, Australian National University, adb.anu.edu.au/biography/vroland-anna-fellowes-12108/text21371, published first in hardcopy 2002, accessed online 4 February 2022.
75 Lambrick to Baer, 'What is to be Our Attitude Towards Communism?', 19 June 1952, series III reel 54, WILPF Papers. For more information on Lambrick, see: Amanda Rasmussen, 'Lambrick, Amelia (1864–1956)', ADB, National Centre of Biography, ANU, adb.anu.edu.au/biography/lambrick-amelia-13038/text23575, published first in hardcopy 2005, accessed online 9 April 2015.
76 Lambrick to Baer, 'What is to be Our Attitude Towards Communism?', 19 June 1952, series III reel 54, WILPF Papers.
77 Lambrick to Baer, 'What is to be Our Attitude Towards Communism?', 19 June 1952, series III reel 54, WILPF Papers.

The WILPF International executive took this seriously and discussed Lambrick's letter at the executive meeting in Geneva in 1952. They agreed with its sentiment and understood the importance of better understanding the attraction of communism but felt that as 'the word implies so many different things for so many different people' it was difficult to even know 'exactly what we mean'.[78] A motion was put that WILPF write a public statement about communism, but it failed 9 votes to 13. It was generally agreed that more harm than good would come of a statement, and they resolved instead to continue to watch 'whether ANY government violated the Charter of Human Rights.'[79] The executive decided 'it would be advisable if the WILPF refrained from comments on communism in all written statements'. Nonetheless, Dr Bussey, on the international executive, maintained that members should be free to criticise both 'Russian Communism and American Capitalism impartially.'[80] WILPF members travelled and gathered information about Russia and China during these years to 'get as complete a picture as possible'. Among them were members of the British section, including Agnes Stapledon, who travelled on a Peace Delegation to Russia in 1952. That same year, Danish member Madame Zeuthen visited China.[81]

As the decade progressed, the Australian section of WILPF became more concerned about 'communist infiltration'. In 1945 WIDF formed and its presence divided women's international organisations into rival camps, drawing them into Cold War divisions. WIDF was primarily anti-fascist and widely considered a 'communist front'.[82] Members of international women's organisations were often fiercely loyal. Even those who were members of multiple groups often had one with which they most strongly identified.[83]

---

78 Resolutions adopted at the meeting of the International Executive Committee of WILPF in Geneva 6–11 August 1952, series I reel 12, WILPF Papers.
79 Resolutions adopted at the meeting of the International Executive Committee of WILPF in Geneva 6–11 August 1952, series I reel 12, WILPF Papers.
80 Resolutions adopted at the meeting of the International Executive Committee of WILPF in Geneva 6–11 August 1952, series I reel 12, WILPF Papers.
81 Stapledon, discussing Lambrick's letter at the exec meeting to Vroland, 26 August 1952, series III reel 54, WILPF Papers. Bussey and Tims, *Pioneers for Peace*, 216.
82 Leila J Rupp, *Worlds of Women: The Making of an International Women's Movement* (Princeton: Princeton University Press, 1997), 47, doi.org/10.1515/9780691221816.
83 Rupp, *Worlds of Women*, 44.

These loyalties meant that international women interacted but remained guarded and sceptical of the workings of one another. WILPF members were not impressed with the women of WIDF, whom they saw as uncritical of communism, stating:

> It was difficult, and sometimes painful, to cast doubts on expressions of solidarity in the cause of peace, freedom and democracy that claimed a mass following in the Eastern-bloc countries and sought to extend this following to the West; but impossible not to do so when these expressions were so at variance with the real conditions of life behind the Iron Curtain and so lacking in criticism of provocative actions by Communist governments.[84]

A major divide between the organisations was in their willingness to support violent decolonisation struggles. While WILPF sympathised with the oppression experienced, they could not support violent tactics as WIDF were willing to do.[85] WIDF were in turn critical of the older women's organisations like WILPF and the International Alliance of Women (IAW) for being too aligned with the 'West' and the status quo of US dominance. WIDF were given consultative status B to the UN before the others, and attempted to block WILPF and the IAW on the charge that they were 'reactionary and pro-Fascist'.[86] Nevertheless, when WIDF had their consultative status revoked by the UN because of Cold War tensions in the General Assembly, WILPF and Gertrud Baer strongly protested on their behalf, appalled at the undemocratic way the issue was handled.

Some sections of WILPF, anxious for cooperation with women in communist countries, believed that they should work closely with WIDF on the international stage. Other sections advocated absolute disassociation. The Australian section experienced a similar tension. In 1952, when Blackburn travelled to Europe on WILPF business, she met with Nancy Wilkinson, an Australian woman from Perth. Wilkinson was in London attending the Friends World Conference, the third international conference of the Quaker organisation, and met several WILPF women at a satellite meeting. She wrote that she was 'impressed with what they were doing', and in discussion with Blackburn 'agreed to gather some interested women

---

84 Bussey and Tims, *Pioneers for Peace*, 197.
85 Katharine McGregor, 'Opposing Colonialism: The Women's International Democratic Federation and Decolonisation Struggles in Vietnam and Algeria 1945–1965', *Women's History Review* 25, no. 6 (1 November 2016): 925–44, doi.org/10.1080/09612025.2015.1083246.
86 Bussey and Tims, *Pioneers for Peace*, 197.

in Perth to meet Doris on her way back to Melbourne.'[87] The Perth branch was then reformed and the organisation began once more to grow in membership. In 1954 the Women's Peace Crusade of Adelaide decided to reconstitute itself as the South Australian branch of WILPF, claiming to be 'proud to become members of such a famous international family'.[88] That same year, a veteran member of the Perth branch, Miss Glasson, who was involved before its dissolution and again after its reformation, corresponded with Vroland about some misinformation regarding the WILPF and WIDF. She claimed to have read in a circular sent by Wilkinson, then heard Blackburn mention on the radio, that the Australian WILPF had affiliated with WIDF.[89] Miss Glasson was shocked by this and wrote: 'you can imagine my horror when I distinctly heard Mrs B make the above statement my first reaction was "so they have captured the old WIL"'.[90] Vroland was quick to reply and to try to gather some proof of the incident. She noted that WILPF 'showed no sign of having changed its principles' and despite the confusion the two remained separate. Assurance that the information was wrong was very welcome to Glasson, who referred to Moore's memory:

> I hope that as far as the Australian branch is concerned there will be no fraternisation whatever—I am sure dear Eleanor Moore would turn in her grave if there were to be.[91]

In September 1955 Vroland and Blackburn travelled to Adelaide to meet with the new section. Mary Broun from the Perth branch also joined them. Broun was 'shocked at the control that the communists had in the Adelaide branch' and wrote personally to Baer in Geneva to share her concern that the 'communist front organisations have decided that they need the prestige that the WIL can give to their movements'.[92] Blackburn, she reported, seemed 'content with the new trend of all peace movements in together' but she, Broun, and her colleague Vroland were concerned about this direction and wanted to 'save' the league. Noting that 'we are dealing with people who are taught to disregard the truth, and to learn the answers to questions which serve the party policy', Broun's letter clearly articulated her anxiety about communists and sought advice on how to extract WILPF from

---

87 Nancy Wilkinson quoted in Heather Williams, *Women and Peace: WILPF an Australian Profile* (WILPF AU 1982), 9.
88 Phyilis Powell to Vroland, 13 July 1954, Box 1722, Papers, WILPF, MS 9377, SLV.
89 Vroland to Glasson, 11 January 1954, Box 1722, Papers, WILPF, MS 9377, SLV.
90 Glasson to Vroland, 16 January 1954, Box 1722, Papers, WILPF, MS 9377, SLV.
91 Glasson to Vroland, 16 January 1954, Box 1722, Papers, WILPF, MS 9377, SLV.
92 Broun to Baer, 10 October 1955, series III reel 55, WILPF Papers.

their influence.⁹³ WILPF members were therefore not immune from the immense difficulties for peace activism in the Cold War era. They reinforced anxieties about communist affiliations by trying to shield themselves from association.

The Sydney branch and interstate conferencing

Taking over the administrative duties of the Geneva office from Gertrud Baer was a woman named Agnes Stapledon, International Vice-Chairman, who is often referred to in the history of WILPF as British. Yet, though married to Olaf Stapledon, a British pacifist and science fiction writer, she had a deeper connection with Australia that was obscured by her marriage. In fact, her youth was spent in Australia where she grew up as Agnes Miller in Sydney.⁹⁴ Correspondence during her administrative tenure often showed signs of a special kinship with Australian women though she had never met them:

> I am an old Australian myself you know, from Sydney, and it is nice to get greetings from Australia. It helps to link the present with my childhood which sometimes seems so far away as to not belong to me!⁹⁵

By the late 1950s Margaret Holmes from Mosman in Sydney became interested in peace activism and joined several peace and justice organisations.⁹⁶ A mother of six, Holmes was in her middle years when her interest in peace activism intensified. By then her children were older and she had time to commit to travel. Learning about WILPF through the journal of the Federal Pacifist Council of Australia, *The Peacemaker*, edited by WILPF member Vivienne Abraham, Holmes joined as an international member and planned a six-month journey to Europe to attend the 1959 Stockholm WILPF congress.⁹⁷ In 1954 Holmes had met with the pacifist Professor Kathleen Lonsdale, president of the British WILPF,

---

93   Broun to Baer, 10 October 1955, series III reel 55, WILPF Papers.
94   For more on Stapledon, see Robert Crossley, *Talking Across the World: The Love Letters of Olaf Stapledon and Agnes Miller, 1913–1919* (Hanover, NH: University Press of New England, 1987).
95   Stapledon to Janet Strong, 3 December 1952, series III reel 54, WILPF Papers.
96   Michelle Cavanagh, *Margaret Holmes: The Life and Times of an Australian Peace Campaigner* (Sydney: New Holland, 2006), 157.
97   Cavanagh, *Margaret Holmes*, 160. For more about *Peacemaker* and Vivienne Abrahams, who was a member of WILPF, see Bobbie Oliver, '*The Peacemaker*'s role in the Anti-Vietnam War Movement', in *Fighting Against War: Peace Activism in the Twentieth Century*, ed. Phillip Deery and Julie Kimber (Albert Park, Vic: Leftbank Press, 2015), 246.

when she visited Australia. It was Lonsdale who first alerted her to WILPF's international work. Holmes was given accreditation to be an 'official observer' and later an alternate delegate of the Australian branch at the 1959 congress. She attended alongside Nancy Wilkinson, president of the Western Australia branch, who acted as the official delegate.[98] Wilkinson gave a speech at the conference discussing the work of the Australian branch and promoting the campaign for justice for Australian Indigenous people. As a member of the Australian Labor Party (ALP), Wilkinson also raised the importance of working within the system and engaging with political parties as a way to achieve peace, accepting that 'peaceworkers are generally reticent to go into politics'. She implored WILPF women to 'take that risk', as 'continuous involvement at the highest level is the only level where total wars can be prevented.'[99]

After the WILPF conference both Holmes and Wilkinson went to the Conference of the International Fellowship of Reconciliation in Austria before returning to Australia. For Holmes this capped off a long journey which included visits to Geneva, the USA, England, France, Germany, Russia, India and China.[100] Holmes' visit to Russia, despite the Australian travel ban that she overcame by applying for the visa in the UK, brought her to the attention of ASIO early in her pacifist activism. Most places she visited included meetings with WILPF women. While in New York she observed sessions of the UN and in London she attended lectures and absorbed campaign strategies from the WILPF women. She stayed in the home of Agnes Stapledon whom she announced the section should 'claim as an Australian'.[101] The travel and opportunity to meet internationalist women had a profound effect on her and she stated when interviewed: 'well, I got so excited and impressed by this marvellous collection of women, I thought "This is what I've been waiting for all my life"'.[102]

Once Holmes returned she was motivated to start building a Sydney branch by the many WILPF women she had met while overseas. Prior to planning her travel in 1959, Holmes met with Vroland in Sydney where they discussed the prospect of inaugurating a Sydney branch. Holmes was drawn to the

---

98 Wilkinson to Vroland, 12 August 1959, Box 1722/25, Papers, WILPF, MS 9377, SLV.
99 Wilkinson, 'Open air meeting—Stockholm 28 July 1959', series III reel 55, WILPF Papers. Wilkinson's husband, Laurie Wilkinson was an ALP senator for Western Australia in 1966–74.
100 Holmes to Tapper, 13 April 1959, series III reel 55, WILPF Papers.
101 Holmes to Hilda Vroland, 8 July 1959, Box 1722/25, Papers, WILPF, MS 9377, SLV.
102 Siobhan McHugh, *Minefields and Miniskirts: Australian Women and the Vietnam War* (Sydney: Doubleday, 1993), 203.

organisation because of WILPF's neutral position in the Cold War discourse, noting that she felt the World Peace Council had the 'reputation of being communist controlled' and she wanted to offer hesitant women 'another, and possibly less militant and more truly peacemaking, organisation and such we believe the WIL to be.'[103]

Gertrud Baer supported Holmes' recruitment attempts, replying; 'we are CERTAINLY NOT COMMUNIST CONTROLLED! I do hope that the material of forty-three years work will convince possible members of that fact.'[104] Holmes was keen to keep the organisation free from suspicions of communism. Even ASIO's reports on Holmes' 'subversive activities' showed the extent to which she was intent on keeping the communist agenda out of WILPF and guarded its non-party affiliation: 'HOLMES is not a member of the CPA, but is very active in the Mosman Peace Group. She is endeavouring to prevent this group becoming a left wing organisation.'[105] The organising practices of communist-controlled groups, which followed centrally dictated lines, were inimical to the philosophy of WILPF. It laid great emphasis on the exercise of individual conscience and sought consensus and cooperation.

In February 1960, Holmes convened a gathering for interested women to meet Blackburn and Miller.[106] They encouraged the women to form a branch and gave them all the information they needed about how to proceed and where they would fit in the national and international structure. The first official Sydney branch meeting occurred on 9 March 1960 at Holmes' house on Military Road in Mosman.[107] Reflecting the non-hierarchical feminist principles of organising which sought to avoid the dominant male forms of politics, the branch decided 'that there should be no vote taken at meetings, but to try for full agreement'. If no agreement could be reached then the proposition should be reframed.[108] The branch meeting also discussed other working examples to model themselves on: 'the British

---

103 Holmes to Baer WILPF Geneva, 20 February 1959, series III reel 55, WILPF Papers.
104 Baer to Holmes, 6 March 1959, series III reel 55, WILPF Papers.
105 Holmes ASIO file volume 1, NAA: A6119, 3362, 25.
106 Annual Report 1961–62, MLMSS 5395/Box 01, State Library of New South Wales (SLNSW). See also Margaret Holmes and Elspeth Christiansen, 'History of WILPF and Activities of NSW Branch', 1990, MLMSS 5395/Box 01, SLNSW.
107 Minutes of the first Sydney branch meeting, 9 March 1960, minute book, MLMSS 5395/Box 01, SLNSW.
108 Minutes of the first Sydney branch meeting, 9 March 1960, minute book, MLMSS 5395/Box 01, SLNSW. See Amy Swerdlow, 'Motherhood and the Subversion of the Military State', in *Women, Militarism, and War: Essays in History, Politics, and Social Theory*, ed. Jean Bethke Elshtain and Sheila Tobias (Totowa, NJ: Rowman & Littlefield, 1988), 3.

section is well informed before writing any letters of support or protest. We should restrain ourselves from such until we have more time to work out details.'[109] Following their example the branch appointed a 'Hansard reader' to keep abreast of issues and perspectives discussed in parliament.[110] Holmes recorded in a history of the branch written in 1990 that within the first year the branch membership grew to 40.[111]

By 1962 there were active WILPF groups in Adelaide, Melbourne, Sydney and Perth. Though the Tasmanian branch had disbanded in 1942, active international members such as Dr Edith Emery remained in contact with other branches. The Tasmanian branch reformed in 1963, as did a branch in Queensland.[112] With women such as Wilkinson, Margery Bowen and Irene Greenwood in the WA branch it became very active, publishing a monthly journal *Peace and Freedom* that was edited by Evelyn Rowland and Greenwood. It became the mouthpiece of the Australian section.[113] Vroland continued to write updates on 'Political Trends in Australia' for *Pax Et Libertas*, the international WILPF paper.[114] Increased activity in disparate locations prompted the branches to turn their energy towards federating the section. Blackburn helped form a provisional committee in 1956 to look at federating, even suggesting two separate east and west branches to accommodate the vast distances needed to travel. WA, however, did not support this suggestion.[115] An Australian constitution was written up and accepted which stated that a national conference was needed to appoint office bearers and executive members.[116] By the 1960s, momentum had at last gathered for WILPF Australia to institute formal section structures. Wishing to federate the branches at a face-to-face meeting the NSW branch organised an interstate conference for 1962, after the international triennial congress held in California.

---

109 Minutes of the first Sydney branch meeting, 9 March 1960, minute book, MLMSS 5395/Box 01, SLNSW.
110 Annual report WILPF NSW 1963–64, MLMSS 5395/Box 01 SLNSW.
111 Holmes and Christiansen, 'History of WILPF and Activities of NSW Branch', 1990, MLMSS 5395/Box 01, SLNSW.
112 See Williams, *Women and Peace;* and Linley Grant et al., *Prevailing for Peace: The History of the WILPF Tasmanian Branch 1920–2013* (North Hobart: WILPF, 2015).
113 *Peace and Freedom*, journal published by WILPF, 1956–present, accessed NLA.
114 Vroland, 'Political Trends in Australia', *Pax Et Libertas* 28, no. 3 (July–September 1963): 10. Accessed at NLA.
115 Blackburn to WILPF international executive, April 1958, series III reel 55, WILPF Papers.
116 Provisional Australian section constitution, as adopted at meeting of the provisional executive committee 16 May 1959, agreed to by majority discussion at meeting of representatives of South Australia, West Australia and Victoria, series III reel 55, WILPF Papers.

Mrs Irene Greenwood, President Peace and Freedom League, Morgan Street, Shenton Park, presents Mrs Pandit with a basket of Western Australian wildflowers.
Source: Image courtesy of the National Archives of Australia. NAA: A1501, A6529/20. See Appendix for a short biography of Irene Greenwood.

The Australian section sent invitations to the international executive suggesting that 'some of the delegates to next year's Congress in California [could] continue or divert their journey to Sydney, New South Wales, before they return home.'[117] Vroland, Jan Symons and Mary Howie were all Australian delegates attending the Californian conference. The west coast of the US was chosen specifically to make it easier for women from the Pacific region to attend, with six women from Japan, three from India, three from Australia and one from New Zealand being able to make the journey.[118] The international congress accepted two new sections, one in Nigeria—

---

117 Hilda Vroland to members of the International Executive, 17 July 1962, series III reel 55, WILPF Papers.
118 Else Zeuthen, 'Women Meet in Sydney', *The Peacemaker* 24 (September–October 1962), 3.

the first African nation to join and the other from Lebanon, the first Arab section.[119] Vroland, in her national section report on Australia, invited any international WILPF member to attend the planned Sydney meeting.[120] Accepting the invitation were Else Zeuthen from Denmark, International Chairman of WILPF, and Stapledon from Britain, international vice-president. Dr Muriel Lloyd Prichard from Auckland University, a senior lecturer in economics, travelled from New Zealand to play a prominent role in the gathering which included women from NSW, WA, SA, Victoria, ACT and Queensland.[121] Baer intended to travel but was prevented at the last minute.

The conference was held at the Women's College at the University of Sydney in August and the Lord Mayor of Sydney, Henry Jensen, welcomed international and interstate visitors at a reception.[122] Blackburn chaired and Dr Prichard addressed the audience about the economy of armaments and the need for centralised planning to avoid mass unemployment after total disarmament. Labor MP Tom Uren spoke of the ALP's position opposing nuclear testing.[123] *The Peacemaker* reported on the gathering, summarising Zeuthen's address to the 100-strong audience about the political aspects of disarmament, where she acknowledged the difficulties of convincing the US and the USSR to total disarmament when they were so distrustful of each other's intentions. She noted that 'disarmament would mean the abandonment of the old power order which would have to be replaced with some new order. This could be the slow development of the UN into a world government'.[124] Zeuthen had a sobering message for the people of the region, noting how 'she had got the impression that some people thought that Australia and New Zealand would not be affected if a war broke out'.[125] Referring to the science fiction novel *On the Beach*, published in 1957 by Australian author Nevil Shute, which described a nuclear war

---

119 '15th International Congress of WILPF report', California 1962, Sklar and Dublin, eds, *Women and Social Movements*, 8.
120 '15th International Congress of WILPF report', California 1962, Sklar and Dublin, eds, *Women and Social Movements*, 8.
121 'Women Meet in Sydney', *The Peacemaker* 24 (September–October 1962), 3. More information about Dr Prichard found in *The University of Auckland Calendar 1961*, 25. Accessed 12 September 2016, cdn.auckland.ac.nz/assets/calendar/archive/1961-calendar.pdf.
122 'Women Meet in Sydney', *The Peacemaker* 24 (September–October 1962), 3. Information on 'Henry Jensen', accessed 16 May 2017, www.sydneyaldermen.com.au/alderman/henry-jensen/.
123 'Women Meet in Sydney', *The Peacemaker* 24 (September–October 1962), 3.
124 'Women Meet in Sydney', *The Peacemaker* 24 (September–October 1962), 3. Zeuthen received other media in the mainstream press, see: 'Nuclear Test Ban "Solution for Peace"', *The Canberra Times*, 22 August 1962.
125 'Women Meet in Sydney', *The Peacemaker* 24 (September–October 1962), 3.

in the northern hemisphere and the gradual contamination of Australia by radiation and nuclear fallout, she mentioned that WILPF UK member and scientist Kathleen Lonsdale had read the manuscript before publication and confirmed that 'the story was scientifically possible'.[126] Stating this possibility reiterated to the section the urgency required in campaigning against nuclear warfare and forced consideration of how Australia would be affected by a nuclear conflict. The tyranny of distance which had for so long plagued and protected Australians offered little comfort in the atomic age.

The conference elected Elspeth Christiansen as president of the Australian section, Holmes as secretary, and Gladys Armstrong as treasurer, effectively moving control of the section away from Melbourne towards Sydney, where all three lived. Holmes observed how the conference motivated WILPF: 'all branches report increased enthusiasm following on the conference, and here in Sydney several new sub branches are about to form.'[127] With tighter networks in place, stronger communication with the international headquarters, institutionalised frameworks for organising, and energised members, the WILPF branches were ready to engage with the serious international issues about to captivate the world's attention.

French nuclear testing in the Pacific

At the 1962 California congress, Baer gave a presentation about the 'extraordinary' progress of the world in the three years since 1959. She pointed out that at least 20 new states had gained independence and were admitted to the UN, as well as drawing attention to the many advancements in technology that proved that 'man *can* conquer and is now conquering time and space.'[128] Yet in certain ways the new modern world was failing:

> the bombing tests are following one another, carried out under instructions which cynically sweep aside the warnings of experts, of sane men and women, of masses of men and women around the globe. Research in atomic biological and radiological warfare is consuming millions of dollars and rubles and francs paid by the very taxes of the future victims of these lethal weapons.[129]

---

126 Nevil Shute, *On the Beach* (Heinemann, 1957). 'Women Meet in Sydney', *The Peacemaker* 24 (September–October 1962), 3.
127 Holmes to Tapper, 15 October 1962, series III reel 55, WILPF Papers.
128 '15th International Congress of WILPF report', California 1962, Sklar and Dublin, eds, *Women and Social Movements*, 24.
129 '15th International Congress of WILPF report', California 1962, 24.

6. THE COLD WAR AND NUCLEAR DISARMAMENT

The Australian section had campaigned vigorously against British nuclear testing on Australian soil in the 1950s and was resolute in their support of total nuclear disarmament. By 1963, however, over 600 atmospheric nuclear tests had been conducted around the world by the US, USSR, UK and France.[130] To the dismay of the Australian section, France announced its intention to build a testing facility in the Pacific in 1963 to continue its nuclear program.

During the nineteenth century France had incorporated groups of islands in the South Pacific into its empire, and at its height in the 1930s was the second largest overseas empire in the world.[131] After World War II, following the brutal experience of German occupation, France was convinced that it should remain a global power and be buttressed by its own nuclear deterrent. It first tested atomic bombs in Algeria in 1960, tests which were conducted during a UN-endorsed moratorium on testing from 1958 to 1961 which the US, USSR and UK all observed.[132] In 1962 Algeria declared independence after a decade of appalling conflict, and France announced construction of the Centre d'Experimentation du Pacifique on the atolls of Mururoa and Fangataufa with administration buildings in Tahiti.[133] In addition, France and China both shunned the Test Ban Treaty of 1963, signed by the US and the USSR, which prohibited testing of nuclear weapons in the atmosphere. This announcement sent the Australian section into action, prompting them to protest and attempt to reason with the French before the testing began. They sent letters to all members of the Australian parliament and maintained a consistent letter writing campaign to the press.[134] WILPF's opposition to the tests was based on two sets of objections. Firstly, they were against all nuclear testing, promoted total disarmament, and felt every nation should do all that was possible to encourage the US and USSR to sign the test ban treaty. Secondly, they were concerned that these tests were to take place in the South Pacific region and considered the proximity to Australia to be a risk to public health.

---

130 For a visual representation of all nuclear bomb tests see: '1945–1998' by Isao Hashimoto, multimedia artwork '2053'—This is the number of nuclear explosions conducted in various parts of the globe up to 1998. Accessed 29 November 2022, www.youtube.com/watch?v=cjAqR1zICA0.
131 Robert Aldrich, *France and the South Pacific Since 1940* (London: Macmillan, 1993), xviii, doi.org/10.1007/978-1-349-10828-2.
132 Ramesh Chandra Thakur, *The Last Bang Before a Total Ban: French Nuclear Testing in the Pacific*, Working Paper, No. 159 (Canberra: Peace Research Centre, ANU, 1995), 2.
133 Aldrich, *France and the South Pacific Since 1940*, 83.
134 For example, see Margaret Holmes, 'Nuclear Test Ban', *The Canberra Times*, 11 November 1963.

'Don't let Strontium 90 poison our children': Women for Peace rally, Sydney, 196-?.

Source: Held in Photographs and slides relating to the peace movement in Australia, ca. 1930–1982, created by the Association for International Co-operation and Disarmament (N.S.W.) Mitchell Library, State Library of NSW PXE 1463.

At their first public demonstration against the testing, WILPF gathered outside the French Embassy in Canberra in June 1963 handing out leaflets outlining their concerns. Margaret Holmes and Dorothy Bendick met with the French Consul-General who, while remaining 'non-committal', agreed to pass their protest on to the French government.[135] To reinforce their concern about contamination of the region by fallout, the women left bottles of milk outside the consulate labelled 'radioactive Strontium 90—causes bone cancer and leukaemia'.[136] In January 1964 the section sent letters to every French company operating in Australia, threatening boycotts of French goods and services. They wrote hoping the 'commercial representatives of France' would urge the government to 'cancel the proposed

---

135 'Sydney Women for Peace say "Aust. Has Purest Milk In World—Let's Keep it That Way"', *Peace Action,* July 1963. Found in Holmes ASIO file NAA: A6119, 3362.
136 'Sydney Women for Peace say "Aust. Has Purest Milk In World—Let's Keep it That Way"', *Peace Action,* July 1963. Found in Holmes ASIO file NAA: A6119, 3362. See also; Holmes and Christiansen, 'History of WILPF and activities of NSW Branch', 1990, MLMSS 5395/Box 01, SLNSW.

test and sign the Partial Test Ban Treaty', noting: 'National prestige is an empty thing if it is built on the resentment and active hostility of millions of people'.[137]

A pamphlet published by the Melbourne branch targeted women to join the campaign, stating: 'French perfume? Yes! French Bomb Tests? No!'. It was a strategic campaign that mobilised the image of French luxury and femininity to encourage women to think more broadly about protest and testing.[138] Holmes and other WILPF members tried a creative spin on the campaign and commissioned a four-page illustrated comic strip called *The Choice*. The comic, drawing on the idea of the sanctity of the family and the image of the vulnerable child, told the story of a family which becomes politicised over the issue of the French testing before ending with two possible outcomes—children dying of leukaemia with anguished parents asking 'oh, why didn't we do something when there was still time?', compared with healthy children playing. The information in the comic made clear the anger at the decisions not just of the French Government, but the inaction of its Australian counterpart. It aimed to call people to action and upheld the power of a women's choice in caregiving responsibilities. The women distributed the pamphlet with a note that it was 'written financed and produced by a group of Sydney mothers because of our concern to warn people of the dangers'.[139]

WILPF members attempted to telephone French President Charles de Gaulle with no success. Members Lorraine Moseley and Jean Richards decided to organise an 'Unofficial Mission to France' which was conceived, not as a protest, but an 'APPEAL for a new spirit in the conduct of national and international affairs.'[140] Richards, a member of the Religious Society of Friends (Quakers), travelled to Paris in March 1964 hoping to use techniques promoted by Quaker ideology to informally meet with de Gaulle. The mission was funded by donations sent in after an appeal that indicated how it would 'give expression to faith in spiritual values, spoken not by a functionary or deputation of citizens to a potentate but by one of God's creatures to

---

137 NSW Branch WILPF to the Manager, Comptoir National d'Escompte de Paris, Sydney, 2 January 1964, MLMSS 5395/Box 01, SLNSW.
138 'Women Say French Perfume? Yes!', November c 1963, Papers, WILPF, MS 9377, SLV.
139 *The Choice*, comic strip financed by 'Sydney mothers'. Copy in Margaret Holmes's ASIO file, NAA: A6119, 3362, 98.
140 Moseley, appeal for sponsorship for Unofficial Mission to France, 13 January 1964, Holmes ASIO file NAA: A6119, 3362.

another'.¹⁴¹ Richards could not meet with de Gaulle, but she felt her mission was not wasted as news of her journey was published in Paris newspapers, and de Gaulle sent her a letter which the women felt showed 'that he did, indeed, understand the spirit of the Mission.'¹⁴² She travelled through France, England and Scotland spreading her message, and on return gave a talk in which she proclaimed the importance of such tactics:

> Before distance shrank under the advance of technology, and man's destructive power grew to its present capacity, it may have been legitimate to leave international concerns in the hands of governments and diplomats, but it is not so today.¹⁴³

The first test occurred in 1966 in the South Pacific. The section continued to monitor the situation and by the 1970s supported union actions such as the mail boycott to France, sending any letters to the French section care of Geneva.¹⁴⁴ They were also very supportive of the Australian and New Zealand governments' challenge in the World Court at The Hague on the issue.¹⁴⁵ Western Australian WILPF member Betty McIntosh noted that WILPF's strength was in 'bringing peace groups together', and that they 'played a big part in getting the cooperation of the trade unions in Australia to go to the World Court and try to stop the French atmospheric testing.'¹⁴⁶ The Australian section of WILPF used their international network to impress on the French section how urgent the situation was, and had the international section urge the French section to take action.¹⁴⁷ As the tests

---

141 Moseley, appeal for sponsorship for Unofficial Mission to France, 13 January 1964, Holmes ASIO file NAA: A6119, 3362.
142 Moseley to The Editor *Woman's Day*, 15 October 1965, MLMSS 5395/Box 01, SLNSW. 'Mrs Newson reported she had written to Mrs. Furrer and Mrs Furrer in turn had sent to news of Jean Richards proposed visit to Paris to newspapers which had published the news.' 12 May 1964 General Meeting minutes MLMSS 5395/Box 01 SLNSW.
143 Jean Richards, paper presented at the CICD Congress 27 October 1964, 'Peace Research and international co-operation—the role of the individual and the churchman', CICD papers, Box 49, Melbourne University Archives.
144 Forte to Ballantyne, 26 August 1973, series III reel 55, WILPF Papers.
145 International Court of Justice, Australia vs France application submitted 9 May 1973, New Zealand vs France, 1974, accessed online, 29 November 2022, www.icj-cij.org/en/case/59.
146 Betty McIntosh interview: Catherine Foster, *Women For All Seasons: The Story of the Women's International League for Peace and Freedom* (Athens: University of Georgia Press, 1989), 174. Australian Dr Helen Caldicott was prominent in this campaign, educating against the nuclear testing. She received a WILPF Peacewoman award in 2015 presented by former Governor General Quentin Bryce. For more on Caldicott see: Helen Caldicott, *A Passionate Life* (Milsons Point, NSW: Random House Australia, 1996). Australian section WILPF Centenary Peacewoman awards, Dr Helen Caldicott 2015, accessed 29 November 2022, www.helencaldicott.com/wilpf-australia-peacewomen-awards/.
147 International Chairmen Ellen Homgaard, Katherine Camp, and Eleanore Romberg, 30 November 1971, series III reel 55, WILPF Papers.

continued intermittently well into the 1990s, after most other established nuclear powers had ceased testing, this was an ongoing campaign for WILPF. It contributed to their cynicism about the misuse of science and technology, prompting the section to create the Committee Against Chemical and Biological Warfare. The committee published leaflets in 1969 titled *What is CBW?* and *New Perversions of Science* which used statements by experts, not just on nuclear weapons and their health impacts, but other forms of germ and chemical warfare which they observed in the Vietnam conflict as defoliants became a characteristic weapon of American modern warfare.[148]

US bases in Australia: Pine Gap and Omega

Connected to the campaign to stop bomb testing and ease tensions during the Cold War was WILPF's opposition to US military installations in Australia and worldwide. Just as the Pacific became a pivotal part of France's military future, so too did it interest the US in the era of decolonisation. After World War II, when the military had fought through various Pacific islands as it advanced on Japan, the US became more involved in the administration of several sites in the region, notably the Marshall Islands which became their 'trust territory'. These islands, inhabited by the Micronesians, comprised several small atolls. From 1945 onwards the US started using the atolls for their own nuclear test programs, the most significant being Bikini atoll where 23 atomic tests were carried out.[149] Escalating involvement in regional conflicts, such as in Korea and Vietnam, called for a more established military presence in the Pacific region. The US maintained bases in Japan on Okinawa, at Sasebo (near Nagasaki), Misawa, Atsugi and Yokosuka. After Curtin's statement that Australia 'looks to America, free of any pangs as to our traditional links or kinship with the United Kingdom' in December 1941, many negotiations occurred for US military installations to be placed on Australian soil to increase the US presence in the Pacific.[150] This made Australia part of the 'Pacific Rim' security chain that 'must be strung with a necklace of American-controlled

---

148 *New Perversions of Science,* printed by WILPF AU, July 1969, and *What is CBW?* Printed by WILPF AU, March 1969, Papers, WILPF, MS 9377, SLV.
149 Richard Rhodes, *Dark Sun: The Making of the Hydrogen Bomb* (New York: Simon & Schuster, 1995), 229.
150 John Curtin [First published in *The Herald* (Melbourne), 27 December 1941], in *Great Words: Speeches That Stirred Australia,* ed. Michael Cathcart and Kate Darian-Smith (Melbourne: Melbourne University Press, 1998), 189.

military bases: from Anchorage to San Diego, Hawaii, Vladivostok, Seoul, Yokahama, Cam Ranh Bay, Subic Bay and Clark, Wellington, Belau and Kwajalein.'[151] By 1989 the US maintained 1,500 military installations on foreign soil, with 144,000 soldiers deployed in Asia and the Pacific.[152] The feminist international relations scholar Cynthia Enloe has noted that the international women's movement opposed the maintenance of military bases, not just because they represented 'military politics', but because they created social upheaval as 'artificial societies created out of unequal relations between men and women of different races and classes.'[153]

By the 1980s there were dozens of US military installations in Australia, but the ones that attracted most concern were:

> the communications station at North West Cape in WA; the satellite ground station at Pine Gap in the Northern Territory, and the satellite ground station at Nurrungar Valley in the Woomera area in SA.[154]

These three bases were the focus for the peace movement as well as an academic community interested in analysing Australia's defence system because the bases were 'vital elements of the US strategic command, control, communications and intelligence system which support[ed] the US strategic nuclear posture'.[155] Desmond Ball from the Peace Research Centre at ANU collated and analysed the available data surrounding the three bases in Australia and became the leading expert in public debate.[156] His contributions highlighted the extreme secrecy and lack of information provided by both the Australian and US governments. Pine Gap, noted Ball, was 'originally called merely a "defence space research facility"' and it

---

151 Cynthia Enloe, *Bananas, Beaches and Bases: Making Feminist Sense of International Politics* (London: Pandora, 1989), 85.
152 Enloe, *Bananas, Beaches and Bases*, 66.
153 Enloe, *Bananas, Beaches and Bases*, 2.
154 Desmond Ball, *A Base for Debate: The US Satellite Station at Nurrungar* (Sydney: Allen & Unwin, 1987), xiii.
155 Ball, *A Base for Debate*, 88.
156 Andrew Mack, *US 'Bases' in Australia: The Debate Continues* (Canberra: Peace Research Centre, ANU, 1988), 2. See also: Desmond Ball, *Pine Gap: Australia and the US Geostationary Signals Intelligence Satellite Program* (Sydney: Allen & Unwin, 1988); Desmond Ball, *The Strategic Implications of American Bases in Australia* (Clayton, Vic: Monash University, Faculty of Economics and Politics, 1974).

was not until 1988 that Labor Prime Minister Bob Hawke gave 'the most informative official explanation of Pine Gap's purpose' in a short statement that referred to the base's function in intelligence data collection.[157]

In response to the increasing number of US bases on Australian soil, and in an attempt to help disseminate much desired information about them, WILPF published a pamphlet in 1971 called *American Bases in Australia: Nuclear Target*.[158] With information assembled from newspaper articles by Peter Robinson in the *Australian Financial Review*, as well as those by Robert Cooksey and Desmond Ball in the *Sydney Morning Herald*, WILPF outlined the establishment of these bases, the 'embarrassed secrecy' with which they were shrouded, and set out WILPF's platform for opposition. Noting that *'Three of these bases are multi-million dollar projects which are absolutely under American control'* (original italics), WILPF echoed concerns that the sovereignty of Australian territory was compromised by the arrangement and that the close partnership hindered Australia's ability to forge its own path in foreign policy relations.[159] Most concerning for WILPF was the fact that the bases at Pine Gap, Nurrungar and the North West Cape implicated Australia in the American nuclear weapons system of deterrence. They believed that it made Australia a nuclear target. Consistent with their modus operandi, WILPF sent the pamphlet to all members of the federal parliament.[160]

The pamphlet described the defence capabilities of each base, starting with the Northwest Cape which was the first US base to open with obvious 'defence significance.'[161] The agreement to build the base was made in 1962 and it became operational from 1968. While negotiations were in progress in 1961, Holmes wrote to the Minister of Defence to gain information on the proposal as media reports speculated it could have been 'the most important defence pact between Australia and the US since WWII' but

---

157 Desmond Ball, foreword, in David Rosenberg, *Inside Pine Gap: The Spy Who Came In From The Desert* (Prahran, Vic.: Hardie Grant Books, 2011), vi. This account was published by an analyst who worked in Pine Gap. He was motivated to write his personal account after Pine Gap's role was officially declassified in 2008, because he attended an exhibition by the Jessie Street National Women's Library in 2009 called 'Remembering Pine Gap' about the women's peace protest, 'was surprised to hear several misconceptions' and he felt he needed to 'set the record straight', 144.
158 Robert Cooksey was a lecturer in international relations at ANU. *American Bases in Australia: Nuclear Target*, WILPF SA Branch, 1971, NLA.
159 *American Bases in Australia: Nuclear Target*, WILPF SA Branch, 1971, NLA.
160 Forte to Ballantyne, 2 November 1971, series III reel 55, WILPF Papers.
161 *American Bases in Australia: Nuclear Target*, WILPF SA Branch, 1971, NLA, 3.

received no reply.¹⁶² Pine Gap was subsequently established after an agreement in 1966 and became operational in 1969. While the agreement was signed in Canberra, it was not brought before parliament. The Labor member for Yarra, Jim Cairns, a leading member of the party left, spoke out in parliament from opposition about the controversy surrounding the base. He was particularly concerned about Australia's financial contribution to it, and, most importantly, the suggestion that it would increase the likelihood of Australia becoming a target for a nuclear attack.¹⁶³ The Minister for Defence, Allan Fairhall, replied that its function was to 'carry out pure research into those aspects of space phenomenon which may have a bearing on the defence of this country'.¹⁶⁴ He reiterated that any further information would be 'of assistance to this country's potential enemies.'¹⁶⁵ This response illustrated once more the secrecy surrounding the project. The same year Pine Gap became operational, the base at the Woomera facility was announced. Fairhall, speaking in defence of the facility, explained cryptically that 'the functioning of this station will make a contribution to free world defence, but I wish you would not ask me how.'¹⁶⁶

In its final section, the WILPF pamphlet set out what the organisation knew about the proposal for the Omega station which at the time was projected to be established either in NSW or Tasmania. Omega was described as 'a very low-frequency (VLF) radio navigation system' intended to 'aid commercial shipping and aviation'.¹⁶⁷ Designed to network with eight other transmitting stations, four of which by 1970 were operational in Hawaii, the US, Trinidad and Norway, the system was intended to provide worldwide coverage improving accuracy of navigation, both militarily and commercially.

WILPF members were sceptical of the claim that this was intended for merchant shipping. From 1970 onwards, when the first media reports and discussions in Hansard about the possibility of a new base were appearing, WILPF monitored and questioned the Omega proposal and helped set

---

162 *American Bases in Australia: Nuclear Target*, WILPF SA Branch, 1971, NLA, 3.
163 Jim Cairns, 'Question—American Installation at Pine Gap—Speech', *CPD*, House of Representatives, 26 February 1969, 155.
164 Allen Fairhall, 'Question—American Installation at Pine Gap', *CPD*, House of Representatives, 26 February 1969, 155.
165 Allen Fairhall, 'Question—American Installation at Pine Gap', *CPD*, House of Representatives, 26 February 1969, 155.
166 *American Bases in Australia: Nuclear Target*, WILPF SA Branch, 1971, NLA, 6.
167 *American Bases in Australia: Nuclear Target*, WILPF SA Branch, 1971, NLA, 6.

up the Sydney-based Stop Omega Committee.[168] In 1973, when the new Labor Government inherited the plans for the Omega installation, they referred the issue to the Joint Committee on Foreign Affairs and Defence for an inquiry.[169] WILPF presented to the government inquiry by providing a written submission, and Holmes drove to Canberra to appear as a WILPF witness before the committee on 9 October 1973 along with Keith Suter, activist and WILPF supporter, who appeared for the Stop Omega Committee.[170] Grateful that the Labor Government was not insistent on secrecy, which characterised the establishment of the other foreign bases, the WILPF submission focused on how this base would continue to 'draw Australia—unwillingly now, we hope—into the big power balance of terror'.[171] Explaining that WILPF already felt Australia was 'compromised by the numerous US bases scattered about the continent', they concentrated their opposition on the idea that strengthening ties with the US reduced independent foreign policy initiative in the region. They wrote:

> can we expect to be taken seriously by our neighbours when we express for; the ASEAN declaration of S.E. Asia as a zone of peace and neutrality; the Sri Lanka proposal that the Indian Ocean be a zone of peace, and our willingness to serve on the UN ad hoc committee to consider the latter proposal?[172]

They then set out to question the assertion that the system was for the purpose of civilian use, asking why the US defence department was so heavily involved and why they would be so willing to 'foot the bill if this is only a peaceful aid to merchant shipping'.[173] WILPF then followed up

---

168 Cavanagh, *Margaret Holmes*, 277.
169 Gough Whitlam, 'Question—OMEGA Navigational Base—Speech', *CPD*, House of Representatives, 26 September 1973, 1507.
170 Joint Standing Committee on Foreign Affairs and Defence, *Omega Navigational Installation Report from the Joint Committee on Foreign Affairs and Defence* (Australian Government Publishing Service, 1975), 116.
171 Wendy Wheelwright to Joint Committee on Foreign Affairs and Defence, 'WILPF Australia Submission on the Possibilities of the Establishment of an Omega Navigational Station in Australia', 2 July 1973, series III reel 55, WILPF Papers.
172 Wendy Wheelwright to Joint Committee on Foreign Affairs and Defence, 'WILPF Australia Submission on the Possibilities of the Establishment of an Omega Navigational Station in Australia', 2 July 1973, series III reel 55, WILPF Papers.
173 Wendy Wheelwright to Joint Committee on Foreign Affairs and Defence, 'WILPF Australia Submission on the Possibilities of the Establishment of an Omega Navigational Station in Australia', 2 July 1973, series III reel 55, WILPF Papers.

their appearance at the inquiry with advertisements purchased in major newspapers that encouraged members of the public to send the form open letter to the prime minister saying 'No to Omega'.[174]

WILPF's presentation gave voice to a number of anxieties. First, it showed how they believed, along with foreign policy experts, that having too close a relationship with the US jeopardised Australia's ability to engage independently in the Pacific region. They recognised the contrast between many other nations stridently calling for self-determination in an era of decolonisation while Australia secretly and willingly ceded sovereignty to the US for military purposes. This position followed the tradition of WILPF asserting that Australia should engage more productively in the region, but it also illustrated a tension in their internationalist ideals. WILPF recognised that campaigning was more likely to hit its mark when the Australian Government had sovereign control over military decisions, whereas their protest would fall on deaf ears in Washington. Second, WILPF was concerned that both governments were attempting to categorise the installations as civilian-focused initiatives when they were in fact an insidious extension of militarism.

To WILPF, the secrecy surrounding the establishment of the bases, and the insistence that the Omega VLF system was not for military purposes, were attempts to subvert the democratic process and allow military hardware to be built without proper endorsement by parliament or oversight from the public. These new bases and VLF systems were central to Western military communication and control, as was the satellite SIGINT information collected at Pine Gap. This kind of technology ultimately made weapons more accurate. The support lent by such facilities for space based reconnaissance, so-called 'national technical means', also helped 'the verification of the Anti-Ballistic Missile (ABM) Treaty, the Strategic Arms Limitation Talks (SALT) constraints on strategic offensive nuclear forces, and other arms control agreements', a point that emerged as a rationale for the bases.[175] Later evolution of global positioning systems (GPS), brought the world closer into line with ideals of international humanitarian law because precision diminished the extent of civilian casualties. Yet WILPF believed such technology enabled weaponry that lowered the threshold for when states were prepared to resort to force. The organisation remained committed to complete disarmament.

---

174 'NO TO OMEGA: An Open Letter to the Prime Minister', *The Australian,* 17 August 1973.
175 Ball, *Pine Gap,* 2.

Finally, and most fearfully, WILPF saw the increasing presence of the US in Australia as connected to the threat of nuclear war. The pamphlet noted how 'it seems that the umbrella of American security bears a frightening resemblance to a mushroom cloud.'[176] Campaigning against the presence of US military bases in Australia during the Cold War was inextricably linked to the fear of the atomic bomb. The women feared not only that nuclear war was possible, with a necessarily devastating impact on the world, but that Australia would also be involved more deeply as a consequence of its integration if such a war ever eventuated. The prospect was something they could not stay silent about.

The increasing prevalence of military bases around the world became a focal point for the international women's movement and other anti-nuclear activists. By the 1980s a number of women's peace camps had been set up around the world to make a statement about the uncertainty and fear of nuclear weapons.[177] The most famous and sustained of the camps was Greenham Common in Berkshire UK. This protest was in response to a decision by the UK parliament to allow the US to base nuclear cruise missiles at the Royal Air Force base.[178] The peace camp started in 1981 and though it began with only a small number of women marching from Cardiff, it continued for 19 years with hundreds of women involved at various times. UK WILPF members were actively engaged, though not the lead organisers, and it motivated them to create the 'Stop The Arms Race' campaign.[179]

The Greenham Common started as a mixed-gender group, but after frustrations that men were doing all the public talking, it became a women-only camp from 1982.[180] Gender, as a result, subsequently became a defining part of the message. Scholars who have written about the peace camp movement in the 1980s note that a major rhetorical strategy was to claim that 'women were acting as guardians of future generations of children, appealing to a maternal function and maternalist feminism.'[181] The international women's peace movement showed solidarity to the women at the peace camp: the Australian section acknowledged their support in

---

176 *American Bases in Australia: Nuclear Target*, WILPF SA Branch, 1971, NLA, 14.
177 Cynthia Cockburn, *From Where We Stand: War, Women's Activism and Feminist Analysis* (London: Zed Books, 2007), 174, doi.org/10.5040/9781350220287.
178 Enloe, *Bananas, Beaches and Bases*, 76.
179 Harriet Hyman Alonso, *Peace as a Women's Issue: A History of the U.S. Movement for World Peace and Women's Rights* (Syracuse, NY: Syracuse University Press, 1993), 229.
180 Cockburn, *From Where We Stand*, 174.
181 Alison Bartlett, 'Feminist Protest and Maternity at Pine Gap Women's Peace Camp, Australia 1983', *Women's Studies International Forum* 34, no. 1 (January 2011): 33, doi.org/10.1016/j.wsif.2010.10.002.

May 1983 reporting that 'most branches joined other women's groups in actions expressing solidarity with the women of Greenham Common.'[182] This rhetoric and the momentum for action flowed into the organising of a peace camp at Pine Gap in Australia in 1983.

The Pine Gap Peace Camp was organised by a coalition of women's groups that took the name Women for Survival. In November 1983 on Remembrance Day, almost 800 women converged at the base, which 'caught the nation's attention through the spectacle of the hundreds of women in the desert'.[183] This protest drew direct inspiration from the Greenham Common peace camp in the UK, once again illustrating the international collaboration of the protest against nuclear weapons. Messages of support were sent to and from both camps, and a sign was put on the fence at Pine Gap with the words 'Greenham Women Are Everywhere'.[184]

Margaret Bearlin, Australian WILPF member, in a Russian fur hat, written on the back 'it was very cold', at Encirclement of Greenham Common, England, 12 December 1982.
Source: Photo courtesy of Margaret Bearlin.

---

182 Australian Section report, '22nd International Congress of WILPF "Women Save the World"', Sweden 1983, accessed through Sklar and Dublin, eds, *Women and Social Movements*. 42.
183 Bartlett, 'Feminist Protest and Maternity at Pine Gap Women's Peace Camp, Australia 1983', 31. See also Megg Kelham, 'War and Peace: A Case of Global Need, National Unity and Local Dissent? A Closer Look at Australia's Greenham Common', *Lilith: A Feminist History Journal*, no. 19 (2013): 76–90.
184 Bartlett, 'Feminist Protest and Maternity at Pine Gap Women's Peace Camp, Australia 1983', 32.

WILPF women in Australia supported the Women for Survival group. Member Yvonne Cunningham attended the protest and was arrested along with 110 other women for breaching the base grounds. Cunningham wrote about the experience for WILPF's international journal, *Pax et Libertas*.[185] As part of the messaging of the protest, she defined herself as a mother protesting to protect the future.

> I am the mother of Justine, Martin and Elizabeth. At 40 I felt the growing of a deep sense of foreboding for the future of our planet. Pine Gap (Australia) Peace Camp gave me the opportunity to physically express my abhorrence to the nuclear and military madness.[186]

Cunningham drove to Alice Springs with five other women and in her report, she detailed the 'demoralising conditions' that the women arrested experienced at the hands of the police. Most of the 111 women gave a false name, 'Karen Silkwood', and were harshly treated for their failure to comply with procedure.[187] Deeply affected by the experience, Cunningham later wrote: 'Pine Gap and Alice Springs exemplify for me the multitude of injustices that plague our society. Racism, sexism, violence and militarism are all bedfellows'.[188] The Pine Gap Peace Camp lasted only two weeks, but has become a highly symbolic event in the history of the Australian women's peace movement. As with many of their previous engagements in public protest, WILPF participated and supported, but were not solely organising the event. Their commitment to long-term education and understanding root causes of conflict meant they continued to campaign on these issues long after the peace camp packed up, and, indeed, well after superpower arsenals were stood down from a near instantaneous posture for attack.

The fear of nuclear war from the 1950s onwards impressed new urgency on women involved with WILPF. This reinvigorated their activism; the campaigns against the arms race became a way for women to avoid feeling helpless and to try to make a difference. The new branch established in Sydney saw the membership grow and these women helped to create more

---

185 Yvonne Cunningham, 'Peace Camps Proliferate … What I Found at Pine Gap', *Pax et Libertas* 49, no. 2 (June 1984): 10.
186 Cunningham, 'Peace Camps Proliferate … What I Found at Pine Gap', 10.
187 Karen Silkwood was an American chemical technician and labour union activist who died in mysterious circumstances in 1974 after raising concerns about health and safety of workers at a nuclear factory. The use of her name highlights again the transnational nature of the protest against nuclear weapons. Cunningham, 'Peace Camps Proliferate … What I Found at Pine Gap', 10.
188 Cunningham, 'Peace Camps Proliferate … What I Found at Pine Gap', 10.

official national branch structures that professionalised Australian WILPF in line with the international branch and their guidelines. In their campaigns against the bomb testing by the British at Emu Field and Maralinga on mainland Australia, and by the French in the Pacific, WILPF often highlighted their roles as the guardians of children whose futures were being placed at risk by nuclear testing, by constant militarisation and, ultimately, by the potential for nuclear war itself.

The campaign against testing on the Australian mainland raised concerns about the treatment of Indigenous communities and their land, which continued WILPF's involvement in campaigns for Indigenous rights. Taking up the fight against the French testing continued WILPF's focus on regional politics. Yet, this 'Cold War' era stretched over decades, and WILPF soon realised that any protest against the threat of nuclear war brought them under suspicion of being 'communist sympathisers'. To remain politically neutral, WILPF tried not to be associated with either communism or capitalism, and they hesitated when criticising or discussing the excesses of the US capitalist system. Coming to terms with this scrutiny and reflecting on the purpose of their protest had a lasting impact on the organisation.

Irene Greenwood's 85th birthday at Cockburn Sound women's peace camp 1983 in Western Australia.
Source: Photo courtesy of Margaret Bearlin, photographer.

7

The anti–Vietnam War movement and women's liberation

One day in 1965, 56-year-old Margaret Holmes hurried towards North Head in Sydney Harbour, where a huge crowd had gathered to mark the departure of a troop ship setting sail for Vietnam. She was accompanied by a small group of middle-aged women carrying a large banner between them. Eventually, when they finally reached the top, the women found themselves standing above a 'more or less just open cliff'. As Holmes later recalled, 'they didn't have fences and things like they have now'.[1] Preparing to unfurl a banner, the women assured onlookers they were simply farewelling the troops as they made their way to the edge and flung the banner down. Luck was not on their side, however, and the banner became caught on a bush. 'I hung on to my young daughter', Holmes would later recall, 'and leant over with my leg and kicked this jolly bush and kicked at the wood—really, I was mad!—and finally it loosened itself and fell right down'.[2] The banner, positioned to be seen by those on the departing troop ship, offered one final message to the departing soldiers: 'YOU GO TO AN UNJUST WAR'.

---

1   Margaret Holmes, quoted in Siobhan McHugh, *Minefields and Miniskirts: Australian Women and the Vietnam War* (Sydney: Doubleday, 1993), 211.
2   Holmes, quoted in McHugh, *Minefields and Miniskirts,* 211.

On her way home, Holmes contacted the media. 'Oh, a terrible thing has just been done on North Head', she exclaimed, in a manoeuvre that only helped garner further publicity for her daring action. With her activism, Holmes regularly baffled people who assumed she was a well-to-do middle-aged Christian woman. When she went to collect the banner and found an angry group about to tear it down, she 'helpfully directed them to the spot and urged them to cut it, which they did—whereupon Margaret rolled it up, hollered "Thank you" and left'.[3]

During the 1960s, the roles and expectations of protesters were fluid and demonstrations with only a small numbers of participants could still gain widespread publicity within the changing media landscape.[4] Indeed, in 1965, Holmes made front page news for staging an action where six women held a banner challenging Dr Hugh Gough, the Anglican Primate of Australia, on his views on Vietnam.[5] Such was the intensity of the public reaction to the Vietnam War that it incited individuals to radical action in spite of the associated risks.

***

The Women's International League for Peace and Freedom (WILPF) celebrated its 50th anniversary in 1965 as the nation became embroiled in another war. In 1962 Australia followed the US in committing advisers to the conflict in Vietnam. By 1965 Australia's involvement had escalated alongside the US, which had by then committed 200,000 troops. Conscription was introduced in 1964 without a national plebiscite, a decision which only exacerbated social and political opposition to the war. The introduction of conscription in Australia stirred the dormant Australian peace movement into action. WILPF's membership increased as women were politicised by anti-war campaigns. They used newspaper advertising and letter writing to influence public opinion, while their vigilance in documenting and understanding the conflict in Vietnam saw them become one of the first organisations to denounce Australia's involvement.

---

3   Holmes, quoted in McHugh, *Minefields and Miniskirts*, 211.
4   Sean Scalmer, *Dissent Events: Protest, the Media and the Political Gimmick in Australia* (Sydney: UNSW Press, 2002), 43.
5   'Protests to Dr Gough', *Sydney Morning Herald*, 9 November 1965, 1.

7. THE ANTI-VIETNAM WAR MOVEMENT AND WOMEN'S LIBERATION

Celebration of 50th anniversary of Women's International League for Peace and Freedom, 28 April, 1965.
Left to right: Lorraine Moseley, Wendy Wheelwright, Janet Finlay, Elspeth Christiansen, Margaret Holmes, Betty Gale, Betty Phillips.
Source: Compiled by Margaret Holmes, Mitchell Library, State Library of New South Wales and the Women's International League for Peace and Freedom (NSW Branch) [PXB 726].

The Vietnam War was a conflict complicated by Cold War tensions in an era of rapid decolonisation. Charges of 'communist sympathies' were rife, and different political alignments caused intense debate within the movement. The Australian peace movement was made up of a constellation of groups and organisations that represented a broad cross-section of views relating to peace. WILPF remained opposed to all violence and war, and was criticised within the movement for being too moderate. Working within a reinvigorated peace movement involved cooperation with groups that had different perspectives, some of whom opposed the Vietnam War but not necessarily all war. Others opposed conscription but supported the intervention. The broader peace movement included the New Left, student groups, and other women-focused groups such as Save Our Sons (SOS) and Women for Peace (WFP).

For WILPF, the debate about how best to articulate dissent and with whom to work was revived. Insistent on producing 'well considered and thoroughly investigated' work, WILPF wanted to present themselves as 'sensible' and 'not revolutionary'.[6] As a consequence of their quest for moderation and stance in favour of nonviolence, they did not support the National Liberation Front, or Viet Cong, the underground South Vietnamese communist force that was supported by some radical groups. Nevertheless, WILPF still had to find ways to work alongside the other groups, despite some viewing WILPF as old-fashioned and overly bureaucratic.[7] Added to this was pressure from Australian Security Intelligence Organisation (ASIO) surveillance that disrupted everyday activities.

In direct response to the sexism many women experienced within the anti-war movement, women on university campuses began organising the Women's Liberation Movement (WLM) from 1969. This new enthusiasm for women's liberation caused a paradigm shift in thinking about women's oppression and challenged the maternalist campaign strategies that WILPF had historically used. WILPF found this confronting and initially had difficulty engaging with new groups involved in the WLM. Holmes recalled their efforts as seeming 'respectable' and distinct from the new generation of radicals 'so that people wouldn't be able to say that the war was only opposed by a ratbag lot of youngsters.'[8] After prioritising involvement with the UN Decade for Women 1975–1985, which required collaboration with other non-government organisations (NGOs), international civil servants, national governments and other feminist groups, WILPF's ideology began to change. This chapter will detail WILPF Australia's involvement in anti-Vietnam War protests, as well as their subsequent transformation after the explosion of feminist activism from the WLM led them to adopt a new language that helped to adapt and renew their radical critique of gender relations and war.

Because of the wider mobilisation of peace activism during the Vietnam War, there has been a large amount of historical scholarship on the peace movement of the 1960s and early 1970s. With widespread opposition to the conflict, pacifists, church groups, political organisations, students and scholars all combined their efforts to end the war.[9] Much of the scholarship published has come from former participants in the movement. Historian

---

6   Agnes Stapledon, 'Head of British Peace League: Left Sydney 40 Years Ago', *Sydney Morning Herald,* 24 November 1966.
7   Amy Swerdlow, *Women Strike for Peace* (Chicago: University of Chicago Press, 1993), 9.
8   Margaret Holmes, 'Proud to be a Proper Peacenik', *The Australian,* 18 July 1990, 3.
9   Kenneth Maddock, 'Opposing the War in Vietnam—The Australian Experience', in *Vietnam and the Antiwar Movement: An International Perspective,* ed. John Dumbrell (Aldershot, Hants, England; Brookfield, USA: Avebury, 1989), 142.

Ann Curthoys published widely about the complexities of writing history as a past participant in the events.[10] She analysed how memory of the events posed a danger of 'self-indulgence' when writing and that it was crucial to 'counteract a tendency to practise selective amnesia, to construct unthinkingly an account of ourselves which is pleasing and comforting'.[11] Curthoys observed in 1992 that 'the dominance by men of the anti-war movement itself seems, so far, to have been reproduced in subsequent historical reconstructions of it'.[12] Histories published by former activists such as Gregory Clark, Michael Hamel-Green and Ralph Summy highlight various aspects of the movement in Australia, such as conscription, the role of students, and the relationship to the longer history of the peace movement.[13] This is important work but as none of these authors were a part of WILPF, they have failed to offer a detailed account of women's contributions. Other works written at the time completely ignored WILPF.[14]

Ann-Mari Jordens and Curthoys have attempted to 'correct the historical impression that the anti-war movement was largely a youth and student movement' by emphasising the role of groups such as WILPF and SOS, the latter a predominantly women's organisation that has recently attracted a detailed study by Carolyn Collins.[15] Michelle Cavanagh and Siobhan

---

10   Ann Curthoys, 'History and Reminiscence: Writing About the Anti-Vietnam-War Movement', *Australian Feminist Studies* 7, no. 16 (December 1992): 116–36, doi.org/10.1080/08164649.1992.9 994666; Ann Curthoys, 'Mobilising Dissent: The Later Stages of Protest', in *Vietnam: Remembered*, ed. Gregory Pemberton (Sydney: Weldon Publishing, 1990): 138–63; Ann Curthoys, '"Vietnam": Public Memory of an Anti-War Movement', in *Memory and History in Twentieth-Century Australia*, ed. Kate Darian-Smith and Paula Hamilton (Melbourne: Oxford University Press, 1994): 113–33; Ann Curthoys, 'The Anti-War Movements', in *Vietnam: War, Myth, and Memory: Comparative Perspectives on Australia's War in Vietnam*, ed. Jeffrey Grey and Jeff Doyle (St Leonards, NSW: Allen & Unwin, 1992): 81–107; Ann Curthoys, interviewed in Greg Langley, *A Decade of Dissent: Vietnam and the Conflict on the Australian Homefront* (North Sydney: Allen & Unwin, 1992), 13.
11   Curthoys, 'The Anti-War Movements', in Grey and Doyle, *Vietnam*, 81.
12   Curthoys, 'Vietnam', in Darian-Smith and Hamilton, *Memory and History in Twentieth-Century Australia*, 116.
13   Gregory Clark, 'Vietnam, China and the Foreign Affairs Debate in Australia: A Personal Account' and Michael Hamel-Green, 'The Resisters: A History of the Anti-Conscription Movement', both in *Australia's Vietnam: Australia in the Second Indo-China War*, ed. Peter King (Sydney: Allen & Unwin, 1983); Ralph V Summy, 'Militancy and the Australian Peace Movement, 1960–67', *Politics* 5, no. 2 (November 1970): 148–62, doi.org/10.1080/00323267008401209.
14   For example see pamphlet: JP Forrester, *Fifteen Years of Peace Fronts* (Sydney: McHugh Printery, 1964).
15   Ann-Mari Jordens, 'Conscription and Dissent: The Genesis of Anti-War Protest', in Pemberton, *Vietnam*: 60-81; Ann Curthoys, '"Shut Up, You Bourgeois Bitch": Sexual Identity and Political Action in the Anti-Vietnam War Movement', in *Gender and War: Australians at War in the Twentieth Century*, ed. Joy Damousi and Marilyn Lake (New York, Melbourne: Cambridge University Press, 1995): 311–41; Carolyn Collins, *Save Our Sons: Women, Dissent and Conscription During the Vietnam War* (Clayton: Monash University Publishing, 2021).

McHugh have each given some attention to the role of WILPF in the anti-war movement. Cavanagh published a biography of WILPF activist Margaret Holmes in 2006 and McHugh's earlier *Minefields and Miniskirts* (1993) relied heavily on interviews with WILPF members to document their involvement in Vietnam protests.[16] These works focused largely on the Australian context of women's peace activism. This chapter contributes to this scholarship by examining the way WILPF engaged in the anti-war campaigns, not just transnationally by adopting some of the techniques of American campaigns, but internationally. WILPF used their international networks to motivate their engagement and directed their energy towards serving as a 'watchdog' of national policy for the international headquarters of WILPF.

Early interest in the Vietnam War

After decades of uncertainty before and during World War II, politicians placed great emphasis on security and prosperity in the postwar years.[17] A long economic boom increased production of goods and services, allowing most Australian families to improve their standard of living and access to consumer goods. Suburbs expanded around major cities, and the population grew from 7.5 million in 1945 to 11.5 million by 1965, with a significant increase in home ownership.[18] Liberal Party leader Robert Menzies, serving from 1949 to 1966, became Australia's longest-serving prime minister. His retirement and the replacement of Opposition Leader Arthur Calwell with Gough Whitlam in 1967 became a symbol of change.[19] The increased accessibility of university education led to a larger population of students, many of whom were interested in challenging the status quo. According to the historian Marilyn Lake: 'convention and security had become suffocating; youth demanded its day'.[20]

---

16 Michelle Cavanagh, *Margaret Holmes: The Life and Times of an Australian Peace Campaigner* (Sydney: New Holland, 2006); McHugh, *Minefields and Miniskirts*.
17 PG Edwards, *A Nation at War: Australian Politics, Society and Diplomacy During the Vietnam War 1965–1975* (St Leonards, NSW: Allen & Unwin in association with the Australian War Memorial, 1997), 3.
18 Edwards, *A Nation at War*, 11.
19 Patricia Grimshaw, Marilyn Lake, Marian Quartly, and Ann McGrath, *Creating a Nation* (Ringwood, Vic: McPhee Gribble, 1994), 299.
20 Grimshaw et al., *Creating a Nation*, 299.

It was during this time of transition that Australia's involvement in Vietnam was announced. At first there was little reaction. While the Australian Labor Party (ALP) was steadfastly opposed to conscription for overseas military service, branches were divided over questions of communism and foreign policy. Various peace conferences in the 1950s and the early 1960s saw the creation of the Association for International Cooperation and Disarmament (AICD), a group WILPF worked closely with. WILPF member Phyllis Latona became the AICD vice-president.[21] However, the AICD and other groups were more concerned with immediate crises relating to nuclear weapons and were slow to grasp the significance of Australia's entry into Vietnam. It was not until Menzies announced the introduction of conscription in late 1964 that the peace movement moved into full swing and began campaigning specifically around the issue of Vietnam.

WILPF reacted earlier to Australia's involvement in Vietnam because of their attention to government policy, and because their international network was already well established. The women of WILPF received their information about the situation in Vietnam from international sources and personal travel experiences. Correspondence between the Australian section and the international headquarters show how eager they were to receive up-to-date reports and articles. This helped them gain a better picture of international events and ensured that their knowledge was not dependent on the Australian press or politicians. Airmail was not cheap for the small budgets of the branches, but it was prioritised as accurate and timely information gave their organisation an informed platform from which to campaign and meant that information would arrive 'while the news is hot'—within days rather than months.[22]

The contact between branches of the organisation, both in Australia and with the headquarters overseas, proved to be WILPF's great strength. Many members subscribed to international papers such as the French newspaper *Le Monde* which had an anti-war editorial position. The national branch of WILPF also received the US pacifist publication *Four Lights*.[23] International information was integral to WILPF's understanding of the severity of the conflict in the early 1960s. Most of their fellow Australians gave little attention to the developments in Vietnam, even as Australia

---

21 Curthoys, 'Shut Up, You Bourgeois Bitch', in Damousi and Lake, *Gender and War*, 319.
22 Tapper to Hilda Vroland, 5 June 1961, series III reel 55, WILPF Papers.
23 Holmes interviewed in McHugh, *Minefields and Miniskirts*, 204. Moesley to Dorothy Hutchinson, 8 April 1967, series III reel 55, WILPF Papers.

gave token support to the French struggle against nationalist forces in the 1950s.[24] Believing that conflict in Vietnam had the potential to erupt into a major war, WILPF in Australia responded to reports of the escalation of Western intervention. As early as 1961 they were expressing concern about US involvement. Secretary Hilda Vroland, sister-in-law of Anna, wrote to WILPF headquarters in Geneva after news that President Kennedy was considering sending additional 'military advisers' to Vietnam: 'We want to add the voice of our Section to any protest you are making or will be making.'[25]

By 1962 Australia had committed to the conflict by sending 30 'advisers', but again this gained little attention from the wider public.[26] The following year the Australian section received reports from Dr Gertrud Woker, from the University of Berne in Switzerland and chairman of the WILPF Committee Against Scientific Warfare, detailing information about defoliants used in conflict zones in Vietnam that was not being reported on widely. WILPF International passed an emergency resolution and wrote to the International Red Cross pleading with them to take action and investigate.[27] Before other protest groups had formed, WILPF members were meeting with government officials to discuss Vietnam and express their concerns over the use of chemical weapons. They argued the conflict was not about a 'communist threat' but rather was a civil war, a position that they came to after studying the history of the country and its decolonisation struggle.[28] They continued to call for an international investigation into the use of chemicals, referred to by the government as simply 'commercial weed-killers', and called for the Australian advisers to be withdrawn, even though their presence had 'passed almost unnoticed' by the wider public.[29]

---

24 Edwards, *A Nation at War*, 24.
25 Hilda Vroland to Mrs Olmsted Geneva office, 18 November 1961, series III reel 55, WILPF International Papers 1915–1978, Sanford, NC: Microfilming Corp. of America, c 1983, accessed at the National Library of Australia (NLA). Hereafter referred to as WILPF Papers.
26 Jordens, 'Conscription and Dissent', in Pemberton, *Vietnam*, 62.
27 Gertrud Woker to the International Red Cross, 12 June 1963, WILPF papers MLMSS 5395/Box 02, State Library of New South Wales (SLNSW).
28 '1964–65 NSW WILPF Annual report', MLMSS 5395/Box 01 SLNSW. Holmes corresponded and met with assistant secretary Mr J Waller from the Department of External Affairs, see Holmes to Mr Waller, 16 August 1963, WILPF papers MLMSS 5395/Box 02 SLNSW and Mr Waller to Holmes, 30 August 1963, MLMSS 5395/Box 02 SLNSW.
29 Holmes to Sir Garfield Barwick, 23 August, series III reel 55, WILPF Papers.

7. THE ANTI-VIETNAM WAR MOVEMENT AND WOMEN'S LIBERATION

Australian WILPF prepared a dossier of their information in July 1964 to send to parliamentarians. Despairing at the lack of information available and the silence surrounding the issue, they felt an 'urgency to take positive action' to make the public and MPs aware of the 'true situation'.[30] The material was sent to the politicians before debate intensified in federal parliament and WILPF was gratified that the Labor opposition used their material in debates. WILPF noted how 'it was thought by many—including the MPs who used our material—that the WILPF was the only source of reliable and valuable information.'[31] Soon more people in the peace movement began to take notice of the conflict. After the Gulf of Tonkin incident in August 1964, which occurred just days before Hiroshima Day, a day of remembrance observed by the peace movement, anti-war groups in Sydney, Melbourne and Brisbane turned their attention to Vietnam. Labor MP Jim Cairns spoke to a large crowd in Melbourne about the incident and echoed many of the concerns WILPF had voiced. Cairns was increasingly recognised as a leader in the anti-Vietnam War protests after this event and always responded positively to WILPF's letter writing.[32]

On 11 August 1964, the Minister for External Affairs, Paul Hasluck, gave a speech to the House of Representatives supporting the notionally retaliatory action by the US. He claimed :

> there is no current alternative to the effort of assisting in South Vietnam to preserve its independence and there is no current alternative to using force as necessary to check the southward thrust of militant Asian Communism.[33]

This announcement spurred WILPF to action and four days later the Australian section paid for an advertisement in the *Australian*. In bold font they asked: 'Is there a current alternative to force in Asia? Yes Mr. Hasluck there is!'[34] They called the US presence 'provocative' and upheld the Vietnamese people's right to self-determination.[35] The advertisement asked people who supported their view to cut it from the paper, add their name

---

30 '1964–65 NSW WILPF Annual report', MLMSS 5395/Box 01 SLNSW.
31 '1964–65 NSW WILPF Annual report', MLMSS 5395/Box 01 SLNSW.
32 Paul Strangio, *Keeper of the Faith: A Biography of Jim Cairns* (Carlton South, Vic: Melbourne University Press, 2002), 146; Edwards, *A Nation at War*, 25.
33 Paul Hasluck, 'International Affairs—Ministerial Statement', *Commonwealth Parliamentary Debates (CPD)*, House of Representatives, 11 August 1964, 21.
34 'Is There a Current Alternative to Force in Asia? Yes Mr Hasluck There Is!', *The Australian*, 15 August 1964.
35 'Is There a Current Alternative to Force in Asia? Yes Mr Hasluck There Is!', *The Australian*, 15 August 1964.

and send it to the minister as a protest against the sentiment expressed in his speech. The office received over 200 copies and Hasluck decided to respond to each one, against the advice of the department, because he felt:

> the cheapest and most effective propaganda is bought with a fivepenny stamp. A large percentage of people who write are not firm in their views and many of them are 'suckers' for organised anti-Western campaigners and a prompt and friendly letter often converts them.[36]

WILPF also received many letters of support and financial contributions for future advertisements, with one correspondent noting: 'I found the lead given by you to be very inspiring'.[37] They regarded this protest as one of their great successes.

After these public protests, the Congress for International Cooperation and Disarmament (CICD, later AICD) held its peace conference in Sydney in October 1964. WILPF sponsored the event along with other organisations, and Holmes served as a member of the preparatory committee.[38] Betty Gale, a member of WILPF, gave the only talk at the conference on Vietnam. The rest of the papers given by activists focused on nuclear disarmament and other areas of conflict such as Indonesia and Malaysia.[39] Gale had visited Vietnam and other countries in South East Asia and she drew on this experience for her talk.[40] Just a few weeks later, on 10 November, Menzies announced the introduction of 'selective conscription' that included overseas service as well as substantial increases to the defence budget.[41] This announcement was not immediately linked with Vietnam, as Menzies referred to Indonesia's 'Confrontation' of the new state of Malaysia and described the pressures of 'cold war and anti-insurgency tasks' on the current force.[42] Nonetheless this decision mobilised other sections of the pacifist community who opposed conscription, though not necessarily war,

---

36 Edwards, *A Nation at War*, 25.
37 F Davis, to WILPF NSW, 17 August 1964, MLMSS 5395/Box 02 SLNSW.
38 Letter about CICD Preparatory Committee attempting to meet with the Prime Minister, and the PM requesting brief information about who they were, 15 May 1964, 'Holmes, Margaret Joan Volume 1' (Canberra, 1964 1957), A6119, 3362, National Archives of Australia (NAA).
39 Jordens, 'Conscription and Dissent', in Pemberton, *Vietnam*, 62. Curthoys, 'Shut Up, You Bourgeois Bitch', in Damousi and Lake, *Gender and War*, 318.
40 B Gale, 'Summary of paper presented by Mrs. B. Gale at Seminar on 26 October on Australia's Relations with Asia', Australian Congress for International Cooperation and Disarmament, Box 49, Series 3/51 CIDC Collection Melbourne University Archives.
41 John Murphy, *Harvest of Fear: A History of Australia's Vietnam War* (St Leonards, NSW: Allen & Unwin, 1993), 114.
42 Murphy, *Harvest of Fear*, 114.

and reminded Australians of the anger and division around conscription dating back to World War I. The ALP strenuously opposed conscription despite being more reserved in debates about Australia's involvement in Cold War era conflicts.[43] The introduction of conscription energised the peace movement and significantly increased opposition to the war in Vietnam.

WILPF, Women for Peace and Save Our Sons

Until the WILPF advertisement in the *Australian*, the Australian section's protests against the Vietnam War mainly consisted of letters to members of parliament and international agencies, talks, conferences and study groups among like-minded sympathisers, and research to obtain more information about the conflict. These were activities that did not generally attract the attention of the press. When it was clear that public opinion was changing, especially on the issue of conscription, WILPF had to decide if it wanted to act as a protest group or remain a 'watchdog', sending letters and hosting meetings but refraining from demonstrations or direct action. Dorothy Bendick, who had been prominent in protest against French nuclear testing, firmly advocated for WILPF to become an organisation for action. She wrote to Holmes after WILPF's advertisement, full of excitement at the fact that many of the letters to the editor supported WILPF's position, exclaiming that WILPF's 'moment in history has arrived. Destiny has presented us with the opportunity to step forward and lead.'[44] Bendick was encouraged by WILPF's prominence in being among the first to agitate on Vietnam.

But not everyone wanted to be part of the protest. Lorraine Moseley, honorary secretary of the NSW branch, believed that WILPF should focus instead on mediation and 'thoughtful negotiation' rather than aggravating tensions through protest. She proudly claimed during her tenure as secretary that she never once sent a 'letter of protest' because 'certain members of the WILPF are only too eager, and too emotionally moved to do anything but condemn'.[45] Moseley was convinced that WILPF's history expressed a conciliatory tradition and their work should be for mediation, though she acknowledged that 'this often makes some of our members impatient … because they want to take a stand, but I am convinced this is not how the WILPF has worked over the last 50 years.'[46]

---

43 Murphy, *Harvest of Fear*, 115.
44 Bendick to Holmes, 17 August 1964, MLMSS 5395/Box 01 SLNSW.
45 Moseley to Marjorie Spencer, 10 March 1965, MLMSS 5395/Box 01 SLNSW.
46 Moseley to Marjorie Spencer, 10 March 1965, MLMSS 5395/Box 01 SLNSW.

Margaret Holmes, Vigil for Peace in Vietnam, Wynyard, Sydney, 12 April 1967.

Source: Item 197: Tribune negatives including a Roland Wakelin art exhibition and Vigil for Peace in Vietnam, Wynyard, Sydney, April 1967 (12 April 1967) / Call Number ON 161/Item 197 (Image 32 of 36) Mitchell Library, State Library of New South Wales and Courtesy SEARCH Foundation. See Appendix for a short biography of Margaret Holmes.

Debates over whether WILPF would be more effective adhering to traditional ideas of how women should behave in public, or whether it should challenge them, caused anxiety among the membership. WILPF women's views did not represent the majority, and research showed that women's attitudes to the Vietnam War in the early 1960s were not significantly different from those of men.[47] Though women's participation in public life was rapidly increasing, women were still received with suspicion and subjected to criticism about their behaviour when showing passion or interest.[48] In a public meeting addressed by Menzies in 1964, a young woman who expressed her opposition to government policy was described by the *Sydney Morning Herald* as 'hysterical'.[49]

---

47   Jordens, 'Conscription and Dissent', in Pemberton, *Vietnam*, 76.
48   Some women were not so quiescent, but mainstream Australia still responded anxiously to passionate and outspoken women. See Grimshaw et al., *Creating a Nation*, 300.
49   'Women in Black Hoods Fail to Shake Menzies At Poll Rally', in *Sydney Morning Herald*, 24 November 1964.

In 1964 WILPF's national branch sent a questionnaire to members asking: 'do you think the WILPF should take part in public demonstrations?' and 'would you be willing to take part yourself in a vigil, march, or deputation to Canberra?'[50] The survey suggested that WILPF understood many of the women involved in WILPF were not willing to engage in any public protest that might compromise their 'respectability'. Holmes envisaged a branch that would appeal to 'the professional women, wives of businessmen, who also long for peace but steer clear of the usual peace organisations.'[51] This attitude reinforced the gendered assumptions about what was considered appropriate for women in public life and what women were capable of. The NSW branch turned down an invitation to visit Vietnam by the Federated Trade Unions of Vietnam after Gale's talk at the CICD conference as

> it was decided a WILPF delegate would be faced with many difficulties, not the least, being a woman. It was also felt trade union representatives would carry a greater impact and be representative of a much larger and more influential group in the community.'[52]

Many of the women involved were middle-aged and had personal experience of the two world wars. Moseley's husband was blinded in World War I, which no doubt motivated her involvement against war and violence. My husband 'has never seen his two children', she wrote in a letter to the Returned Servicemen's League. 'I want them to grow up being taught to love their fellow-men—not hate them—so that they will help create a better world.'[53] The women's movement in Australia during the 1950s and 1960s was also affected by Cold War tensions as 'feminism was increasingly identified with subversive forces, threatening the stability of family and community'.[54] Feminist agendas were not popular in the mainstream press, which partly explains why Holmes was so prescriptive about the type of women WILPF should aim to recruit. Nonetheless Gertrud Baer explicitly stated in 1962 that in spite of difficulties for the movement caused by global tensions, she hoped that WILPF women would own the feminist label. Acknowledging that even WILPF members 'pretend that equality has been acquired' and 'even asseverate that they are not "feminists"', she went on to describe her

---

50 'Special Notice Sent to Branch Members', c1964, MLMSS 5395/Box 01 SLNSW.
51 Holmes to Tapper WILPF Geneva, 18 March 1959, series III reel 55, WILPF Papers.
52 'NSW WILPF Executive Minutes', 4 November 1964, MLMSS 5395/Box 01 SLNSW.
53 Moseley to Returned Servicemen's League, 16 July 1964, MLMSS 5395/Box 01 SLNSW.
54 Marilyn Lake, *Getting Equal: The History of Australian Feminism* (St Leonards, NSW: Allen & Unwin, 1999), 204.

pride at having a 'militant feminist' mother and declared herself 'a feminist as long as I can remember'.[55] Baer saw feminism as essential to WILPF's core purpose, noting that 'only if we can speak for the millions of women still inarticulate are we women entitled to demand from and bear influence upon, those in power at home and at the United Nations'.[56]

In NSW, however, there was an impression that the organisation 'drew most of its membership from Sydney's well-to-do North Shore'.[57] Their concern about presentation meant that their group remained small while other groups were created around them.[58] Many members wanted to make a nonviolent but visible stand. Among them was Ann Michaelis, a psychologist, who felt constrained by the excessive caution of other WILPF NSW members. She was a WILPF representative to the AICD and noted that instead of strictly representing WILPF she 'represented what [she] thought needed to be done for the people of Vietnam'.[59] She felt it was 'ridiculous' to be overly concerned with 'offending anyone' or being thought of as a communist.[60]

For women such as Michealis and Bendick who wanted to demonstrate their opposition to war more actively, a new 'WILPF inspired' organisation was created called Women for Peace (WFP).[61] WFP had many WILPF members and even held organising meetings at Holmes' house. Holmes argued that WFP should dissolve and work through WILPF but the group decided against this course.[62] It saw itself as a movement rather than an organisation, with 'no dues, no memberships, no board, no officers. Each community's women are organised as much or as little as they like'.[63] They modelled themselves on the group Women Strike for Peace (WSP) in the US, sharing solidarity with their concept of a women's strike 'against the unprecedented threat to life from a nuclear holocaust' which held major

---

55   Gertrud Baer, report on Commission on the Status of Women, '15th International Congress of WILPF' California 1962, accessed through database edited by Kathryn Kish Sklar and Thomas Dublin, *Women and Social Movements, International—1840 to Present*, 53.
56   Baer, '15th International Congress of WILPF', 53.
57   Curthoys, 'Shut Up, You Bourgeois Bitch', in Damousi and Lake, *Gender and War*, 322.
58   Curthoys, 'Shut Up, You Bourgeois Bitch', in Damousi and Lake, *Gender and War*, 322.
59   McHugh, *Minefields and Miniskirts*, 250.
60   McHugh, *Minefields and Miniskirts*, 250.
61   Holmes and Christiansen, 'History of WILPF and Activities of NSW Branch', 1990, MLMSS 5395/Box 01, SLNSW.
62   'Holmes, Margaret Joan Volume 1' (Canberra, 1964 1957), A6119, 3362, NAA. This ASIO file showed that meetings were held at Holmes' house.
63   'Women Strike for Peace in Victoria', August 1963, Box 1723/16, Papers, WILPF, MS 9377, SLV.

rallies in US cities with mothers and children in strollers in 1961.⁶⁴ The WSP in the US, not unlike WFP in Australia, was created in response to growing discontent with WILPF's hierarchical structure. In Australia the main membership of WFP were WILPF members who wanted a way around WILPF's resistance to protest. It gave active members 'interested in taking part in demonstrations' a forum to engage without upsetting those WILPF members who felt the organisation should remain 'respectable' and focused on international advocacy at the UN.⁶⁵

The WFP's first actions were the 'women in mourning' protests in November 1964 which featured over 40 women wearing black veils in a silent but visually powerful statement against conscription.⁶⁶ First protesting at a campaign speech by Menzies in Hornsby on Sydney's North Shore, the women stood during his talk and filed out of the room, causing uproar at the meeting.⁶⁷ Advertisements placed in local papers such as the *North Shore Times* explained that the women were in mourning for 'the youths who will be trained to kill their brother man' and 'for the loss of the individual's right to decide how best to serve his country'.⁶⁸ They continued the metaphor at actions in shopping centres where they also handed out leaflets to the public. This was the first recorded public opposition by Australian women to the reintroduction of conscription.⁶⁹

Conscription motivated many other groups to oppose the militarisation of Australian society. Another group comprising mostly married middle-aged women, Save Our Sons, drew a large following after its creation in 1965. Founded by Joyce Golgerth and Noreen Hewett from the Union of Australian Women (UAW) in Sydney, the non-party affiliated organisation opposed conscription but did not have any official policy on the war.⁷⁰ Critics accused the organisation of being a self-interested group of mothers who were over-protective of their own sons. Indeed, some members did drop out of the movement once their sons were not directly threatened.⁷¹

---

64 'Women Strike for Peace in Victoria', August 1963, Box 1723/16, Papers, WILPF, MS 9377, SLV. See also Harriet Hyman Alonso, *Peace as a Women's Issue: A History of the U.S. Movement for World Peace and Women's Rights* (Syracuse, NY: Syracuse University Press, 1993), 202; Swerdlow, *Women Strike for Peace*, x.
65 '1964–65 NSW WILPF Annual report', MLMSS 5395/Box 01 SLNSW.
66 '1964–65 NSW WILPF Annual report', MLMSS 5395/Box 01 SLNSW.
67 'Women in Black Hoods Fail to Shake Menzies At Poll Rally', *Sydney Morning Herald*, 24 November 1964.
68 'We are Women in Mourning', *North Shore Times*, 2 December 1964.
69 Collins, *Save Our Sons*, 2.
70 Jordens, 'Conscription and Dissent', in Pemberton, *Vietnam*, 79.
71 McHugh, *Minefields and Miniskirts*, 208.

However, for many of the women who joined, 'sons' was a figurative term that conveyed their opposition to any individual forced into combat. Women gained experience and confidence from the movement which encouraged their wider participation in political activity.[72] SOS groups formed in Newcastle, Wollongong, Adelaide, Perth, Townsville and Melbourne, and although they collaborated on federal representations to parliament, each group set its own agenda.[73] Men were permitted to join as associates, but the leadership roles were reserved for women. Jean McLean, a member of the ALP and later a Victorian Legislative Councillor, founded the Melbourne group after hearing an address by Nola Barber who was president of the Victorian ALP Women's Central Organising Committee. The Melbourne group had a close relationship with the ALP.[74]

'Mothers reject conscription': Women for Peace rally, Sydney, 196-?.
Source: Held in Photographs and slides relating to the peace movement in Australia, ca. 1930–1982, created by the Association for International Co-operation and Disarmament (N.S.W.) Mitchell Library, State Library of NSW PXE 1463.

---

72 Jordens, 'Conscription and Dissent', in Pemberton, *Vietnam*, 79; McHugh, *Minefields and Miniskirts*, 206.
73 Collins, *Save Our Sons*, xii.
74 Murphy, *Harvest of Fear*, 142. 'Jean McLean profile', The Australian Women's History Register, accessed 12 December 2016, www.womenaustralia.info/biogs/AWE1230b.htm.

Not unlike WILPF, SOS women were concerned with the way that they were depicted by the media. At their first meeting in Sydney they discussed the need to 'preserve our reputation' and to be tactically prudent in order to maintain an image of respectability and avoid 'being dismissed as militants'.[75] One activist of the era recalled that their strategy was a 'hats and gloves' approach: to 'infiltrate "nice" society and show them that people who really cared were opposed to the war and, as such, they weren't necessarily to be feared.'[76] This group was similar to the US group WSP, who saw their protest as 'feminine, not feminist', and defined their role as mothers and caregivers of society.[77] Sydney women were certainly aware of the work of WSP, as the US WILPF member Ava Pauling had talked about her experience of a WSP conference at a meeting arranged by WILPF when she was in Australia for the CICD 1964 conference. Her husband Linus Pauling, a well-known scientist and peace activist, was presented at the CICD as an international guest.[78] Amy Swerdlow, who was herself a participant in WSP from its formation in 1961, noticed that the women who joined WSP were expressing their 'sense of male betrayal of the agreement they, as women, had made with society to sacrifice their own personal interests and career goals in favour of raising the next generation'. At the same time, they 'were trying to speak to the American people in a language they believed would be understood and accepted'.[79]

WFP, SOS and WILPF in Australia all used maternalist arguments against nuclear warfare, conscription and the Vietnam War, even as they tried to understand and redefine the limited role 'respectable' women were expected to fulfil in public. Moseley wrote often about her motivation in joining WILPF as a mother and grandmother not wanting her 'beautiful new grandson [to] grow up in a world made ugly and terrifying because mothers and grandmothers did not try to stop it when they had the chance'.[80] Building on traditional ideas of feminine identity, as earlier women's rights activists had done, and emphasising the importance of women's roles as mothers, this rhetoric helped to reinforce gender roles. Such activities received criticism

---

75 Murphy, *Harvest of Fear*, 143.
76 Curthoys, 'Shut Up, You Bourgeois Bitch', in Damousi and Lake, *Gender and War*, 325.
77 Swerdlow, *Women Strike for Peace*, x.
78 These connections show once more the wide and diverse networks of international WILPF, connected through marriage, friendship and other means international leaders of the peace community. Ava Pauling to Moseley, 15 June 1964, MLMSS 5395/Box 01 SLNSW.
79 Swerdlow, *Women Strike for Peace*, 235.
80 Moseley to The Editor, *Woman's Day*, 15 October 1965, MLMSS 5395/Box 01 SLNSW.

from detractors who rejected their political action with accusations of: 'why aren't you at home doing the washing'.[81] This stereotyping was something that women in the emerging WLM reacted strongly against.

WILPF collaborated closely with SOS and other groups such as the UAW and Christian Women Concerned in organising events to protest the Vietnam War.[82] Both WILPF and SOS organised silent vigils and attended court proceedings for conscientious objectors. They also both referred young conscripts to WILPF member Vivienne Abraham, a lawyer and editor of *Peacemaker*, who helped give advice on their rights.[83] But WILPF also separated itself from SOS by focusing on their international significance, historical network and commitment to understanding the root causes of war. Honorary secretary of the NSW branch, Michaelis, wrote to the *Sydney Morning Herald* to clarify when the paper had confused and conflated the organisations explaining that 'the two organisations are quite independent, and neither is an offshoot or subsidiary of the other'.[84] She pointed out how SOS women were specifically opposed to conscription while WILPF recognised conscription 'as one aspect of a total situation'.[85]

WILPF's history was a strength that members were eager to promote as it connected their current activity to an international movement with traditions that outlived any controversy over communism. To raise awareness of this history, the NSW branch placed another paid announcement in the *North Shore Times*, reprinting the 'I Am Woman' article written by Eleanor Moore in 1916 about the conscription plebiscite during the World War I. Titled 'Women ... Think!' it explained the origin of the piece and wondered whether society had really 'progressed at all'.[86] WILPF women also dressed as suffragettes and paraded on a lorry singing 'we'll bring the boys back' at a demonstration on the wharves when the first conscripts were sent overseas in April 1966. It was, perhaps unconsciously, echoing a similar protest WILPF made at a May Day march in 1924, when women dressed in white and holding placards rode on the back of a 'peace lorry' decorated

---

81   Curthoys, 'Shut Up, You Bourgeois Bitch', in Damousi and Lake, *Gender and War*, 325.
82   Fiona Wilson, 'Women in the Anti-Vietnam War, Anti-Conscription Movement in Sydney 1964–72' (BA (Hons) thesis, University of New South Wales, 1985), 32.
83   Bobbie Oliver, '*The Peacemaker*'s role in the Anti-Vietnam War Movement', in *Fighting Against War: Peace Activism in the Twentieth Century*, ed. Phillip Deery and Julie Kimber (Albert Park, Vic: Leftbank Press, 2015), 257.
84   Ann Michaelis, to the editor *Sydney Morning Herald*, 9 April 1966, MLMSS 5395/Box 01 SLNSW.
85   Ann Michaelis, to the editor *Sydney Morning Herald*, 9 April 1966, MLMSS 5395/Box 01 SLNSW.
86   'Women ... Think!', in *North Shore Times*, 23 November 1966.

with wisteria blooms.[87] In 1966, however, Michaelis and Elizabeth Morrow radicalised the image by attempting to chain themselves to the gates of the dockyard where they were freed by the police using bolt cutters. They were arrested but later dismissed without charge.[88]

Under surveillance: ASIO and WILPF

The women involved in WILPF suspected that their activities were being monitored and several made vocal disavowals of communist connections. Government files were kept on all those actively involved in WILPF with many containing lists of participants at meetings as well as reports on discussions and planned actions.[89] In certain files it is clear that the information was used by government ministers to assess whether particular protesters were communist; for example, Menzies asked for information on the CICD delegation he declined to meet. He 'requested advice on the security status of the persons named' which, when sent to him, described WILPF as 'an organisation penetrated by the Communist Party of Australia'.[90] It was also presumably penetrated by ASIO. The thought of being under surveillance unsettled many WILPF women who were concerned about maintaining a respectable middle-class reputation. In a later interview, Michaelis recalled that awareness of surveillance prompted members to suspect each other of being agents of ASIO and she wondered herself if Holmes was a plant.[91] This mirrored the events in the US, though on a smaller scale, where the WILPF section was nearly paralysed by the anti-communist paranoia of the McCarthy era.[92] One incident worth recounting occurred in 1966 and involved files on Michaelis, leading to a public discussion on the nature of information gathered by the organisation, who had access to it, and for what purpose it was to be used.

---

87 Eleanor M Moore, *The Quest for Peace, As I Have Known It in Australia* (Melbourne, 1948), 84.
88 McHugh, *Minefields and Miniskirts*, 212. 'R-Riot Ends Clash', *The Australian*, 16 April 1966.
89 For example see 'Holmes, Margaret Joan Volume 1' (Canberra, 1964 1957), A6119, 3362, NAA; 'VROLAND, Anna' (Canberra, 1970 1939), A6119, 2419, NAA; 'Phyllis LATONA' (Canberra, 1962 1926), A6119, 565, NAA.
90 Holmes NAA file, ASIO report on Australian Congress for International Co-operation and Disarmament, Prime Minister's Enquiry, 15 May 1964, A6119, 3362, NAA.
91 McHugh, *Minefields and Miniskirts*, 240.
92 Harriet Alonso, 'Mayhem and Moderation', in *Not June Cleaver: Women and Gender in Postwar America, 1945–1960,* ed. Joanne Meyerowitz (Philadelphia: Temple University Press, 1994), 129.

Michaelis' teenage son Robert attended Sydney Grammar School where cadet training was part of the curriculum. Unimpressed with this requirement, he decided to make a stand and refused to participate when the cadets were ordered to 'take part in a "search and destroy" exercise against soldiers dressed as Vietcong'.[93] The headmaster took a hard line and declared that Robert would have to participate or leave the school.[94] This protest became public with national newspapers reporting that he faced expulsion and that his mother supported his stand. The ALP member for Grayndler, Fred Daly, opposed to the war in Vietnam, supported the boy's stand in parliament, only attracting more publicity to the family.[95] This led the Minister for the Army, Malcolm Fraser, to respond by suggesting that the protest was coordinated by the boy's mother and he provided information about her in parliament that noted her membership with the AICD and WILPF.[96]

Labor member Tom Uren praised WILPF and the AICD, calling them a 'distinguished group of women' associated with the UN.[97] Prime Minister Harold Holt, however, defended Fraser's actions and restated the ASIO information, including Michaelis' street address in parliament. He argued that the minister had to 'test the good faith' and the 'genuineness of the episode' because it had received widespread publicity.[98] Some newspapers such as the *Telegraph* wrote sensationalist articles about Michaelis' alleged 'red' leanings.[99] Yet the majority of public criticism shown in letters to the editor and from the Labor opposition was aimed at Holt and Fraser for misusing ASIO information. Church groups held rallies in support of Michaelis, with Reverend Alan Walker noting that the incident 'raised serious questions concerning the activities of the Security Service and the use of security dossier material by politicians.'[100] The *Australian* newspaper denounced the government's 'stupidity' and both the *Age* and *Sydney Morning Herald*, which had editorial lines supportive of the war, called the event 'unfortunate' and 'distasteful'.[101] This is an example of where WILPF played strongly on their respectability to secure public sympathy and support, leading parts of the establishment to concede that the suspicion of 'communism' went too far. Robert transferred to the local public school.

---

93   'Cadet Faces Expulsion Threat', *The Canberra Times*, 26 September 1966.
94   McHugh, *Minefields and Miniskirts*, 225.
95   Fred Daly, *CPD*, House of Representatives, 28 September 1966, 1401.
96   Malcolm Fraser, *CPD*, House of Representatives, 28 September 1966, 1403.
97   Tom Uren, *CPD*, House of Representatives, 29 September 1966, 1497.
98   Harold Holt, *CPD*, House of Representatives, 29 September 1966, 1416.
99   'Mother in Red-Inspired Committee', *The Telegraph*, September 1966.
100 'Attack on School Cadet System at Church Rally', *The Canberra Times*, 10 October 1966.
101 Edwards, *A Nation at War*, 128.

7. THE ANTI-VIETNAM WAR MOVEMENT AND WOMEN'S LIBERATION

How Australia's involvement in Vietnam influenced WILPF

The Vietnam War lasted seven years, making it Australia's longest overseas military conflict at the time. Murray Goot and Rodney Tiffen have shown that opinion polls during this time are unreliable as true indicators of public opinion because of politically loaded 'wide-ranging and clear-cut cases of manufacture of opinion'.[102] That said, the trend in opinion did show a shift from majority support for Australian and American intervention from 1965 to majority support for a withdrawal from 1969 onwards.[103] The peace movement contributed to this overall shift, though polls also showed that attitudes towards anti-war demonstrators were negative, illustrating why WILPF and more middle-class protesters often tried to distance themselves from more radical parts of the movement.

Nevertheless, in 1970 and 1971, WILPF became a sponsor of the moratorium marches, demonstrations that attracted huge crowds and entrenched the anti-war movement in historical memory as a high point in peace activism. The protests included actions by many new groups at this time, such as the manifold movements of the New Left, conscientious objectors, draft resisters, and the student movement on university campuses which, in many ways, changed the political landscape in Australia. Though WILPF aimed to remain a respectable organisation within this changing milieu, their growing connections to a radical section of society highlight their determined, if still restrained, desire to be part of these momentous social changes. Ted Wheelwright, a lecturer in economics at the University of Sydney, was one of the first academics at the university to radicalise students during 'teach ins'.[104] Many students from conservative families did not join the movement straight away, contrary to the impression of the era being 'flower-bedecked, long-haired student radicals'.[105] Wheelwright was in fact married to Wendy Wheelwright, the treasurer of NSW WILPF and editor of *Peace and Freedom* journal in 1983.[106] By examining radical

---

102 Murray Goot and Rodney Tiffen, 'Public Opinion and the Politics of the Polls', in King, *Australia's Vietnam*, 164.
103 Goot and Tiffen, 'Public Opinion and the Politics of the Polls', in King, *Australia's Vietnam*, 164.
104 'Giant Man with a Mind to Match', *Sydney Morning Herald*, 10 August 2007, accessed 29 November 2022, www.smh.com.au/national/giant-man-with-a-mind-to-match-20070810-gdqtnx.html.
105 Jordens, 'Conscription and Dissent', in Pemberton, *Vietnam*, 75.
106 Australian Section report, '22nd International Congress of WILPF' Sweden 1983, Sklar and Dublin, eds, *Women and Social Movements*, 42.

activity through familial relationships we can see how interconnected groups were, and how discussion, education and debate flowed through personal connections and shaped political commitments.

By 1969 the changing attitudes to Vietnam were beginning to favour the ALP electorally and in December 1972 Labor, led by Gough Whitlam, was elected to government in a victory that ended a long succession of Liberal governments. Many WILPF women were connected with the ALP and shared the optimism for progressive change ushered in by the new government. 'It is a great and exhilarating feeling to win an election when you know it is going to mean so much', wrote Evelyn Rothfield.[107] WILPF women were pleased with Whitlam's initial response to the Vietnam War, not least as he released all draft resisters in his first few days of office. In January 1973 the government declared an end to Australia's involvement and the troops were withdrawn by June. WILPF pointed out how worthwhile the victory was in terms of Australia becoming more clearly aligned to the UN, as the government took a 'stand on declaring the Indian Ocean a zone for peace' and started the process of establishing diplomatic relations with China.[108] At both national and international levels, WILPF felt very strongly that China should be recognised by the UN. In their eyes, the institution could only work if it were truly representative. As they had noted in 1971: 'any disarmament question or other world problem cannot be fully solved without the active participation of the People's Republic of China, with a population of one quarter of mankind.'[109] Whitlam's victory encouraged WILPF Australia to enter the era with a sense of optimism.

The dramatic federal reform implemented by the new government exacerbated a long-running tension in the ideology of WILPF. They felt the more progressive side of politics was listening to their proposals, which gave the organisation confidence that they were helping to shape the future towards their goals. Some realised that promoting local candidates whose views were aligned with their own would have a greater impact on policy than focusing on the international networks. As a result, the nation-state increasingly shaped their activism. Around the issue of the Vietnam War their action often had a national focus as WILPF campaigned against conscription and Australian involvement in the war. Yet the organisation still wanted to promote an international understanding of the conflict,

---

107 Rothfield to Ballantyne, 6 December 1972, series III reel 55, WILPF Papers.
108 Rothfield to Ballantyne, 6 December 1972, series III reel 55, WILPF Papers.
109 *Peace and Freedom* 8, no. 1 (March 1971), series III reel 55, WILPF Papers.

as did many members who became frustrated by the obsession with local parochial politics at the expense of a more internationalist mindset. Many members remained focused on their international connections, while others joined with WFP to undertake creative actions against conscription and the war within a locally minded peace movement.

While the international connections remained strong, some believed that there should be a sharper focus on the local and national. In May 1966 Holmes wrote to the Geneva headquarters to explain that they could not increase their international membership fees because

> Australia is AT WAR and we are fighting a desperate struggle against our own government and our country's ever-increasing involvement in United States policy, and we must have money to carry on this struggle.[110]

For members like Lorraine Moseley, the international was more important, and the focus on the local was a frustration that diverted the energy of the section:

> I did not want to continue on just to be busy, or to make myself feel better, but rather to work with others with an INTERNATIONAL AND GLOBAL viewpoint. Ah! But there's the rub! I found people in WILPF so concerned with local affairs that they had no time for a global viewpoint.[111]

Moseley became an international observer for WILPF at the Economic Commission for Asia and the Far East Conferences in 1968 and 1969 in Canberra, and used this as a way to keep her attention on regional internationalism while others focused on local issues.[112] It was a challenge to engage with internationalism as most political engagement required action at the national level. This debate would surface again over the next decades when WILPF became more focused on their lobbying efforts at the UN and their evolving identity as an NGO.

---

110 Holmes to Stahle, 22 May 1966, series III reel 55, WILPF Papers.
111 Moseley to Ellen Holmgaard, 18 March 1972, series III reel 55, WILPF Papers.
112 Heather Williams, *Women and Peace, WILPF An Australian Profile*, accessed through WILPF, 1982, 13.

SISTERS IN PEACE

The women's liberation movement

By 1970 new energy was being injected into the organised women's movement through the radical experiences of women activists in the peace protests against the Vietnam War. Life was changing for women in Australia. Scientific developments offered the promise of revolutionary emancipation in sexual relationships, with reliable contraception in the form of the pill as well as effective and rapid treatment for sexually transmitted diseases that were prevalent at the time.[113] While many of the ideas about sex and sexuality had been championed by radicals long before the 1960s, the wider acceptance of various social changes, along with the radicalising protests of the Vietnam War, turned the decade into an era 'encrusted with legend'.[114]

Ground-breaking feminist books gave a new language to the women's movement. Simone de Beauvoir's *The Second Sex,* published in 1949 and translated into English in 1953, was still influencing other writers such as Betty Friedan, who published *The Feminine Mystique* in 1963. The latter articulated the limitations of women's social role within the family, calling it 'the problem that has no name'.[115] Kate Millett's *Sexual Politics*, published in the US in 1969, popularised the term 'patriarchy' as a way of understanding male power and privilege, while Germaine Greer's *The Female Eunuch*, published the following year, became an international bestseller.[116] These were radical and provocative books that had far-reaching impacts. Beyond the sexual revolution they also stimulated new interest in women's history. It was not long before new histories of women were having a significant impact on the understanding of women's place in society in Australia and abroad.[117]

---

113 Lake, *Getting Equal*, 220.
114 Frank Bongiorno, *The Sex Lives of Australians: A History* (Collingwood, Vic: Black Inc, 2012), 222.
115 Simone de Beauvoir, *The Second Sex* (New York: Knopf, 1952); Betty Friedan, *The Feminine Mystique* (Melbourne: Penguin, 1963).
116 Kate Millett, *Sexual Politics* (London: Rupert Hart-Davis, 1970), 25; see discussion of this in Susan Magarey, *Dangerous Ideas: Women's Liberation—Women's Studies—Around the World* (Adelaide: University of Adelaide Barr Smith Press, 2015), 7, doi.org/10.20851/dangerous-ideas; Germaine Greer, *The Female Eunuch* (London: Paladin, 1971). For more information see biography of Greer, Christine Wallace, *Greer, Untamed Shrew* (Sydney: Pan Macmillan Australia, 1997).
117 Anne Summers, *Damned Whores and God's Police*, 2nd rev. ed. (Camberwell, Vic; Penguin Books, 2002); Beverley Kingston, *My Wife, My Daughter, and Poor Mary Ann: Women and Work in Australia* (Melbourne: Thomas Nelson Australia, 1975); Miriam Dixson, *The Real Matilda: Woman and Identity in Australia 1788 to the Present* (Sydney: UNSW Press, 1976); Edna Ryan and Anne Conlon, *Gentle Invaders: Australian Women at Work 1788–1974* (Melbourne: Thomas Nelson Australia, 1975).

The latest wave of women's organising, inspired by novel theories of gender and equipped with a new language of 'sex roles' and 'sexism' to discuss it, began on university campuses and within peace movements in the late 1960s. 'Sexism' in particular offered a framework in which to discuss structural inequalities, though analysis usually focused on the individual rather than women's role in the family. Sexuality and bodily autonomy were primary concerns. This emphasis differed from previous women's rights campaigns in acknowledging women's desire for sex and aiming to achieve sexual liberation through access to contraception and abortion rather than through repression.[118] Women also had new economic and career aspirations that underpinned their call for change. As the historians Patricia Grimshaw and Marilyn Lake (among others) have shown, the WLM was a 'generational rebellion' that rejected women's biological destiny as mothers as well as the demands and expectations of motherhood.[119]

Women who engaged in the Vietnam War protests were encouraged to think about oppression from the perspective of the national struggle of the Vietnamese. Through direct experience and theoretical contemplation in the anti-war movement they began to think more deeply about their own liberation. The name women's liberation movement (WLM) was consciously chosen to mirror the Vietnamese liberation movement. Many young women became frustrated with the condescension from male comrades in the peace movement. Activist Kate Jennings gave a speech at a Vietnam War moratorium march in Sydney in 1970 that controversially pointed out the inconsistencies of men in the New Left. Jennings proclaimed,

> [O]ur brothers of the left and in the peace movement … will think that what I am about to say is not justified, this is a moratorium … Women are conscripted every day into their personalised slave kitchens. Can you with your mind filled with the moratorium, spare a thought for their freedom, identity, minds, and emotions?[120]

Women like Jennings wanted to have a louder and distinctive voice in the male-dominated anti-war campaigns. They also did not want to be subordinated to perform menial tasks within the movement.

---

118 Marilyn Lake, 'Sexuality and Feminism: Some Notes in Their Australian History', *Lilith: A Feminist History Journal*, no. 7 (1991): 29. See also Lake, *Getting Equal*, 223.
119 Grimshaw et al., *Creating a Nation*, 301.
120 Kate Jennings, *Trouble: Evolution of a Radical: Selected Writings 1970–2010* (Melbourne, Vic: Black Inc, 2010), 8.

WILPF and its interaction with the WLM

For WILPF, whose membership in the 1970s consisted primarily of older married women, some of the views being promoted by the WLM were confronting. The focus on abortion, contraception and sexuality certainly challenged some church-going members. In Australia and internationally, WILPF was not at the forefront of the WLM. That said, many WILPF members had been the targets of insults as a result of their efforts in the Vietnam peace movement, similar to those endured by the politicised WLM women. Holmes and other members bristled at being asked to 'why aren't you back at home looking after your husbands and kids?'[121] Though women like Holmes sympathised with WLM women, they had grown up in an era of rigid gender segregation and did not politicise the experience in the same way as the younger generation, instead seeking to instrumentalise the philosophy and values underpinning a more traditional gender order to advance their politics. WILPF saw itself as a peace organisation. When it was clear that women's suffrage 'had not put an end to or even diminished wars', their commitment to their feminist identity was constantly questioned.[122]

The rising transnational WLM provoked WILPF to reassert its identity as a peace organisation, rather than a feminist one. In fact, serious discussions took place about whether it should remain a women's group at all. In 1968 British WILPF member Margaret Tims wrote a circular letter to the international membership advocating that WILPF should no longer be a women's organisation, because 'the two causes—of peace and freedom in the general sense and of women's freedom in the particular sense—are no longer synonymous and should be treated separately.'[123] As women were no longer 'outside' politics but part of the system as enfranchised citizens, they had joint responsibility for its failures and achievements. With more women in positions of power, especially in Australia—not least as a result of the rise of 'state feminism' instituted by 'femocrats' working within the political system and the rising critique of white feminists by Indigenous activists—it became harder for WILPF to assert that they spoke for all women, or to argue that women were not complicit in decisions about war and violence.[124]

---

121 Holmes quoted in McHugh, *Minefields and Miniskirts*, 239.
122 Catherine Foster, *Women for All Seasons: The Story of the Women's International League for Peace and Freedom* (Athens: University of Georgia Press, 1989), 40.
123 Margaret Tims, April 1968 circular letter to WILPF, quoted in Foster, *Women for All Seasons*, 55.
124 Lake, *Getting Equal*, 253. Patricia O'Shane, *Aboriginal Political Movements: Some Observations* (Armidale, NSW: University of New England-Armidale, 1998).

7. THE ANTI-VIETNAM WAR MOVEMENT AND WOMEN'S LIBERATION

The ambitions of the peace movement did not necessarily align with those advanced by feminists. For example, when the Australian feminist Anne Summers made a proposal in the 1990s that women should be admitted to full combat duties, arguing that 'women were getting killed anyway; but as long as their access to the military was restricted, they were being denied the opportunity to rise up the ranks of an important public service employer', she was advancing a feminist argument that directly contradicted WILPF's stance against normalising militarism in society.[125]

Tims' suggestion that WILPF women should abandon their status as a women's organisation was not acted upon; however, the Danish section did remove 'Women's' from their title in 1969. They were congratulated by the international chair, Elise Boulding, for doing so. '[P]erhaps our sisters are right and its time for women to become people', wrote Boulding.[126] By 1974, when Kay Camp was international president of WILPF, her husband William Camp became a member of WILPF. More men also joined, including the Australian pacifist Dr Keith Suter after hearing about Camp's membership.[127] Some WILPF leaders such as Baer determinedly tried to maintain the link between women and peace, but the League gradually 'evolved into being a peace organisation whose members happened to be women', though with the acceptance of male members even this had changed.[128]

Although some WILPF members were sceptical and somewhat defensive about associating with the WLM, they still promoted women's issues and equality more generally. Their concerns about new feminist ideologues were with their insistence on an equality that did not account for women's 'difference'. The US section of WILPF wrote about the relationship of WILPF with the WLM in 1970, noting that: 'WILPF was born of the suffrage movement … Our criticism is that some feminists equate equality and similarity—the idealization of masculine attributes.'[129] When members of WILPF were asked if they were feminists, many were quick to draw the distinction between the organised WLM, with which they were not involved, and general support for women's equality. As Betty McIntosh, president of the WA WILPF branch in the 1970s, explained:

---

125 McHugh, *Minefields and Miniskirts*, 263.
126 Foster, *Women for All Seasons*, 56.
127 Cavanagh, *Margaret Holmes*, 302. Erika Rathgeber to Edith Ballantyne, 5 July 1978, Box 53/4 WILPF, SCPC, University of Colorado at Boulder Archives (CU Archives). Ballantyne reply, 10 July 1978, WILPF, SCPC, CU Archives.
128 Foster, *Women for All Seasons*, 32.
129 Foster, *Women for All Seasons*, 56.

> I don't feel I want to drop other things I'm doing for the sake of pursuing feminism, and yet I have always been strongly in favour of women's rights and personally involved in a number of areas where recognition of women is very important ... I think there's a difference between organised feminism and feeling the strength of feminism. I think when we use the term loosely, we do refer to organised feminism. And I've just never had the time to devote to that.[130]

While WILPF leaders ensured that the organisation kept its distance from the WLM, the new movement energised individual members. Irene Greenwood, in her 70s at the time, enjoyed the new 'awakened consciousness' fostered by WLM but felt it was 'no new phenomenon'.[131] She nonetheless saw the new wave's differences, with its 'advantages of higher education, knowledge of the realities of economics and politics, experience in student militancy, and financial independence from their parents' control.' Greenwood specifically acknowledged their mobility. The new generation of activists

> poured across national and international borders and met, speaking and singing together, picking up the phrases of a new culture: 'We shall overcome'. The words on their banners might have been different, but the expression was, like the Women's Movement I grew up with, for freedom and a challenge to power systems.[132]

A certain intergenerational solidarity connected some WILPF women with WLM.

This solidarity, significant though it was, did not resolve the tension between the two organisations. WILPF's reluctance to become involved with this new wave of organised women's groups points to the difficulties women had organising across generations with different motivations, perspectives and experiences. Indeed, Stella Cornelius, the Australian vice-president of WILPF in 1987, believed that WILPF members tended 'to be matriarchs', and while they would 'very happily [work] with other women's groups that attract younger women', they were more 'like a motherly organisation in the women's activities for peace'.[133] Suellen Murray has noted that in the women's peace movement of the 1980s, 'while many involved ... would not

---

130 Betty McIntosh interviewed in 1985 in Foster, *Women for All Seasons*, 176.
131 Irene Greenwood, 'Chronicle of Change', in *As a Woman: Writing Women's Lives*, ed. Jocelynne A Scutt (Melbourne: Artemis Publishing, 1992), 113.
132 Greenwood, 'Chronicle of Change', in Scutt, *As a Woman*, 113.
133 Stella Cornelius, 'Peace Worker and Businesswoman', in *The Matriarchs*, ed. Susan Mitchell (Ringwood, Vic: Penguin, 1987), 130.

have claimed to be radical feminists, the politics of radical feminism was influential'.[134] WILPF was not intimately involved in the new direction of the movement, but they were starting to reconceptualise the indissoluble links between violence and gender. Influenced by feminist theory, WILPF began articulating the link between international violence and domestic forms of violence such as rape and battery. The US section held a conference in 1967 called 'Women's Response to the Rising Tide of Violence'.[135] And in Western Australia in 1971 the WILPF branch held a symposium called 'The Understanding of Human Aggressiveness' where they invited a sociologist, psychologist, psychiatrist and biologist to address the issue. While it was not made explicit that it was male violence and aggressiveness under examination, the report used gendered pronouns throughout to discuss 'mankind', 'man' and 'his very nature'.[136]

Anti-nuclear march through George and Pitt Streets, Sydney, the AICD banner celebrating 20 years dates this picture as 1979.
Source: 'Women's International League for Peace and Freedom', held in Photographs and slides relating to the peace movement in Australia, ca. 1930–1982, created by the Association for International Co-operation and Disarmament (N.S.W.) Mitchell Library, State Library of NSW, PXE 1463.

---

134 Suellen Murray, '"Make Pies Not War": Protests by the Women's Peace Movement of the Mid 1980s', *Australian Historical Studies* 37, no. 127 (1 April 2006): 81, doi.org/10.1080/10314610608601205.
135 Foster, *Women for All Seasons*, 41.
136 Roma Brown and Betty King, *The Understanding of Human Aggressiveness Seminar Report*, 24 June 1971, Western Australian Branch of WILPF, NLA.

The membership of WILPF was aging, and many sections had difficulty recruiting a cohort of younger members. In the Australian branch, new member Jennifer Fischhof joined after the Vietnam War protests. Her youth and vitality were much feted by the older membership, with members writing: 'She is just the sort of woman we need, young, active and tremendously motivated.'[137] Fischhof became active in WILPF and tried to engage older members with the campaigns run by the WLM. She was a member of the newly formed Women's Electoral Lobby, which was established in 1972. She spoke of the difficulty she had in interesting older members in the WLM in a letter to Edith Ballantyne at the Geneva office:

> WILPF in Australia is unknown!!! I have tried hard this year to put WILPF on the map in Australia, but there seems to be a fear that by working with other groups that WILPF will lose its identity. I feel discrimination against women is a WILPF issue, but cannot get anyone in WILPF to work with Women's lib and a new big group here, the Women's Electoral Lobby.[138]

Just as many WILPF women involved in peace activism did not want to engage directly with the WLM, many in women's liberation were sceptical of joining the peace movement. There was a concern that 'peace activism could be tied too closely to particular discourses about femininity, ones that feminists were working hard to challenge.'[139] Maternity and nurturance were often invoked in discussions of peace. This did not serve the interests of feminists preoccupied with 're-imagining gender well beyond the confines of motherhood and wifedom'.[140] In the 1970s and 1980s, with the emergence of SOS and the Pine Gap Peace Camp that referenced maternalism as a rhetorical device, the equality/difference debate again divided feminists and pacifists. For some Women's Liberationists there was a fear 'that any form of women's pacifism may be positively subversive of feminist purpose'.[141] However, unlike other more conservative women's groups such as the National Council of Women (NCW) and the Country Women's Association, WILPF did not expressly criticise the aims of WLM, despite the difficulty they often had in finding a place for themselves within their

---

137 Rothfield to Ballantyne, 11 May 1974, series III reel 55, WILPF Papers.
138 Jennifer Fischhof to Ballantyne, 15 February 1974, series III reel 55, WILPF Papers.
139 Suellen Murray, 'Taking the Toys from the Boys', *Australian Feminist Studies* 25, no. 63 (March 2010): 5, doi.org/10.1080/08164640903499893.
140 Murray, 'Taking the Toys from the Boys', 5.
141 Jo Vellacott, 'A Place for Pacifism and Transnationalism in Feminist Theory: The Early Work of the Women's International League for Peace and Freedom', *Women's History Review* 2, no. 1 March 1993: 24, doi.org/10.1080/09612029300200021.

ranks.¹⁴² Fischhof remained involved in both peace activism and feminism, and attended international meetings in the UN Decade of Women. She was among a small handful of young women who remained committed to participating in both WILPF and the WLM, working to weave together the rhetoric of peace and feminism.

While WILPF may not have been at the forefront of second wave feminism, the wider social and political transformations triggered by the movement nevertheless substantially transformed the organisation. Increased scholarship on gender and peace, largely produced by women who were beginning to establish themselves in university departments, gave WILPF a new lens through which to examine their core purpose. In 1983 Cynthia Enloe, an American academic and member of WILPF, published *Does Khaki Become You? The Militarisation of Women's Lives,* which explored how militarism relied upon individual men and women performing conventional gender roles.¹⁴³ Such scholarship prompted WILPF to rethink the nature of their organising. Also relevant in connection with WILPF's relationship to contemporary feminism was the work of the philosopher Sara Ruddick and her book *Maternal Thinking*, which revived the maternalist perspective and helped encourage the transnational WLM to reflect on the strengths of WILPF's approach.¹⁴⁴ Ruddick, in her description of motherhood and the politics of caring, maintained that men could fulfil the roles traditionally left to women. In such ways, entire patriarchal order was under scrutiny, and WILPF did try to find ways to bring their own activism into dialogue with wider public debates. At the 1986 WILPF triennial congress in the Netherlands, the keynote speaker, Dr Catharina Halkes, gave a speech that unpacked the word 'patriarchy'—made popular in the 1970s by feminist scholars—and linked it to the idea of peace.¹⁴⁵ Her talk sought to understand how the structure of patriarchal societies was a major root cause of war, and explore how this could help provide the justification for WILPF's decision to organise autonomously.

---

142 The NCW often forwarded letters from affiliates to politicians critical of the WLM, and a new group Women Who Want to be Women would purposely sabotage WLM conferences, see Judith Smart and Marian Quartly, *Respectable Radicals: A History of the National Council of Women of Australia 1896–2006* (Melbourne: Monash University Publishing, 2015), 390 and 396.
143 Cynthia H Enloe, *Does Khaki Become You? The Militarisation of Women's Lives* (Boston: South End Press, 1983).
144 Sara Ruddick, *Maternal Thinking: Towards a Politics of Peace* (London: Women's Press, 1990).
145 Catharina JM Halkes, 'Women's Work for Peace in a Patriarchal Society', in '23rd International Congress of WILPF "Women Unite for Justice and Peace"', The Netherlands, 1986, Sklar and Dublin, eds, *Women and Social Movements*, 26. This talk was edited and reproduced as 'Peace and Patriarchy', *Pax et Libertas* 51, no. 4 (December 1986).

Halkes said that the 'rigid role distribution' that made women 'accustomed to think that they have to keep peace only in the house, in the family and in personal relations' which would 'influence their husbands and children ... to help avoid war' was wrong.[146] Women, she argued, were not inherently more peaceful than men. Rather, the 'differences between the sexes stem from social conditioning—learned behaviour by which women and men come to see the world, and act in it, in substantially different ways.'[147] Halkes reinforced the idea that it was not men who were the problem, but 'the patriarchal system which dehumanizes many men' and encourages them to 'kill the enemy of tenderness, love and care within themselves. The linking of male sexuality to aggression is the root of both patriarchy and war'.[148] Furthermore, Halkes suggested that 'peace is not possible in a patriarchal society' and that opposing male aggression with 'feminine motherliness' only reinforces patriarchal ideas about men and women having different moral codes. The way forward for peace was to 'throw off shackles of fear and lack of self-confidence'.[149]

From 1989 onwards, all congresses of WILPF referred to 'patriarchy' as a root cause of war and recognised the need to dismantle the oppression of women as part of their program to move towards a more peaceful society. Though it did not happen all at once, and while WILPF was not immediately on board with second wave feminist activism, WILPF eventually adopted a radical interpretation of feminist theory into their core ideas and vocabulary.

***

With the anti-war movement running parallel to rapid changes in women's social position, the WLM began to discuss ideas about femininity, women in the workforce and family responsibilities. Curthoys has noted that the older women in the anti–Vietnam War movement, especially WILPF, with its legacy stretching back to World War I, came from a 'more sharply sexually segregated culture than their younger sisters' and 'tended to take for granted the necessity to work with other women to achieve political goals'.[150] New political ideas about equality meant that radicalised young feminists found the value of female solidarity 'less obvious'.[151] Their concept

---

146 'Peace and Patriarchy', *Pax et Libertas* 51, no. 4, December 1986.
147 'Peace and Patriarchy', *Pax et Libertas* 51, no. 4, December 1986.
148 'Peace and Patriarchy', *Pax et Libertas* 51, no. 4, December 1986.
149 'Peace and Patriarchy', *Pax et Libertas* 51, no. 4, December 1986.
150 Curthoys, 'Shut Up, You Bourgeois Bitch', in Damousi and Lake, *Gender and War*, 338.
151 Curthoys, 'Shut Up, You Bourgeois Bitch', in Damousi and Lake, *Gender and War*, 338.

of autonomous collective action, while drawing on ideas of sisterhood, came from experiences of marginalisation rather than from ideas of maternalism. Engaging with this new and subversive movement in the 1970s required a change in WILPF's approach.

Herself a participant in the 1970s WLM, Curthoys recognised how women in the movement 'anxiously distinguished' themselves from activists who had come immediately before them in established groups such as the UAW and WILPF.[152] She described the lack of knowledge and arrogance the movement showed in thinking it was an entirely new as 'matricidal feminism', with women 'shaking hands with our sisters yet rejecting our mothers.'[153] The movement fragmented, with different groups promoting different priorities, all responding to backlash and criticism from outside the movement and from other women.

WILPF was confronted by this 'matricidal feminism', which they felt excluded their ideas and devalued their history. Yet, despite this rejection, the organisation eventually absorbed ideas generated by the WLM. The concept of 'patriarchy', in particular, gave WILPF the language to articulate the gendered focus of their organisation and interpret their activities with a radical framework seeking to dismantle gendered oppression.

The Vietnam era changed Australian society. Newly politicised university students became vocal and sometimes militant opponents to the status quo while young women spoke out about the marginalisation they experienced in Vietnam War protests. This altered configuration posed a challenge to WILPF, which was confronted by new ideas about gender equality and feminism.[154] Recruiting younger women remained a problem for the organisation. Margaret Forte, who was a long-time secretary in the SA branch, argued in the 1980s how necessary it was for WILPF to embrace new techniques and engage with the WLM. She believed 'the old secretary's day is done'.[155] Certainly, it was not easy for women with careers to give leadership to voluntary organisations, but this was the challenge they must meet. 'We must stop building up files of papers and be out in the community, speaking on television and from public platforms, organizing

---

152 Ann Curthoys in preface to Barbara Curthoys and Audrey McDonald, *More Than a Hat and Glove Brigade: The Story of the Union of Australian Women* (Sydney: Bookpress, 1996), ii.
153 Curthoys, *More Than a Hat and Glove Brigade*, ii.
154 Lake, *Getting Equal*, 221.
155 Margaret Forte, *Peace and Freedom*, 1985, papers of Meredith Stokes Box 5/35 NLA.

conferences and demonstrations,' Forte declared. We must be 'seen and heard.'[156] WILPF, along with other voluntary organisations like the NCW, trade unions, political parties and even religious congregations, began experiencing 'organisational decline' from the 1960s onwards. Despite their efforts to engage younger women, this would continue to pose a threat into the twenty-first century.[157]

---

[156] Margaret Forte, *Peace and Freedom*, 1985, papers of Meredith Stokes Box 5/35 NLA.
[157] Smart and Quartly, *Respectable Radicals*, 419.

8

Women, peace and security: The United Nations Women's conferences and Security Council Resolution 1325

In December 1987, the US warship USS *Missouri* had an open day for the public while it was docked in Sydney Harbour. Barbara Meyer, otherwise known as Bobi, went on board with the crowd. Unbeknown to those around her, Meyer was not an ordinary warship visitor. Underneath her clothes her body was covered in paint: 'NO NUKE SHIPS' had been written on her legs and, with the help of a friend, 'GREENHAM GRANNIES AGAINST THE NUKES' was printed on her back above her bra. On her upper chest was a peace sign.[1] Climbing aboard the warship, Meyer chose a prominent site on the upper deck and 'swallowing her misgivings, took off her dress'.[2] While shocked onlookers and sailors gathered around, unsure of how to react, she gave a '20 minute anti-nuclear speech' in her underwear.[3] Police eventually arrived, covering her with a blanket and escorting her from the ship, but not before hundreds saw her anti-war message where she discussed being a mother of eight and a grandmother of five. The media delighted in the story, *The Canberra Times* leading with the headline 'Granny Strips'.[4]

---

1   'Vale—Barbara (Bobi) Meyer ACT Branch', *Peace and Freedom* 52, Issues 1 and 2 (April 2013), 13.
2   'Vale—Barbara (Bobi) Meyer ACT Branch', *Peace and Freedom* 52, Issues 1 and 2 (April 2013), 13.
3   'Granny Strips, Two Men Arrested in N-Protests', *The Canberra Times*, 28 December 1987, 3.
4   'Granny Strips, Two Men Arrested in N-Protests', *The Canberra Times*, 28 December 1987, 3.

Older members of the Women's International League for Peace and Freedom (WILPF) were dedicated members of the anti-war movement in Australia, often attracting surprised reactions when they attended protests. Those defying stereotypes and breaking conventions frequently drew the attention of the media. New South Wales member Launa Gilmour noted in a media interview how 'photographers always go straight for my sister, who is in her 80s. Her age apparently lends some authority'.[5] Individual members continued to stage creative and personal protests to gain media attention for their anti-war agenda, even as the structure of WILPF became more focused on lobbying at international forums. It remained one of WILPF's strengths that they were able to combine the local and personal aspects of grassroots activism with international and political action. The 1980s were a productive period for WILPF in Australia. A new ACT branch created in 1982 brought a significant increase in membership, and peace groups across the country were energised by large nuclear disarmament and Palm Sunday rallies in all major cities.[6] It seemed, according to one journalist, that since the women's liberation movement 'offered ordinary women the confidence to speak up', women 'not only held their own within the movement, but have also taken control of it'.[7] Gilmour herself believed the rapid increase in WILPF membership was partly 'a rebellion against a world run by men'.[8] A greater number of members were working but still found time for volunteering, which Gilmour believed reflected a particularly feminine engagement with politics; 'unlike men, women make time for everything'.[9]

***

The year 1975 was declared International Women's Year by the United Nations (UN). It was followed by a 'Decade for Women' where an official conference was planned every five years, first in Mexico City (1975), then Copenhagen (1980) and Nairobi (1985), with a follow up conference in Beijing (1995).[10] Three themes were chosen to structure the first conference:

---

5   'Peace? It's Up to the Women', *Sydney Morning Herald*, 3 June 1984.
6   Australian Section report, '22nd International Congress of WILPF "Women Save the World"' Sweden, 1983, accessed through database edited by Kathryn Kish Sklar and Thomas Dublin, *Women and Social Movements, International—1840 to Present*, 42.
7   'Peace? It's Up to the Women', *Sydney Morning Herald*, 3 June 1984.
8   'Peace? It's Up to the Women', *Sydney Morning Herald*, 3 June 1984.
9   'Peace? It's Up to the Women', *Sydney Morning Herald*, 3 June 1984.
10 For more on IWY see: Jocelyn Olcott, 'Globalizing Sisterhood' in *The Shock of the Global: The 1970s in Perspective,* ed. Niall Ferguson et al., (Cambridge, Mass: Belknap Press of Harvard University Press, 2010), 281–93, doi.org/10.2307/j.ctvrs8zfp.21; and Roland Burke, 'Competing for the Last Utopia? The NIEO, Human Rights, and the World Conference for the International Women's Year, Mexico City, June 1975', *Humanity* 6, no. 1 (2015), doi.org/10.1353/hum.2015.0000.

equality, development and peace. The influences of new women's groups and the UN Decade of Women set the tone for WILPF in the 1970s and 1980s, with members committed to highlighting the peace pillar within a growing network of women's advocacy groups and organisations focused on international action.

WILPF's strength was often seen to lie in its reputation as a grassroots organisation with widespread membership. Its engagement with the UN Decade for Women and the World Conference on Women in Beijing in 1995 saw a new dual identity emerge as it started to modernise into a professional non-government organisation (NGO), integrating with the UN lobbying structure. WILPF centralised its focus on lobbying the UN and other international bodies, with the New York office becoming fundamental to the international section. In the 1990s the staff of the New York office took a leadership role in lobbying for the passing of Security Council Resolution (SCR) 1325 on women, peace and security, which became a watershed moment for the movement. National branches then began a campaign to pressure governments to create National Action Plans for local implementation of 1325 goals, all the while continuing to promote feminist foreign policy priorities.[11]

Trying to promote the peace agenda at the Decade for Women conferences was not always easy or straightforward, despite peace being a stated theme. The limited discussion of peace and conflict was highly politicised, not least as a result of a resolution that equated Zionism with racism, which caused countries that were supportive of Israel to abstain from voting for the various plans of action.[12] At the 1980 conference in Copenhagen, for example, Australia voted against the whole plan of action due to the use of the word Zionism. The focus on the Arab–Israeli conflict, the discussion of liberation groups during the era of decolonisation and problems of economic development created a complex political environment. WILPF members also debated the need to work with groups like the Women's International Democratic Federation (WIDF) who many felt were supportive of violence in liberation struggles. Like the generations of WILPF women that had

---

11   Catia Cecilia Confortini, *Intelligent Compassion: The Women's International League for Peace and Freedom and Feminist Peace* (Oxford: Oxford University Press, 2012), 133, doi.org/10.1093/acprof:oso/ 9780199845231.001.0001.

12   Kristen Ghodsee, 'Revisiting the United Nations Decade for Women: Brief Reflections on Feminism, Capitalism and Cold War Politics in the Early Years of the International Women's Movement', *Women's Studies International Forum* 33, no. 1 (January 2010): 6, doi.org/10.1016/j.wsif.2009.11.008.

come before them, they were concerned about any action that might contradict or erode their commitment to nonviolence. Their passion and determination had endured: WILPF Australia's involvement in the UN Decade for Women conferences and their role in campaigns during the 1990s played an important role in the SCR 1325 being passed by the UN.

The peace agenda at the UN women's conferences has sometimes been dismissed by anti-communist critics as Cold War propaganda. Indeed, the political momentum for the UN to host the conferences emerged from Cold War rivalries, and the 'peace' pillar was for many a 'catch-all term used for issues that the United States delegation preferred to keep off the agenda, such as nuclear disarmament, apartheid, racial discrimination, and national sovereignty'.[13] Some critics thought the conferences fatally divided between the 'first world' feminist priorities of equality versus 'third world' issues of development.[14] The entire decade was politically turbulent, with national governments often limiting delegation and individual participation and the international media portraying the conferences as chaotic. Yet WILPF continued to participate, hoping to advance their cause without being mistaken as communist sympathisers. Their efforts nevertheless were seen by some to have been coopted by anti-Western initiatives. WILPF's participation was nonetheless distinctive in its attachment to nonviolent methods. One WILPF Australia member took stock after the 1975 conference, realising: 'We are in the midst of a period of violent social change without a clear policy on how we, who believe in nonviolent change, fit in to the picture.'[15] WILPF women were confronted by the violence of national liberation movements and often found themselves trying to articulate a position denouncing violence in an arena where many approved of conflict if used in struggles against oppression.

---

13   Jocelyn Olcott, *International Women's Year: The Greatest Consciousness-Raising Event in History* (New York: Oxford University Press, 2017), doi.org/10.1093/oso/9780195327687.001.0001.
14   Olcott, *International Women's Year*. See also Challen Nicklen, 'Rhetorics of Connection in the United Nations Conferences on Women, 1975–1995' (PhD thesis, Pennsylvania State University, 2008).
15   Rothfield to Ballantyne, 11 March 1976, Box 53/4 WILPF, SCPC, University of Colorado at Boulder Archives (CU Archives).

1975 Mexico City Conference and the Arab–Israeli Conflict

In 1975, Elizabeth Reid, as the Australian prime minister's adviser on women's affairs, organised the 'Women in Politics Conference' to discuss theoretical and practical issues facing women interested in getting involved in Australian politics. It was International Women's Year (IWY) and the credibility given to the women's movement by increased funding provided by the Whitlam Government made the conference a significant part of government business. The atmosphere was electric. Irene Greenwood, a prominent member of the WILPF in Australia, was appointed by Reid to the advisory committee of the government's IWY program.[16] As a stalwart of the women's movement, introduced at a young age into feminist activism in Western Australia by her mother, Mary Driver, a noted activist of her time, Greenwood's knowledge of the movement before the burst of activity in 1975 was something the women's liberation movement (WLM) sorely needed.[17] Speaking as a keynote at the conference in Canberra, 76-year-old Greenwood encapsulated the excitement of the year and praised the energy of the movement: 'whether we like it or not, I think the lid's off and the steam's out from what I can judge from here today'.[18] Greenwood recognised the significance of the moment. Even so, she was not afraid to put young feminists in their place when it came to their lack of interest in a feminist legacy they had mainly failed to discover. 'I am amazed', she declared:

> to find the young women of this new women's liberation movement totally unaware of the fact that there were women who protested, women who struggled, women who marched, that there were women who accepted the very same principles as they are accepting and advocated them sixty, seventy, eighty, ninety, a hundred years ago.[19]

Greenwood proceeded to share memories from her own long career in women's activism and broadcasting in Australia in an attempt to counter assumptions widely held by younger women activists that their predecessors were 'slow', or 'didn't appreciate' the vote they were 'given'. Critics had often

---

16 Michelle Arrow, *The Seventies: The Personal, the Political, and the Making of Modern Australia* (Sydney: NewSouth Publishing, 2019), 113.
17 Mary Driver profile, Daphne Popham, *Reflections: Profiles of 150 Women who helped make Western Australia's History* (Carroll's Pty Ltd, 1978), 64.
18 Irene Greenwood, 'A Lifetime of Political Activity', in *Women and Politics Conference Volume 1* (Canberra: Australian Government Publishing Service, 1977), 58.
19 Greenwood, 'A Lifetime of Political Activity', *Women and Politics Conference Volume 1*, 58.

pointed to the underrepresentation of women in parliament as proof of women's apathy.[20] She countered: 'And so they think we weren't working. We were working but you see there were many things working against us.'[21] Her call for greater historical understanding represented one of the core functions of the activities of WILPF over the life of the organisation from its founding in 1915: to educate people about social change and the activities of those working towards peace instead of war, and to change the way we understand history. She positioned the women's movement within a longer historical narrative, questioning what it is we remember and commemorate, and why.

The number of international NGOs and intergovernmental organisations dramatically increased over a short period of time, from 2,795 NGOs in 1972 to 12,686 by 1984.[22] It was a development that transformed the international political arena. The Whitlam Government was active in engaging with international political framework. Whitlam renewed Australia's commitment to internationalism by entering into over 133 international treaties in just three years and used international legal commitments as a way of expanding federal government power.[23] Whitlam was eager to involve Australian society in the UN Decade for Women. The government had appointed Reid as the first women's adviser, and to celebrate IWY, it allocated over two million dollars of funding towards grants for events and projects.[24]

Reid had the difficult job of bringing together the various sections of the women's movement during the year and, despite her efforts, the International Women's Year National Advisory Committee was criticised by the mainstream media and sections of the movement itself. The media represented IWY as 'feminism as excess, equated with the extravagance attributed to the Whitlam government in general'.[25] Women's liberation activists such as Mavis Robertson criticised the allocation of funding for not being feminist enough and prioritising non-feminist proposals over WLM

---

20 Greenwood, 'A Lifetime of Political Activity', *Women and Politics Conference Volume 1*, 61.
21 Greenwood, 'A Lifetime of Political Activity', *Women and Politics Conference Volume 1*, 61.
22 Akira Iriye, *Global Community: The Role of International Organizations in the Making of the Contemporary World* (Berkeley: University of California Press, 2002), 129, doi.org/10.1525/9780520936126.
23 Michael Kirby, 'Whitlam as Internationalist: A Centenary Reflection', *Melbourne University Law Review*, 39 (2016): 850, accessed 3 November 2022, law.unimelb.edu.au/__data/assets/pdf_file/0012/2061021/04-Kirby.pdf, 3.
24 Marilyn Lake, *Getting Equal: The History of Australian Feminism* (St Leonards, NSW: Allen & Unwin, 1999), 258.
25 Lake, *Getting Equal*, 259.

projects.²⁶ WILPF members were also disappointed, noting how peace was constantly dropped from the agenda. While pleased that IWY events were well attended and 'spectacular', WILPF remained worried that 'nothing is ever said by anyone except us about the third objective, namely peace. So that is what we are concentrating on'.²⁷

WILPF women decided to put their energy towards the conference planned by the UN for IWY in Mexico City. Unable to have many observers at the main UN event, WILPF's main arena of engagement was through the Tribune satellite conference organised for the many NGOs that arrived to participate in the women's conference. The Tribune hosted over 6,000 women and was open to 'any woman who could get there and wanted to have her say'.²⁸ Both the official conference and the satellite conferences were considered lively and controversial, and represented the 'NGO-ization of activism, particularly transnational women's activism'.²⁹ The media characterised the official conference as being dominated by 'wives of Prime Ministers and Presidents', dubbed 'wifey-poos', and the Tribune conference as being disruptive and divisive.³⁰ Feminists Betty Friedan and Germaine Greer wrote about their experiences of both the UN conference and the Tribune, criticising the national delegations for promoting national interests rather than engaging in a genuine discussion of sexism and its impacts on worldwide gender equality.³¹ Reid, representing Australia at the official proceedings and leading an official delegation that included Margaret Whitlam, was among the few delegates to confront directly issues such as sexism. She decried the focus on women as 'instruments' for national goals rather than acknowledging them as people in their own right.³²

---

26   Lake, *Getting Equal*, 259.
27   Rothfield to Ballantyne, 14 March, 1975, Box 53/4, WILPF, SCPC, CU Archives.
28   Philippa Day Benson, 'Looking to Australia for a Lead in Women's Policies', *Australian Women's Weekly*, 30 July 1975, 4–5.
29   Jocelyn Olcott, 'Globalizing Sisterhood', in Ferguson, *The Shock of the Global*, 287.
30   Day Benson, 'Looking to Australia for a Lead in Women's Policies', 4–5.
31   Betty Friedan, *It Changed My Life: Writings on the Women's Movement* (New York: Dell Publishing Company, 1977), 343; Germaine Greer, *The Madwoman's Underclothes: Essays and Occasional Writings* (New York: Atlantic Monthly Press, 1987), 200.
32   'Australia Wants Changes in Plan', and 'Ms Reid Hits Back' in *Xilonen*, Mexico City, 24 June 1975. See also Elizabeth Reid, 'Between the Official Lines', *Ms. Magazine*, November 1975.

Evelyn Rothfield, 'Handcrafts of All Nations' exhibition, Melbourne, December 1956.

Over forty nations sent exhibits to Australia for a 'Handcrafts of All Nations' exhibition held in Melbourne in December. It was organised by the All Nations Cultural Centre which aims to establish contact on all cultural levels between people of all nations — the Secretary of the All Nations Cultural Centre, Mrs Evelyn Rothfield, arranging the Pakistani exhibit at the exhibition. The Pakistani Government sent all the exhibits.

Source: Photographer J. Fitzpatrick. Image courtesy of the National Archives of Australia. NAA: A1501, A470/1. See Appendix for a short biography of Evelyn Rothfield.

Australian WILPF president Evelyn Rothfield organised a delegation of 35 Australian women to attend the satellite Tribune conference.[33] Women from NGOs were given grants to travel to the Tribune conference, including feminist and labour movement activist Edna Ryan, Aboriginal rights activist Pat Eatock, and President of the National Council of Women Australia Joyce McConnell.[34] Rothfield felt buoyed by the conference, stating: 'I really think we hadn't realised the extent of the anger and frustration of the women of the world. Something very positive has come out of this.'[35] Yet, at the same time, Rothfield felt disappointed by the reluctance of attendees at the UN conference and the Tribune to focus on the 'peace' pillar.[36] International general secretary of WILPF Edith Ballantyne worked alongside Rothfield to organise a 'peace caucus' that released a statement pushing for the UN to convene a world disarmament conference, but they were told that 'such matters would unnecessarily "politicize" the decade'.[37]

The one occasion when peace was raised did indeed become highly divisive and politicised. Leah Rabin, delegate from Israel and wife of Israeli Prime Minister Yitzhak Rabin, was giving a speech to the UN conference when many delegations participated in a coordinated 'walk out' which was widely covered by the press.[38] Rabin said as the walkout occurred: 'countries may have their differences and their misunderstandings, but not to sit down and listen to each other is to miss the point of being here'.[39] Jahan el-Helou, attending from Palestine, responded when asked about the speech by reporters of the conference newspaper *Xilonen*: 'we will sit down with Jews, but not with Zionists and imperialists.'[40] The equating of Zionism with racism and imperialism was controversial and disruptive, characterised as a way to mount the 'soviet agenda' of criticising US foreign policy.[41] In the final world action plan, Zionism was inserted into a resolution about Palestinian and Arab women:

---

33 Rothfield, quoted in Day Benson, 'Looking to Australia for a Lead in Women's Policies', 4–5.
34 Department of Foreign Affairs, 'World Conference for International Women's Year', news release no. 137, 17 June 1975, accessed 12 December 2022, parlinfo.aph.gov.au/.
35 Department of Foreign Affairs, 'World Conference for International Women's Year', news release no. 137, 17 June 1975, accessed 12 December 2022, parlinfo.aph.gov.au/.
36 Rothfield to Ballantyne, 18 July 1975, Box 53/4, WILPF, SCPC, CU Archives.
37 Catherine Foster, *Women for All Seasons: The Story of the Women's International League for Peace and Freedom* (Athens: University of Georgia Press, 1989), 76.
38 'Walkout Staged on Israel', *Xilonen*, Mexico City, 25 June 1975.
39 'Walkout Staged on Israel', *Xilonen*, Mexico City, 25 June 1975.
40 'Walkout Staged on Israel', *Xilonen*, Mexico City, 25 June 1975.
41 Ghodsee, 'Revisiting the United Nations Decade for Women', 6.

> The World Conference of the International Women's Year …
> Considering that international cooperation and peace require national independence and liberation, the elimination of colonialism, neo-colonialism, fascism, Zionism, apartheid and foreign occupation, alien domination and racial discrimination in all its forms and also respect for human rights … Appeals to all states and international organisations to extend assistance—moral and material—to the Palestinian and Arab women and people in their struggle against Zionism.[42]

Eighty-nine countries voted in favour of the document, three opposed and eighteen abstained.[43] The Australian delegation voted in favour of the plan, despite the resolution, because they agreed with everything else in the declaration. Other delegations who voted no to the declaration, such the US, Israel and Denmark, were shocked. The Declaration on the Equality of Women document became the first international document to label Zionism as racism. For US feminist Betty Friedan, who had previously had little interest in Zionism, this incident motivated her to become 'suddenly dedicated to the Zionist cause'.[44] She lamented, however, that the issue had become a 'scapegoat' to blame for the decade's failures and was the 'prevention of real action on women's rights'.[45] Discussing the conflict was one of the few ways in which the conference intended to advance the 'peace' plank of the agenda. But, rather than advancing the peace cause, it deepened divisions and depleted the goodwill required for interpersonal solidarity within the women's movement.

Evelyn Rothfield, as a non-governmental delegate, tried to persuade the Australian delegation to abstain and made her views known to Reid after the conference. '[W]hy single out Zionism?' she asked, encouraging Reid to take a 'more principled stand'.[46] Rothfield was angry. In a letter to Ballantyne she admitted that the 'deliberate singling out of Israel for attack at international forums is becoming an issue of great anxiety to me'.[47] A progressive woman and activist in the Jewish community, experienced in advocating for peace

---

42 Report of the World Conference of the International Women's Year, Mexico City 19 June – 2 July 1975 (New York: United Nations publications, 1976), Sklar and Dublin, *Women and Social Movements*, 110.
43 Ghodsee, 'Revisiting the United Nations Decade for Women', 6.
44 Gil Troy, *Moynihan's Moment: America's Fight Against Zionism as Racism* (New York: Oxford University Press, 2013), 85.
45 Troy, *Moynihan's Moment*, 85.
46 Rothfield to Reid, 21 July 1975 reproduced in Evelyn Rothfield, *The Future Is Past* (self-published: Copy available at the State Library of Victoria, 1992), 65.
47 Rothfield to Ballantyne, 18 July, 1975, Box 53/4, WILPF, SCPC, CU Archives.

in the Middle East, Rothfield did not identify as a Zionist, but the emotive debate at the Mexico City conference made her angry enough to consider doing so.[48]

Evelyn Rothfield and her husband Norman had migrated to Australia from England in 1939.[49] Both were heavily involved in progressive causes and the peace movement through their engagement in the Australian Peace Council (APC) and its successor organisations. Norman Rothfield helped established the Australian Jewish Peace Movement in 1952 and was a delegate to the Vienna Peace Assembly.[50] A mother of three children, herself from a Jewish family, Evelyn had many cultural and personal connections to Europe and to the future of Israel. She first visited Palestine in 1947 and subsequently 'visited Israel more times than I can count'.[51] On her many travels, Rothfield wrote for Australian newspapers such as the *Argus* as a correspondent reporting on the UN.[52] She then published two small booklets about Palestine and the creation of a Jewish state. *Whither Palestine*, published in March 1947, detailed the history of Jews in Palestine while *Israel Reborn* was published after the UN declaration in November 1947 partitioning Palestine between Jews and Arabs and providing for the formation of Israel as a Jewish state the following year.[53] These two works detailed Evelyn's position on the creation of Israel and her belief that peace between the two parties in conflict could be achieved through recognition, understanding and 'good neighbourliness'.[54]

The Australian section of WILPF supported the UN decision in 1947 to create the state of Israel. Doris Blackburn was a prominent signatory to a pamphlet called *Australia and Israel* (1948) written by Brian Fitzpatrick, a prominent historian, journalist, civil libertarian and socialist, which encouraged people to 'ask their government to give official recognition to Israel's government.'[55] By the 1970s Rothfield had many family connections in Israel, which gave a personal dimension to reports of conflict. While she was critical of many of Israel's aggressive policies towards the Palestinians,

---

48 Rothfield to Ballantyne, 18 July, 1975, Box 53/4, WILPF, SCPC, CU Archives.
49 Rothfield, *The Future Is Past*, 25. See biography in the Appendix.
50 Philip Mendes, *The New Left, the Jews and the Vietnam War, 1965–1972* (North Caulfield, Vic: Lazare, 1993), 18.
51 Rothfield, *The Future Is Past*, 55.
52 For example see: Evelyn Rothfield, 'Australian Girls at UN', *The Argus*, 18 October 1949.
53 Evelyn Rothfield, *Israel Reborn* (Melbourne: Dolphin Publications, 1948); Evelyn Rothfield, *Whither Palestine* (Melbourne: Dolphin Publications, 1947).
54 Rothfield, *Israel Reborn*, 2.
55 Brian Fitzpatrick, *Australia and Israel* (Melbourne: July 1948), NLA.

she also remained sensitive towards what she saw as disproportionate scrutiny of Israel from the left which she felt was 'motivated purely and simply by expediency and morality and justice, as usual, have very little to do with it'.[56]

The Rothfields were widely recognised for their contribution to promoting peace and discussion of human rights in Australia. In 1984 they were involved in the founding of the Australian Jewish Democratic Society (AJDS) which aimed to be 'a progressive voice among Jews and a Jewish voice among progressives'.[57] *Paths to Peace*, the journal they jointly published about the Middle East conflict, was awarded a United Nations Association of Australia (UNAA) peace media prize in 1979, an award which was established by Stella Cornelius, another prominent WILPF member.[58] The ceremony was held in Sydney and Yehudi Menuhin, an internationally renowned violinist and brother to Hephzibah Menuhin, president of WILPF UK, distributed the award, with another going to Australian WILPF for their journal *Peace and Freedom*. Recognition did not end there. In 1998, Norman and Evelyn were both awarded the Medal of the Order of Australia for 'service to the promotion of peace and human rights in Australia and internationally.'[59]

Evelyn Rothfield shared with Libby Frank, a US Jewish member of WILPF, in the belief that discussion over the nature of Zionism distracted from the search for peaceful solutions. The resolutions by the UN conference equating Zionism with racism were simply 'used as politically expedient tools by "the most hawkish and intransigent of the Israelis and the Americans" and by Arab regimes' to rally people to causes and further accentuate the 'us and them' divide in the Middle East.[60]

---

56   Rothfield to Ballantyne, 21 November 1973, series III reel 55, WILPF International Papers 1915–1978, Sanford, NC: Microfilming Corp. of America, c 1983, accessed at the National Library of Australia (NLA). Hereafter referred to as WILPF Papers.
57   Australian Jewish Democratic Society, accessed 3 November 2022, www.ajds.org.au. For more information about the Rothfields' involvement, their son Robin Rothfield was interviewed for an oral history project, see: 'AJDS Oral History Project: Interview with Robin Rothfield 01/05/2014', Mixcloud, accessed 17 October 2015, www.mixcloud.com/AJDS/ajds-oral-history-project-interview-with-robin-rothfield-01052014.
58   Norman Rothfield, *Many Paths to Peace: The Political Memoirs of Norman Rothfield* (Melbourne: Yarraford, 1997), 141.
59   Evelyn Rothfield OAM, 26 January 1998, accessed 3 November 2022, honours.pmc.gov.au/honours/awards/882176.
60   Catia Cecilia Confortini, 'How Matters: Women's International League for Peace and Freedom's Trips to the Middle East, 1931–1975', *Peace & Change* 38, no. 3 (1 July 2013): 301, doi.org/10.1111/pech.12023.

Stella Cornelius of the International Year of Peace Secretariat completes the chain of 10,000 peace banners, 30 March 1986.
Source: Photographer Brendan Read, the *Sydney Morning Herald* and *The Age*. Photos, Fairfax Media Archives. See Appendix for a short biography of Stella Cornelius.

WILPF International's position on this issue changed profoundly from its founding to the 1970s. In her work on the history of WILPF, Catia Confortini has detailed the evolution of policy on the Middle East and demonstrated how various missions to the region by WILPF members informed the organisation's policy direction.[61] Fact-finding missions to conflict areas had a long tradition. WILPF did not rely blindly on media or government reports when formulating policy, often attempting to understand issues on the ground for themselves and obtain information unfiltered by media and governments. The first mission to the Middle East occurred in 1931 when Swedish member Elisabeth Waern-Bugge travelled to Palestine at a time when WILPF had a large Jewish constituency and few national sections outside of Europe.[62] Colonial authorities sympathetic to the Jewish population of Palestine facilitated the trip and her report detailed a position influenced by the Zionist narrative. After the creation of the state of Israel in 1948, the official position of WILPF reproduced ideas

---

61 Confortini, 'How Matters'.
62 Confortini, 'How Matters', 287.

of 'hateful and belligerent Arab enemies surrounding a weak new state', and juxtaposed Israel's 'pioneering and technologically innovative spirit with Arab backwardness'.[63]

In 1958 Haitian WILPF member Madeleine Boucherau again travelled to the Middle East and reported on the situation. She offered a more balanced interpretation of the conflict, making clear that in certain cases Israel had misappropriated Palestinian land and calling for a return to the partition plan. She made contacts in the region that eventually led to the creation of the Lebanese section of WILPF in 1962, which changed the dynamics of discussions on the conflict.[64] Nevertheless, as Confortini has argued, WILPF still 'unquestioningly reproduced the myth of pre-Israel Palestine as a sparsely populated area, which the Israeli transformed into fertile land'.[65] WILPF delegates travelled once more to the region in 1967, but it was not until the 1975 Middle East mission that the organisation officially changed its policy on the nature and root cause of the conflict. The political context of the conflict had changed. By 1974 Yasser Arafat had appeared before the UN General Assembly to present his famous 'olive branch' speech which aligned the Palestinian struggle with decolonisation movements. Then, in 1975, the US State Department acknowledged Palestinians' claims. Libby Frank and Edith Ballantyne travelled on the 1975 WILPF mission and wrote a report that contrasted with previous ones in its recognition of more similarities than differences between Arab and Jewish women.[66]

Following on from the report, Frank and Ballantyne hosted a workshop for the International Executive Committee of WILPF to create a new official policy statement. Not all sections were happy with this change in direction. Ballantyne felt the WILPF section in Israel had 'turned the section into a propagandistic arm of the Israeli government'.[67] These discussions precipitated a rupture with the Israeli section which led to its disbanding after 1975. The new statement recognised self-determination for both Palestinian and Jewish communities and condemned the militarisation of the region. Frank acknowledged that the new, more balanced position led several WILPF members to leave the organisation but organising in the area soon returned when the Israeli section reformed in 1982. Only a few years later, in 1989, a Palestinian section was formed.[68]

---

63 Confortini, 'How Matters', 291.
64 Confortini, 'How Matters', 291.
65 Confortini, 'How Matters', 291.
66 Confortini, 'How Matters', 298.
67 Confortini, 'How Matters', 302.
68 Confortini, 'How Matters', 303.

Rothfield remained a member of WILPF and supported the new position which closely aligned with her own personal view on the conflict and its resolution. As friends, Ballantyne and Rothfield often debated and disagreed over various aspects of the conflict—just as the organisation continued to do in an effort to try and reach a consensus. Rothfield was insistent, however, that the Palestinian Liberation Organisation (PLO) should recognise Israel before any peaceful negotiations could commence.[69] In 1979 Rothfield and her husband visited Egypt, Jordan, Syria and Israel as part of a tour organised by the Australian Institute of International Affairs.[70] At a meeting with Yasser Arafat in Damascus, the Rothfields made a point of asking if the PLO would recognise Israel. Norman wrote:

> I asked him, if Menachem Begin recognised a Palestinian state in part of Palestine, would he, Yasser Arafat, recognise Israel and agree to make peace? He replied with the question 'Has Begin made any such offer?' At this, Evelyn immediately called out from the back of the room, 'You're just like a Jew; you answer one question with another.' Arafat was a bit stunned at this. As for me I nearly fell through the floor.[71]

On the one hand, Rothfield felt she had a lot of support from within the British, French and Scandinavian sections of WILPF for her position on the conflict. On the other, she 'got a lot of flack from the Americans and their allies' and realised that she was a 'thorn in the side of many in WILPF'.[72] Nevertheless she remained active in monitoring and critiquing WILPF's positions on world affairs. In 1987 she wrote to the US publication of *Peace and Freedom* requesting to be taken off the mailing list because of their coverage of a meeting between WILPF and Soviet women, which she felt lacked the 'slightest criticism of anything done by the Soviet Union'.

> If you cannot convince them of the errors of their government, in the same way that they convince you of the errors of yours, it is all rather a waste of time and not contributing to the peace *with freedom*, to which we all aspire.[73]

---

69 Rothfield to Ballantyne, 11 April, 1974 Box 53/4 WILPF, SCPC, CU Archives.
70 Rothfield to Ballantyne, 13 February 1979, Box 53/4, WILPF, SCPC, CU Archives.
71 Rothfield, *Many Paths to Peace*, 107.
72 Rothfield, *The Future Is Past*, 59.
73 Evelyn Rothfield, 'WILPF and the USSR Letter to the Editor', *Peace and Freedom* 47, no. 4 (June 1987), 4.

1980 Copenhagen, WILPF as an NGO

By the time of the UN conference in Copenhagen in 1980, the Australian section of WILPF had elected Erika Rathgeber as president with Elizabeth Mattick as secretary. Rathgeber (née Regener) was married to the physicist Henri Rathgeber and had migrated to Australia from Germany. Both she and her husband had mothers who had been involved in the founding of WILPF in Europe.[74] Rothfield became international vice-president of WILPF from 1980 to 1983. Around this time, the Queensland branch was increasing its activity with Heather Williams becoming a regular correspondent with Geneva. The Australian section inaugurated the Junior Media Peace Prize in 1980 that aimed at encouraging youth interest in peace research. The national body also decided to highlight the 'position of Aboriginal children in Australia' as a special project for the International Year of the Child in 1979 and prepared a detailed submission to the prime minister.[75]

In 1979 Edith Ballantyne from the Geneva office was elected to head the UN Conference of Non-Governmental Organisations. This made WILPF central in setting the agenda for the NGO forum that ran alongside the 1980 UN Copenhagen Women's conference.[76] WILPF was better prepared and organised than in 1975, and were far more satisfied with the amount of discussion peace received on the agenda. The NGO forum had over 8,000 registered participants. WILPF organised 11 workshops on peace, which were 'extremely well attended'.[77] Those WILPF members attending the forum felt that the event gave them hope that the trend of peace being left to the 'politicians and experts' was being reversed.[78] Rathgeber led the Australians at the NGO forum and was a WILPF observer to the UN conference. At the official UN conference, however, the issue of Zionism once again threatened to derail the proceedings. An item on Palestinian women and refugees was put on the agenda months before and made most national delegations anxious about the politicisation of the conference.[79]

---

74 WILPF Bulletin, report on the 70th Birthday Party of WILPF, 27 April 1985, Box 54/1 WILPF, SCPC, CU Archives.
75 Rothfield to Ballantyne, 13 February 1979, Box 53/4, WILPF, SCPC, CU Archives. See also WILPF Australian Section, 'Open Submission to the Prime Minister, Education—Health—Housing of Aboriginal Children, A Blueprint for the 1980s', Box 54/1, WILPF, SCPC, CU Archives.
76 Foster, *Women for All Seasons,* 77.
77 'What Happened in Copenhagen', *Pax et Libertas* 45, no. 3 September 1980.
78 'What Happened in Copenhagen', *Pax et Libertas* 45, no. 3 September 1980.
79 Ghodsee, 'Revisiting the United Nations Decade for Women', 6.

Members of the National Women's Advisory Council (NWAC), established by Prime Minister Malcolm Fraser, led the official Australian delegation to the UN conference.[80] There they initiated a resolution on women and development assistance programs and co-sponsored resolutions on 'battered women'.[81] In a resolution recognising the root causes of women's disadvantage, and which listed a number of 'isms' (including Zionism, along with racism, neo-colonialism and imperialism), the Australian delegation attempted to have the word 'sexism' added, reprising their efforts at Mexico City. It sparked an intense debate with many countries claiming sexism did not exist. The Soviet Union claimed that sexism was 'such a foreign concept that there was no word for it in the Russian language.'[82] The word was finally placed in a footnote to the final plan of action. Despite Australia's serious engagement with the program, when the final vote came on the document, Australia voted against it along with the US, Canada and Israel. This was a decision by politicians at home rather than the delegation itself who were forced to vote against the plan of action because of the references to Zionism. WILPF thought the action by the four countries was 'a shocker'.[83] They hoped that nations would 'nevertheless apply the provisions' since the sections of concern were so small. Ballantyne wrote:

> I cannot believe that the women will allow them not to implement the major part of the programme even if they won't touch the measures of assistance to Palestinian women … The Australian women have certainly work before them.[84]

For WILPF internationally, leading the NGO forum created new contacts and resulted in the creation of two new sections, one in French Polynesia and another in the Netherlands which was a revival of an older section that had previously folded.[85] It also cemented WILPF's emerging identity as a major NGO at the UN. However, despite WILPF's 1971 policy change which 'accepted that oppressed people feel a need for revolution', members still withheld approval of violence in these international forums.[86] After a

---

80   Marilyn Lake and Natasha Campo, 'International Activism and Organisations—Theme', *The Encyclopedia of Women and Leadership in Twentieth-Century Australia*, accessed 21 November, 2015, www.womenaustralia.info/leaders/biogs/WLE0200b.htm.
81   Patrick Kilby, *NGOs and Political Change: A History of the Australian Council for International Development* (Canberra: ANU Press, 2015), 80, doi.org/10.22459/NPC.08.2015.
82   Ghodsee, 'Revisiting the United Nations Decade for Women', 7.
83   Ballantyne to Phyllis Wild, 14 October 1980, Box 53/4, WILPF, SCPC, CU Archives.
84   Ballantyne to Phyllis Wild, 14 October 1980, Box 53/4, WILPF, SCPC, CU Archives.
85   WILPF conference report, 1983, Sklar and Dublin, *Women and Social Movements*, 52.
86   Confortini, *Intelligent Compassion*, 73.

public meeting associated with the NGO gathering at Copenhagen, which focused solely on women and national liberation, some European members of WILPF tried to organise a protest against what they thought was too great an emphasis on supporting violence and not enough on WILPF's pacifist objectives. Ballantyne recognised that the radicalism of the US participants and the 'presence of women who had themselves been involved in liberation struggle' had a 'traumatizing effect on many of our European members'.[87]

This ongoing tension within WILPF and the wider women's anti-war movement over violence and oppression once again highlighted WILPF's difficulty in engaging with violent insurgencies. Ballantyne felt the failure of some WILPF members to sympathise with national liberation struggles showed

> that we have failed in self-education, in developing toward the 21st century as a coherent international organisation. We must change that if we are to survive or be an effective women's peace organisation.[88]

Here the 'eurocentrism' of WILPF became an issue as the wider international women's movement broadened.

1985 Nairobi, and the Pacific regional conference

Concerned that WILPF and the wider international NGO community were too focused on the northern hemisphere, especially as decolonisation was rapidly transforming the Pacific region, WILPF Australia organised the Australian Pacific Women's Peace Conference in Sydney in 1985.[89] More than 300 women participated from over twenty Pacific nations, all providing personal insight into their struggles against imperialism and oppressive regimes. The gathering made clear that 'there can be no peace without justice' and pointed to specific forms of injustice relating to the region. They identified transnational corporations working alongside states as being primary oppressors which acted 'intentionally or otherwise in

---

87   Ballantyne to Phyllis Wild, 14 October 1980, Box 53/4, WILPF, SCPC, CU Archives.
88   Ballantyne to Phyllis Wild, 14 October 1980, Box 53/4, WILPF, SCPC, CU Archives.
89   Kath Gibson, 'Pacific Women Speak Out', *Pax et Libertas* 50, no. 3 (September 1985). Statements from the Australian Pacific Women's Peace Conference, Sydney 28–30 June 1985, Box 54/1, WILPF, SCPC, CU Archives.

denying the fruits of development from many of the people of the region.'[90] Capitalism and imperialism were identified as major forces of oppression as foreign powers continued to build military bases and test nuclear weapons. The conference called out 'continuing suffering, violence and abuse of Human Rights in East Timor, West Papua, Australia, Aotearoa [New Zealand], Belau, Kanaky, Polynesia, Philippines and Easter Island.'[91] WILPF recognised the rights of Indigenous people and supported calls for land rights in Australia and self-determination in the rest of the Pacific. They never advocated violence in resisting oppression but engaged in letter writing campaigns expressing criticism of oppressor powers.[92] Kath Gibson, who reported on the conference to *Pax et Libertas*, felt that it 'succeeded in creating and strengthening a Pacific consciousness'. As we have seen, it might also be seen a returning to the regional preoccupations of the organisation during the interwar years. WILPF Australia hoped to continue meeting with their Pacific colleagues into the future.[93]

WILPF NSW branch president Elizabeth Mattick subsequently led a group that travelled to Nairobi, Kenya, for the third UN women's conference after the Sydney Pacific conference in July 1985. She took with her a document drafted for circulation to the wider international community which outlined the statements Pacific women had made. As at the 1980 Copenhagen conference, Ballantyne chaired the UN NGO conference planning committee as secretary general of WILPF.[94] At WILPF's insistence, a 'Peace Tent' was established where issues thought to be 'too political' could be openly discussed. The 'Peace Tent' was declared a great success as it became a 'focal point for intense discussion of the reasons of conflict'. It was an important and necessary initiative, not least because at the official UN conference many issues were not discussed due to US officials threatening to boycott if apartheid, militarism, imperialism or the Palestinian question were debated.[95]

---

90   Statements from the Australian Pacific Women's Peace Conference, Sydney 28–30 June, 1985, Box 54/1, WILPF, SCPC, CU Archives.
91   Statements from the Australian Pacific Women's Peace Conference, Sydney 28–30 June, 1985, Box 54/1, WILPF, SCPC, CU Archives.
92   For example in 1983 WILPF wrote to the UN expressing concern about the plebiscite in the Republic of Palau (Belau), which would give 'free association' with the US. In 1981 Palau adopted a nuclear-free constitution, but the US wanted to use the territory to store nuclear weapons. WILPF believed that the US had not ensured 'adequate time for political education with Palau' and asked for the plebiscite to be postponed. The vote was very contentious and was not accepted until 1994. Elizabeth Mattick to Girma Abebe, UN Trusteeship Council NY, 10 January 1983, Box 54/1, WILPF, SCPC, CU Archives.
93   Gibson, 'Pacific Women Speak Out'.
94   Foster, *Women for All Seasons*, 95.
95   Ghodsee, 'Revisiting the United Nations Decade for Women', 8. See also Foster, *Women for All Seasons*, 95. Janet Bruin and Ballantyne, 'What Happened in Nairobi?', *Pax et Libertas* 50, no. 3 (September 1985).

Outside the Peace Tent at the Nairobi UN NGO conference July 1985, artwork reads a quote from Virginia Woolf, *Three Guineas* (1938).
Source: Photo courtesy of Margaret Bearlin, photographer.

The NGO conference at Nairobi became the largest of all three women's conferences. It had almost 15,000 participants and journalists, overshadowing the UN event which had only 1,500 attendees. Observing the official conference, Mattick found that 'compared with the forum, the conference could only be described as dull. Indeed many official delegates found it much more interesting to attend forum workshops.'[96] The issue of Zionism was still hotly debated at the 1985 conference but a compromise was negotiated where the phrase 'all forms of racial discrimination' replaced the contentious word Zionism. This allowed the conference document to be adopted by consensus and the conference ended the decade on a more positive and inclusive note than it had begun.[97]

---

96 Elizabeth Mattick, 'Nairobi, Report to the Australian Section', 1985, quoted in Foster, *Women for All Seasons*, 96.
97 Ghodsee, 'Revisiting the United Nations Decade for Women', 9.

8. WOMEN, PEACE AND SECURITY

The issue of Zionism at the various UN women's conferences was an important one for the US, as well as for the US section in WILPF. Gil Troy noted how 'mostly Democratic Jewish feminists' from the US delegation allied with their 'ideological enemies, the Reagan Republicans' to 'liberate the international women's movement from its Zionist obsession'.[98] US President Ronald Reagan's daughter Maureen was appointed head of the US delegation and was instructed to walk out if the conference demonised Zionism. However, the preparation done by activists within the conference meant that most national delegations now saw the issue as a distraction from the real feminist agenda.[99] Friedan reported that 'every reference to Zionism [was] gone', a significant step for the anti-Zionist movement as the first resolution that began to roll back the 'Zionism as racism' campaign.[100]

1989 triennial conference in Sydney

The 1980s came to a close with WILPF Australia hosting the triennial conference in 1989 in Sydney, the first time it was held in the southern hemisphere. Themed 'women building a common and secure future', over 300 women from around the world travelled to Australia to be a part of the proceedings held at Sancta Sophia College at the University of Sydney.[101] In setting the direction for the conference, the Australian section used the opportunity to focus WILPF's attention on the Pacific and issues specific to the Asia-Pacific region. With visiting members from countries such as Fiji, Guam, Rarotonga and Belau, the keynote speaker, Senator Margaret Reynolds, told the conference:

> It is important that women from the rest of the world, attending this Congress, hear women from the Pacific speak about issues of importance to them, including the indigenous Pacific people's movement to be nuclear free and independent. This Congress helps give the Pacific people's struggle international publicity and support.[102]

---

98   Troy, *Moynihan's Moment*, 243.
99   Troy, *Moynihan's Moment*, 243.
100 Troy, *Moynihan's Moment*, 243.
101 'Report of the Twenty-Fourth Congress of the Women's International League for Peace and Freedom', Sydney, Australia 14–25 July 1989, Sklar and Dublin, *Women and Social Movements*.
102 'Report of the Twenty-Fourth Congress of the Women's International League for Peace and Freedom', Sydney, Australia 14–25 July 1989, Sklar and Dublin, *Women and Social Movements*.

Bettina Glass, *Feminine strength*. Portrait of Margaret Reynolds, 1990. Painting, acrylic on canvas, 118.9 x 119 cm.
Source: National Library of Australia, viewed 11 April 2022, nla.gov.au/nla.obj-136227576.

Bundjalung woman Kaye Mundine, a member of WILPF and long-time campaigner for peace and social justice, officially opened the conference with a welcome to country.[103] WILPF Australia had supported Mundine to attend the World Congress for Women in Moscow in 1987 to discuss issues relating to Indigenous Australia, reconfirming their commitment to helping amplify the voices of active Indigenous women.[104] In her welcome

---

103 Gai Smith, 'Remembering a Fearless Champion—Kaye Mundine (1947–2016)', *South Sydney Herald*, 9 August 2016, accessed 3 November 2022, www.southsydneyherald.com.au/remembering-a-fearless-champion-kaye-mundine-1947-2016/.
104 'Report of the Twenty-Fourth Congress of the Women's International League for Peace and Freedom', Sydney, Australia 14–25 July 1989, Sklar and Dublin, *Women and Social Movements*, 57.

8. WOMEN, PEACE AND SECURITY

address, Mundine gave a short history of Indigenous issues and the violence of colonisation as well as the continuing disadvantage experienced by Indigenous peoples. She also called the conference to action:

> You cannot walk away from here, thinking this is an Australian problem. You have a responsibility to know and understand the issues. For what I am saying today, may also be happening in your country in relation to Indigenous peoples.[105]

Continuing the conversation was a keynote from Barbara Shaw, an Indigenous activist from Alice Springs, who discussed specific issues relating to 'the plight of Aboriginal women'.[106] The conference ended with a seminar 'for Indigenous Women and Women from Developing Countries' which again demonstrated WILPF's commitment to combatting racism and dealing with issues of decolonisation and economic development. However, following traditions of the Black Power movement that had influenced many anti-racism movements since the 1960s, the organising committee, consisting of representatives of Aboriginal women's organisations and 'representatives of third world communities', were polarised on the question of whether European women should be present at the seminar. It was decided that while they were not to be entirely excluded, European women were only allowed limited participation. Many criticised the decision which they felt 'stifled the all-important educational opportunity for WILPF members all over the world to gain an intimate understanding of the problems faced by indigenous women from the Pacific area'.[107]

1995 Beijing Peace Train

In the 1990s WILPF's activity maintained a regional focus. They campaigned on a range of issues, from traditional owners' land rights and environmental issues to the mining and export of uranium and regional conflicts, with specific focus on East Timor, Bougainville and Cambodia.[108] WILPF also opposed Australia's role in the Gulf War, joining with other peace groups to

---

105 Kaye Mundine, 'Report of the Twenty-Fourth Congress of the Women's International League for Peace and Freedom', Sydney, Australia 14–25 July 1989, Sklar and Dublin, *Women and Social Movements*, 2.
106 Judith Smart and Shurlee Swain, eds, 'Shaw, Barbara Catherine (1952–)', *The Encyclopedia of Women and Leadership in Twentieth-Century Australia*, 2 May 2014, accessed 19 July 2019, www.women australia.info/leaders/biogs/WLE0712b.htm.
107 'Report of the Twenty-Fourth Congress of the Women's International League for Peace and Freedom', Sydney, Australia 14–25 July 1989, Sklar and Dublin, *Women and Social Movements*, 178.
108 'Report of the Twenty-Fifth Congress of the Women's International League for Peace and Freedom', St Cruz Bolivia 1–6 July 1992, Sklar and Dublin, *Women and Social Movements*, 59.

stage demonstrations and hold public meetings. The ACT branch was active in opposing the government's decision to host an Australian International Defence Exhibition (AIDEX) in Canberra in 1991. The event was the largest exhibition of military hardware held in Australia and drew large protests from the combined anti-war movement.[109] WILPF women held placards around intersections in Canberra away from other protesters with slogans such as 'THE ARMS TRADE MAKES US POORER NOT SAFER' and tried to talk directly with the community. As they had at the height of the feminist and women's liberation movement, they sought to 'negotiate our own expression of protest' rather than participating in the 'violence is entertainment' media.[110] Many protesters complained of misrepresentation through the media's sensationalised reporting, and the protests were marked by allegations of extensive police violence, with over 200 arrests.[111] The ACT branch sent out a media release on Mother's Day, May 8, urging the cancellation of AIDEX '91, to cease participation in the arms trade, and to reclaim 'the original idea' of the day which was conceived as a time 'when everyone should dedicate themselves anew to the task of bringing about world peace', as 'mothers do not raise their sons to kill other women's sons'.[112]

National financial membership of WILPF Australia remained steady at around 300 members. In the lead up to WILPF's participation in the 1995 Fourth UN Conference on Women, however, the branch was able to apply for government funding which expanded the reach of WILPF's activities and encouraged more young women to join. WILPF, with its older membership profile, was always keen to recruit younger peace activists. Australian feminism during this time followed a state-sponsored approach with senior women taking on roles in the public service to extend the reach and resources of their activism. These women, labelled 'femocrats', had a significant impact on government policy which was 'noted with interest by the rest of the world'.[113] Positions were created within government to keep gender issues on the national agenda, with one of the first appointees to the role of Minister Assisting the Prime Minister for the Status of Women being a WILPF member, Senator

---

109 For more on these protests see: Iain McIntyre, 'The AIDEX '91 Protest: A Case Study of Obstructive Direct Action' (Masters thesis, University of Melbourne, 2011).
110 'Piecing it Together: Hearing the Stories of AIDEX '91', prepared by the Friends of the Hearings, 1991–1995 (Curtin ACT: Penniless Publications, 1995), 195.
111 McIntyre, 'The AIDEX '91 Protest: A Case Study of Obstructive Direct Action'.
112 ACT Branch of WILPF, 'Women's International League for Peace and Freedom—General Representations', media release, 8 May 1991 (item, Canberra, 4 December 1986), A463, 1989/2011 PART 4, National Archives of Australia (NAA).
113 Verity Burgmann, *Power, Profit and Protest. Australian Social Movements and Globalisation* (Crows Nest, NSW: Allen & Unwin, 2003), 151.

8. WOMEN, PEACE AND SECURITY

Margaret Reynolds. An Office for the Status of Women (OSW) was created by the Hawke Labor Government, replacing the advisory council established by Fraser. The new office monitored issues relating to violence against women internationally and nationally, ran public awareness campaigns, and even released a women's budget statement that outlined the budget's repercussions for women's lives.[114] In 1993–1994 the Labor Government also allocated funding to national women's organisations through a National Agenda for Women Grants Program, and WILPF received a grant that allowed the opening of a national office.[115] WILPF, encouraged by the changing cultural and political landscape, began implementing more modern feminist organising techniques by auditing documents and advocating use of 'non-sexist language in all WILPF publications'.[116]

'ACT Arms Trade makes us poorer not safer' posters created for the AIDEX protests in 1991. Used again here in the mid-2000s by Margaret Bearlin and Annie Didcott at GDAMS (Global Day of Action on Military Spending) demonstration in Canberra.
Source: Photo courtesy of Margaret Bearlin.

---

114 Burgmann, *Power, Profit and Protest*, 151.
115 'Report of the Twenty-Sixth Congress of the Women's International League for Peace and Freedom', Helsinki Finland, 1–6 August 1995, Sklar and Dublin, *Women and Social Movements*, 55.
116 'Report of the Twenty-Fifth Congress of the Women's International League for Peace and Freedom', St Cruz Bolivia 1–6 July 1992, Sklar and Dublin, *Women and Social Movements*, 60.

The mid-1990s saw attention again focus on the UN women's conferences with the fourth conference, held in Beijing in 1995, designed to function as a review and update to the previous conferences. As on previous occasions, WILPF in Australia spent significant time and energy preparing for the program, especially their contribution to the parallel NGO forum and lobbying the government's delegation to the conference to ensure adequate attention was paid to peace issues.[117] Internationally, WILPF organised their triennial conference, celebrating 80 years of organising, in Helsinki, Finland, in 1995 to leave enough time for a Peace Train of women travelling overland through St Petersburg, Kiev, Bucharest, Sofia, Istanbul, Almaty and into China for the UN women's conference.[118] There were 230 women who undertook the journey, including a significant cohort of Australians. The women involved spoke of the trip as a transformative experience. The train compartments 'hummed with activity' as women spent days walking through the cities where they stopped, talking to local groups and learning about local conditions for women. Young participants also learnt from discussions with older members: 'we would stumble and sway as we crossed between the coaches to the meeting cars to attend workshops ranging from alternative economics to sewing circles'.[119] Travelling through the former Soviet countries and into China during this time with an expressly political agenda of peace and internationalism was cause for concern in some countries they passed through. It seemed, wrote Heather Cummings, that 'a simple act of women meeting women provoked our hosts … [who] feared the impact of "radical" women mostly from Western Europe, the United States and Australia upon local women'.[120] Women noticed they were followed on public buses while in Turkey, and the Chinese Government refused to allow the train to stop in Urumchi, sending a 'train with 70 security and government representatives to escort us through the country'.[121]

---

117 'Report of the Twenty-Sixth Congress of the Women's International League for Peace and Freedom', Helsinki Finland, 1–6 August 1995, Sklar and Dublin, *Women and Social Movements*, 53.
118 Heather Cummings, 'The WILPF Peace Train: Training for Peace from Helsinki to Beijing', *International Peace Update* 60, no. 5–6 (November 1995): 22.
119 Cummings, 'The WILPF Peace Train', 23.
120 Cummings, 'The WILPF Peace Train', 22.
121 Cummings, 'The WILPF Peace Train', 22.

The Australian delegation to the 1995 WILPF conference in Helsinki.
Left to right: Jenni Dall, Yumi Lee, Felicity Hill, Hellen Cooke and Leonie Ebert pictured.
Source: Photo courtesy of Margaret Bearlin, photographer.

While in Beijing, NGO groups found that access to the UN conference was much more limited than it had been at previous conferences.[122] WILPF therefore spent its time organising a peace caucus through the NGO parallel conference that monitored the UN Platform for Action and released an alternative declaration when it felt the positions taken by governments were too weak. They challenged governments to 'radically transform the social, economic and political structures that oppress women worldwide'.[123] The NGO conference opened with more than 30,000 participants in the Beijing Olympic Stadium and followed on with plenaries and forums in nearby Huairou. Once again, by organising a Peace Tent at the conference, WILPF created a meeting space for people to 'network, listen and learn, to build friendships and solidarity, and to give shelter.'[124] Much more than just participating in the bureaucratic processes of conferencing, women recounted feeling 'empowered by being with so many women from different parts of the world working for peace and justice and the rights of women'.[125]

---

122 'World Women's Conference', *International Peace Update* 60, no. 5–6 (November 1995), 10.
123 'Beijing NGO Declaration', *International Peace Update* 60, no. 5–6 (November 1995), 24.
124 'Ten Busy Days at the NGO Forum', *International Peace Update* 60, no. 5-6 (November 1995), 9.
125 'Ten Busy Days at the NGO Forum', *International Peace Update* 60, no. 5-6 (November 1995), 9.

Security Council Resolution 1325

After the election of the Liberal–National Coalition Government led by John Howard in 1996, WILPF's federal funding dried up. By 1998 they were considered 'too international' even to qualify for funding through the OSW, and the decline in funds began to reduce the scope of their activity.[126] The new conservative agenda of the government had a narrow view of the national interest. Nonetheless WILPF, familiar with surviving on limited funds and volunteer commitment, continued their work despite the difficulties with member Yumi Lee representing the organisation on the Department of Foreign Affairs' National Consultative Committee for Peace and Disarmament.[127] They did not hesitate to publish a newspaper advertisement calling the government to withdraw from military involvement in the Persian Gulf.[128] WILPF did not need to fear criticising a government that was no longer providing funding.

Internationally, the WILPF office was focused on the platform of action that resulted from the Beijing conference and interested in finding a way for the 'critical area of concern—Women and Armed Conflict' to be advanced in a meaningful way by the UN.[129] Australian WILPF member Felicity Hill had been an active participant who travelled on the Peace Train to the 1995 conference. The following year she was the disarmament intern for WILPF International before becoming the director of the New York office of WILPF which was primarily responsible for lobbying the UN.[130] In 1998 the Commission on the Status of Women (CSW) reviewed the Beijing platform of action in a two-week long session. WILPF coordinated a group of international NGOs known as the 'Women and Armed Conflict Caucus' who drafted an outcome document. As the feminist and scholar Cynthia Cockburn noted in her account of the efforts of women's organisations lobbying the UN in the 1990s and early 2000s, it was here that there was a subtle shift away from getting conflict on the UN's 'women

---

126 'Report of the Twenty-Seventh International Congress of the Women's International League for Peace and Freedom', Baltimore USA, 24–31 July 1998, Sklar and Dublin, *Women and Social Movements*, 70.
127 'Report of the Twenty-Seventh International Congress of the Women's International League for Peace and Freedom', Baltimore USA, 24–31 July 1998.
128 'Report of the Twenty-Seventh International Congress of the Women's International League for Peace and Freedom', Baltimore USA, 24–31 July 1998.
129 Cynthia Cockburn, *From Where We Stand: War, Women's Activism and Feminist Analysis* (London: Zed Books, 2007), 139, doi.org/10.5040/9781350220287.
130 Felicity Hill, 'Reaching Critical Will', in *Listen to Women for a Change*, ed. Irmgard Heilberger and Barbara Lochbihler (WILPF German Section, October 2010), 27.

8. WOMEN, PEACE AND SECURITY

agenda' to getting 'women and armed conflict' on the main agenda.[131] 'They set their sights on the Security Council', wrote Cockburn, turning their attention to 'the power centre of the UN, responsible for the maintenance of international peace and security'.[132]

This lobbying culminated in the historic passing of the SCR 1325 in 2000. Participants in the NGO working groups included Amnesty International, International Alert, the Hague Appeal for Peace, the Women's Commission for Refugee Women and Children, the International Peace Research Association and WILPF, with former secretary General Edith Ballantyne, Barbara Lochbihler and Felicity Hill convening and coordinating the efforts of the NGOs. These women led the lobbying movement with determination and skill but, as Cockburn noted, they would not have been effective without organisational backing and:

> A full list would run into hundreds, perhaps thousands, and would include a web of women spreading from the United Nations Plaza in New York to the killing fields of many war-afflicted countries.[133]

Painstaking effort by the NGOs of the working group was put into the promotion of the women, peace and security agenda in the lead-up to the passing of UNSCR 1325. It was a resolution for which 'the groundwork, the diplomacy, and lobbying, the drafting and redrafting, was almost entirely the work of civil society, and certainly the first in which the actors were almost all women'.[134] Cultivating allies within the UN system, the NGO group approached the Namibian Ambassador, Martin Andjaba, who was due to take up the presidency of the Security Council in October 2000. The presidency rotated between member states monthly, and each president was allowed to initiate a theme. Andjaba agreed to sponsor a session on 'Women, Peace and Security'. 'Wilpfers were jubilant', noted Felicity Hill in response to its announcement.[135] From then on the NGOs compiled documents and reading lists for members of the Security Council, lobbied them relentlessly, and drafted the resolution that was eventually adopted by the council on 31 October 2000.[136]

---

131 Cockburn, *From Where We Stand*, 140.
132 Cockburn, *From Where We Stand*, 140.
133 Cockburn, *From Where We Stand*, 139–40.
134 Cockburn, *From Where We Stand*, 141.
135 Cockburn, *From Where We Stand*, 141.
136 Cockburn, *From Where We Stand*, 141.

UNSCR 1325 consisted of 18 points, grouped in three themes.[137] First, there was protection, which called for a recognition of gender-specific needs in time of war and the 'protection of women and girls from gender-based violence, particularly rape and other forms of sexual abuse, and an end to impunity for these crimes.'[138] Participation was the second theme and called for the inclusion of women in all levels of peace negotiations, from the local and national to the international. The last theme called for the inclusion of a gendered perspective in UN peacekeeping, especially gender sensitive training in measures of demobilisation, reintegration and reconstruction after war. After its passing by the council, the NGO group continued its activity to ensure that the issue remained a priority and was implemented by member states and the UN. The Ford Foundation also now provided funding to the NGO group to employ a coordinator so Felicity Hill was able to return to her WILPF work, while WILPF received an additional grant to fund the creation of the PeaceWomen website. That provided information to the wider activist community on UNSCR 1325 and monitored the UN systems to ensure the organisation included gender awareness in all its work.[139] While WILPF undoubtedly played a significant role in the NGO activity around UNSCR 1325, they did not necessarily see themselves as the driver of the overall campaign that had 'so many involved'.[140] It is also not the case that all WILPF members were comfortable with the pathway the organisation was taking. While many celebrated the passing of the resolution, others criticised the new direction of WILPF lobbying.

WILPF was more explicitly feminist than the other NGOs that were active in the working group, and was the only one to be unequivocally anti-militarist. Therefore, many members felt disappointed that the resolution made no mention of ending war itself, and only talked briefly about women's role in preventing war.[141] Some saw it as cooperative, with the emphasis on 'protection' focusing only on women as victims and the absence of a strong anti-war theme simply 'trying to make war safer for women'. Hill, as a key player in the adoption of the resolution, recognised how the radical elements of WILPF's ideology became muted in a need to adapt to the reality of the UN bureaucracy. Writing on the significance and impact of UNSCR 1325,

---

137 United Nations Security Council Resolution 1325 (2000), Adopted by the Security Council at its 4213th meeting, on 31 October 2000, accessed 3 February 2022, www.un.org/womenwatch/osagi/wps/#resolution.
138 Cockburn, *From Where We Stand*, 141.
139 See: www.peacewomen.org/ (accessed 23 July 2019).
140 Cockburn, *From Where We Stand*, 146.
141 Cockburn, *From Where We Stand*, 147.

8. WOMEN, PEACE AND SECURITY

she explained how the NGOs succeeded only 'by being self-effacing and self-censoring, using information, persuasion, and rhetorical entrapment to bring along the UN personnel, civil servants and diplomats concerned.'[142] Many academics have also criticised how the resolution 'left the war system essentially undisturbed'.[143] Hill recognised the limitations of the resolution in its failure to theorise gender in a complex way. Discussing the revolutionary power of the resolution at a roundtable, she noted that the resolution could:

> transform ways of understanding how security is conceived, protected and enforced. It could make photos of only male leaders at peace negotiating tables starkly outdated. But for this to happen, the focus has to move from women to men, and this still hasn't happened.[144]

The UN failed to interrogate militarised masculinities, or masculinity more generally, in grappling with the over-representation of men in the war system.

After the passing of UNSCR 1325 Australian WILPF focused on encouraging the federal government to develop a National Action Plan. As the responsibility for implementation of UNSCR 1325 lay with member states of the UN, realisation of the action plan became a national issue, allowing WILPF once again to apply for grants from the OSW. In 2003 they received $10,000 to assist in creating educational packages about the resolution to be distributed to secondary schools, community groups and parliamentarians.[145] The funds also helped WILPF Australia improve their online presence and make information about UNSCR 1325 more widely available. In 2009 WILPF received another large government grant to 'undertake community consultations and prepare a draft report on the content of a National Action Plan.'[146] The resulting discussion paper was submitted to the government, which responded by creating an inter-departmental working group to develop a plan 'informed by key suggestions from WILPF Australia's network'. The 'Australian National Action Plan on Women, Peace

---

142 Felicity Hill, 'How and When Has Security Council Resolution 1325 (2000) on Women, Peace and Security Impacted Negotiations Outside the Security Council?' (Masters thesis, Uppsala University Programme of International Studies, 2004); Cockburn, *From Where We Stand*, 148.
143 Cockburn, *From Where We Stand*, 148.
144 Felicity Hill, quoted in Carol Cohn, Helen Kinsella and Sheri Gibbings, 'Women, Peace and Security Resolution 1325', *International Feminist Journal of Politics* 6, no. 1 (1 January 2004): 137, doi.org/10.1080/1461674032000165969.
145 'Report of the Twenty-Eighth International Congress of the Women's International League for Peace and Freedom', Sweden, August 2004, Sklar and Dublin, *Women and Social Movements*, 95.
146 'WILPF International Congress Report', Costa Rica, 2011, Sklar and Dublin, *Women and Social Movements*, 103; WILPF Australian section, *Developing a National Action Plan on United Nations Security Council Resolution 1325*, report compiled by Di Zetlin (School of Political Science and International Studies, Peace and Conflict Studies and Gender Studies, University of Queensland, 2009).

and Security 2012–2018' was launched on International Women's Day on 8 March 2012.[147] The Australian Government subsequently claimed its international reputation as a leader in implementing UNSCR 1325 and became the largest contributor to the Women's Peace and Humanitarian Fund.[148] The implementation of the National Action Plan 'played a pivotal role in a successful campaign for a non-permanent seat on the Security Council (2013–2014).'[149]

Chris Henderson and Melody Kemp, national launch of the Children of the Gulf War photo exhibition, March 2003, Brisbane City Hall.

The event was the Brisbane City Hall opening of the Children of the Gulf War exhibition, March 2003, on the eve of the global rally to stop the planned war on Iraq. Fifty-eight photographs depicted the impact of war and depleted uranium on Iraqi women, children and the environment, taken by Japanese photojournalist Takashi Morizumi. Melody and I were co-organisers of the project. This subsequently became the launch of an extended national tour of the exhibition to cities and towns around the country.

Source: Photographer Sean Kemp.

---

147 Department of Families, Housing, Community Services and Indigenous Affairs, 'Australian National Action Plan on Women, Peace and Security 2012–2018', accessed 12 December 2022, www.dss.gov.au/our-responsibilities/women/publications-articles/government-international/australian-national-action-plan-on-women-peace-and-security-2012-2018?HTML.

148 Barbara K Trojanowska, 'Norm Negotiation in the Australian Government's Implementation of UNSCR 1325', *Australian Journal of International Affairs* 73, no. 1 (2019): 30, doi.org/10.1080/10357718.2018.1548560.

149 Trojanowska, 'Norm Negotiation in the Australian Government's Implementation of UNSCR 1325', 29.

Other activities pursued alongside the focus on UNSCR 1325 were often driven by individual members who wanted to be more radical in opposing war rather than exclusively engaging with the flawed UN system. The Iraq War created another crisis that spurred WILPF to public protest. Members again joined with other anti-war activities around the country in 2003 to encourage the Australian Government to avoid going to war. War, ironically, helped with recruitment and Mary Ziesak lamented the core paradox of WILPF's organising; 'a bitter sweet gain that we have to have the imminent threat of war to recruit new members.'[150] When Australia did enter the Iraq War, WILPF member Ruth Russell made the personal decision to travel to Iraq in 2003 with an organised group of protesters to become 'human shields'. One of the great motivators for her dramatic and dangerous action was to circumvent the national media in gathering information. Russell, like many women before her, wanted to 'report back independent of any censoring'.[151] WILPF Australia also purchased a photographic exhibition called 'Children of the Gulf War' by Japanese photographer Takashi Morizumi and organised exhibitions, led by members Melody Kemp and Christine Henderson, all over the country during 2004.[152] Noting the 'profound impact' the images had on viewers, WILPF felt they were an 'effective method of lobbying' in that they reminded people of the emotional reality of war: 'everyone who views this exhibition is moved, some to tears'.[153]

The emphasis on mainstreaming the women, peace and security agenda reminded many in the organisation of WILPF's own unconventional history and traditions. While it was important to have a gender perspective included in the workings and policy decisions of government, WILPF was an organisation that had long refused to be mainstreamed itself. In the historian and feminist Marilyn Lake's words:

> It remains a woman-based and woman-focused organization able to invoke the common interests and solidarity of women across the world—able to make a persuasive international case in support of the interests of women and children.[154]

---

150 'Report of the Twenty-Eighth International Congress of the WILPF', (2004), 95.
151 Ruth Russell, *Human Shield in Iraq: Finding a Way Forward for Peace* (Adelaide: Seaview Press, 2005), 5.
152 'Report of the Twenty-Eighth International Congress of the WILPF', (2004), 95.
153 'Report of the Twenty-Eighth International Congress of the WILPF', (2004), 95.
154 Marilyn Lake, WILPF Centenary Exhibition Launch Speech, Canberra Museum and Art Gallery, 27 February 2015.

Nonetheless, WILPF's focus on engaging the UN and its various forums, like the CSW, made it an attractive organisation for young women interested in the workings of international diplomacy and the increasingly professionalised international sphere. The Young WILPF (YWILPF) network was developed in 2011, and younger feminists encouraged a reinvigoration of the program in Australia.[155] WILPF's membership in Australia remained relatively stable, as it was always a small and committed membership that drove its activity; they were able to sustain activity despite contending with the associational decline that had affected many community groups and trade unions from the 1970s onwards.[156]

In 2010 WILPF invited Professor Marilyn Lake to speak to the ACT branch where she gave a talk on the topic of 'Rediscovering Australia's Peace History'.[157] The talk moved many in the organisation to think seriously about understanding the history of WILPF women in Australia. In the lead-up to the 2015 centenary of WILPF's organising in Australia, the section became focused on publicising their history. From 2011 onwards the gathering of stories for the anniversary was a high priority in all their reports. Branch coordinators Ruth Russell and Barbara O'Dwyer began calling on members to collect and sort through personal archives to submit resources to the National Library of Australia for use in exhibitions.

In researching this history, I was able to network with leading members Margaret Bearlin and Hellen Cooke who had become very active in trying to promote WILPF's history. They were generous in opening their archives to my research efforts in the interests of a rigorous and critical appraisal of WILPF's efforts over the course of a century. Russell and O'Dwyer asked members to think critically about war remembrance in Australia:

> We need to ask ourselves, friends and others—does this Anzac myth really define you as an Australian? Is mateship and support for others in times of distress, not really a universal characteristic? Are there not other better more defining characteristics that we would want to highlight to show Australians in a more progressive light?[158]

---

155 *Peace and Freedom* 48, Issue 3 (December 2011): 11.
156 Judith Smart and Marian Quartly, *Respectable Radicals: A History of the National Council of Women of Australia 1896–2006* (Melbourne: Monash University Publishing, 2015), 419.
157 WILPF posters, accessed 3 November 2022, www.wilpf.org.au/wilpf-history/.
158 Ruth Russell and Barbara O'Dwyer, 'National Coordinators Report', *Peace and Freedom* 52, Issues 1 and 2 (April 2013): 2.

'We join with historian Marilyn Lake', Hellen Cooke wrote, 'in reclaiming Australia's true history'.[159] Efforts to recover their history were inherently political to the women of WILPF. A centenary exhibition was held at the Canberra Museum and Gallery, showcasing the ephemera and documents from WILPFs extensive archives.

By the 2015 centenary conference of WILPF, held at The Hague in the Peace Palace—the same venue as the conference in 1915—WILPF women were finding inspiration in reflecting on their history as an organisation and reconsidering its future direction. President Kozue Akibayashi wrote in the conference report of how relevant the ideas of the founding women in 1915 were to the work of WILPF women today:

> Our founders' analysis—that wars start in the violence of our daily lives, and that they are perpetuated and made to seem natural and inevitable by the intertwined systems of patriarchy, militarism, and an economy based on profits rather than needs—remains relevant to us today.[160]

WILPF conference attendees outside the Peace Palace, The Hague, 2015.
Source: Photo by the author.

---

159 Hellen Cooke, *Peace and Freedom* 49, Issues 2 and 3 (September 2012), 9.
160 Kozue Akibayashi, 'Congress Report 2015', 1. Digitised report available online (accessed 15 December 2022): issuu.com/wilpf/docs/congress_report_spreads_final.

Delegates to the WILPF conference at The Hague holding a handmade quilt depicting historical women from the Australian branch, 2015.

Source: Photo by the author. Quilt made by Peaceknits project in Queanbeyan.

Building on the new momentum inspired by their own history, WILPF produced a new manifesto which was adopted by the conference. Written by Cockburn, it focused on the need for WILPF to return to discussions of root causes of war. The organisation committed to agitating for reform of the flawed structures of the UN rather than accepting and working within them.[161]

After the fall of the Berlin Wall, when the Cold War dichotomies dissolved and the world entered a new economic and diplomatic order, WILPF was forced to adapt their campaign focus in a changing globalised system that brought new challenges to equality and individual freedoms. Internationally, this saw WILPF focus on an institutional route that involved directing their energies into the systems and forums of the UN and associated bodies. Many activists felt that the compromises necessary to work within these bureaucratic structures were important, and that women had to 'risk getting our hands dirty if we are to make a contribution to resolving armed conflict and ending war itself.'[162] Despite its weaknesses and shortcomings, there was a sense that UNSCR 1325 had provided more leverage and tools for activists working in conflict zones to promote issues of gender and conflict, especially as its passing by the Security Council meant the UN publicly acknowledged gender-specific issues of women in war.

The explosion in other women's NGOs meant WILPF was part of a larger international arena and had to find ways to stand out and make strong statements in ways that would be productive and recognised. WILPF embraced the modern, institutionalised NGO identity throughout the UN Decade for Women. Yet its structure and history always made it different from other professional NGOs. While it functioned as a lobbying organisation to the UN, alongside other organisations like Amnesty International and the International Committee of the Red Cross, WILPF always maintained and encouraged recruitment on a local level, relying on participation. It performed the important role of connecting women from all walks of life to the international arena. Focusing on their wider membership similarly gave WILPF stronger lobbying potential, especially as the UN became more directed by national government decisions made outside the UN. WILPF contributed to this political environment that continued a tradition of women's transnationalism that had 'a dynamic of its own which is not subordinate to or simply a proxy for the political battles fought by men.'

---

161 'WILPF Manifesto 2015', accessed 15 December 2022, www.wilpf.org/publications/wilpf-manifesto-2015/.
162 Cockburn, *From Where We Stand*, 155.

Conclusion

'The only way you can preserve peace is to prepare for war.'[1] In 2022, during an election campaign on Anzac Day, the defence minister in a Liberal–National Coalition Government, Peter Dutton, had unknowingly answered Doris Blackburn's question of 1947: 'Is preparation for war the best means of preserving peace?' The minister was responding to rising conflict between China and the West, which raised the spectre of war over the future of Taiwan, and the outbreak of an actual European war in February 2022, when Russia invaded Ukraine in an act of aggression that shocked the world.

The largest land incursion in Europe since World War II has shattered two complacent assumptions that had become widespread about modern warfare: that nuclear weapons were no longer a threat, and that technology and the globalised financial system meant conventional wars between dominant powers were a thing of the past. Horrifying images have spread around the world, rapidly assisted by social media showing civilian casualties and a refugee crisis. Those images clearly demonstrate the gendered impact of the modern war and the all-too-familiar use of rape as an instrument of warfare. Ukrainian woman Antonina Medvedchuk spoke with journalists about her fear of sexual violence: 'Every break between curfew and bombing I was looking for emergency contraception instead of a basic first aid kit,' she said.

---

1   Peter Dutton comments on Nine's *Today* show, quoted in Angus Thompson, '"Reality of our Time": Dutton Warns Australians to Prepare for War', *The Age,* 25 April 2022, accessed 25 April 2022, www.theage.com.au/politics/federal/reality-of-our-time-dutton-warns-australians-to-prepare-for-war-20220425-p5afuy.html.

> My mother tried to reassure me: 'This is not a war like that, they don't exist anymore, they are from old movies.' I have been a feminist for eight years, and I cried in silence, because all wars are like this.[2]

The images coming out of Ukraine that reveal the horrors of war and a renewed understanding of the threat of nuclear weapons have cast new relevance on this history of women's anti-war activism. The urgency of trying to find alternative ways to achieve peace and security without militarising to address a military threat has become paramount. The central purpose of the existence of the Women's International League for Peace and Freedom (WILPF) remains painfully necessary. And indeed WILPF have again contributed to the debate by condemning the illegal actions of Russia and its violation of Ukrainian independence while also urging that we continue to look more deeply at the root causes of war. The secretary general of WILPF, Madeleine Rees, in an open letter to the UN Security Council, simply stated: 'militarism is literally killing everything.'[3]

***

WILPF has provided a platform that fostered Australian women's political activism over the twentieth century and into the twenty-first. The task was always momentous and formidable: to pursue peace in an imperfect world. The extensive archives of the organisation illuminate the ways Australian women dealt with the distinctive challenges of internationalism as a political project almost invariably without governmental or institutional support, while contributing to an effective international community of advocacy. From WILPF's origins in World War I peace activism, women who joined the organisation connected with a worldwide network that allowed them to cultivate an international outlook. This perspective, for Australian women, gave new direction and understanding to their campaigns against conscription, imperialism, militarism in school textbooks, and government spending on war. WILPF members did not shy away from discussing contentious and complex issues. Their insistence on interrogating their own perspectives on difficult topics extended from militarism, war and racism to nationalism, self-determination and communism. Their language

---

2   Bethan McKernan, 'Rape as a Weapon: Huge Scale of Sexual Violence Endured in Ukraine Emerges', *The Guardian,* 4 April 2022, accessed 4 April 2022, www.theguardian.com/world/2022/apr/03/all-wars-are-like-this-used-as-a-weapon-of-war-in-ukraine.

3   Madeleine Rees, '"War 'Over' Ukraine—Militarism Is Killing Us All," Writes WILPF Secretary General In An Open Letter To The United Nations Security Council', 28 January 2022, accessed 4 April 2022, www.wilpf.org/war-over-ukraine-militarism-is-killing-us-all/.

CONCLUSION

and frameworks changed significantly throughout the decades. Yet their willingness to confront their own shortcomings illustrated a commitment to active engagement in a wide range of domains.

The triennial congresses of WILPF held in different cities of the world provided an important space for international women to develop their politics. Meeting with women of other nationalities, even at times from states officially at war with one another, political women were able to form common bonds and empathise in a community beyond the limitations of nationalism, though disagreement arose from differences in national circumstances. The nature of WILPF members' travels was consequently highly political, each interaction being an opportunity to recruit, each conversation being a chance to disseminate their worldview for the sake of progressive change.

Each WILPF congress produced resolutions and changes to the operation of the organisation. These reports and press releases demonstrated how seriously the women took the output of the conferences and the impact they might have on the wider international political arena. However, often personal reports of the gatherings showed levels of frustration at conference procedure and the practical difficulties of bringing together many women with different languages, ideas and experiences in a productive way. For some Australian participants, the ability to be part of the physical space and be connected to the women separated by huge distances was more valuable than the resolutions they debated. Edith Abbott at the conference in 1949 wrote:

> To me the lasting value and joy of meeting such women and talking freely with them between sessions and on 'time off' was of more interest than the actual work of the congress.[4]

Having all the sections as 'seemingly disparate cities of the world' connected into a 'common global space' gave a concrete meaning to internationalism that could not always be reflected in formal policy documents.[5] As this reflection demonstrates, the apparatus of conferencing and the locations of the gatherings reflected as much about their political priorities as the resolutions at the end.

---

4   Edith Abbott, report to Australian WILPF section on the 1949 conference, 28 March 1950, Box 1728/3 Papers, WILPF, MS 9377, State Library of Victoria (SLV).
5   Jake Hodder, 'Conferencing the International at the World Pacifist Meeting, 1949,' *Political Geography* 49 (November 2015): 9, doi.org/10.1016/j.polgeo.2015.03.002.

Internationalism was personally transformative for the women involved in WILPF. On return from the conferences, and in the interwar period when a wider appetite for pacifist sentiment was prevalent, WILPF members began to question national policies in light of their new insights. Publicly discussing the White Australia Policy (WAP) and looking to promote regional engagement signalled a significant departure from prevailing modes of thought, which had been cornerstones of the early twentieth-century Australian progressivism from which WILPF had emerged. While they were not able to provide a definitive denunciation of racial exclusion, their deliberations were significant for the time and a clear representation of how internationalist connection and exposure could provoke discussion and lay the foundations for change. Questioning the WAP of itself was, for this milieu, a highly unusual break from consensus. This re-evaluation continued with their engagement with the Pan-Pacific Women's movement between the wars.

Anti-gun campaigner, 88-year-old Eve Masterman of WILPF holds a sign reading 'Destroy guns and let people live' at a rally in the park outside the Tasmanian Parliament House, in the days after the Port Arthur massacre, Hobart, Tasmania, 4 May 1996.

Source: *The Age*, picture by Jason South, Fairfax Media Archives. See Appendix for a short biography of Eve Masterman.

Those involved were not able to dispense entirely with national interests in formulating their contributions to international policy. However, they utilised the international connections whenever possible to promote national issues internationally, as shown in the mobilisation of the international network over issues relating to Aboriginal rights from the 1950s onwards. Utilising new channels after the creation of the UN and new language once the Universal Declaration of Human Rights was adopted, WILPF was moved to refashion its existing idealism, tying its anti-war philosophy to wider issues of human rights and social justice. A new interstate network for the national section of WILPF, formed during the 1960s, illustrated how WILPF in Australia brought the section into line with the international structure, enacting its transformation into a modern non-government organisation (NGO).

Over the years, WILPF expressly cultivated a personal form of internationalism among its members. The Maison Internationale in Geneva acted as the 'heart' of the organisation and became a place for women to meet and interact through their travels.[6] It was a site of pilgrimage for members. For women who could not afford to travel, it held a meaningful place in their mind as a physical representation of the international network through which WILPF's correspondence and publications flowed. Many women became very devoted to the cause. Historian and feminist Leila Rupp has written of women who 'worked hard, sacrificed their health, and overcame obstacles that stood in the way of full-time commitment'.[7] They did this because they found joy and fulfilment in their work. For many, it was a place to learn new skills, and gain confidence and support, especially for women unused to public roles. They felt satisfaction in giving to something bigger than themselves, something of immense importance. WILPF facilitated international friendships, promoted universality and strengthened international identities alongside national ones.

Small organisations were crucial in the promotion of internationalism in Australia.[8] WILPF in Australia was never huge, and internationally by 1926 its estimated membership was only 50,000.[9] Nonetheless they were well

---

6   Leila J Rupp, *Worlds of Women: The Making of an International Women's Movement* (Princeton: Princeton University Press, 1997), 166, doi.org/10.1515/9780691221816.
7   Rupp, *Worlds of Women*, 182.
8   Joy Damousi, 'Does Feminist History have a Future?', *Australian Feminist Studies* 29, no. 80 (2014): 199, doi.org/10.1080/08164649.2014.928188.
9   Laura Beers, 'Advocating for a Feminist Internationalism Between the Wars', in *Women, Diplomacy and International Politics since 1500*, ed. Glenda Sluga and Carolyn James (New York: Routledge, 2015), 203, doi.org/10.4324/9781315713113-13.

placed to capitalise on the renewed interest in internationalism that surged after 1918, when a war-weary public was receptive to a new ideas in political life and international affairs. The creation of the League of Nations meant that Australia, as a signatory to the Treaty of Versailles, became a voting nation-state, thereby drawing interest from the women's movement in the possibilities of a state-sponsored internationalism.[10]

Lobbying the League of Nations became a significant ritual of power in the global imaginary of the women's movement, as the covenant of the league explicitly stated that 'all positions under and in connection with the League ... shall be open to men and women'.[11] WILPF joined in with other women's groups which campaigned to have female representation on the Australian delegation to the league, gaining regular alternate delegates (who were non-voting), with Jessie Street being the first actual delegate in 1946 at the new United Nations (UN). But WILPF did not, as other women's organisations did, define their internationalism by the need to have national accreditation. WILPF women continued to travel with accreditation by their voluntary organisation and utilised its specific advantages of 'informal' influence to have an impact in the international sphere. This continued after the League of Nations was replaced by the UN in 1945, and Australian WILPF woman Irene Greenwood gave first-hand experience of this in a reflection in 1975, noting:

> when you go to the United Nations you don't just sit in a seat with earphones on as an observer and have the right to speak or make submissions, but also you go into the corridors behind and you meet comparable groups and then you lobby the leaders of the various countries for certain things that are brought forward on the agenda. And so our influence at the United Nations has been rather more than I indicated, but again it was an indirect influence.[12]

Tracing the travel and funding arrangements of the organisation, it is clear that WILPF, like other women's organisations, had to overcome limitations specific to their gender. For women to become involved in political activism throughout the twentieth century, especially internationalist activism, where travelling was time-consuming and costly, there had to be certain conditions

---

10 Fiona Paisley, 'Being International at Home: Australian Public Opinion in the League Era', *Journal of Australian Studies* 43, no. 4 (2 October 2019): 429–46, doi.org/10.1080/14443058.2019.1672205.
11 Jill Roe, 'What has Nationalism Offered Australian Women?' in *Australian Women: Contemporary Feminist Thought,* ed. Norma Grieve and Ailsa Burns (Oxford: Oxford University Press, 1994), 36.
12 Irene Greenwood, 'A Lifetime of Political Activity', in *Women and Politics Conference Volume 1* (Canberra: Australian Government Publishing Service, 1977), 63.

that would enable them to overcome socialised gendered expectations. Eleanor Moore worked independently as a stenographer and could rely on income from a familial rental investment property.[13] For others like Edith Waterworth and Margaret Holmes, wealthy families and hired domestic help facilitated political involvement. The scarcity of women in public and political roles has been due to the 'historical connection between women, housework and childcare'.[14] Many WILPF women regularly travelled with their husbands, making time for WILPF work overseas, or they had partners who were fellow activists and encouraged their public activities.

Financial freedom for women throughout the history of WILPF has been a significant factor in shaping the organisation. In the early years of its operation, unpaid domestic work, along with simple social and legislative impediments, often meant women did not have access to funds outside the family. Discrimination against women in employment and financial matters remained pervasive and widespread.[15] Members had to work creatively to find ways to fund and support their campaigns without institutional backing. Meetings were often held in private spaces, in living rooms and backyards instead of boardrooms. Wealthier members subsidised travel opportunities for others, and craft stalls and fetes were held regularly, such as the annual fete at Janie Kerr's residence in Melbourne during the early years of WILPF, where the proceeds of arts and craft sales went to building up funding reserves. These methods of fundraising maintained a close coupling with the domestic space and domestic economy. Subscriptions were collected for publications such as *Peacewards*, *Woman Voter* and *Peace and Freedom*, and most of the time spent campaigning, collecting signatures, attending meetings and maintaining the organisation was volunteered—another way in which women's work remained unpaid while men in established political roles were often remunerated. While this made some things difficult, it also gave the organisation a distinctive voice, where the discussion of grand global struggles was conducted in intimate spaces separate from any intermediating bureaucratic systems. The symbolism of

---

13 Malcolm Saunders, *Quiet Dissenter: The Life and Thought of an Australian Pacifist: Eleanor May Moore 1875–1949* (Canberra: Peace Research Centre, Australian National University, 1993), 52.
14 Marilyn Lake and Farley Kelly, eds, *Doubletime: Women in Victoria, 150 Years* (Ringwood, Vic: Penguin, 1985), ix.
15 Patricia Grimshaw, Marilyn Lake, Marian Quartly, and Ann McGrath, *Creating a Nation* (Ringwood, Vic: McPhee Gribble, 1994), 301.

domestic organising reminds us that despite the rhetoric of international affairs, which often talks of nation-states and conflict in the abstract, these serious international questions ultimately reach into these intimate spaces.

WILPF in Australia was especially prone to taking direction from dominant members because the membership over time fluctuated and institutional knowledge became centralised. Disavowal of hierarchical organising structures and the promotion of consensus building, which often characterised women's organising, were not always borne out in operations. By the 1930s WILPF had a membership of about 250 across branches in Melbourne, Hobart, Newcastle and Rockhampton, and leader Eleanor Moore noted:

> we have never made a push to obtain a large membership, finding that we can work to better effect with a small band of thoroughly convinced pacifists than with a large gathering of uncertain ones.[16]

Judy Horacek cartoon: Centenary Gift to WILPF Australia.
Source: Used with permission of Jenny Darling.

---

16   Moore to Drevet, 11 August 1931, series III reel 54, WILPF International Papers 1915–1978, Sanford, NC: Microfilming Corp. of America, c 1983, accessed at the National Library of Australia (NLA). Hereafter referred to as WILPF Papers.

CONCLUSION

It is difficult to determine through the archives the extent of involvement of the branch rank and file, those women who attended meetings and paid dues but were not the prominent letter writers or minute takers. As is characteristic of voluntary organisations, it was the women of the executive who took on most of the work to which their names were signed. Yet, driven by the most passionate, the group was still sustained by the enthusiasm of a much broader cohort who lent what time and funds they could in often constrained circumstances.

The wider impact of the Australian section's activism, considering their modest place in national affairs, is difficult to quantify. As a history based on memoir and archives, this book has not specifically analysed the broader public perceptions of WILPF or sought to provide a full account of its policy impacts. Internationally, however, WILPF remains a significant organisation worthy of study as it boasts being one of the oldest international peace organisations in the world and it pioneered a style of advocacy that brought a cohort of women into international affairs. Close examination of their operating style also demonstrates the practical tensions that have plagued the women's movement throughout the twentieth century, and how different sections of the movement interacted with contradicting but arguably justifiable forms of applying evolving feminist theory. Today, it prides itself on being one of the oldest NGOs, gaining consultative status with the League of Nations in the 1920s and formalising its position with the UN in 1948.[17] The longevity of the organisation has been due to its adaptability, the international organising structure, and its core focus of women's empowerment, peace and freedom, which were major concerns of the twentieth century. While today a challenge remains of building membership and making the transition to more digital engagement, its strength continues to lie in the organisation's willingness to engage with all issues through a gendered lens.

War memorials and other well-funded war commemorations maintain the importance of honouring individuals, and WILPF women too recognised each person who worked for peace. From early in WILPF's history, the women of WILPF tried to document peace workers to match the honour rolls of the military, with Margaret Nimmo's death in 1933 prompting the tribute: 'we salute her indomitable spirit as it passes from among us, and

---

17 Mary Meyer, 'The Women's International League for Peace and Freedom: Organizing Women for Peace in the War System', in *Gender Politics in Global Governance*, ed. Elisabeth Prügl and Mary K Meyer (Lanham, Maryland: Rowman & Littlefield Publishers, 1999), 110.

are proud to inscribe her name on the lasting Honour Roll of the Heroines of Peace.'[18] Looking at the history of WILPF as an organisation over time reveals how an alternative world order has been imagined and pursued by actors who sat far from the levers of formal power. Their example encourages us to look beyond the militarism that has been so normalised in public life, despite the certainty of its destructive results.

---

18   *Peacewards*, 1 July 1933, Box 1731/6 Papers, WILPF, MS 9377, SLV.

Appendix: Biographies of WILPF leaders

Janet Julia Fullarton Strong née Denniston (1844–1919)

Janet (Jessie) Julia Fullarton Denniston was born in Greenock, Scotland. She married Dr Charles Strong in 1872 and moved with him to Melbourne. According to Strong's biographer, she was:

> intelligent, well read and a decided personality. She was an excellent musician and a better German scholar than Charles Strong. She shared his interests and gave him unfailing support in all his undertakings.[1]

Together they had eight children; five sons and three daughters. When Charles Strong founded the Australian Church in Melbourne in 1885 she was a pivotal part of its practical philanthropic mission. She had a great interest in helping women and children, volunteering her time to become the leader of many of the societies associated with the church's programs for social improvement, and other women groups concerned with social reform. Janet Strong was a founding member of the National Council of Women Victoria in 1902 and remained an executive member until 1915. That year she helped to found the Sisterhood of International Peace (the Sisterhood) through the Australian Church. Media reports show her work was respected and recognised. She was 'public spirited and unselfish', though she remained humble and 'cannot be induced to speak of her work'.[2] Active and supportive of the peace movement during World War I, she became

---

1   Colin Robert Badger, *The Reverend Charles Strong and the Australian Church* (Melbourne: Abacada Press on behalf of the Charles Strong Memorial Trust, 1971).
2   'Mrs Charles Strong', *Weekly Times,* 18 April 1914, 9.

ill in 1919 and died at her home in Armadale, Melbourne.[3] Her husband Charles then put his energies into pacifist activity through the Australian Church until his death in 1942.

Eleanor May Moore (1875–1949)

Eleanor Moore was born on 10 March 1875 in Lancefield, a rural town north of Melbourne. She was one of seven children.[4] In the 1880s, the Moore family moved to the wealthy suburb of Toorak in Melbourne, living at 40 Evelina Road, where Eleanor continued to reside until her death in 1949. Moore went to local primary schools and won a scholarship to attend the Presbyterian Ladies' College (PLC).[5] Her family were members of the Australian Church congregation from its foundation in 1885 and were 'liberal religious thinkers'.[6] In the mid-1890s, Moore took a secretarial course and trained as a stenographer. Staying in the family home all her adult life, the unmarried Moore contributed to the family budget, but was never dependent on work to survive. This gave her the opportunity to pursue her love of literature. It also gave her the energy and security to commit her volunteer labour to the Sisterhood and the Women's International League for Peace and Freedom (WILPF). From the founding in 1915, Evelina Road became the mailing address through which all major correspondence with the Australian section of WILPF flowed. Moore remained active and involved in politics until her death in October 1949. In the last year of her life, she wrote her memoir containing her recollections of the peace movement in her time. Tributes to Moore after her death detailed her extended commitment to peace. One eulogy published in the War Resisters International journal, an organisation with which WILPF worked closely, detailed how through international communication close relationships were formed, despite geographical distance and an inability to meet in person:

> Eleanor M. Moore died on 1st October, 1949, at the age of seventy-four. She was the first contact the W. R. I. had with Australia, acting as correspondent for the Women's International League (Melbourne). Although I had never met her, I felt that it made very little difference—I knew her. She was one with whom

---

3   'Death of Mrs. Charles Strong', *The Age*, 25 April 1919.
4   Malcolm Saunders, *Quiet Dissenter: The Life and Thought of an Australian Pacifist: Eleanor May Moore 1875–1949* (Canberra: Peace Research Centre, Australian National University, 1993), 21.
5   Kathleen Fitzpatrick, *PLC Melbourne: The First Century, 1875–1975* (Burwood: Presbyterian Ladies' College, 1975).
6   Saunders, *Quiet Dissenter*, 42.

I often used to consult and her response was always prompt and reliable ... The death of Eleanor Moore will not only be a loss to our friends in Australia but to an even larger number in many other parts of the world, who did not actually know her.[7]

Mabel Drummond née Gardner (1877–1968)

Mabel Drummond was a founding member of the Sisterhood and remained closely associated with WILPF throughout most of her life. Born Mabel Gardner in 1877, she completed her education at PLC in East Melbourne, where she excelled in English and gained skills in public speaking. In 1899 she married Robert Charles Goodyear and moved to Queensland, where she gave birth to Guy and Cecily. Robert died in 1903, leaving her widowed at 25 with small children, at which point she moved back to Melbourne to be with her family. She gained employment as a secretary for a merchant on Flinders Lane.[8] During this time, she taught herself to speak Esperanto, and developed her interest in the 'universal' nature of the language. In June 1914 she married her second husband, William Drummond. Mabel and William, like Eleanor Moore and Vida Goldstein, were members of the Australian Church congregation and were recruited to pacifism by Dr Charles Strong.[9] William also shared her passion for Esperanto and both were members of the Melbourne Esperanto Club. She travelled with her husband to the Esperanto World Congress held in Nuremberg in 1923.[10] Drummond initially became one of the corresponding secretaries and the Esperanto secretary of the Sisterhood in 1915. She was to hold many positions with the organisation, including general secretary from 1917 to 1928, vice-president in 1929, and president in 1930–1932 and again in 1938–1939.[11] From the outset, she and Moore became close friends and supported each other in the administration of the WILPF. Drummond was integral to the organisation of WILPF in Melbourne and all of her time was volunteered. She administered the Peace Scholarship that WILPF sponsored between the war and was active in all WILPF's domestic advocacy. In 1955 she recorded her attendance at the 40th anniversary of the league held at Ormond College

---

7   HRB, *The War Resister*, no. 56 (Winter 1949). Reel 54, WILPF International Papers 1915–1978, Sanford, NC: Microfilming Corp. of America, c 1983, accessed at the National Library of Australia (NLA).
8   Janet Morice, *Six-Bob-a-Day Tourist* (Ringwood, Vic: Penguin Books, 1985), 20.
9   Morice, *Six-Bob-a-Day Tourist*, 45. See also Badger, *The Reverend Charles Strong and the Australian Church*.
10 Eleanor M Moore, *The Quest for Peace, As I Have Known It in Australia* (Melbourne, 1948), 66.
11 Moore, *The Quest for Peace*, 174.

at Melbourne University.¹² Drummond remained a committed member of WILPF and was made an honorary permanent member in 1967. She died in 1968 aged 91.

Doris Blackburn née Horden (1889–1970)

Doris Horden was born at Hawthorn in Melbourne and educated at Hessle College, Camberwell, a progressive school where she was encouraged to think about politics. She joined the Women's Political Association (WPA) led by Vida Goldstein and became the campaign manager for Goldstein's run for the senate in 1913.[13] There she met Maurice Blackburn, who she married in 1914, and together they were active in many progressive organisations. Maurice encouraged her involvement in the labour movement.[14] They had four children and alongside being a mother she focused her political energy on WILPF, the Women's Christian Temperance Union (WCTU), the free kindergarten movement, and other groups focused on maternal and child health needs. By World War II Doris Blackburn moved away from WILPF as she did not agree with the group's increasingly isolated position within the peace movement and instead joined the International Peace Campaign and the Movement Against War and Fascism (MAW&F). She was a member of the Australian Labor Party (ALP) but resigned in 1938 after a political clash. She was supported in 1946 by a breakaway group from the ALP and won the federal seat of Bourke, which Maurice had held until his defeat at the 1943 election, the year before his death. Her victory made her the second woman to enter the House of Representatives. As one of the few female federal politicians, and as an independent, she was isolated on the crossbench. Nonetheless, she was a vocal politician with a coherent message that focused on the needs of women and children. She only served one term, as a redistribution changed her seat, and after her period in office she returned her political energies to leading WILPF into the 1950s. She also helped found the Aborigines Advancement League.[15] She died in 1970.

---

12   Mabel Drummond, entry in personal diary, 28th April 1955. Diary transcribed by Janet Morice, access courtesy of WILPF 2014.
13   Carolyn Rasmussen, 'Blackburn, Doris Amelia (1889–1970)', *Australian Dictionary of Biography* (ADB), National Centre of Biography, Australian National University, adb.anu.edu.au/biography/blackburn-doris-amelia-9517/text16755, published first in hardcopy 1993, accessed online 17 October 2022.
14   Carolyn Rasmussen, *The Blackburns: Private Lives, Public Ambitions* (South Carlton: Melbourne University Publishing, 2019).
15   Richard Broome, *Fighting Hard: The Victorian Aborigines Advancement League* (Canberra: Aboriginal Studies Press, 2015).

Anna Fellowes Vroland née White (1902–1978)

Anna White was born at Ascot Vale in Melbourne in 1902. She was educated at the Methodist Ladies' College (MLC) in Kew and became a schoolteacher.[16] She taught at private and state schools around Melbourne, including in 1954 the MLC where she was a student, and later in 1961 she became the headmistress of Woodstock Girls School in Albury, New South Wales. Her teaching methods were experimental, and many viewed them as unorthodox. She became the secretary of WILPF in 1950 until 1957 and was very active in the New Education Fellowship. She encouraged WILPF to become involved in the Aboriginal rights movement, recognising the different needs of urban and rural communities and raising those concerns in international networks and forums. However, her conspicuous membership of WILPF led to her dismissal from Woodstock College after the school board decided that her political commitments indicated communist sympathies.[17] Anna married her husband Anton Vroland in 1947 at the Australian Church in Melbourne, where he was the secretary. He too was a teacher interested in new pedagogical methods, and he worked closely with Indigenous communities around Victoria. They were both very interested in human rights, education and social improvement. Anton died in 1957, after which Anna withdrew from active political engagement, jaded about the possibility of progressive reform. She remained involved with the wider WILPF network, but frequently worked alone.[18] She died in 1978 at Box Hill.

Stella Cornelius née Cohen (1919–2010)

Stella Cohen was born in Sydney in 1919. Her father, Isador Cohen, had fled Russia to live in Australia and worked as a draper and tailor. She had to leave school at 14, helping her father as a pattern maker and designer.[19] She met Max Cornelius, a Jewish German refugee who arrived in Australia in 1938 and enlisted in the Australian army, and they married in Sydney

---

16 Sitarani Kerin and Andrew Spaull, 'Vroland, Anna Fellowes (1902–1978)', ADB, National Centre of Biography, Australian National University, adb.anu.edu.au/biography/vroland-anna-fellowes-12108/text21371, published first in hardcopy 2002, accessed online 17 October 2022.
17 Jodi Kok, 'An "Ordinary Great Woman": Anna Vroland', 31 March 2021, State Library of Victoria Blog, accessed 18 October 2022, blogs.slv.vic.gov.au/family-matters/an-ordinary-great-woman-anna-vroland/.
18 Sitarani Kerin, *'An Attitude of Respect': Anna Vroland and Aboriginal Rights, 1947–1957* (Clayton, Vic: Monash University, 1999).
19 Stella Cornelius, 'Peace Worker and Businesswoman' in *The Matriarchs*, ed. Susan Mitchell (Ringwood, Vic: Penguin, 1987), 126.

in 1943.[20] They had one daughter, Helena, born in 1944. Max was a furrier and together they established Cornelius Furs. Stella was heavily involved in the business, making a point of employing women and giving them flexible working conditions. She was often the only woman buyer at international auctions. Stella remained interested in history and literature and read widely, developing a passion for peace and world affairs and initiating a Peace and Conflict Resolution Program for the United Nations Association of Australia (UNAA). By 1978 they had sold their business when Max died suddenly. Stella then put all her energies into peace activities. She became the vice-president of WILPF Australia and in 1985 she established a National Consultative Committee on Peace and Disarmament. She also established the Australian Media Peace Awards through the UNAA. In 1986 she was appointed by the Australian Government as the director of the International Year of Peace. She was awarded the Order of Australia in 1987. Cornelius campaigned for the Centre for Conflict Resolution at Macquarie University in 1988, where she was awarded an Honorary Doctor of Letters. In 2003 she was appointed to a National Committee on Human Rights Education.

Evelyn Rothfield née Dell (1910–2006)

Evelyn Dell was born in England, raised in a Jewish family. She married her husband Norman Rothfield in 1934 and together they migrated to Australian in 1939. They had three children. Evelyn and Norman were inspired to work for peace after living through World War II and being concerned for family in Europe. They were active in the Melbourne Jewish community; Evelyn became president of the Melbourne branch of the National Council of Jewish Women in 1946. She joined the UNAA and participated in the Model Parliament of Women. Evelyn also worked as a journalist reporting on the UN for Australian newspapers, often focusing on women's contributions, and she later became a travel consultant and travelled widely. When Rothfield was president of the Australian section, Hephzibah Menuhin was president of the UK branch and the two worked closely together on these issues. Menuhin, from a Jewish family and sister to violinist Yehudi Menuhin, was a musician and human rights advocate. Rothfield and Menuhin met when Menuhin lived in Australia after her

---

20 Malcolm Brown, 'Cornelius, Stella (1919–2010)', Obituaries Australia, National Centre of Biography, Australian National University, oa.anu.edu.au/obituary/cornelius-stella-16826/text28721, accessed 18 October 2022.

marriage to Lindsay Nicholas.[21] Evelyn first attended an international WILPF meeting in 1970, became the WILPF Australia president in 1975, and was elected to the international executive in 1980, becoming international vice-president in 1980–83.[22] In 1974 Evelyn and Norman began publishing a journal called *Paths to Peace*. In 1998 both Evelyn and Norman were awarded the Medal of the Order of Australia for promoting peace and human rights.[23]

Margaret Holmes née Read (1909–2009)

Margaret Read was born in Wahroonga on Sydney's North Shore on 24 January 1909. Both her father and uncle enlisted in 1914 and, as the family wished to remain close when leave was granted, Margaret, her mother and siblings moved to England, returning to Australia in August 1915. Educated at Abbotsleigh private girls school, she then went to the University of Sydney where she lived at the Women's College form 1927 to 1931. She began studying medicine in 1929, one of only seven women in the cohort of 100 students, and met her husband, Thomas Holmes. Her years at university helped broaden her experience and her politics from the conservative and privileged upbringing she had been raised in, and Margaret was a member of the Students' Representative Council in 1930.[24] Moving to Mosman in Sydney, she and her husband had six children. Despite limited time for political activity, she was a subscriber to the Left Book Club, and to *The Peacemaker*, where she learnt about WILPF.[25] In 1959, with her children more independent, she planned a solo journey to Europe where she attended the WILPF triennial congress in Stockholm.[26] Holmes also set up the WILPF Sydney branch in 1960. This well-respected, community-minded woman from a wealthy family on the North Shore was

---

21 Rothfield wrote a tribute after Menuhin's death in 1981 in *Pax et Libertas* 46, no. 1 (March 1981).
22 Evelyn Rothfield, *The Future Is Past* (self-published: Copy available at the State Library of Victoria, 1992), 59.
23 Steve Brook, '"Peacenik" who Never Gave up Ideals', obituary for Norman Rothfield, *The Sydney Morning Herald*, 12 June 2010, accessed 19 October 2022, www.smh.com.au/national/peacenik-who-never-gave-up-ideals-20100611-y3p2.html.
24 Information about Holmes' early life from Michelle Cavanagh, *Margaret Holmes: The Life and Times of an Australian Peace Campaigner* (Sydney: New Holland, 2006).
25 Cavanagh, *Margaret Holmes*.
26 Siobhan McHugh, *Minefields and Miniskirts: Australian Women and the Vietnam War* (Sydney: Doubleday, 1993), 203.

an enigma to the Australian Security Intelligence Organisation (ASIO) and the government, who were intrigued by her decision to become part of the radical peace movement. She died aged 100 in October 2009.[27]

Irene Greenwood née Driver (1898–1992)

Irene Adelaide Driver was born in Albany, Western Australia, in December 1898, the eldest of five children.[28] Her mother, Mary Anne Driver, was a committed women's rights advocate and president of the WCTU, founded in WA in 1892. She attended the Perth Modern School on a scholarship.[29] Irene completed a year at the University of Western Australia, before briefly entering the public service where she met her husband, Albert Greenwood. They married in 1920 and had two children.[30] During the 1920s Greenwood began radio broadcasting with the Australian Broadcasting Commission (ABC) and wrote radio scripts on 'women in the international news' every week. In 1930 she and her husband moved to Sydney where she met activist Jessie Street, whom Greenwood came to see as a 'mother figure'.[31] Her friendship with Street and others such as Ruby Rich and Linda Littlejohn at this time revolutionised her thinking. Not content with merely asking for reform, Street and Littlejohn encouraged Greenwood to think about the political system as a whole and the need for systemic reform.[32] Greenwood and her family moved back to WA in 1935. She returned to broadcasting, hosting a daily session called *Woman to Woman*, where she interviewed important guests, gave book reviews and promoted women's organisations and achievements.[33] She also broadcast 'travel adventure' stories, fictions that focused on female protagonists and demonstrated her worldly interests.[34]

---

27 Michelle Cavanagh, 'Powerful Voice for Peace and Freedom—Margaret Holmes, 1909-2009', *The Sydney Morning Herald*, 3 October 2009, accessed 17 October 2022, www.smh.com.au/comment/obituaries/powerful-voice-for-peace-and-freedom-20091002-ggg6.html; Michelle Cavanagh, 'Margaret Holmes Obituary', *The Guardian*, 26 November 2009, accessed 17 October 2022, sec. 'Australia News', www.theguardian.com/world/2009/nov/25/margaret-holmes-obituary.
28 Kay Murray, *Voice for Peace: The Spirit of Social Activist Irene Greenwood 1898–1992* (Bayswater, WA: Kay Murray Productions, 2005), 1.
29 Irene Greenwood, 'Chronicle of Change', in *As a Woman: Writing Women's Lives*, ed. Jocelynne A Scutt (Melbourne: Artemis Publishing, 1992), 109.
30 Murray, *Voice for Peace*, 20.
31 Greenwood, 'Chronicle of Change', in Scutt, *As a Woman*, 111.
32 Murray, *Voice for Peace*, 40.
33 Cora V Baldock, 'Irene Adelaide Greenwood 1992', *Australian Feminist Studies* 8, no. 17 (1 March 1993): 2, doi.org/10.1080/08164649.1993.9994672.
34 John Richardson, 'New and Strange Ways: The Radio Broadcasts of Irene Greenwood', *Continuum* 2, no. 2 (1 January 1989): 51, doi.org/10.1080/10304318909359364.

WILPF WA re-formed in 1952 with Evelyn Rowland. The branch produced the journal *Peace and Freedom* that Rowland edited until her death in 1961, when Greenwood took over. This journal became the paper for the national organisation, and Greenwood utilised the platform to communicate local and international peace issues for a decade. She became president of the WA branch from 1966 until 1969. She only travelled overseas once, in 1965, as a delegate for the WILPF triennial anniversary conference.[35] In 1975 Greenwood was a member of the Advisory Committee for International Women's Year.[36] This gave her a prominent position in developing programs in Australia focused on the UN Decade for Women, 1975–1985. That same year, for International Women's Year, the WILPF published a book called *Listen to Women for a Change: Fifty World Feminists on Equality, Development, Peace*.[37] Compiled by the international president of WILPF, Kay Camp, it included seven Australian women, and Greenwood was honoured to be among them. Greenwood's activities and associations made her a pivotal figure in the history of Australian feminism. In 1981 she was awarded the UNAA silver peace medal and life membership. She also had the flagship of the state ships fleet named in her honour, the MV *Irene Greenwood*.

Evelyn (Eve) Masterman (1907–2014)

Eve Masterman was born in the United Kingdom in 1907 and moved with her family to Chauncy Vale, Tasmania in 1912. She was sent to St Michael's Collegiate boarding school at a young age. In 1933 she was awarded a degree at the University of Tasmania; she became a poet and also became the first qualified librarian in the Parliamentary Library. Eve was a staunch Quaker and became involved in WILPF in 1964 to protest the Vietnam War and conscription.[38] She became the president of Tasmanian WILPF in 1974 and 1978, was a delegate to the WILPF international congress in 1968 and was the international vice-president four years later. Eve travelled widely and was a keen bushwalker. She was instrumental in the establishment of the International Peace Park in Berriedale, Tasmania, where she helped maintain a community garden. She became a Member of the Order of Australia in 1976, received an international award from the United Nations, and was

---

35 Murray, *Voice for Peace*, 150.
36 Greenwood, 'Chronicle of Change', in Scutt, *As a Woman*, 119.
37 Kay Camp, *Listen to the Women for a Change: Fifty World Feminists on Equality, Development, Peace* (Women's International League for Peace and Freedom, US Section, 1975), 19.
38 Linley Grant et al., *Prevailing for Peace: The History of the WILPF Tasmanian Branch 1920–2013* (North Hobart: WILPF, 2015), 7.

inducted to the Tasmanian Women's Honour Roll in 2009. Masterman lived to 106, passing away in 2014. An adjournment speech was given in the federal parliament by Senator Lisa Singh to acknowledge her life's work.[39] WILPF Tasmania established the Eve Masterman Peace Poetry Prize in her honour in 2014.

---

39   Lisa Singh, 'Adjournment', *Commonwealth Parliamentary Debates*, Senate, Tuesday 13 May 2014, 2523.

Acknowledgements

This work began its life in the form of a PhD thesis which I started in 2013. I was looking for an opportunity to continue my interest in the historical experience of women in politics in Australia, and I moved to Melbourne to work with one of the leading historians of the field, Professor Marilyn Lake, as my supervisor. I have therefore had the Women's International League for Peace and Freedom (WILPF) and its history on my mind for almost 10 years now, finding new stories of its activity throughout the twentieth century. With 10 years of research comes many people to thank for the final production of this book.

I would first like to acknowledge and thank my PhD supervisors, Marilyn Lake and Roland Burke, for helping to shape and structure the material for the thesis and for their encouragement and help with turning the material into a book for a more general readership. Both supervisors have generously given time for references and essential feedback; however, any mistakes or inaccuracies throughout are my own.

I would like to thank Frank Bongiorno from The Australian National University (ANU) who has given substantial time to the manuscript, helping to get it into shape. I would also like to thank Marian Sawer, the ANU Press Social Sciences Editorial Board, the anonymous reviewers and the editorial staff, particularly Emily Gallagher, for all their help with the publication. The publication of this work was made possible by an ANU Press Publication Subsidy for which I am thankful. Thank you to Beth Battrick for copyediting.

I have used material from a large number of libraries and archives, including the National Library of Australia, the National Archives of Australia, the Mitchell Library at the State Library of New South Wales, the State Library of Victoria, Latrobe Bundoora Library, Melbourne University Library and Archives, United Nations Archives at Geneva, the Boulder University archives in Colorado, who facilitated access from afar, and the Australian War Memorial Research Centre and I thank all staff and archivists who have helped me access various collections. Material from this book has been published in different forms in *History Australia, the La Trobe Journal,* and in the edited collections *Contesting Australian History,* and *Charles Strong's Australian Church,* and I thank the editors of those collections for their help in publishing.

The post-PhD transition is a difficult one in the current climate of the higher education industry. Navigating this challenging terrain has been made more enjoyable by the network of other PhD candidates and early career researchers in history, including among others Lucy Davies, James Keating, Sarah O'Connor, Cath Bishop, Nikita Vanderbyl and the Australian Women's History Network. Thank you to Diane Kirkby, Melanie Oppenheimer, Carolyn Strange, and Marion Maddox, for helping me remain research active while precariously employed.

Thank you to the Society of Friends who gave permission to access the papers of WILPF member Margaret Watts, and to Angela Dury, Public Officer People for Nuclear Disarmament NSW Inc who gave permission to publish images in the PND collection. I am thankful to Judy Horacek for permission to publish her cartoon image. Women involved in WILPF still active today have been keen supporters of my research over the last few years. I met or corresponded with many women who provided me with material on WILPF, including Michelle Cavanagh, Del Cuddhity, the Young Women's International League for Peace and Freedom, Helen Cooke, Margo Pearson, Margaret Geddes, Janette McLeod and Joyce and Colin Clague. I want to thank Margaret Reynolds for providing the foreword, and Ruth Russell, Chris Henderson, Barbara O'Dwyer, Cynthia James and especially Margaret Bearlin who has gone above and beyond to share her insights, photos and amazing experiences with me and that have made the work more interesting.

Finally, I would like to thank my family and friends, who all helped my progress in various ways. Thank you to Liz Williams and Paul McGahen, to my sisters Amelia Laing, Gemma Piat and Teresa Laing, and my mother Julie Johnson who always shared a love of history and has been an excellent editor. Most importantly, thank you to my partner Adrian McGahen and my daughters Audrey and Monica for your unwavering support, patience and encouragement.

Bibliography

Archives

National Library of Australia (NLA)

American Bases in Australia: Nuclear Target. WILPF, Royston Park, SA, [1971].

Brown, Roma and Betty King. *The Understanding of Human Aggressiveness: A Report on a Seminar Held by the Women's International League for Peace and Freedom* (WA Branch) on 24 June 1971.

Drevet, Camile and Edith Pye. *Report of the WILPF Delegation to China.* Geneva 1928, P 172.4 DRE.

Fitzpatrick, Brian. *Australia and Israel.* Melbourne, July 1948.

The Hydrogen Bomb: The World in Danger. WILPF publication, Melbourne 1955.

Man and his Environment: A Report on a Series of Lectures Delivered to the WILPF, W.A. Branch during 1969–1970. 107 The Esplanade, Mt. Pleasant, WA 6153.

Moore, Eleanor. *What Shall we Do With the Japanese?* North Fitzroy, Vic: Publications Dept., Federal Pacifist Council of Australia, (194–).

New Perversions of Science. WILPF, Australian Section Committee Against Chemical and Biological Warfare, Mosman, NSW, 1969.

Papers of Anton William Rutherford Vroland, 1876–1974 [manuscript], MS 3991.

Papers of Irene Greenwood 1912–1981 [manuscript], MS 7737.

Papers of Jessie Street, circa 1914–1968 [manuscript], MS 2683.

Papers of Margaret Holmes, circa 1920–circa 1989 [manuscript], MS 9034, MS Acc07.010.

Papers of Meredith Stokes, circa 1970–1997 [manuscript], MS 9486, MS Acc10.127.

Papers of RS Ross, MS 3222.

Papers of Ruby Rich, 1906–1984 [manuscript], MS 7493.

Papers on various Australian women [19–] [manuscript], MS 842.

Papers of Vivienne Abraham 1938–1989 [manuscript], MS 9152.

Papers of William Morris Hughes, circa 1865–1958 [manuscript], MS 1538.

Pax et Libertas. ISSN 0031-3327, Geneva, v. 6, no. 5 – v. 59, no. 4; Nov.–Dec. 1950 – Dec. 1994.

Pax International. Journal of WILPF Geneva, began 1926; ceased July/Aug. 1939.

Peace and Freedom. Journal of WILPF Western Australia, 1956–1994.

Records of the Women's International League for Peace and Freedom. Australian Section, 1943–1998 [manuscript] MS 7755, MS Acc06.149, MS Acc08.153, MS Acc11.160.

Report of the Australian Delegation. The Pan-Pacific Women's Conference. Sydney: George A. Jones Printer, 1928–.

Vida Goldstein 1869–1949 January 1966 [manuscript], MS 1637.

Women and Politics Conference Volumes 1 & 2. Canberra: Australian Government Publishing Service, 1977.

Women of the Pacific: A Record of the Proceedings of the ... Conference of the Pan-Pacific Women's Association. [Vancouver, B.C.: The Association, 1937–1955?] 4th (1937) – 7th (1955).

Women's International League for Peace and Freedom papers, 1915–1978 [microform]. Series III: National Sections and Other Countries, 1914–1979. Australia Folders 6-30, Reel 54-55, Sanford, N.C: Microfilming Corp. of America, [c1983], 114 microfilm reels; 35 mm.

State Library of Victoria (SLV)

Commonweal and *Peacewards* (Melbourne, Vic.). Australian Church 1908–1942, Vol. 15, no. 12 (Aug 1, 1908) – v. 49, no. 7 (Mar. 1942).

Education Gazette and Teachers Aid (Victoria), Vol. 1, no. 1 (1900) – v. 91, no. 9 (10 Dec. 1991).

Maurice Blackburn, Papers, 1911–1971 [manuscript]. MS 11749.

Papers of Anna Vroland, 1947–1973 [manuscript]. Accession no. MS 10301.

The Peacemaker (Melbourne, Vic). Federal Pacifist Council of Australia 1939–1971, Vol. 1, no. 1 (Sep. 1939) – v. 33, no. 9–12 (Sept.–Dec. 1971).

Records of the Women's International League for Peace and Freedom, 1915–1973 [manuscript]. Australian Section, Accession no. MS 9377.

Rothfield, Evelyn. *Israel Reborn*. Melbourne: Dolphin Publications, 1948. Record ID 57796. Digitised at: viewer.slv.vic.gov.au/?entity=IE6801980&mode=browse.

Rothfield, Evelyn. *Whither Palestine*. Melbourne: Dolphin Publications, 1947. Record ID 142301. Digitised at: viewer.slv.vic.gov.au/?entity=IE2995766&mode=browse.

The School Paper for Grades VII and VIII. Melbourne: Education Dept., Victoria 1912–1962, Rare Books.

The Woman (Melbourne, Vic). Australian Women's National League, Vol. 1, no. 1 (21st. Sept., 1907) – v. 26, no. 11 (Jan. 1st, 1934).

White, Anna. *Who Goes Where?* (Mildura, Vic: Sunraysia Daily Print, 1938).

State Library of New South Wales (SLNSW)

Eleanor M. Moore papers, 1887–1953. MLMSS 4170.

Irina Dunn papers, ca. 1980–1984, with papers collected relating to early feminists, 1873–1983. MLMSS 5324.

Religious Society of Friends (Quakers) in Australia – papers concerning Margaret Watts, 1914–1982. MLMSS 7097 access courtesy of the Society of Friends.

Women's International League for Peace and Freedom. NSW Branch – Records, 1960–1990. MLMSS 5395/Boxes 1–3 MLMSS 5395/Item 4X.

Women's International League for Peace and Freedom. NSW Branch further records, 1960–1995, 2004. MLMSS 9015, MLOH 716.

Melbourne University Archives

Campaign for International Co-Operation and Disarmament (CICD), 1892–1988; 1991 [Most 1953–1988], 79/152; 87/92; 87/93; 88/107; 88/121.

The Woman Voter [microform]. No. 1 (Aug. 1909) – no. 326 (Dec. 18, 1919). Baillieu Library.

University of Colorado at Boulder Archives, USA (CU Archives)

Women's International League for Peace and Freedom (WILPF). Swarthmore College Peace Collection Accession (1915–2000).

Women's International League for Peace and Freedom. 2nd Accession (1915–1998).

League of Nations Archives, Geneva

Disarmament Conference 7B 32813 31155—Correspondence with the Women's International League for Peace and Freedom. United Nations Archives Geneva.

Disarmament Conference registry no. 7B 34621, 34619, 1928–1932. United Nations Archives Geneva.

Mandates committee, boxes R33 and R34 – Australia's mandate for New Guinea, 1921. United Nations Archives Geneva.

Nous Desarmons … Visions de la Conference pour la Réduction et la Limitation des Armements – Genève 1932. United Nations Archives Geneva.

Records of the Conference for the Reduction and Limitation of Armaments Series: A Verbatim Records of Plenary Meetings. Volume 1, February 2 to July 23, 1932. United Nations Archives Geneva.

Australian War Memorial Research Centre

Gardner, Thomas Oliver, Private. 7 Battalion, 59 Battalion, AIF b: 1881 d: 1918, PR90/157. www.awm.gov.au/collection/PR90/157/.

National Archives of Australia (NAA)

'Anna F. Vroland (Mrs) Re Welfare of Natives Northern Territory'. Canberra, 1954 1948. A431, 1950/730.

'BROWN, Freda Yetta (Aka LEWIS) Volume 1'. Canberra, 1958 1943. A6119, 4905.

'Holmes, Margaret Joan Volume 1'. Canberra, 1964 1957. A6119, 3362.

'Holmes, Margaret Joan Volume 2'. Canberra, 1973 1964. A6119, 3363.

'Intelligence Reports on Enemy Trading and Other Suspicious Actions'. MP95/1.

'Mrs Ada BROMHAM'. Canberra, 1959 1952. A6126, 168.

'Phyllis LATONA'. Canberra, 1962 1926. A6119, 565 REFERENCE COPY.

'THORP, Miss Margaret – Travelled to London and Europe. Interests Are Pacifism, Revolutionary Pacifism, Socialism, pro-Germanism and pro-Bolshevism. Queensland'. Canberra, 1922 1922. A402, W245.

'VROLAND, Anna'. Canberra, 1970 1939. A6119, 2419.

'Women's International League for Peace and Freedom—General Representations'. Media release, 8 May 1991. Item, Canberra, 4 December 1986, A463, 1989/2011 PART 4.

Other

Behrendt, Larissa, dir. *Maralinga Tjarutja*. ABC Blackfella Films, 2020.

Department of the House of Representatives. *Annual Report 1988–89*. Canberra: Australian Government Publishing Service, 1989.

Drummond, Mabel. Personal Diaries provided by Janet Morice, granddaughter. Access courtesy of WILPF.

Grant, Linley, and Audrey Moore, Hilary Martin, and Kay Binet. *Prevailing for Peace; The History of the WILPF Tasmanian Branch 1920-2013*. North Hobart: published by WILPF, 2015.

Morgan, Alec, and Gerry Bostock, dir. *Lousy Little Sixpence*. Ronin Films, 1982.

'Piecing it Together: Hearing the Stories of AIDEX '91'. Prepared by the Friends of the Hearings, 1991–1995. Curtin ACT: Penniless Publications, 1995. Access courtesy of Helen Cooke.

Williams, Heather. *Women and Peace; WILPF An Australian Profile*. Unpublished access courtesy of WILPF, 1982.

Newspapers and magazines

The Advocate
The Age
The Argus
The Australian
The Australian Women's Weekly
The Australian Worker
The Ballarat Star

The Canberra Times
The Daily Express (London)
The Daily Herald
The Daily News
The Daily Standard
The Guardian
The McIvor Times and Rodney Advertiser
The Mercury
The Mirror
Ms. Magazine
North Shore Times
The Portland Guardian
The Sun
The Sydney Morning Herald
The Telegraph
Townsville Daily Bulletin
The Weekly Times
The West Australian
Windsor and Richmond Gazette
The Woman
The Woman Voter
The World
Xilonen (Mexico City)
International Peace Update

Books, theses and journal articles

Acheson, Ray. *Banning the Bomb, Smashing the Patriarchy*. Rowman & Littlefield, 2021.

Addams, Jane. *Women at The Hague: The International Congress of Women and Its Results*. Urbana, Illinois: University of Illinois Press, 1915.

Aldrich, Robert. *France and the South Pacific Since 1940*. London: Macmillan, 1993. doi.org/10.1007/978-1-349-10828-2.

Allen, Judith. *Rose Scott: Vision and Revision in Feminism*. Melbourne: Oxford University Press, 1994.

Alonso, Harriet Hyman. *Peace as a Women's Issue: A History of the U.S. Movement for World Peace and Women's Rights*. Syracuse, New York: Syracuse University Press, 1993.

Anderson, Benedict R O'G. *Imagined Communities: Reflections on the Origin and Spread of Nationalism*. London; New York: Verso, 1983.

Arnold, Lorna, and Mark Smith. *Britain, Australia and the Bomb: The Nuclear Tests and Their Aftermath*. 2nd ed. New York: Palgrave Macmillan, 2006. doi.org/10.1057/9780230627338.

Arrow, Michelle. *The Seventies: The Personal, the Political and the Making of Modern Australia*. Sydney: NewSouth, 2019.

Attwood, Bain. *Rights for Aborigines*. Crows Nest, NSW: Allen & Unwin, 2003.

Badger, Colin Robert. *The Reverend Charles Strong and the Australian Church*. Melbourne: Abacada Press on behalf of the Charles Strong Memorial Trust, 1971.

Baldock, Cora V. 'Irene Adelaide Greenwood 1992'. *Australian Feminist Studies* 8, no. 17 (1 March 1993): 1–4. doi.org/10.1080/08164649.1993.9994672.

Ball, Desmond. *A Base for Debate: The US Satellite Station at Nurrungar*. Sydney: Allen & Unwin, 1987.

———. *Pine Gap: Australia and the US Geostationary Signals Intelligence Satellite Program*. Sydney: Allen & Unwin, 1988.

———. *The Strategic Implications of American Bases in Australia*. Clayton, Vic: Monash University, Faculty of Economics and Politics, 1974.

Bartlett, Alison. 'Feminist Protest and Maternity at Pine Gap Women's Peace Camp, Australia 1983'. *Women's Studies International Forum* 34, no. 1 (January 2011): 31–38. doi.org/10.1016/j.wsif.2010.10.002.

Barwick, Diane. 'A Little More than Kin: Regional Affiliation and Group Identity Among Aboriginal Migrants in Melbourne'. PhD thesis, ANU, 1963.

Beaumont, Joan. *Broken Nation: Australians in the Great War*. Allen & Unwin, 2013.

Beauvoir, Simone de. *The Second Sex*. 1st American ed. New York: Knopf, 1952.

Blackwell, Joyce. *No Peace Without Freedom: Race and the Women's International League for Peace and Freedom, 1915–1975*. Carbondale, Illinois: Southern Illinois University Press; London, 2004.

Blake, LJ. *Vision and Realisation: A Centenary History of State Education in Victoria*. Melbourne: Education Department of Victoria, 1973.

Bomford, Janette M. *That Dangerous and Persuasive Woman: Vida Goldstein*. Carlton, Vic: Melbourne University Press, 1993.

Bongiorno, Frank. *The Sex Lives of Australians: A History*. Collingwood, Vic: Black Inc, 2012.

Boutilier, Beverly Lynn. 'Educating for Peace and Co-Operation: The Women's International League for Peace and Freedom in Canada, 1919–1929'. MA thesis, Carleton University (Canada), 1988. doi.org/10.22215/etd/1988-01474.

Broome, Richard. *Fighting Hard: The Victorian Aborigines Advancement League*. Canberra: Aboriginal Studies Press, 2015.

———. 'Tracing the Humanitarian Strain in Black–White Encounters'. *Latrobe Journal* 43 (Autumn 1989): 37–38.

Burgmann, Meredith. 'The Women Against Rape in War Collective's Protests Against ANZAC Day in Sydney, 1983 and 1984'. *Cosmopolitan Civil Societies Journal* 6, no. 3 (2014): 4222. doi.org/10.5130/ccs.v6i3.4222.

Burgmann, Verity. *Power, Profit and Protest. Australian Social Movements and Globalisation*. Crows Nest, NSW: Allen & Unwin, 2003. doi.org/10.4324/9781003116745.

Burke, Roland. 'Competing for the Last Utopia? The NIEO, Human Rights, and the World Conference for the International Women's Year, Mexico City, June 1975'. *Humanity* 6, no. 1 (2015): 47–61. doi.org/10.1353/hum.2015.0000.

———. *Decolonization and the Evolution of International Human Rights*. Philadelphia: University of Pennsylvania Press, 2010.

Bussey, GC, and Margaret Tims. *Pioneers for Peace: Women's International League for Peace and Freedom, 1915–1965*. 2nd ed. London: Allen & Unwin, 1965.

Caine, Barbara, ed. *Australian Feminism: A Companion*. Melbourne: Oxford University Press, 1998.

Caldicott, Helen. *A Passionate Life*. Milsons Point, NSW: Random House Australia, 1996.

Camp, Kay. *Listen to the Women for a Change: Fifty World Feminists on Equality, Development, Peace*. Women's International League for Peace and Freedom, US Section, 1975.

Carey, Jane, and Claire McLisky. *Creating White Australia*. Sydney: Sydney University Press, 2009. doi.org/10.30722/sup.9781920899424.

Cathcart, Michael, and Kate Darian-Smith, eds. *Great Words: Speeches That Stirred Australia*. Melbourne: Melbourne University Press, 1998.

Cavanagh, Michelle. *Margaret Holmes: The Life and Times of an Australian Peace Campaigner*. Sydney: New Holland, 2006.

Clark, Anna, Alecia Simmonds, and Anne Rees. *Transnationalism, Nationalism and Australian History*. Singapore: Palgrave Macmillan, 2017. doi.org/10.1007/978-981-10-5017-6.

Cockburn, Cynthia. *From Where We Stand: War, Women's Activism and Feminist Analysis*. London: Zed Books, 2007. doi.org/10.5040/9781350220287.

Cohn, Carol, Helen Kinsella, and Sheri Gibbings, 'Women, Peace and Security Resolution 1325'. *International Feminist Journal of Politics* 6, no. 1 (1 January 2004): 130–40. doi.org/10.1080/1461674032000165969.

Colligan, Mimi. 'Brothers and Sisters in Peace: The Peace Movement in Melbourne 1900–1918'. BA (Hons) thesis, Monash University, 1973.

Collins, Carolyn. *Save Our Sons: Women, Dissent and Conscription During the Vietnam War*, Monash University Publishing, 2021.

Confortini, Catia Cecilia. 'How Matters: Women's International League for Peace and Freedom's Trips to the Middle East, 1931–1975'. *Peace & Change* 38, no. 3 (1 July 2013): 284–309. doi.org/10.1111/pech.12023.

———. *Intelligent Compassion: The Women's International League for Peace and Freedom and Feminist Peace*. New York: Oxford University Press, 2012. doi.org/10.1093/acprof:oso/9780199845231.001.0001.

Cook, Megan, Barbara Etschmann, Rahul Ram, Konstantin Ignatyev, Gediminas Gervinskas, Steven D Conradson, Susan Cumberland, Vanessa NL Wong, and Joël Brugger. 'The Nature of Pu-Bearing Particles from the Maralinga Nuclear Testing Site, Australia'. *Scientific Reports* 11, no. 1 (21 May 2021): 10698. doi.org/10.1038/s41598-021-89757-5.

Coper, Michael, Tony Blackshield, and George Williams, eds. *The Oxford Companion to the High Court of Australia*. Oxford: Oxford University Press, 2001. doi.org/10.1093/acref/9780195540222.001.0001.

Crisp, LF. *Ben Chifley: A Biography*. London: Longmans, 1961.

Crossley, Robert. *Talking Across the World: The Love Letters of Olaf Stapledon and Agnes Miller, 1913–1919*. Hanover, New Hampshire: University Press of New England, 1987.

Curthoys, Ann. 'History and Reminiscence: Writing About the Anti-Vietnam-war Movement'. *Australian Feminist Studies* 7, no. 16 (1 December 1992): 116–36. doi.org/10.1080/08164649.1992.9994666.

Curthoys, Ann, and Marilyn Lake. *Connected Worlds: History in Transnational Perspective*. Canberra: ANU Press, 2005. doi.org/10.22459/CW.03.2006.

Curthoys, Ann, and John Merritt. *Australia's First Cold War, 1945–1953 Volume 1*. Sydney: George Allen & Unwin, 1984.

———. *Better Dead Than Red: Australia's First Cold War, 1945–1953 Volume 2*. Sydney: George Allen & Unwin, 1984.

Curthoys, Barbara, and Audrey McDonald. *More Than a Hat and Glove Brigade: The Story of the Union of Australian Women*. Sydney: Bookpress, 1996.

Damousi, Joy. 'An Absence of Anything Masculine: Vida Goldstein and Women's Public Speech'. *Victorian Historical Journal* 79, no. 2 (November 2008): 251–64.

———. 'Does Feminist History Have a Future?' *Australian Feminist Studies* 29, no. 80 (3 April 2014): 189–203. doi.org/10.1080/08164649.2014.928188.

———. *The Labour of Loss: Mourning, Memory, and Wartime Bereavement in Australia*. Cambridge, UK; New York: Cambridge University Press, 1999. doi.org/10.1017/cbo9780511552335.012.

———. 'Socialist Women and Gendered Space: The Anti-Conscription and Anti-War Campaigns of 1914–1918'. *Labour History*, no. 60 (May 1, 1991): 1–15. doi.org/10.2307/27509044.

Damousi, Joy, and Marilyn Lake, eds. *Gender and War: Australians at War in the Twentieth Century*. New York; Melbourne: Cambridge University Press, 1995.

Damousi, Joy, Kim Rubenstein, and Mary Tomsic, eds. *Diversity in Leadership*. Canberra: ANU Press, 2014, doi.org/10.22459/DL.11.2014.

Darian-Smith, Kate, and Paula Hamilton. *Memory and History in Twentieth-Century Australia*. Melbourne: Oxford University Press, 1994.

Davidson, Dianne. *Women on the Warpath: Feminists of the First Wave*. Nedlands, WA: University of Western Australia Press, 1997.

Deery, Phillip, and Frank Bongiorno, 'Labor, Loyalty and Peace: Two Anzac Controversies of the 1920s'. *Labour History*, no. 106 (May 2014): 205–28. doi.org/10.5263/labourhistory.106.0205.

Deery, Phillip, and Julie Kimber, eds. *Fighting Against War: Peace Activism in the Twentieth Century*. Albert Park, Vic: Leftbank Press, 2015.

Dennis, Peter, Jeffrey Grey, Ewan Morris, Robin Prior, and Jean Bou. *The Oxford Companion to Australian Military History*. 2nd ed. Oxford: Oxford University Press, 2008. doi.org/10.1093/acref/9780195517842.001.0001.

Devereux, Annemarie. *Australia and the Birth of the International Bill of Human Rights, 1946–1966*. Annandale: Federation Press, 2005.

D'Itri, Patricia Ward. *Cross Currents in the International Women's Movement, 1848–1948*. Bowling Green, Ohio: Bowling Green State University Popular Press, 1999.

Dixson, Miriam. *The Real Matilda: Woman and Identity in Australia 1788 to the Present*. Sydney: UNSW Press, 1976.

Dumbrell, John. *Vietnam and the Antiwar Movement: An International Perspective*. Aldershot, England; Brookfield, USA: Avebury, 1989.

Edwards, PG. *A Nation at War: Australian Politics, Society and Diplomacy During the Vietnam War 1965–1975*. St Leonards, NSW: Allen & Unwin in association with the Australian War Memorial, 1997.

Elshtain, Jean Bethke, and Sheila Tobias. *Women, Militarism, and War: Essays in History, Politics, and Social Theory*. Totowa, New Jersey: Rowman & Littlefield, 1988.

Enloe, Cynthia. *Bananas, Beaches and Bases: Making Feminist Sense of International Politics*. London: Pandora, 1989. doi.org/10.1525/9780520957282.

———. *The Big Push: Exposing and Challenging the Persistence of Patriarchy*. Oxford: Myriad Editions, 2017. doi.org/10.1525/9780520969193.

———. *Does Khaki Become You? The Militarisation of Women's Lives*. Boston: South End Press, 1983.

Ferguson, Niall, Charles S. Maier, Erez Manela, and Daniel J. Sargent, eds. *The Shock of the Global: The 1970s in Perspective*. Cambridge, Massachusetts: Belknap Press of Harvard University Press, 2010.

Ferrell, Robert H. *Peace in Their Time: The Origins of the Kellogg–Briand Pact*. Hamden, Connecticut: Archon Books, 1968.

Fitzpatrick, Kathleen. *PLC Melbourne: The First Century, 1875–1975*. Burwood: Presbyterian Ladies' College, 1975.

Forrester, JP. *Fifteen Years of Peace Fronts*. Sydney: McHugh Printery, 1964.

Foster, Carrie A. *The Women and the Warriors: The U.S. Section of the Women's International League for Peace and Freedom, 1915–1946*. Syracuse, New York: Syracuse University Press, 1995.

Foster, Catherine. *Women For All Seasons: The Story of the Women's International League for Peace and Freedom*. Athens, Georgia: University of Georgia Press, 1989.

Foster, Kevin. 'The Diseased Orchard: Australia's Collective Moral Failures in Afghanistan'. *Australian Book Review*, no. 446 (September 2022).

Friedan, Betty. *It Changed My Life: Writings on the Women's Movement*. New York: Dell Publishing Company, 1977.

———. *The Feminine Mystique*. Melbourne: Penguin, 1963.

Furmage, Lorene. 'Making It to the Platform: The Involvement of Women in the Peace Movement in Tasmania From the Crimean War to the End of the Vietnam War'. MA thesis, University of Tasmania, 1993.

Ghodsee, Kristen. 'Revisiting the United Nations Decade for Women: Brief Reflections on Feminism, Capitalism and Cold War Politics in the Early Years of the International Women's Movement'. *Women's Studies International Forum* 33, no. 1 (January 2010): 3–12. doi.org/10.1016/j.wsif.2009.11.008.

Glendon, Mary Ann. *A World Made New: Eleanor Roosevelt and the Universal Declaration of Human Rights*. New York: Random House, 2001.

Goedde, Petra. *The Politics of Peace: A Global Cold War History*. Oxford: Oxford University Press, 2019. doi.org/10.1093/oso/9780195370836.001.0001.

Goodall, Heather. *Invasion to Embassy: Land in Aboriginal Politics in New South Wales, 1770–1972*. Sydney: Sydney University Press, 2008.

Gowing, Margaret. *Reflections on Atomic Energy History*. The Rede Lecture series. Cambridge: Cambridge University Press, 1978.

Grant, Linley, Kay Binet, and Alison Alexander. 'Margot Roe: An Appreciation'. *Tasmanian Historical Research Association Papers and Proceedings* 63, no. 2 (July 2016): 102–03.

Greer, Germaine. *The Female Eunuch*. London: Paladin, 1971.

———. *The Madwoman's Underclothes: Essays and Occasional Writings*. 1st American ed. New York: Atlantic Monthly Press, 1987.

Grey, Jeffrey, and Jeff Doyle. *Vietnam: War, Myth, and Memory: Comparative Perspectives on Australia's War in Vietnam*. St Leonards: Allen & Unwin, 1992.

Grieve, Norma, and Ailsa Burns. *Australian Women: Contemporary Feminist Thought*. Melbourne: Oxford University Press, 1994.

Grimshaw, Patricia, Marilyn Lake, Marian Quartly, and Ann McGrath. *Creating a Nation*. Ringwood, Vic: McPhee Gribble, 1994.

Gwinn, Kristen E. *Emily Greene Balch: The Long Road to Internationalism*. Urbana, Illinois: University of Illinois Press, 2010.

Haan, Francisca de, Margaret Allen, June Purvis, and Krassimira Daskalova. *Women's Activism: Global Perspectives from the 1890s to the Present*. Hoboken: Taylor and Francis, 2012. doi.org/10.4324/9780203081143.

Habel Norman, ed. *Remembering Pioneer Australian Pacifist Charles Strong*. Melbourne: Morning Star Publishing, 2018.

Heilberger, Irmgard, and Barbara Lochbihler, eds. *Listen to Women for a Change*. WILPF German Section, October 2010.

Hellawell, Sarah. 'Antimilitarism, Citizenship and Motherhood: The Formation and Early Years of the Women's International League (WIL), 1915–1919'. *Women's History Review*, 22 February 2017. doi.org/10.1080/09612025.2017.1292625.

Henderson, Leslie. *The Goldstein Story*. North Melbourne: Stockland Press, 1973.

Hiernaux, Jean, and Michael Banton. *Four Statements on the Race Question*. Paris: UNESCO, 1969. Accessed 16 April 2017. unesdoc.unesco.org/images/0012/001229/122962eo.pdf.

Hill, Felicity. 'How and When Has Security Council Resolution 1325 (2000) on Women, Peace and Security Impacted Negotiations Outside the Security Council?' Masters Thesis, Uppsala University Programme of International Studies, 2004.

Hinder, Eleanor M. 'Pacific Women'. *Pacific Affairs* 1, no. 3 (1 July 1928): 9–12. doi.org/10.2307/3035494.

Hodder, Jake. 'Conferencing the International at the World Pacifist Meeting, 1949'. *Political Geography* 49 (November 2015): 40–50. doi.org/10.1016/j.polgeo.2015.03.002.

Holbrook, Carolyn. *Anzac: The Unauthorised Biography*. Sydney: NewSouth Publishing, 2014.

Holbrook, Carolyn, Lyndon Megarrity, and David Lowe, eds. *Lessons from History*. Sydney: NewSouth Publishing, 2022.

Holl, Karl. 'German Pacifist Women in Exile, 1933–1945'. *Peace & Change* 20, no. 4 (1995): 491–500. doi.org/10.1111/j.1468-0130.1995.tb00248.x.

Holland, Alison. *Breaking the Silence: Aboriginal Defenders and the Settler State 1905–1939*. Carlton, Vic: Melbourne University Press, 2019.

———. 'Wives and Mothers like Ourselves? Exploring White Women's Intervention in the Politics of Race, 1920s–1940s'. *Australian Historical Studies* 32, no. 117 (1 October 2001): 292–310. doi.org/10.1080/10314610108596166.

Holt, Betty, and Women's International League for Peace and Freedom. *Women for Peace and Freedom: A History of the Women's International League for Peace and Freedom in New Zealand*. Wellington: The League, 1985.

Hopkins, Lekkie, and Lynn Roarty. *Among the Chosen; The Life Story of Pat Giles*. Fremantle: Fremantle Press, 2010.

Horner, David. *The Spy Catchers, Volume I: The Official History of ASIO, 1949–1963*. Crows Nest, NSW: Allen & Unwin, 2014.

Hudson, WJ. *Australia and the League of Nations*. Sydney: Sydney University Press in association with the Australian Institute of International Affairs, 1980.

Hutching, Megan. 'Turn Back this Tide of Barbarism: New Zealand Women who were Opposed to War, 1896–1919'. MA thesis, University of Auckland, 1990.

Immerman, Richard H, and Petra Goedde, eds. *Oxford Handbook of the Cold War*. Oxford: Oxford University Press, 2012. doi.org/10.1093/oxfordhb/9780199236961.001.0001.

Iriye, Akira. *Global Community: The Role of International Organizations in the Making of the Contemporary World*. Berkeley: University of California Press, 2002.

Jauncey, Leslie Cyril. *The Story of Conscription in Australia*. London: Allen & Unwin, 1935.

Jennings, Kate. *Trouble: Evolution of a Radical: Selected Writings 1970–2010*. Melbourne: Black Inc, 2010.

Jordan, Deborah. '"Women's Time": Ina Higgins, Nettie Palmer and Aileen Palmer'. *Victorian Historical Journal* 79, no. 2 (November 2008): 269–313.

Keating, James. *Distant Sisters: Australasian Women and the International Struggle for the Vote, 1880–1914*. Manchester: Manchester University Press, 2020. doi.org/10.7765/9781526140968.

Kelham, Megg. 'War and Peace: A Case of Global Need, National Unity and Local Dissent? A Closer Look at Australia's Greenham Common'. *Lilith: A Feminist History Journal*, no. 19 (2013): 76–90.

Kerin, Rani. *Doctor Do-Good: Charles Duguid and Aboriginal Advancement, 1930s–1970s*. North Melbourne, Vic: Australian Scholarly Publishing, 2011.

Kerin, Sitarani. *'An Attitude of Respect': Anna Vroland and Aboriginal Rights, 1947–1957*. Clayton, Vic: Monash University, 1999.

Kilby, Patrick. *NGOs and Political Change: A History of the Australian Council for International Development*. Canberra: ANU Press, 2015. doi.org/10.22459/NPC.08.2015.

King, Peter. *Australia's Vietnam: Australia in the Second Indo-China War*. Sydney: Allen & Unwin, 1983.

Kingston, Beverly. *My Wife, My Daughter, and Poor Mary Ann: Women and Work in Australia*. Melbourne: Thomas Nelson Australia, 1975.

Kirby, Michael. 'Whitlam as Internationalist: A Centenary Reflection'. *Melbourne University Law Review* 39 (2016): 850–95. Accessed 3 November 2022. law.uni melb.edu.au/__data/assets/pdf_file/0012/2061021/04-Kirby.pdf.

Kirkby, Diane, ed. *Sex, Power and Justice: Historical Perspectives of Law in Australia*. Melbourne: Oxford University Press, 1995.

Knight, Louise W. *Jane Addams: Spirit in Action*. New York: W.W. Norton, 2010.

Koven, Seth, and Sonya Michel, eds. *Mothers of a New World: Maternalist Politics and the Origins of Welfare States*. New York: Routledge, 1993.

Laing, Kate. 'Peace Politics and Women's Liberation'. In *Contesting History Australia: Essays in Honour of Marilyn Lake*, edited by Joy Damousi and Judith Smart, 51–65. Melbourne: Monash University Publishing, 2019.

———. '"The White Australia Nettle": Women's Internationalism, Peace, and the White Australia Policy in the Interwar Years'. *History Australia* 14, no. 2 (2017): 218–36. doi.org/10.1080/14490854.2017.1319736.

———. 'World War and Worldly Women; The Great War and the Formation of the Women's International League for Peace and Freedom in Australia'. *La Trobe Journal*, no. 96 (2015): 117–34.

Laing, Kate, and Lucy Davies. 'Intersections of the Local and the International: Joyce Clague's Activist Journeys'. *Women's History Review* 30, no. 4 (11 June 2020): 574–93. doi.org/10.1080/09612025.2020.1776485.

Laing, Kate, and Lucy Davies. 'The Leadership of Women in the 1967 Referendum'. *Agora* 56, no. 1 (March 2021).

Lake, Marilyn. *Faith: Faith Bandler, Gentle Activist.* Crows Nest, NSW: Allen & Unwin, 2002.

———. 'Female Desires: The Meaning of World War II'. *Australian Historical Studies* 24, no. 95 (1 October 1990): 267–84. doi.org/10.1080/10314619008595846.

———. 'Feminism and the Gendered Politics of Antiracism, Australia 1927–1957: From Maternal Protectionism to Leftist Assimilationism'. *Australian Historical Studies* 29, no. 110 (1 April 1998): 91–108. doi.org/10.1080/10314619808596062.

———. *Getting Equal: The History of Australian Feminism.* St Leonards, NSW: Allen & Unwin, 1999.

———. '"This Great America": H. B. Higgins and Transnational Progressivism'. *Australian Historical Studies* 44, no. 2 (May 31, 2013): 172–88. doi.org/10.1080/1031461x.2013.791708.

———. *Progressive New World: How Settler Colonialism and Transpacific Exchange Shaped American Reform.* Cambridge, Massachusetts: Harvard University Press, 2019. doi.org/10.4159/9780674989993.

———. 'Sexuality and Feminism: Some Notes in Their Australian History'. *Lilith: A Feminist History Journal*, no. 7 (1991): 29–45.

Lake, Marilyn, and Farley Kelly, eds. *Doubletime: Women in Victoria, 150 Years.* Edited by the Victorian 150th Anniversary Publications Sub-committee. Ringwood, Vic: Penguin, 1985.

Lake, Marilyn, and Henry Reynolds. *Drawing the Global Colour Line: White Men's Countries and the Question of Racial Equality.* Australian ed. Carlton, Vic: Melbourne University Press, 2008.

Lake, Marylin, and Henry Reynolds, eds. *What's Wrong With Anzac? The Militarisation of Australian History.* Sydney: University of NSW Press, 2010.

Langley, Greg. *A Decade of Dissent: Vietnam and the Conflict on the Australian Homefront.* North Sydney: Allen & Unwin, 1992.

Larsson, Marina. *Shattered ANZACs: Living with the Scars of War.* Kensington: University of New South Wales Press, 2009.

Laville, Helen. *Cold War Women: The International Activities of American Women's Organisations*. Manchester; New York: Manchester University Press, Distributed in the USA by Palgrave, 2002.

Locke, Elsie. *Peace People: A History of Peace Activities in New Zealand*. Christchurch: Hazard Press, 1992.

Mack, Andrew. *US 'Bases' in Australia: The Debate Continues*. Canberra: Peace Research Centre, 1988.

MacMillian, Catherine, and Charlotte Smith, eds. *Challenges to Authority and the Recognition of Rights: From Magna Carta to Modernity*. Cambridge: Cambridge University Press, 2018. doi.org/10.1017/9781108554336.

Magarey, Susan. *Dangerous Ideas: Women's Liberation—Women's Studies—Around the World*. Adelaide: University of Adelaide Barr Smith Press, 2015. doi.org/10.20851/dangerous-ideas.

Manela, Erez. *The Wilsonian Moment: Self-Determination and the International Origins of Anticolonial Nationalism*. Oxford; New York: Oxford University Press, 2009.

Matthews, Jill Julius. *Good and Mad Women: The Historical Construction of Femininity in Twentieth Century Australia*. Sydney: Allen & Unwin, 1984.

May, Elaine Tyler. *Homeward Bound: American Families in the Cold War Era*. New York: Basic Books, 1988.

McCarthy, Helen. *The British People and the League of Nations: Democracy, Citizenship and Internationalism, c. 1918–45*. Manchester: Manchester University Press, 2013. doi.org/10.7765/9781847794284.

McGregor, Katharine. 'Opposing Colonialism: The Women's International Democratic Federation and Decolonisation Struggles in Vietnam and Algeria 1945–1965'. *Women's History Review* 25, no. 6 (1 November 2016): 925–44. doi.org/10.1080/09612025.2015.1083246.

McHugh, Siobhan. *Minefields and Miniskirts: Australian Women and the Vietnam War*. Sydney: Doubleday, 1993.

McIntyre, Iain. 'The AIDEX '91 Protest: A Case Study of Obstructive Direct Action'. Masters thesis, University of Melbourne, 2011.

McKernan, Michael. *The Australian People and the Great War*. Sydney; London: Collins, 1984.

Mendes, Philip. *The New Left, the Jews and the Vietnam War, 1965–1972*. North Caulfield, Vic: Lazare, 1993.

Meyerowitz, Joanne J. *Not June Cleaver: Women and Gender in Postwar America, 1945–1960*. Philadelphia: Temple University Press, 1994.

Miller, Carol, '"Geneva—the Key to Equality": Inter-war Feminists and the League of Nations'. *Women's History Review* 3, Issue 2 (1994): 219–45. doi.org/10.1080/09612029400200051.

Millett, Kate. *Sexual Politics*. London: Rupert Hart-Davis, 1970.

Mitchell, Susan. *The Matriarchs*. Ringwood, Vic: Penguin, 1987.

Moore, Eleanor M. *The Quest for Peace, As I Have Known It in Australia*. Melbourne: Self-published, 1948.

Morgan, Robin. *Sisterhood is Global: The International Women's Movement Anthology*. Garden City, NY: Anchor Press/Doubleday, 1984.

Morice, Janet. *Six-Bob-a-Day Tourist*. Ringwood: Penguin Books, 1985.

Morton, Peter. *Fire Across the Desert: Woomera and the Anglo-Australian Joint Project 1946–1980*. Canberra: Defence Science & Technology, 2017.

Murphy, John. *Harvest of Fear: A History of Australia's Vietnam War*. St Leonards, NSW: Allen & Unwin, 1993.

Murray, Kay. *For the Love of Peace: Women and Global Peace Building*. Sydney: Kay Murray, 1995.

———. *Voice for Peace: The Spirit of Social Activist Irene Greenwood 1898–1992*. Bayswater, WA: Kay Murray Productions, 2005.

Murray, Suellen. '"Make Pies Not War": Protests by the Women's Peace Movement of the Mid 1980s'. *Australian Historical Studies* 37, no. 127 (1 April 2006): 81–94. doi.org/10.1080/10314610608601205.

———. 'Taking the Toys from the Boys'. *Australian Feminist Studies* 25, no. 63 (March 2010): 3–15. doi.org/10.1080/08164640903499893.

Nicklen, Challen. 'Rhetorics of Connection in the United Nations Conferences on Women, 1975–1995'. PhD thesis, Pennsylvania State University, 2008.

Noel-Baker, Philip. *The First World Disarmament Conference, 1932–1933 and Why It Failed*. Oxford; New York: Pergamon Press, 1979.

Olcott, Jocelyn. *International Women's Year: The Greatest Consciousness-Raising Event in History*. New York: Oxford University Press, 2017. doi.org/10.1093/oso/9780195327687.001.0001.

Oldstone, Michael BA. *Viruses, Plagues, and History: Past, Present, and Future*. Rev. and updated ed. Oxford; New York: Oxford University Press, 2010.

Oppenheimer, Melanie. *The Power of Humanity: 100 Years of Australian Red Cross 1914–2014*. Sydney South: HarperCollins Australia, 2014.

Osborne, Graeme. 'A Socialist Dilemma'. *Labour History*, no. 35 (1 January 1978): 112–28. doi.org/10.2307/27508339.

O'Shane, Patricia. *Aboriginal Political Movements: Some Observations*. Armidale, NSW: University of New England, 1998.

Overy, RJ. *The Morbid Age: Britain Between the Wars*. London: Allen Lane, 2009.

Paisley, Fiona. 'Being International at Home: Australian Public Opinion in the League Era'. *Journal of Australian Studies* 43, no. 4 (2 October 2019): 429–46. doi.org/10.1080/14443058.2019.1672205.

———. *Glamour in the Pacific: Cultural Internationalism and Race Politics in the Women's Pan-Pacific*. Honolulu: University of Hawai'i Press, 2009. doi.org/10.21313/hawaii/9780824833428.001.0001.

———. *Loving Protection? Australian Feminism and Aboriginal Women's Rights 1919–1939*. Carlton South: Melbourne University Press, 2000.

Palfreeman, AC. *The Administration of the White Australia Policy*. Carlton: Melbourne University Press, 1967.

Palmowski, Jan. *A Dictionary of Contemporary World History*. 3rd ed. Oxford: Oxford University Press, 2008.

Parnaby, MR. 'The Socially Reforming Churchman: A Study of the Social Thought and Activity of Charles Strong in Melbourne 1890–1900'. BA (Hons) thesis, University of Melbourne, 1975.

Paulson, Ross Evans. *Women's Suffrage and Prohibition: A Comparative Study of Equality and Social Control*. Glenview, Illinois: Scott, Foresman, 1973.

Pemberton, Gregory. *Vietnam: Remembered*. Sydney: Weldon Publishing, 1990.

Pesman, Ros. *Duty Free: Australian Women Abroad*. Melbourne: Oxford University Press, 1996.

Plastas, Melinda. *A Band of Noble Women: Racial Politics in the Women's Peace Movement*. Syracuse: Syracuse University Press, 2011.

Popham, Daphne. *Reflections: Profiles of 150 Women who Helped Make Western Australia's History*. Carroll's Pty Ltd, 1978.

Prügl, Elisabeth, and Mary K Meyer. *Gender Politics in Global Governance*. Lanham, Maryland: Rowman & Littlefield Publishers, 1999.

Rasmussen, Carolyn. *The Blackburns: Private Lives, Public Ambition*. Carlton: Melbourne University Press, 2019.

———. *The Lesser Evil? Opposition to War and Fascism in Australia, 1920–1941*. Parkville, Vic: History Department, University of Melbourne, 1992.

Reekie, Gail. 'Market Research and the Post-War Housewife'. *Australian Feminist Studies* 6, no. 14 (1 December 1991): 15–27. doi.org/10.1080/08164649.1991.9994625.

Rhodes, Richard. *Dark Sun: The Making of the Hydrogen Bomb*. New York: Simon & Schuster, 1995.

Richardson, John. 'New and Strange Ways: The Radio Broadcasts of Irene Greenwood'. *Continuum* 2, no. 2 (1 January 1989): 50–76. doi.org/10.1080/10304318909359364.

Rischbieth, Bessie. *March of Australian Women: A Record of Fifty Years Struggle for Equal Citizenship*. Perth, WA: Paterson Brokensha, 1964.

Robertson, John. *J.H. Scullin: A Political Biography*. Nedlands, WA: University of Western Australia Press, 1974.

Robson, LL. *Australia and the Great War, 1914–1918: Narrative and Selection of Documents*. South Melbourne: Macmillan of Australia, 1969.

Roe, Jill. *Beyond Belief: Theosophy in Australia 1879–1939*. Kensington: New South Wales University Press, 1986.

Roe, Jill, and Margaret Bettison. *A Gregarious Culture: Topical Writings of Miles Franklin*. St Lucia: University of Queensland Press, 2001.

Rosenberg, David. *Inside Pine Gap: The Spy Who Came in From the Desert*. Prahran, Vic: Hardie Grant Books, 2011.

Rothfield, Evelyn. *The Future Is Past*. Self-published. Copy available at the State Library of Victoria, 1992.

Rothfield, Norman. *Many Paths to Peace: The Political Memoirs of Norman Rothfield*. Melbourne: Yarraford, 1997.

Rowse, Tim, and Richard Nile. *Contesting Assimilation*. Perth: API Network, 2005.

Ruddick, Sara. *Maternal Thinking: Towards a Politics of Peace*. London: Women's Press, 1990.

Rupp, Leila J. *Worlds of Women: The Making of an International Women's Movement.* Princeton: Princeton University Press, 1997. doi.org/10.1515/9780691221816.

Russell, Ruth. *Human Shield in Iraq: Finding a Way Forward for Peace.* Adelaide: Seaview Press, 2005.

Ryan, Edna, and Anne Conlon. *Gentle Invaders: Australian Women at Work 1788–1974.* Melbourne: Thomas Nelson Australia, 1975.

Sandell, Marie. 'Regional versus International: Women's Activism and Organisational Spaces in the Inter-War Period'. *The International History Review* 33, no. 4 (2011): 607–25. doi.org/10.1080/07075332.2011.620737.

Saunders, Malcolm. 'Are Women More Peaceful than Men? The Experience of the Australian Section of the Women's International League for Peace and Freedom, 1915–39'. *Interdisciplinary Peace Research* 3, no 1 (1 May 1991): 45–61. doi.org/10.1080/14781159108412732.

———. 'An Australian Pacifist: The Reverend Dr. Charles Strong, 1844–1942'. *Biography* 18, no. 3 (1995): 241–53. doi.org/10.1353/bio.2010.0089.

———. 'The Early Years of the Australian Section of the Women's International League for Peace and Freedom: 1915–49'. *Journal of the Royal Australian Historical Society* 82, no. 2 (December 1996): 180–91.

———. *Quiet Dissenter: The Life and Thought of an Australian Pacifist: Eleanor May Moore 1875–1949.* Canberra: ANU Peace Research Centre, 1993.

Saunders, Malcolm, and Ralph Summy. *The Australian Peace Movement: A Short History.* Canberra: Peace Research Centre, Australian National University, 1986.

———. 'Odd Ones Out: The Australian Section of the Women's International League for Peace and Freedom: 1919–41'. *Australian Journal of Politics & History* 40, no. 1 (7 April 2008): 83–97. doi.org/10.1111/j.1467-8497.1994.tb00093.x.

Sawer, Marian. *Removal of the Commonwealth Marriage Bar: A Documentary History.* Canberra: University of Canberra, 1997.

———. *A Woman's Place: Women and Politics in Australia.* 2nd ed. Sydney: Allen & Unwin, 1993.

Scalmer, Sean. *Dissent Events: Protest, the Media and the Political Gimmick in Australia.* Sydney: UNSW Press, 2002.

Scates, Bruce. *A Place to Remember: A History of the Shrine of Remembrance.* Port Melbourne, Vic: Cambridge University Press, 2009.

Schott, Linda K. *Reconstructing Women's Thoughts: The Women's International League for Peace and Freedom before World War II*. Stanford, California: Stanford University Press, 1997. doi.org/10.1515/9781503623873.

Scott, Ernest. *The Official History of Australia in the War of 1914–1918*. Volume 11, *Australia During the War*. Sydney: Angus & Robertson, 1936.

———. *A Short History of Australia*. London: Oxford University Press, 1916.

Scutt, Jocelynne A. *As a Woman: Writing Women's Lives*. Women's Voices, Women's Lives No. 2. Melbourne: Artemis Publishing, 1992.

———. *Taking a Stand: Women in Politics and Society*. Melbourne: Artemis Publishing, 1994.

Shute, Nevil. *On the Beach*. London: Heinemann, 1957.

Sluga, Glenda. '"Add Women and Stir": Gender and the History of International Politics'. *Humanities Australia*, no. 5 (2014): 65–72.

———. *Internationalism in the Age of Nationalism*. Philadelphia: University of Pennsylvania Press, 2013. doi.org/10.9783/9780812207781.

Sluga, Glenda and Caroyln James, eds. *Women, Diplomacy and International Politics Since 1500*. London: Routledge, 2015. doi.org/10.4324/9781315713113.

Smart, Judith. 'The Right to Speak and the Right to Be Heard: The Popular Disruption of Conscriptionist Meetings in Melbourne, 1916'. *Australian Historical Studies* 23, no. 92 (1989): 203–19. doi.org/10.1080/10314618908595809.

———. 'Women Waging War: The National Council of Women of Victoria 1914–1920'. *Victorian Historical Journal* 86, no. 1 (June 2015): 64.

Smart, Judith, and Marian Quartly. *Respectable Radicals: A History of the National Council of Women of Australia 1896–2006*. Clayton: Monash University Publishing, 2015.

Souter, Gavin. *Lion and Kangaroo: The Initiation of Australia*. New ed. Melbourne: Text Publishing, 2001.

Sparrow, Jeff. *Radical Melbourne*. Carlton North, Vic: Vulgar Press, 2001.

Stanner, WEH. 'The Great Australian Silence'. In *After the Dreaming: The 1968 Boyer Lectures*, 18–29. Australian Broadcasting Commission, 1969.

Strangio, Paul. *Keeper of the Faith: A Biography of Jim Cairns*. Carlton South, Vic: Melbourne University Press, 2002.

Strangio, Paul, and Brian J Costar, eds. *The Victorian Premiers 1856–2006*. Annandale, NSW: Federation Press, 2006.

Street, Jessie MG, and Lenore Coltheart. *Jessie Street: A Revised Autobiography*. Annandale, NSW: Federation Press, 2004.

Summers, Anne. *Damned Whores and God's Police*. 2nd rev. ed. Camberwell; London: Penguin Books, 2002.

Summy, Hilary. 'From Hope … to Hope: Story of the Australian League of Nations Union, Featuring the Victorian Branch, 1921–1945'. PhD thesis, University of Queensland, 2007.

———. *Peace Angel of World War I: Dissent of Margaret Thorp*. Brisbane: Australian Centre for Peace and Conflict Studies, 2006.

Summy, Ralph V. 'Militancy and the Australian Peace Movement, 1960–67'. *Politics* 5, no. 2 (1 November 1970): 148–62. doi.org/10.1080/00323267008401209.

Swerdlow, Amy. *Women Strike for Peace*. Chicago: University of Chicago Press, 1993.

Symonds, JL. *A History of British Atomic Tests in Australia*. Canberra: Australian Government Publishing Service, 1985.

Tavan, Gwenda. *The Long, Slow Death of White Australia*. Carlton North, Vic: Scribe, 2005.

Taylor, AJP. *The Oxford History of England*. Volume 15, *English History, 1914–1945*. Oxford: Clarendon Press, 1966.

Thakur, Ramesh Chandra. *The Last Bang Before a Total Ban: French Nuclear Testing in the Pacific*. Canberra: ANU Peace Research Centre, 1995.

Thompson, JA. 'Lord Cecil and the Pacifists in the League of Nations Union'. *The Historical Journal* 20, no. 4 (1 December 1977): 949–59. doi.org/10.1017/s0018246x00011481.

Tickner, Ann. *Gender in International Relations: Feminist Perspectives on Achieving Global Security*. New York: Columbia University Press, 1992.

Tickner, J Ann, and Jacqui True. 'A Century of International Relations Feminism: From World War I Women's Peace Pragmatism to the Women, Peace and Security Agenda'. *International Studies Quarterly* 62, no. 2 (1 June 2018): 221–33. doi.org/10.1093/isq/sqx091.

Towns, Deborah. '"Youth and Hope and Vigor in Her Heart": Clara Weekes, a "Born Teacher" and First-Wave Feminist'. *Victorian Historical Journal* 79, no. 2 (November 2008): 277–95.

Trojanowska, Barbara K. 'Norm Negotiation in the Australian Government's Implementation of UNSCR 1325', *Australian Journal of International Affairs* 73, no. 1 (2019): 29–44. doi.org/10.1080/10357718.2018.1548560.

Troy, Gil. *Moynihan's Moment: America's Fight Against Zionism as Racism*. New York: Oxford University Press, 2013.

True, Jacqui. *The Political Economy of Violence against Women*. Oxford, New York: Oxford University Press, 2012. doi.org/10.1093/acprof:oso/9780199755929.001.0001.

Tyrrell, Ian R. *Woman's World/Woman's Empire: The Woman's Christian Temperance Union in International Perspective, 1880–1930*. Chapel Hill: University of North Carolina Press, 1991.

Vellacott, Jo. 'A Place for Pacifism and Transnationalism in Feminist Theory: The Early Work of the Women's International League for Peace and Freedom'. *Women's History Review* 2, no. 1 (March 1993): 23–56. doi.org/10.1080/09612029300200021.

Vroland, Anna F. *Their Music Has Roots*. Box Hill, Vic: Anna F Vroland, 1951.

Walker, David, and Agnieszka Sobocinska, eds. *Australia's Asia: From Yellow Peril to Asian Century*. Crawley, Western Australia: UWA Publishing, 2012.

Wallace, Christine. *Greer, Untamed Shrew*. Sydney: Pan Macmillan Australia, 1997.

Wheelhouse, Frances. *Eleanor Mary Hinder, an Australian Woman's Social Welfare Work in China Between the Wars*. Sydney: Wentworth Books, 1978.

Wilson, Deborah. 'Different White People: Communists, Unionists and Aboriginal Rights 1946–1972', PhD thesis, University of Tasmania, 2013.

———. *Different White People: Radical Activism for Aboriginal Rights 1946–1972*. Crawley: UWAP Scholarly, 2015.

Wilson, Fiona. 'Women in the Anti-Vietnam War, Anti-Conscription Movement in Sydney 1964–72'. BA (Hons) thesis, UNSW, 1985.

Wilson, Paul. 'A Question of Conscience: Pacifism in Victoria 1938–1945'. PhD thesis, La Trobe University, 1984.

Windschuttle, Elizabeth. *Women, Class and History: Feminist Perspectives on Australia, 1788–1978*. Sydney: Fontana/Collins, 1980.

Wittner, Lawrence S. *The Struggle Against the Bomb*. Stanford: Stanford University Press, 1993.

Woollacott, Angela. 'Inventing Commonwealth and Pan-Pacific Feminisms: Australian Women's Internationalist Activism in the 1920s–30s'. *Gender & History* 10, no. 3 (November 1998): 425–48. doi.org/10.1111/1468-0424.00112.

———. *To Try Her Fortune in London: Australian Women, Colonialism and Modernity*. Oxford: Oxford University Press, 2001.

Wright, Clare. '"A Splendid Object Lesson": A Transnational Perspective on the Birth of the Australian Nation'. *Journal of Women's History* 26, no. 4 (2014): 12–36. doi.org/10.1353/jowh.2014.0069.

Young, Nigel, ed. *The Oxford International Encyclopaedia of Peace*. Online version. Oxford: Oxford University Press, 2010.

Ziino, Bart. 'Enlistment and Non-Enlistment in Wartime Australia: Responses to the 1916 Call to Arms Appeal'. *Australian Historical Studies* 41, no. 2 (2010): 217–32. doi.org/10.1080/10314611003713603.

Online sources

Aeria, Gillian, and Evelyn Leckie. 'Fallout from Nuclear Tests at Maralinga Worse than Previously Thought'. *ABC News*, 22 May 2021. Accessed 11 April 2022. www.abc.net.au/news/2021-05-22/maralinga-nuclear-particles-more-reactive/100157478.

'AJDS Oral History Project: Interview with Robin Rothfield 01/05/2014'. *Mixcloud*. Accessed 17 October 2015. www.mixcloud.com/AJDS/ajds-oral-history-project-interview-with-robin-rothfield-01052014/.

Aristophanes. *Lysistrata*. Translated by Jack Lindsay. 411 AD. Accessed 1 June 2016. www.gutenberg.org/ebooks/7700.

Australian Dictionary of Biography, produced by the National Centre of Biography at The Australian National University. Accessed 1 June 2016. adb.anu.edu.au/.

Australian Women's Archives Project, an initiative of The National Foundation for Australian Women (NFAW) in conjunction with the University of Melbourne. Accessed 1 June 2016. www.womenaustralia.info/awap.html.

Clark, Anna. 'Friday Essay: The "Great Australian Silence" 50 Years On'. *The Conversation*, 3 August 2018. Accessed 3 August 2018. theconversation.com/friday-essay-the-great-australian-silence-50-years-on-100737.

Commonwealth Parliamentary Debates, Hansard Documents. Accessed 22 May 2017. www.aph.gov.au/Parliamentary_Business/Hansard.

Department of Families, Housing, Community Services and Indigenous Affairs. 'Australian National Action Plan on Women, Peace and Security 2012–2018'. Accessed 29 November 2022. www.dss.gov.au/our-responsibilities/women/publications-articles/government-international/australian-national-action-plan-on-women-peace-and-security-2012-2018.

Department of Foreign Affairs. 'World Conference for International Women's Year'. News release no. 137, 17 June 1975. Accessed 29 November 2022. parlinfo.aph.gov.au/.

Giles, Patricia. 'World Women Parliamentarians for Peace'. Press release, 7 September 1990. Accessed 11 April 2022. parlinfo.aph.gov.au/parlInfo/download/media/pressrel/HNC062015050919/upload_binary/HNC062015050919.pdf;fileType=application%2Fpdf#search=%22world%20women%20parliamentarians%20for%20peace%22.

Joint Standing Committee on Foreign Affairs and Defence. *Omega Navigational Installation Report from the Joint Committee on Foreign Affairs and Defence.* Report. Canberra: Australian Government Publishing Service, 1975. Accessed 17 May 2017. www.aph.gov.au/parliamentary_business/committees/House_of_Representatives_Committees?url=/report_register/bykeylist.asp?id=1497.

Kok, Jodi. 'An "Ordinary Great Woman": Anna Vroland'. 31 March 2021, State Library of Victoria Blog. Accessed 18 October 2022. blogs.slv.vic.gov.au/family-matters/an-ordinary-great-woman-anna-vroland/.

Lake, Marilyn. WILPF Centenary Exhibition Launch Speech. Canberra Museum and Art Gallery, 27 February 2015. Accessed 15 December 2022. web.archive.org/web/20180919165619/http://www.wilpf.org.au/images/downloads/Centenary/Marilyn_Lake_WILPF_Centenary_Exhibition_Launch.pdf.

Lake, Marilyn, and Natasha Campo. 'International Activism and Organisations'. *The Encyclopedia of Women and Leadership in Twentieth-Century Australia.* Blog post. Accessed 21 November 2015. www.womenaustralia.info/leaders/biogs/WLE0200b.htm.

Mackie, Vera. 'Radical Objects: Origami and the Anti-Nuclear Movement'. *History Workshop Online*, 3 August 2015. Accessed 29 November 2022. www.historyworkshop.org.uk/radical-objects-origami-and-the-anti-nuclear-movement/.

McCarthy, Helen. 'Women, Peace and Transnational Activism, a Century on: Symposium Papers'. 30 March 2015. *History and Policy.* Accessed June 9, 2015. www.historyandpolicy.org/index.php/dialogues/discussions/women-peace-and-transnational-activism-a-century-on.

Monash University. 'From Fire to Dust: Plutonium Particles from British Nuclear Testing in Outback Australia More Complex than Previously Thought, Scientists Warn'. 21 May 2021. Accessed 11 April 2022. www.monash.edu/science/news/current/from-fire-to-dust-plutonium-particles-from-british-nuclear-testing-in-outback-australia-more-complex-than-previously-thought,-scientists-warn.

Obituaries Australia, produced by the National Centre of Biography at The Australian National University. Accessed 1 June 2016. oa.anu.edu.au/.

Pankhurst v Porter [1917] HCA 52 (2 October 2017). Accessed 17 November 2020. www.austlii.edu.au/cgi-bin/sinodisp/au/cases/cth/HCA/1917/52.html?stem=0&synonyms=0&query=pankhurst.

Peace Women Project. Women's International League for Peace and Freedom, United Nations Office. Accessed 1 June 2016. www.peacewomen.org/.

Rees, Madeleine. '"War 'Over' Ukraine—Militarism Is Killing Us All," Writes WILPF Secretary General In An Open Letter To The United Nations Security Council'. 28 January 2022. Accessed 4 April 2022. www.wilpf.org/war-over-ukraine-militarism-is-killing-us-all/.

Sklar, Kathryn Kish, and Thomas Dublin, eds. *Women and Social Movements, International—1840 to Present.* Accessed through Melbourne University Library. Accessed 29 November 2022. search.alexanderstreet.com/wasi.

The Encyclopedia of Women & Leadership in Twentieth-Century Australia. The Australian Women's Archives Project, 2014. Accessed 1 June 2016. womenaustralia.info/leaders/index.html.

United Nations History Project. United Nations, April 2015. Accessed 13 September 2016. unhistoryproject.org/.

Victorian Parliamentary Debates, Hansard Documents. Accessed 29 November 2022. www.parliament.vic.gov.au/hansard.

Way, Amy. 'Best We Forget: Excluding Women, Rape and Protest From the Anzac Myth and Memorial'. *Making History at Macquarie,* 18 November 2013. Accessed 20 October 2022. makinghistoryatmacquarie.wordpress.com/2013/11/18/best-we-forget-excluding-women-rape-and-protest-from-the-anzac-myth-and-memorial/.

WILPF (Women's International League for Peace and Freedom). 'Manifesto 2015'. Accessed 24 July 2019. wilpf.org/wp-content/uploads/2015/07/Manifesto-2e-print-bleed.pdf.

WILPF (Women's International League for Peace and Freedom) Australian Section. *Developing a National Action Plan on United Nations Security Council Resolution 1325*. Report compiled by Di Zetlin. School of Political Science and International Studies, Peace and Conflict Studies and Gender Studies, University of Queensland, 2009. Accessed 17 November 2020. www.dss.gov.au/sites/default/files/documents/05_2012/finalreportjuly2009.pdf.

Women's International League for Peace and Freedom. 'Congress Report 2015'. The Hague, The Netherlands. Accessed 24 July 2019. wilpf.org/wp-content/uploads/2016/03/Congress-Report_FINAL-with-budgets.pdf.

Women's International League for Peace and Freedom. Academic Network Webpage. Accessed 20 May 2016. wilpf.org/academic-network/.

www.ingramcontent.com/pod-product-compliance
Lightning Source LLC
Chambersburg PA
CBHW071811230426
43670CB00013B/2426